Is the Environment a Luxury?

The purpose of this collection of essays is to shed some light on the complex relationship between environmental quality and the distribution of income. Are the preferences of the poor towards a cleaner environment really different from those of the rich?

Environmental economists have traditionally focused on efficiency issues. In their analyses the quality of the environment is usually related to aggregate or average variables, like per capita income; policy recommendations are usually formulated considering efficiency with no regard for equity and also the predicted effects of policies are evaluated in aggregate terms.

The essays collected in this volume go into the problem of the relationship between environmental quality and income distribution. The book's opening essay shows how different theories of economic growth and environmental quality seem to suggest that the higher the level of income the higher the value of environmental protection. The essays that follow, a mix of already published papers and papers solicited for this book, analyse the relationship between environmental quality and income distribution from different perspectives (both micro and macro) and on the basis of more than one methodology.

This book highlights that the preferences of the poor towards a cleaner environment may differ from those of the rich, but income is also very likely to represent only one factor affecting them. The essays consider other relevant factors affecting preferences for environmental quality. What clearly emerges is that the distribution of costs and benefits of environmental policies is the key for their successful implementation, and that further research is needed to both address the distributional effects themselves and the strategies to mitigate them.

Silvia Tiezzi is Assistant Professor of Economics at the University of Siena, Italy.

Chiara Martini is Assistant Professor of Economic Policy at Roma Tre University, Italy.

Routledge explorations in environmental economics
Edited by Nick Hanley
University of Stirling, UK

1. **Greenhouse Economics**
   Value and ethics
   Clive L. Spash

2. **Oil Wealth and the Fate of Tropical Rainforests**
   Sven Wunder

3. **The Economics of Climate Change**
   Edited by Anthony D. Owen and Nick Hanley

4. **Alternatives for Environmental Valuation**
   Edited by Michael Getzner, Clive Spash and Sigrid Stagl

5. **Environmental Sustainability**
   A consumption approach
   Raghbendra Jha and K.V. Bhanu Murthy

6. **Cost-Effective Control of Urban Smog**
   The significance of the Chicago cap-and-trade approach
   Richard F. Kosobud, Houston H. Stokes, Carol D. Tallarico and Brian L. Scott

7. **Ecological Economics and Industrial Ecology**
   Jakub Kronenberg

8. **Environmental Economics, Experimental Methods**
   Edited by Todd L. Cherry, Stephan Kroll and Jason F. Shogren

9. **Game Theory and Policy Making in Natural Resources and the Environment**
   Edited by Ariel Dinar, José Albiac and Joaquín Sánchez-Soriano

10. **Arctic Oil and Gas**
    Sustainability at risk?
    Edited by Aslaug Mikkelsen and Oluf Langhelle

11. **Agrobiodiversity, Conservation and Economic Development**
    Edited by Andreas Kontoleon, Unai Pascual and Melinda Smale

12. **Renewable Energy from Forest Resources in the United States**
    Edited by Barry D. Solomon and Valeria A. Luzadis

13. **Modeling Environment-Improving Technological Innovations under Uncertainty**
    Alexander A. Golub and Anil Markandya

14. **Economic Analysis of Land Use in Global Climate Change Policy**
Thomas Hertel, Steven Rose and Richard Tol

15. **Waste and Environmental Policy**
Massimiliano Mazzanti and Anna Montini

16. **Avoided Deforestation**
Prospects for mitigating climate change
Edited by Stefanie Engel and Charles Palmer

17. **The Use of Economic Valuation in Environmental Policy**
Phoebe Koundouri

18. **Benefits of Environmental Policy**
Klaus Dieter John and Dirk T.G. Rübbelke

19. **Biotechnology and Agricultural Development**
Robert Tripp

20. **Economic Growth and Environmental Regulation**
Tim Swanson and Tun Lin

21. **Environmental Amenities and Regional Economic Development**
Todd Cherry and Dan Rickman

22. **New Perspectives on Agri-Environmental Policies**
Stephen J. Goetz and Floor Brouwer

23. **The Cooperation Challenge of Economics and the Protection of Water Supplies**
A case study of the New York City watershed collaboration
Joan Hoffman

24. **The Taxation of Petroleum and Minerals**
Principles, problems and practice
Philip Daniel, Michael Keen and Charles McPherson

25. **Environmental Efficiency, Innovation and Economic Performance**
Massimiliano Mazzanti and Anna Montini

26. **Participation in Environmental Organizations**
Benno Torgler, Maria A. García-Valiñas and Alison Macintyre

27. **Valuation of Regulating Services of Ecosystems**
Pushpam Kumar and Michael D. Wood

28. **Environmental Policies for Air Pollution and Climate Change in New Europe**
Caterina De Lucia

29. **Optimal Control of Age-Structured Populations in Economy, Demography and the Environment**
Raouf Boucekkine, Natali Hritonenko and Yuri Yatsenko

30. **Sustainable Energy**
Edited by Klaus D. John and Dirk Rubbelke

31. **Preference Data for Environmental Valuation**
Combining revealed and stated approaches
John Whitehead, Tim Haab and Ju-Chin Huang

32. **Ecosystem Services and Global Trade of Natural Resources**
Ecology, economics and policies
Edited by Thomas Koellner

33. **Permit Trading in Different Applications**
Edited by Bernd Hansjürgens, Ralf Antes and Marianne Strunz

34. **The Role of Science for Conservation**
Edited by Matthias Wolff and Mark Gardener

35. **The Future of Helium as a Natural Resource**
Edited by W.J. Nuttall, R. H. Clarke and B.A. Glowacki

36. **The Ethics and Politics of Environmental Cost–Benefit Analysis**
Karine Nyborg

37. **Forests and Development**
Local, national and global issues
Philippe Delacote

38. **The Economics of Biodiversity and Ecosystem Services**
Edited by Shunsuke Managi

39. **Analyzing Global Environmental Issues**
Theoretical and experimental applications and their policy implications
Edited by Ariel Dinar and Amnon Rapoport

40. **Climate Change and the Private Sector**
Scaling up private sector response to climate change
Craig Hart

41. **Game Theory and Fisheries**
Essays on the tragedy of free for all fishing
Ussif Rashid Sumaila

42. **Government and the Environment**
The role of the modern state in the face of global challenges
Edited by Laura Castellucci

43. **Is the Environment a Luxury?**
An inquiry into the relationship between environment and income
Edited by Silvia Tiezzi and Chiara Martini

Is the Environment a Luxury?

An inquiry into the relationship between environment and income

Edited by
Silvia Tiezzi and Chiara Martini

Routledge
Taylor & Francis Group
LONDON AND NEW YORK

First published 2014
by Routledge
2 Park Square, Milton Park, Abingdon, Oxon OX14 4RN

and by Routledge
52 Vanderbilt Avenue, New York, NY 10017

First issued in paperback 2020

Routledge is an imprint of the Taylor & Francis Group, an informa business

British Library Cataloguing in Publication Data
A catalogue record for this book is available from the British Library

Library of Congress Cataloging in Publication Data
Is the environment a luxury? : an inquiry into the relationship between environment and income / edited by Silvia Tiezzi and Chiara Martini.
pages cm
1. Environmental policy. 2. Economic development—Environmental aspects.
3. Income distribution. I. Tiezzi, Silvia, editor of compilation.
II. Martini, Chiara, editor of compilation.
HC79.E518296 2014
333.7—dc23
2013048743

ISBN 13: 978-0-367-66954-6 (pbk)
ISBN 13: 978-0-415-69059-1 (hbk)

Typeset in Times New Roman
by Swales & Willis Ltd, Exeter, Devon

Contents

List of figures ix
List of tables x
List of contributors xi
Foreword by Maurizio Franzini xii
Acknowledgements xiv

1 **Introduction** 1
CHIARA MARTINI AND SILVIA TIEZZI

PART I
Income and environmental quality: theory and empirics 11

2 **Willingness to pay for environmental quality: testable empirical implications of the growth and environment literature** 13
DEBRA ISRAEL AND ARIK LEVINSON

3 **The income elasticity of the impact of climate change** 34
DAVID ANTHOFF AND RICHARD S.J. TOL

PART II
The distributional incidence of benefits of environmental improvements 49

4 **Environmental goods and the distribution of income** 51
UDO EBERT

5 **How much do we care about air quality improvements? Evidence from Italian households** 76
CHIARA MARTINI AND SILVIA TIEZZI

PART III
The distributional incidence of the costs of environmental policies: the case of carbon/energy taxes 99

6 Household-level studies on the distributional impact of carbon/energy taxes 101
CHIARA MARTINI

7 Carbon pricing and distributional effects on firms: a methodological survey 128
ROSSELLA BARDAZZI AND MARIA GRAZIA PAZIENZA

8 Distributional effects of carbon pricing in Ireland: a computational general equilibrium approach 157
STEFANO VERDE

PART IV
The role of fairness and distributional weights in environmental public goods provision 189

9 Distributional weights in cost-benefit analysis: should we forget about them? 191
OLOF JOHANSSON-STENMAN

10 Fair air: distributive justice and environmental economics 213
OLOF JOHANSSON-STENMAN AND JAMES KONOW

Index 237

Figures

2.1	Individual preferences explanation	15
2.2	Dirtiest technology explanation	18
2.3	Institutional cost explanation	19
2.4	Returns to scale explanation	21
2.5	Country coefficients from Table 2.2	28
4.1	Income and substitution effect	64
5.1	Index of air quality 2002–2006	89
5.2	Index of air quality by region 2002–2006	89
8.1a	Industries' demand in GTAP-E	165
8.1b	Industries' demand in G-EMH	166
8.2	Wind and hydro's production functions	166
8.3	Government and household demand in G-EMH	167
8.4a	Irish industries' emissions	171
8.4b	Irish industries' emissions intensities	171
8.4c	Share of electricity in total costs of Irish industries	171
8.5	Impacts on nominal income across income distribution	179
8.6	Impacts on real income (CPI adjusted nominal income) across income distribution	180

Tables

2.1	Descriptive statistics from the World Values Survey	24
2.2	Linear probability model of yes/no responses to World Values Survey environment question on WTP higher prices for environmental protection	26
Appendix	Country averages from the World Values Survey	31
3.1	The eight alternative cases for the effect of development on the damage by climate change	37
3.2	FUND regions	39
3.3	Estimated income elasticities when net climate change impacts are harmful	41
3.4	Estimated income elasticities when net climate change impacts are beneficial	43
4.1	Income and price elasticities of demand	73
5.1	The data	88
5.2	First-step probit estimates	90
5.3	Mean household budget shares, w_j, expenditure elasticities, e_j and Hicksian elasticities e^*_{ij}	91
5.4	WTP for air quality improvements	92
5.5	WTP by household location	93
5.6	Rate of change of WTP over time and with respect to the index of air quality	94
7.1	Measure of climate policy impact on firms and indicators by level of analysis	133
8.1	Aggregation of sectors, regions and primary factors	170
8.2	Emissions by user and fuel	172
8.3	Earned income by factor	172
8.4	Distribution of earned income by factor and household	173
8.5	Distribution of income sources (GDP) by household	175
8.6	Macroeconomic effects and emissions abatement	177
8.7	Consumer price index by income decile	179
A1	CES elasticities in production structure	182
A2	Irish households' budget shares	183
A3	Closure and closure swaps	183

Contributors

David Anthoff is Assistant Professor at the University of Michigan, School of Natural Resources and Environment.

Rossella Bardazzi is Associate Professor of Economic Policy at the University of Florence, Italy.

Udo Ebert has been a Professor of Public Economics and is currently a Professor Emeritus at the University of Oldenburg, Germany.

Maurizio Franzini is Professor of Economic Policy at the University of Rome La Sapienza, Italy.

Debra Israel is Associate Professor at Indiana State University, Economics Department.

Olof Johansson-Stenman is August Röhss Professor of Economics, Economics and Law University of Gothenburg, Sweden.

James Konow is Professor at Loyola Marymount University, Economics Department.

Arik Levinson is Professor at Georgetown University, Economics Department.

Chiara Martini is Assistant Professor of Economic Policy at Roma Tre University, Italy.

Maria Grazia Pazienza is Associate Professor of Public Finance at the University of Florence, Italy.

Silvia Tiezzi is Assistant Professor of Economics at the University of Siena, Italy.

Richard S.J. Tol is Professor at the University of Sussex (UK), Economics Department.

Stefano Verde is Researcher at the Climate Policy Research Unit, European University Institute, San Domenico di Fiesole, Italy.

Foreword

Maurizio Franzini

Environmental economists traditionally have been little concerned with distributional issues. In their analyses the quality of the environment is usually related to aggregate or average variables, like per capita income; policy recommendations are formulated taking efficiency as the only gauge for judgement, with no regard for equity, also, the predicted effects of policies are evaluated in aggregate terms.

This lack of concern for distributional issues connects to the widespread use of the fictitious representative agent that strongly undermines the explanatory capacity of economic models. In a world where agents are heterogeneous and inequality exists many phenomena can be the result of processes that are precluded to models based upon the representative agent.

Environmental economics is not the only field where distributional issues have not received the attention they deserve. For example, the impact that income inequality can have on economic growth has been overlooked for a very long time, as well as its likely effects on many other dimensions that have a bearing on individual and social well-being. The strength and also the sign of these effects are nowadays the subject of lively disputes and much progress is still to be made. However, our understanding of real-world phenomena will be flawed unless distributional issues are integrated into the analysis.

Distributive considerations can enrich several aspects of environmental economics. Environmental quality can depend not only on how high average income is but also on its dispersion: rich and poor behave differently and this may have deep implications for the environment too. However, it is not an easy task to identify those implications and to establish whether they differ according to the environmental dimension that we refer to.

In addition, changes in the quality of environment can have differentiated impacts across the population. In particular, the benefits of a better quality environment can be unevenly distributed, both because people may not have the same access to such improvements (due to geographical location, culture, age, etc.) or because their evaluations, usually measured by the willingness to pay, are different.

A better knowledge of how the benefits stemming from an improved environment are distributed has positive implications from a number of points of view. The first is equity: it is interesting to know the extent and the characteristics of what could be called ecological inequality. But it is even more interesting to broaden the analysis beyond this sole dimension and take a multidimensional view of equity and equality. In a multidimensional perspective what matters, among other things, is whether environmental benefits and income are correlated and the signs of such correlation. Should it be positive, inequality in the multidimensional space would be higher than in each of the original dimensions.

The second point of view is the design itself of environmental policies; in fact, some effort should be devoted to aligning the distribution of the benefits with the distribution of the costs originated by the policy measures, so as to avoid sharp inequalities in the distribution of the net benefits. Mitigating such inequalities can pave the way to the successful adoption of pro-environment policies. There are, indeed, good reasons for believing that a major obstacle is the opposition of those who do not gain enough from or are damaged by those policies.

In recent times such issues have begun to be considered in the literature, within a more general resurgence of interest among scholars in the causes and consequences of inequality.

However, we still know too little and many results are not yet clear or robust enough. Moreover, the full implications of these results for the design and assessment of environmental policies have to be worked out.

The chapters collected by Chiara Martini and Silvia Tiezzi in this very useful book discuss the problem of the relationship between environmental quality and income distribution. The book offers a broad and very interesting analysis of different aspects of this relationship and has the virtue of analysing the problem from different perspectives (both micro and macro) and on the basis of more than one methodology. It provides excellent food for thought and adds a lot to our knowledge of a relationship that is crucial not only for the future of environmental economics but also for social and environmental sustainability.

Acknowledgements

The following publishers have kindly granted permission to reprint the following material that appears in the book:

With kind permission from Springer Science+Business Media: Environmental & Resource Economics, Fair Air: Distributive Justice and Environmental Economics, Volume 46, Jan 1, 2010, Full text, Olof Johansson-Stenman.

With kind permission from Springer Science+Business Media: Environmental & Resource Economics, Environmental Goods and the Distribution of Income, Volume 25, Jan 1, 2003, Full Text, Udo Ebert.

Johannson-Stenman, Olof. “Distributional Weights in Cost-Benefit Analysis: Should We Forget About Them?” Originally Published in *Land Economics* 8.3 (2005): 337–352. © 2005 by the Board of Regents of the University of Wisconsin System. Reproduced by the permission of the University of Wisconsin Press.

1 Introduction

Chiara Martini and Silvia Tiezzi

What this book is about

The relationship between environmental quality and income is at the very foundation of the environmental sustainability versus economic growth divide. An inverted "U" finding linking pollution and economic growth seems to offer evidence that the net benefits of environmental regulation increase at higher income levels, implying that they are progressively distributed. In fact such a pattern is consistent with different theories linking economic growth and environmental quality and each of them has different implications for the pattern of people's Marginal Willingness to Pay (MWTP) for improvements in environmental quality. Moreover, the empirical relationship between income and MWTP may differ in different countries and may not conform to the predictions of the theory (Israel and Levinson, 2004). In particular, it is not clear whether in low-income countries MWTP is initially low and then increases until a switch point is reached. This is crucial because the MWTP for improvements in environmental quality identifies the reservation value people attach to environmental improvements, i.e. it is a money measure of the benefits people experience from environmental policies. What these different theories seem to have in common is the idea that the poor and the wealthy assign different priority to environmental protection: the proposed construction of new buildings on the Sardinian coasts could produce cries from middle- and upper-income inhabitants, who might perceive the associated loss of natural resources as a welfare loss, and yet it could be welcomed as a source of new jobs at a time of high unemployment rates by individuals in lower-income brackets. This is a controversial and important issue which calls for further investigation and suggests that any Cost–Benefit Analysis (CBA) should carefully consider not only the absolute level of the costs and benefits of environmental protection, but also the distribution of both the costs and the benefits of environmental policies (Johansson-Stenman, 2005). While the distributional impact of costs is fairly straightforward to assess using standard economic analysis, because market policies often translate into higher prices for households and firms, assessing the distributional impact of benefits poses additional challenges, as they are usually not traded in markets. This is probably the reason why the literature on benefits distribution is much less developed than that on the distribution of costs

(Kristrom, 2006). Yet, any sound CBA of environmental policies should take both aspects into account.

Even though CBA constitutes a direct link from economic analysis to recommendations for political decision makers, one of the most important problems with it is the practice of focusing solely on efficiency, by simply comparing aggregate maximum willingness to pay (WTP) figures with costs. In fact, for the political debate, distributional issues, especially concerning environmental issues, are often extremely important. Distributional issues are at the core of debates over reforms that will affect other countries or generations where identifying potential winners or losers, and in particular how environmental policies' net benefits and costs will be distributed by income levels, is important (Tol, 2001; Narita et al., 2010). By ignoring the redistributive effects of an environmental policy, we may either unintentionally harm certain groups in society or, alternatively, undermine the program politically (Johansson-Stenman and Konow, 2010).

Distributional issues are also crucial in the context of international climate negotiations: Tol (2001) shows how the adoption of different criteria when defining emission reduction commitments implies different results, in terms of both efficiency and equity (respectively, total emissions and inequity level). Narita et al. (2010) highlight that burden sharing in international climate treaties does not account for international equity: the EU proposal for a post-Kyoto treaty appears generous in monetary terms, but not so in utility terms. More generally, fairness perceptions by individuals about alternative environmental policy instruments may be particularly important to reach a consensus on environmental policy and in international negotiations (Johansson-Stenman and Konow, 2010).

The purpose of this collection of essays is to shed some light on the complex relationship between environmental quality and the distribution of income. Are the preferences of the poor towards a cleaner environment really different from those of the rich?

The main aim of any environmental policy measure is to reduce environmental damages caused by production and consumption activities or, stated differently, to increase social welfare. Depending upon the distribution of benefits, environmental policies may favor the rich, in the sense that net benefits are larger for individuals with high incomes than for those with lower incomes. Environmental benefits, expressed as a fraction of income, are progressively distributed when they rise with income. In this case they are considered pro-rich. They are, instead, regressively distributed, and considered pro-poor, when they fall with income. The opposite is true for environmental costs, which are pro-rich when they are regressively distributed and pro-poor when their distribution is progressive.

The degree of progressiveness of environmental benefits may limit a policy's political appeal, because further implementation of environmental policies may result in a redistribution against lower-income groups. In contrast, the case for government intervention is strengthened in situations where net benefits are positive and large across income groups. Correctly measuring the incidence of environmental benefits, besides costs, is therefore crucial for policy purposes.

Since the quantity demanded of most environmental goods is rationed, the relevant parameter is not the income elasticity of demand but the income elasticity of willingness to pay (WTP) for a fixed quantity of the public good. When the income elasticity of WTP is considered, the literature has produced evidence of a value consistently smaller than one (Kristrom and Riera, 1996), which argues against the idea that the environment is a luxury and that the growing concern with environmental protection is an "upper-class" movement (Harry, Gale and Hendee, 1969).

Finding an income elasticity of WTP for environmental benefits less than one has striking policy implications. First, growth in income and in environmental quality could be decoupled, as higher-income groups would not show a higher willingness to pay for environmental quality than lower-income groups do (Martini and Tiezzi, 2013). Second, CBA of environmental projects would also be affected, because ignoring the real incidence of social projects may produce decisions that are "biased" against the poor. Therefore, finding that environmental benefits are regressively distributed suggests using appropriate weights that take into account the distribution of costs and benefits (Johansson-Stenman, 2005). Third, the income elasticity of environmental benefits is important for shaping efficient environmental policies. In international agreements for curbing carbon dioxide emissions, poorer countries should be allocated larger shares of the total number of emissions' rights at an efficient allocation, if the income elasticity of WTP is between zero and one (Chichilnisky and Heal, 1994). Finally, recent research (Cai, Cameron and Gerdes, 2010) empirically demonstrates that the distributional consequences of alternative environmental policies can have strongly significant effects on individuals' WTP, meaning that it may not be possible to adequately design an efficient policy measure without taking its distributional consequences into account.

One issue that clearly emerges from this book is that information on the distributional effects of costs is much larger and more detailed than information on the distributional effects of benefits of environmental policies. This makes the evaluation of the distribution of the net benefits of environmental policies more difficult. The book's opening essay shows how different theories of economic growth and environmental quality do not offer precise predictions on the distribution of the benefits of environmental protection, but they seem only to suggest that the higher the level of income, the higher is the value of environmental protection. The chapters that follow, a mix of already published papers and of papers solicited for this book, analyze the complex issue of benefits and costs distribution in more details.

The distributional incidence of the costs of environmental policies can be analyzed with partial equilibrium analysis focusing on households or firms, or with general equilibrium analysis considering the entire economy. This book considers carbon/energy taxes as one prominent example of environmental policy and discusses their distributional effects from a variety of methodological standpoints. Carbon/energy taxes can increase firms' net output prices in carbon-supplying industries and raise costs in industries that intensively employ fossil fuels as inputs. They can also produce two types of disparities in households' welfare: the first is due to a change in environmental quality, the second is linked to the distribution of financial effects, such as direct or indirect compliance costs (Tiezzi, 2005; Verde and Tol, 2009; Martini, 2010). The overall distributive incidence of environmental policies also includes more indirect effects on public finance, labor markets and international trade, which can be best analyzed adopting a general equilibrium approach.

Our answer to the opening question is that the preferences of the poor towards a cleaner environment may differ from those of the rich, but income is also very likely to represent only one factor affecting them. Other relevant factors affecting preferences for environmental quality could be the age and education of households' members, the production structure and competitiveness profile of firms, and the vulnerability of countries to specific environmental damages. What clearly emerges is that the distribution of costs and benefits is key to the successful implementation of environmental policies, and that further research is needed to address both the distributional effects themselves and the strategies to mitigate them.

What the chapters are about

The book is divided into four parts. The first part considers the environmental quality/income distribution nexus from a macroeconomic viewpoint. Chapter 1 by Debra Israel and Arik Levinson, "Willingness to pay for environmental quality: testable empirical implications of the growth and environment literature," is a streamlined version of a paper published in 2004 on the *Contributions Tier* of the *BEJEAP*. This contribution shows very clearly how the macroeconomic theories linking economic growth and environmental quality are connected to the microeconomic theories on individual preferences and then to WTP. The empirical analysis performed by the authors represents a very valuable example of this connection. The different theories examined all imply an inverse "U" relationship between per capita income and pollution, but offer a different explanation for it and imply a different pattern of individual MWTP. The "technological constraint" hypothesis implies that poor countries will always trade worse environmental quality for more income. In the alternative "institutional constraints" explanation, poor countries cannot afford the fixed costs of developing environmental protection agencies until their economies grow. Finally, in the "returns to scale" explanation, as countries become richer abatement becomes cheaper. The authors then empirically explore the relationship between national income and MWTP using the World Values Surveys. A strong relationship is found between MWTP and individual characteristics, such as age, income, and education, but little evidence that MWTP varies systematically with economic growth. We are left with no clue as to which theory is consistent with the observed patterns of MWTP and economic growth. This suggests that more empirical research is needed to explore the link between MWTP and national income.

Chapter 3, by David Anthoff and Richard Tol, uses the integrated assessment model FUND to compute the income elasticity of climate change total impact for different world regions over time. This macroeconomic approach allows us to consider a wide range of both beneficial and harmful impacts, in developed and developing countries. Limited support is found for the Schelling Conjecture that development might be the best defense against climate change impacts, and for the Sterner Conjecture that the impacts from climate change might be akin to a "luxury good." By contrast, no support is obtained for the Weitzman Conjecture that impacts are independent of development. Impacts are highly heterogeneous across time and space. A very important factor is considering the country-specific relevance of environmental damages. For very poor societies, a strong confirmation of the Schelling Conjecture is obtained, since harmful health impacts initially prevail and then rapidly disappear as societies get richer. This seems to be an area for future research: if some regions stay poor throughout the century, it is highly likely that even small increases in wealth might be the best way to lower the harmful impacts from climate change. For wealthier regions, climate impacts show characteristics of a "luxury good" in the medium term, consistently with the Sterner Conjecture. This effect disappears in the long run as the composition of damages changes.

The second part deals with the distributional incidence of the benefits of environmental improvements, with specific emphasis on the role of the income elasticity of demand for environmental quality and of demand drivers different from income. This part includes chapters by Udo Ebert, "Environmental goods and the distribution of income," and Chiara Martini and Silvia Tiezzi, "How much do we care about air quality improvements? Evidence from Italian households." Chapter 4 by Udo Ebert, reprinted in this book, is a milestone in this literature and aims at presenting a thorough theoretical investigation of the benefits from environmental commodities and of their effect on the income distribution. This chapter also clarifies the theoretical linkages between demand theory, as used in Chapter 5, and incidence parameters such as the income elasticity of demand and the income elasticity of the WTP for environmental quality. The magnitude of the income elasticity of MWTP for an environmental good turns out to be the crucial variable determining progressivity of benefits. The author points out that even normality of an environmental good does not necessarily imply that the income elasticity of MWTP is positive. For this reason, benefits incidence should be examined empirically. Furthermore, if the assumption of equal preferences is dropped, individual characteristics other than income influence consumers' choices. Consistently with other empirical studies included in this volume (Israel and Levinson, Chapter 1; Martini, Chapter 6), Chapter 5 by Chiara Martini and Silvia Tiezzi empirically confirms the relevance of demand drivers different from income.

In Chapter 5, WTP for air quality improvements is estimated using a novel approach (Ebert, 2007) and a unique dataset, obtained by merging data on Italian households' monthly current expenditure and unique information on a bundle of air pollutants' concentrations. WTP is found to vary by geographical location, the level of air quality, and over time, maybe signaling a change of preferences. Higher WTP values are observed for the Northwest and the Centre, the macro-regions where the big metropolitan areas are located; WTP for air quality is declining as the level of air quality improves, and also shows a negative time trend, confirming results obtained from other studies (Noonan, 2011).

The environmental benefits associated with environmental policies may be counteracted by the adverse consequences of such policies on specific income groups. Such consequences may be the main obstacle to implementing environmental reforms, complicating their political acceptability. Part III of the book deals with the distributional incidence of the costs of environmental policies, with particular reference to the case of carbon/energy taxes. It includes three chapters reviewing the literature on the distributional incidence of carbon taxes on households (Chapter 6, by Martini), on firms (Chapter 7, by Bardazzi and Pazienza), and on the whole economy in a specific country (Chapter 8, by Stefano Verde). The first and second chapters provide a useful methodological synthesis of the different approaches available for investigating costs distribution at household and firm level respectively. Chiara Martini's chapter is focused the distributional implications of Environmental Tax Reforms (ETR), especially for low- and middle-income households which may be disproportionately affected by carbon taxation. Evidence on the presumed regressivity of ETRs seems not to be unanimous. Household income seems not be the only relevant variable for assessing potential regressive impacts. In fact, demographic variables, such as household composition, age and employment status of its members, car and other energy-related goods ownership variables, although not widely investigated, turn out to be relevant in analyses of distributional effects. This essay additionally points out that the inclusion of revenue recycling options and of compensation measures (rather than environmental tax structure modification or the introduction of special provisions) is the key strategy to compensate potential adverse distributional effects which are better dealt with outside the taxation system itself. Finally, combining different approaches for investigating costs distribution could be a promising research strategy, and the availability of different methodological approaches could represent a significant value added in this direction.

Rossella Bardazzi and Maria Grazia Pazienza focus on the firm side, clarifying the impact of carbon/energy taxes in terms of profits and competitiveness, and considering the modeling tools available for an empirical estimation of the distributional impact of carbon pricing policy. Even though distributional analyses for firms have been performed mainly at sector level, they are nevertheless strategic, as the heterogeneity among firms is even higher than that among households. The empirical literature reviewed in this essay identifies positive signals for environmental policies: fuel and factor elasticities are non-negligible and the profitability and competitiveness impacts appear non-prohibitive, especially in those cases where a double dividend can be identified. Depending on the agent's ability to offset increasing costs, the burden of carbon pricing can be totally or partially shifted to other sectors of society, through a price increase or a consistent decrease in demand. Some of the limitations concerning firms' substitution analysis could be overcome by increasing the level of disaggregation, thus taking energy inputs and firms' heterogeneity into account. Also in the case of this second methodological review, the potential of combining different modeling approaches is highlighted.

In particular, the integration of the micro-simulation with the macroeconomic approach would allow estimation of very specific parameters and to simultaneously consider all major interactions at the general equilibrium level.

In Chapter 8 Stefano Verde, using Computational General Equilibrium (CGE) analysis, simulates the medium-term impacts of a carbon tax in Ireland, with a special focus on income distribution and revenue recycling, i.e. on whether both lower emissions and greater welfare can be achieved by means of carbon pricing and revenue recycling. A variant of the Global Trade Analysis Project (GTAP) model, G-EMH, has been developed, combining two existing versions of the model, one linking together energy-related CO_2 emissions and the economy, and the second allowing for multiple representative households. Over time, firms respond to environmental policy by modifying their own demands for production factors. At the same time, some workers may be discouraged to supply labor. Changes in the remuneration and employment of primary factors determine additional distributional effects. The chapter's main findings are that the impact of carbon pricing in Ireland is regressive over the medium term. Only if the proceeds of the carbon tax are redistributed to households through progressive transfers is the impact on real incomes virtually neutral. Five alternatives for revenue recycling are considered in this paper: (a) progressive household transfers, and lower taxes on (b) consumption, (c) labor, (d) labor income, and (e) capital income. While the carbon tax proves to be environmentally effective, none of the recycling schemes produced the second dividend, intended as a positive effect on real GDP. The four schemes differ in the magnitude, and even in the sign, of the effects across income distribution. When the tax on capital income is lowered, a large part of the benefit is not appropriated by the resident households, and as a result the average distributional impact is more adverse than in all other scenarios. By contrast, a lower tax on consumption turns out to make all households across income distribution better off.

After having provided some insights on the distribution of benefits and costs separately, it appears worth investigating the potential link between distributional effects and CBA. Since distributional aspects are so important, should distributional weights be used in the social appraisal of public projects involving environmental goods? Part IV of the book tries to offer an answer to this question. Many argue that it is socially inefficient to use distributional weights in CBA, because it implies large inefficiency losses. Instead, distributional matters can be dealt with through income taxation. However, other contributions in this book (Chapter 6) point out how adverse distributional effects are better dealt with outside the taxation system itself. Chapter 9, "Distributional weights in cost-benefit analysis: should we forget about them?" by Olof Johansson-Stenman, offers a theoretical investigation demonstrating that the commonly expressed perception that using distributional weights generally implies large efficiency losses appears to be incorrect. When the Hicks-Kaldor compensation criterion is used, a project resulting in a regressive (pro-poor) distribution of environmental benefits is less likely to pass than a project that would primarily benefit high-income groups. This is because the social profitability of the project is decided by the sum of WTPs, and rich people have a higher WTP than poor people (Hökby and Söderqvist, 2003). Therefore, finding that environmental benefits are regressively distributed suggests using appropriate weights that take into account the distribution of costs and benefits of projects. The author shows a large range of cases in which distributional weights are (second-best) optimal to use. More generally, taking fairness perceptions about alternative environmental policy instruments into account can be important to reach a consensus on environmental policy and in international negotiations, as pointed out by other contributions, for example Cai, Cameron and Gerdes (2010).

Chapter 10, "Fair air: distributive justice and environmental economics," by Olof Johansson-Stenman and James Konow, investigates the concept of fairness and distributive justice in environmental economics. This concept concerns moral preferences over the distribution of social and economic benefits and burdens among a group of individuals. The authors argue that fairness considerations are relevant to both descriptive and prescriptive analysis in environmental economics. In particular, they have important implications in environmental economics through the analysis of (1) individual behavior, (2) the behavior of other decision makers such as policy makers and international negotiators, and also through (3) the overall social objective function. The benefits in terms of greater empirical predictive power, as well as greater theoretical and policy relevance, of incorporating fairness concerns in the analysis often dominate the associated costs in terms of greater complexity. The authors further point out that one particularly important avenue of investigation is the empirical analysis of fairness perceptions about alternative policy instruments. The complexity of many environmental policy instruments implies that reaching a consensus may be the result of an informed and thoughtful process. Thus, future work in this field might build, in particular, on experimental studies, which have been shown to generate consensus about policies with important distributive consequences.

References

Cai, B., T. A. Cameron and G. Gerdes (2010) Distributional Preferences and the Incidence of Costs and Benefits in Climate Change Policy. *Environmental and Resource Economics*, 46, pp. 429–458.

Chichilnisky, G. and G. Heal (1994) Efficient Abatement and Marginal Abatement Costs. Working Paper, Columbia University.

Ebert, U. (2007) Revealed preferences and household production. *Journal of Environmental Economics and Management*, 53, pp. 276–289.

Harry, J., R. Gale and J. Hendee (1969) Conservation: an Upper Class Social Movement. *Journal of Leisure Research*, 2(2), pp. 123–126.

Hökby, S. and Söderqvist, T. (2003) Elasticities of demand and willingness to pay for environmental services in Sweden. *Environmental and Resource Economics*, 26, pp. 361–382.

Israel, D. and A. Levinson (2004) Willingness to Pay for Environmental Quality: Testable Empirical Implications of the Growth and Environment Literature. *B. E. Journal of Economic Analysis and Policy* (Contributions tier), 3(1), pp. 1–31.

Johansson-Stenman, O. (2005) Distributional Weights in Cost-Benefit Analysis: Should We Forget about Them? *Land Economics*, 81(3), pp. 337–352.

Johansson-Stenman, O. and J. Konow (2010) Fair Air: Distributive Justice and Environmental Economics. *Environmental and Resource Economics*, 46, pp. 147–166.

Kristrom, B. (2006) Framework for Assessing the Distribution of Financial Effects of Environmental Policy. In *The Distributional Effects of Environmental Policy*, edited by Y. Serret and N. Johnstone, Paris and Cheltenham: OECD, Edward Elgar Publishing, pp. 79–136.

Kristrom, B. and P. Riera (1996) Is the Income Elasticity of Environmental Improvements Less Than One? *Environmental and Resource Economics*, 7, pp. 45–55.

Martini, C. (2010) The Distributive Effects of Carbon Taxation in Italy. In *Critical Issues in Environmental Taxation Volume VIII*, edited by C. Dias Soares, J. Milne, H. Ashiabor, K. Deketelaere and L. Kreiser, Oxford University Press.

Martini, C. and S. Tiezzi (2013) Is the Environment a Luxury? An Empirical Investigation using Revealed Preferences and Household Production. Forthcoming, *Resource and Energy Economics*. DOI: 10.1016/j.reseneeco.2013.11.014.

Narita, D., R. S. J. Tol and D. Anthoff (2010) International Climate Policy and Regional Welfare Weights. *Environmental Science and Policy*, 13, pp. 713–720.

Noonan, D. S. (2011) How Much Do We Care About the Air? Evidence on the Value of Air Quality Improvements, AEI (American Enterprise Institute) Working Paper 2011–07.

Tiezzi, S. (2005) The Welfare Effects and the Distributive Impact of Carbon Taxation on Italian Households. *Energy Policy*, 33, pp. 1597–1612.

Tol, R. S. J. (2001) Equitable Cost-Benefit Analysis of Climate Change Policies. *Ecological Economics*, 36, pp. 71–85.

Verde, S. F. and R. S. J. Tol (2009) The Distributional Impact of a Carbon Tax in Ireland. *The Economic and Social Review*, 40, pp. 317–338.

Part I

Income and environmental quality

Theory and empirics

2 Willingness to pay for environmental quality

Testable empirical implications of the growth and environment literature

Debra Israel and Arik Levinson[1]

1 Introduction

This chapter is a condensed version of a research paper that appeared in the *Berkeley Electronic Journal of Economic Analysis and Policy* (Israel and Levinson, 2004). Empirical evidence has documented some forms of local pollution (airborne lead, sulfur) that have declined significantly in industrialized countries despite robust economic growth. Poor countries appear relatively unpolluted, middle-income countries more polluted, and rich countries clean again.[2] Because this evidence comes from reduced-form, country-level regressions of pollution on per capita gross domestic product (GDP), the cause of this inverse-U pattern is uncertain and the policy implications are ambiguous. Some have inferred that poor countries are not efficiently regulating externalities. Others have concluded that environmental progress eventually becomes an automatic consequence of economic growth.[3] If nothing else, these disparate claims highlight the need for a causal explanation of the relationship between economic growth and environmental quality.

Several theoretical explanations have been proposed to explain these findings. Because these theories were designed to generate inverse-U-shaped pollution–income patterns, they cannot be distinguished empirically on the basis of those patterns. However, the theories have different implications for people's marginal "willingness to pay" for environmental cleanup, and therefore may have testable empirical predictions using international surveys of environmental priorities.

We begin by noting that the inverse-U-shaped pollution–income relationship may be based entirely on individual preferences. This "individual preferences" explanation demonstrates that the observed pattern of pollution and income is not sufficient evidence that low-income countries set either Pareto-efficient or inefficient policies. Without any institutional barriers to accommodating individual preferences, this explanation has no implications for policy. Moreover, the stark prediction of this explanation is that people's marginal willingness to pay (MWTP) for environmental quality will be the same at different income levels, *ceteris paribus*.

We then identify three theoretical explanations that depend on institutional differences between countries with varying levels of per capita GDP. These include constraints on technologies, constraints on government institutions, and returns to scale in pollution abatement. Some of the models predict that MWTP increases with income, some predict increasing and then decreasing MWTP, while still others have no implications for the pattern of MWTP and income. Furthermore, because the models rely on different mechanisms to generate the inverse-U-shaped pollution–income path, they have different policy implications.

In what follows we examine patterns of willingness to pay across households with different incomes and countries with different levels of GDP, using household-level data from the third wave of the World Values Survey (WVS), a poll of about 70,000 respondents in 48 countries. Among other questions, the survey asked "would you be willing to pay 20 percent higher prices to protect the environment?" While this does not conform to standard contingent valuation protocols, we are not seeking specific dollar measures of willingness to pay. Instead, we wish only to see whether the patterns of MWTP conform to those predicted by the models. For this purpose the WVS provides a reasonable first look at these previously unstudied empirical implications of the growth and environment theories.[4]

2 Theories of growth and environmental quality

One commonly heard explanation for the observed inverse-U-shaped pollution–income path is that it reflects the natural progression of economic development, from clean agrarian economies to dirty industrial economies to clean service economies. This explanation has no normative implications for the future pattern of pollution and economic growth, since we cannot forecast the nature of the next phase of economic development after service economies. A related explanation is that rich countries become cleaner by importing those products whose manufacture creates the most pollution. This suggests that the pattern cannot be repeated indefinitely, because the poorest countries will never have poorer countries from which they can import their polluting goods.

Alternatively, the entire curve may be explained by individual preferences. Perhaps the inverse-U-shaped pollution–income path merely represents non-monotonic income expansion paths, or Engel curves, as pictured in Figure 2.1. No economic theory implies that goods must be normal or inferior in all ranges of income, and cannot switch back and forth. While it may seem improbable that poor people choose clean environments, middle-income people prefer to trade clean environments for other goods, and rich people prefer clean environments, no economic fundamentals would be violated by such a pattern. Furthermore, if the curve is a function of individual preferences alone, then the per capita GDP of the country in which a person resides should be irrelevant to that person's MWTP for environmental improvements. If we could estimate individuals' MWTP as a function of household characteristics, including income, the coefficient on per capita GDP in that regression should be irrelevant.[5]

In contrast, three recent explanations rely on institutional characteristics of economies. We have labeled these explanations "technology constraints," "institutional constraints," and "returns to scale." The technology constraint explanation, represented by Stokey (1998) and John and Pecchenino (1994), is that poor

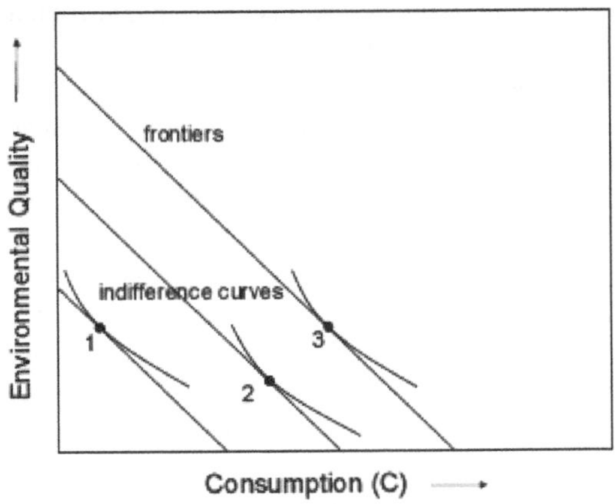

Figure 2.1 Individual preferences explanation

countries are as polluting as they can possibly be, given available resources and technologies. In these papers, there is some most-polluting form of production. Poor countries would like to use even dirtier and cheaper technologies, but none exist. As poor economies expand, they become both dirtier and richer. Once a country is sufficiently wealthy and polluted, the marginal cost of abating pollution becomes worthwhile, and pollution begins to decrease gradually with economic growth as less polluting, more expensive technologies are employed. The normative implication of this explanation is that the observed inverse-U shape can represent a Pareto-optimal response to technological constraints. If we were to relax those constraints somehow, poor countries would only become more polluted faster. In these models, the only efficient way to become less polluted is to grow.

The institutional constraint explanation is that some obstacle prevents poor countries from establishing the social institutions necessary to regulate pollution. An example would be the political-economic barriers in Jones and Manuelli (2001). Once a country is wealthy enough, these fixed costs become worth incurring, environmental agencies are established, and pollution begins to decline with economic growth. A normative implication of this explanation is that the well-being in developing countries might be improved by assistance in overcoming the fixed costs of establishing environmental agencies.

The returns to scale explanation, represented by Andreoni and Levinson (2001), is that as economies become larger, abating the marginal unit of pollution becomes cheaper, and larger economies therefore abate more. In this case, the empirical observation of an inverse-U pattern has no normative policy implications. With only one agent, all decisions are by definition Pareto-optimal. With multiple agents, both the decentralized (sub-optimal) and centralized equilibria exhibit inverse-U shapes, with the difference being that the decentralized pattern reaches a peak pollution level at higher income and with more pollution. Merely observing an inverse-U is therefore neither necessary nor sufficient evidence that the underlying pattern is efficient or inefficient.

Each of these three explanations predicts that pollution levels will rise and then fall with economic growth. They are, therefore, indistinguishable empirically using only data on countries' incomes and pollution levels. Each has, however, a different prediction about the pattern of households' MWTP for environmental improvements as a function of national income.

In the technology constraint explanation, poor countries start with low MWTP (they would trade worse environmental quality for more income). But no technology exists that can reduce pollution at such low marginal cost, and so poor countries do no abatement. As they become richer and more polluted, they become more willing to trade income for environmental improvements. At some point a country is rich and polluted enough that it becomes worthwhile to invest in a marginal amount of abatement technology, and pollution begins to decline gradually with economic growth. MWTP increases with income up to the point where the technological constraint is relaxed. Beyond that point, the pattern of MWTP and income depends upon other factors. Under the parameters in Stokey (1998), MWTP continues to increase with income.

In the institutional constraints explanation, poor countries cannot afford the fixed costs of developing environmental protection agencies. As their economies grow, they become richer and more polluted until it becomes worthwhile incurring those fixed costs. At that point an environmental agency is established, externalities are internalized, pollution declines, and MWTP stops increasing and declines. After the externalities are internalized, the pattern of MWTP is indeterminate.

In the returns to scale explanation, as countries become richer abatement becomes cheaper. At the same time, if clean air is a normal good, as people are richer they will have higher MWTP. The pattern of MWTP and incomes thus depends on whether, as incomes rise, abatement costs fall faster or slower than preferences for abating pollution rise.

Together, these theoretical explanations for the observed inverse-U-shaped pollution–income path generate separate predictions for the patterns of MWTP and national income. If the observed path is due to individual preferences, or to the returns-to-scale story of Andreoni and Levinson (2001), MWTP need not exhibit any particular pattern with respect to national income. If the path is due to technological constraints, as in Stokey (1998), MWTP will increase with national income, at least for poor countries. And if the path is due to institutional constraints, as in Jones and Manuelli (2001), MWTP will rise and then fall with national income.

Before turning to international survey data to look for evidence of these patterns of MWTP, we first demonstrate the theoretical arguments in more detail. First we derive the MWTP in the technology constraint model. We then depict MWTP in both the technology constraint and institutional constraint models graphically, using standard indifference curves and budget constraints. Finally, we generalize both models to incorporate the returns to scale story.

Technology constraint

Stokey (1998) describes a static model with a choice of production technologies with varying degrees of pollution. John and Pecchenino (1994) present an overlapping generations model in which environmental quality is a stock resource that degrades over time unless maintained by investment. Both models yield pollution–income relationships that are inverse-V shaped, peaking when the equilibria switch from corner solutions with zero environmental investment to interior optima with positive investment.

Each of these stories involves the conclusion that at low levels of income, countries are somehow endowed with an *excess* of environmental quality. Stokey's producers would like to use an even more polluting but cheaper technology, were one available. Since it is not, they use the dirtiest available technology and pollution increases steadily with production until such time as they begin to value the environment and switch to cleaner technologies. Similarly, John and Pecchenino's citizens would like to trade environmental quality for other goods, but cannot, so they slowly degrade their environment with polluting production until they reach an income threshold beyond which they care about pollution and begin to invest in environmental quality.

Stokey starts with representative agent utility function:

$$U(C, P) = V(C) - h(P) \tag{1}$$

where C is consumption and P is pollution, and $V()$ and $h()$ are subutility functions. Stokey assumes that consumption is produced from potential income (M) using some technology, indexed by $\theta \in (0,1]$, where $\theta = 1$ is the dirtiest possible technology. Consumption is equal to θM, and pollution generated is

$P = \varphi(\theta)M$, where $\varphi(0) = 0$, $\varphi'(0) = 0$, $\varphi(1) = 1$, $\varphi'(1) = 1$, and $\varphi''(0)>0$. The government's role is to choose θ to maximize (1) subject to these constraints, yielding the first-order condition

$$\frac{h'}{V'} \leq \frac{1}{\phi'} \tag{2}$$

The left-hand side of (2) is the MWTP for a decrease in pollution.

Stokey then defines M^* as the threshold level of potential income (the economy's endowment) below which it will always be optimal to choose $\theta^*(M) = 1$ for all $M < M^*$. Above M^*, $\theta^*(M) < 1$, which means that some pollution abatement takes place in the form of cleaner technologies employed.

Figure 2.2 depicts this setup.[6] The downward-sloping concave lines represent the available tradeoffs between pollution and consumption, defined by the function $\varphi(\theta)$. For $M < M^*$, preferences are such that the MWTP for abatement is less than the marginal rate of technical substitution implied (assumed to be $\varphi(1) = 1$), and no abatement takes place. In Figure 2.2 when the economy is small, with endowment of potential income M_l, the indifference curve is steeper than the consumption possibility frontier, and we are at a corner solution where consumption is M_l and pollution is P_l.

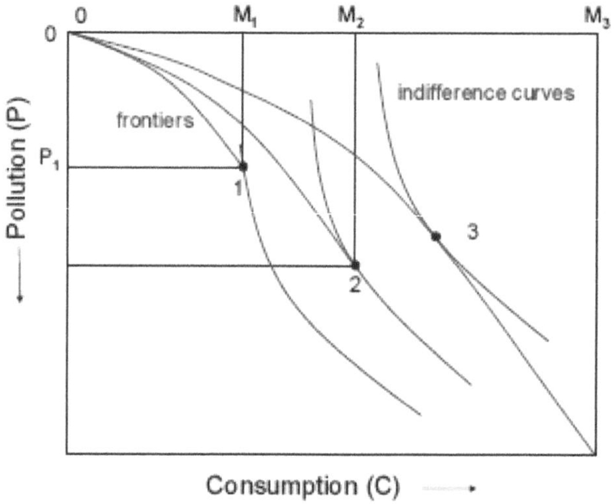

Figure 2.2 Dirtiest technology explanation

As the economy grows, so long as $M < M^*$, $\theta = 1$, the dirtiest technology is employed, pollution increases, and the MWTP increases (the slopes of the indifference curves at corner solutions like 1 and 2 become flatter). At some point, the economy grows sufficiently and becomes sufficiently polluted that the slope of the indifference curve equals the slope of the technology frontier, and we move to an interior solution. Such an interior is depicted at point 3. Notice that pollution increases and then decreases as income grows.

Algebraically, MWTP is $h'(M\varphi(\theta))/V'(\theta M)$ in equation (2). So long as $M < M^*$, this is equal to $h'(M)/V'(M)$. And, so long as pollution is a normal good, and the marginal utility of consumption is diminishing, MWTP increases with income.

When $M > M^*$, and cleaner technologies become optimal, the pattern of MWTP with respect to income is less clear. Stokey uses the following functional forms as an example:

$$\varphi(\theta) = \theta^{\beta}$$

$$V(C) = \frac{c^{1-\sigma} - 1}{1-\sigma} \tag{3}$$

$$h(P) = \frac{bP^{\gamma}}{\gamma}$$

where $\beta > 1$, $\sigma > 0$, $\gamma > 1$, $b > 0$. In this case, the MWTP is

$$MWTP = b\theta^{\beta(\gamma-1)+\sigma} M^{\gamma+\sigma-1} \tag{4}$$

and $\partial MWTP/\partial M > 1$, so MWTP increases with income even after the technology threshold is passed, though this is not necessarily the case for all values of the parameters.

The empirical implication of this technology-constraint explanation is that, all else equal, richer countries will have *higher* MWTP than poor countries, at least up until the point where pollution starts to improve with income. This implication is in theory testable using international survey data. Before describing the test, however, we derive contrasting implications from the competing theoretical explanations for the inverse-U-shaped pollution–income pattern.

Institutional constraints

A second explanation is that some institutional constraints block poor countries from enacting legislation to clean up their economies. Jones and Manuelli's (2001) model consists of two overlapping generations in which the younger generation sets pollution regulations. Depending on the voting mechanism, the pollution–income relationship can be an inverted U, monotonically increasing, or even a "sideways-mirrored-S" (what others have called "N-shaped"). In their model, all of the dynamics come from the political economy. Pollution is a flow, lasting only one period, and is suffered only by the older generation. Consequently, much of the intuition in their model can be described in a static framework along the lines of the technology constraint discussion.

Figure 2.3 depicts this model graphically. Begin with the smallest endowment economy, the rectangle bordered by M_I. The resource constraint faced by a representative consumer is the kinked thick line. The short segment along the bottom right corner of the box represents the fixed costs of enacting regulation (political-economic costs in Jones and Manuelli). Once these fixed costs are incurred, the

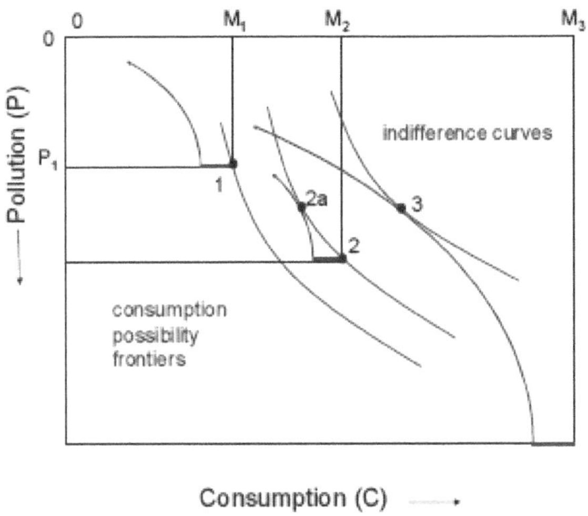

Figure 2.3 Institutional cost explanation

economy can abate pollution at some cost of foregone consumption. The highest indifference curve this small economy can attain is in the lower right corner of the endowment box, where no abatement takes place. As the economy expands, and M grows, MWTP increases until at some point the optimum will jump from the corner solution of no abatement (such as point 2 in the graph), to an interior solution with abatement (such as point 2a).

The pattern of MWTP here is distinct. So long as the economy is at the corner solution, where no abatement takes place, as M increases MWTP increases, just as in the Stokey model when $M < M^*$. At the threshold where abatement takes place, however, in this scenario there is a discrete jump from the corner to an interior solution. Pollution falls suddenly, and MWTP falls from point 2 to point 2a in Figure 2.3. Beyond this threshold, the pattern of MWTP with respect to income depends on other things.

Note that, depicted this way, the institutional constraint explanation of Jones and Manuelli is a special case of the technology constraint explanation of Stokey. In both stories, poor economies are stuck at the corner solution of no abatement – the southeast corner of their endowment boxes in Figures 2.2 and 2.3. As the economies grow, MWTP increases. The difference is that in Figure 2.2, the possibility frontier is concave, so when the economy moves off the corner it does so gradually, and pollution is gradually abated. In Figure 2.3, the frontier is convex, and so the economy jumps discretely from the corner to some interior solution.

Returns to scale

A third model relies on returns to scale in the technology for abating pollution. Andreoni and Levinson (2001) describe a one-agent, one-good, consumption model, with no technological or institutional constraints on consumption or pollution abatement, in which returns to scale in the abatement technology generate an inverse-U-shaped pollution–income path. They start with a general version of Stokey's utility function from equation (1):

$$U = U(C, P) \tag{5}$$

where $U_C > 0$ and $U_P < 0$. Next, they assume that gross pollution is created as a byproduct of consumption, but that pollution can be abated by devoting effort to cleanup.

$$P = C - A(C,E) \tag{6}$$

where A () is the abatement function, E is cleanup effort, and $A_C > 0$ and $A_E > 0$. The single agent is endowed with resources (M) that can be divided among consumption (C) and abatement effort (E).

$$M = C + E \tag{7}$$

Maximizing (5) subject to (6) and (7), and rearranging terms, yields the first-order condition

$$\frac{-U_P}{U_C} = \frac{1}{1-(A_C - A_E)} \tag{8}$$

The left-hand side of (8) is the MWTP for environmental improvement. It is the slope of an indifference curve, plotted with consumption on the bottom axis and pollution on the left axis, and it will always be positive in the optimum.[7]

To find what happens to MWTP as income (M) increases, note that the derivative of (8) with respect to M will have the same sign as the derivative of (A_C-A_E) with respect to M:

$$\begin{bmatrix} A_{CE} - A_{EE} \\ + \quad\; - \end{bmatrix} + \begin{bmatrix} A_{CC} - 2A_{CE} + A_{EE} \\ - \quad\;\; + \quad\;\; - \end{bmatrix} \underset{+}{\frac{\partial C}{\partial M}} \tag{9}$$

As long as the abatement function has diminishing marginal product of C and E ($A_{CC} < 0$, $A_{EE} < 0$), and the marginal product of E is increasing in C ($A_{CE} > 0$), and C is a normal good ($\partial C/\partial M>0$), then the sign of (9) is ambiguous. The left bracketed term is positive, the right bracketed term is negative, and $\partial C/\partial M$ is positive.

Figure 2.4 depicts what is happening graphically. The smallest rectangle represents the endowment (M_1) of a small economy. If the agent consumes nothing, no pollution is created. If the agent consumes the entire endowment M_1, devoting nothing to abatement, P_1 units of pollution are generated. The consumption possibility frontier, derived from $A()$, depicts the tradeoff between pollution and consumption facing the economy. Given convex indifference curves, the agent will optimize at some point as depicted. The MWTP in this case is the inverse of the slope of the indifference curve at that tangency point.

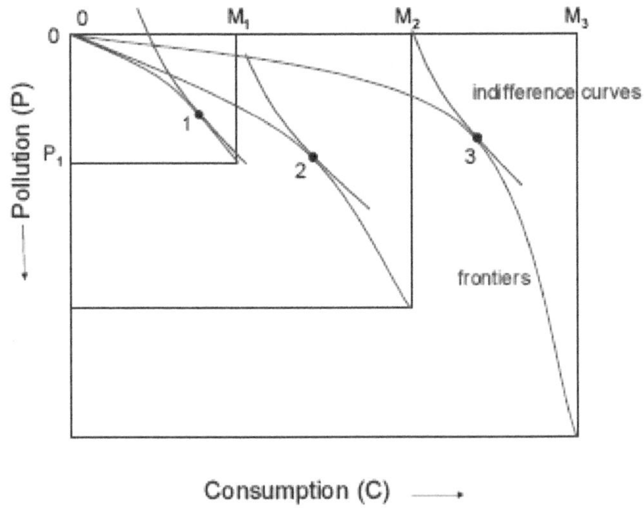

Figure 2.4 Returns to scale explanation

Richer economies, with successively larger endowments M_2 and M_3, are represented by increasingly larger rectangles. Andreoni and Levinson show that if the abatement function A () has increasing returns to scale and environmental quality is a normal good, the new point of tangency will at some point begin to have higher consumption and lower pollution levels. As depicted, pollution increases and then decreases with the wealth of the economy.

Unlike the technology or institutional constraint explanations, this returns to scale story is consistent with *any* pattern of MWTP. Thus, although we can never rule out returns to scale using MWTP data, if we do find evidence against the technology or institutional constraints, we now have a substitute explanation for the inverse-U-shaped pollution pattern.

All of these institutional explanations have different implications for the pattern of MWTP and national income per capita. Under the technology constraint story, MWTP will increase with income until the point that the threshold is passed and less-polluting technologies are chosen. After that point, MWTP is uncertain, but under Stokey's functional form and parameters, it continues rising. Under the institutional constraints explanation, MWTP rises until the point where environmental agencies are established, falls once the externalities are internalized, and is indeterminate beyond that point. Finally, the returns to scale explanation has no prediction for the pattern of MWTP and income.

To look for support for these models, we turn to international survey data on environmental valuations from the World Values Survey, and examine the empirical patterns of people's expressed willingness to pay for environmental improvement as a function of household and national incomes.

3 Empirics

Perhaps the ideal way to examine the empirical relationship between MWTP and national income would be to conduct an international contingent valuation (CV) study.[8] One could survey individuals' MWTP for an extra unit of some local air pollutant that has been shown to increase and then decrease with national income, following established CV protocol, asking people to vote yes or no for a well-defined environmental benefit, with a well-defined payment mechanism. In the absence of such an internationally comparable survey, we turn to what is arguably the next best alternative: the World Values Survey (WVS).

The WVS is designed to be a representative survey carried out using consistent methodologies across numerous countries. We focus on the third wave of the survey, carried out predominantly from 1995 to 1996, with some countries surveyed in 1997 or 1998.[9] We combine the WVS with national income data from the World Bank (2002). Thirty-three countries had consistent data on the environmental questions, national income, and associated household characteristics. The countries are listed, along with some descriptive statistics, in the appendix.

While none of the WVS environment questions conforms to standard contingent valuation protocols, some come close enough to make comparisons of responses across households and countries worthwhile. For example, one question asks "would you be willing to pay 20 percent higher prices to protect the environment?" Respondents are asked to pick from among four choices, "strongly agree," "agree," "disagree," and "strongly disagree."[10] Though the question is not a referendum, we can group the two first and two last responses to simulate what a yes/no question would have yielded. The question does seem to ask about *marginal* willingness to pay, as opposed to *total*, and the pattern of responses across incomes supports that interpretation.[11]

A larger problem with the "higher prices" question is that it does not ask about a specific environmental problem. If we find that MWTP does not follow a pattern predicted by a particular theory, that could be because the theory is wrong, or because the question is about an environmental problem that does not follow an inverse-U-shaped pollution–income path, or because different countries face different environmental problems and interpret the question differently. Moreover, by asking about a price increase, the question implicitly imposes a higher absolute cost on high-income respondents than on low-income respondents. Though this concern will be partially mitigated to the extent we can control for household income, as we will describe, that control turns out to be problematic.

In sum, if our goal were to place a precise dollar value on people's willingness to pay, we would be concerned about a number of features of these questions. However, our goal is not to identify people's MWTP precisely. Rather, we merely wish to establish the relationships among people's MWTP, their individual household incomes, and the national income of the countries in which they reside.

Table 2.1 presents some descriptive statistics. Of the 36,375 observations, a little fewer than half (48 percent) said "yes" they would be willing to pay higher prices to protect the environment. (This is the sum of those who "agreed" and "strongly agreed.") Not surprisingly, this is highly correlated with respondents' opinions about the importance of environmental protection relative to economic growth, and with respondents' propensity to choose environmental products and to contribute to environmental organizations.

The per capita GDP of people who said "yes" they would pay higher prices for the environment is lower than that of people who said "no." While the GDP difference is statistically insignificant, people who support the environmental improvement are significantly more likely to be female and younger.

The household income variable is a ranking of ten income categories for each country. Households with higher relative incomes (categories 5 through 10) are more likely to respond "yes" to the environmental questions (although this difference is statistically significant only for the top income category). Households with low relative incomes (categories 2 through 4) are less likely to respond "yes," as would be expected if environmental quality is a normal good. However, for some reason, households in the lowest category of incomes are more likely to respond "yes," although the difference in responses is small (half of a percentage point) and only marginally significant. Respondents with at least some university education and those living in bigger cities were more likely to respond "yes" to paying for environmental improvements.

Table 2.1 Descriptive statistics from the World Values Survey

	Willing to pay higher prices to protect the environment?	
Variable	Yes	No
Environment a priority over growth.[a]	0.64	0.46*
Choose environmental products.[a]	0.50	0.41*
Contribute to environmental organization.[a]	0.17	0.11*
Per capita GDP using purchasing power parity exchange rates ($1000)	8.60(8.11)	8.65(8.45)
Age	39.79(15.36)	42.51(16.22)*
Female	0.52	0.50*
Income category 1	0.119	0.113†
Income category 2	0.127	0.145*
Income category 3	0.136	0.143†
Income category 4	0.124	0.129
Income category 5	0.124	0.120
Income category 6	0.091	0.089
Income category 7	0.086	0.084
Income category 8	0.075	0.073
Income category 9	0.062	0.058
Income category 10	0.057	0.045*
Education: none	0.026	0.036*
Education: some primary	0.054	0.064*
Education: complete primary	0.120	0.132*
Education: some secondary	0.145	0.149
Education: complete secondary	0.394	0.404†
Education: some university	0.079	0.068*
Education: university degree	0.181	0.148*
City size: < 2000	0.109	0.140*
City size: 2–5000	0.130	0.135
City size: 5–10000	0.073	0.083*
City size: 10–20000	0.076	0.072
City size: 20–50000	0.113	0.115
City size: 50–100000	0.087	0.075*
City size: 100–500000	0.177	0.163*
City size: > 500000	0.234	0.217*
Observations	17435	18940

Notes: Sample standard deviations for continuous variables in parentheses.

* Differences statistically significant at 5 percent.

† Differences statistically significant at 10 percent.

a These environmental questions had slightly fewer responses: 30809, 30401, and 34338, respectively.

The models outlined in section 2 all describe a single representative agent. In the WVS, of course, respondents are heterogeneous. There are rich respondents in poor countries and vice versa. Hence, our goal is to describe how MWTP changes with national income, controlling for household characteristics. Our strategy is to estimate a linear probability model, where the dependent variable is equal to one if the respondent agrees with the environmental question posed, and zero otherwise. We control for the respondent's age, sex, income, education, and city size, and we include a set of country-specific dummy variables, or fixed effects.

The key role played by the country dummies is that we can plot their coefficients against GDP per capita to see whether, in relative terms, rich countries' citizens have higher or lower propensities to answer "yes" to the environmental question. Under the technology constraint story, the country dummy coefficients should increase with income for low-income countries. Under the institutional constraint story, the coefficients should increase and then decrease.

Before we turn to the results, one final problem with the data needs to be addressed. For household income, respondents were asked to place themselves in one of ten income brackets, defined by specific monetary ranges (e.g. \$0–\$10,000, \$10,000–\$20,000, etc.). These brackets were different for each country, and were meant to correspond to the income deciles for each country. However, it is clear from the survey responses that the categories rarely matched income deciles. As a consequence, we have only a rough idea of the relative income of households in each country. A person in income category 5 in a poor country may be poorer in absolute terms than a person in income category 5 in a rich country. The income categories are *relative* rankings of income, and differ by country. If we were to ignore this problem and simply regress MWTP on household income bracket dummies and country dummies, the country dummies would pick up both country-level income per capita and individual respondents' incomes. If the country fixed effect for a rich country were higher than for a poor country, we would not be able to say for certain whether that was due to individual preferences of richer people, or the institutional characteristics of richer societies. Absolute household income would be an important omitted variable that is correlated with GDP per capita.

We deal with this concern in two main ways. First, we include in the regression demographic characteristics associated with human capital: age, sex, education, and city size. To the extent that these capture absolute household income, the omitted variable bias is mitigated. (We must interpret carefully those ancillary coefficients, as they reflect both the direct effect of the demographics on MWTP, and the indirect effect via income.) Second, we interact the ten income categories with the per capita GDP of the respondents' country. This means that the regression includes relative income (the income categories), per capita GDP (embodied in the fixed effects), and the interaction between the two, which we interpret as absolute household income. In the original paper we also presented results controlling for absolute household income for nine of the 33 countries which had complete-enough documentation available to assign absolute household incomes (Israel and Levinson, 2004).

Table 2.2 presents the results from the linear probability model where the dependent variable is one if the respondent answered "agree" or "strongly agree"

Table 2.2 Linear probability model of yes/no responses to World Values Survey environment question on WTP higher prices for environmental protection.

	Parameter estimate (standard error)
Age	–0.0017* (0.0002)
Female	0.025* (0.005)
Income category 1	–0.046* (0.022)
Income category 2	–0.113* (0.022)
Income category 3	–0.077* (0.021)
Income category 4	–0.073* (0.021)
Income category 5	–0.045* (0.021)
Income category 6	–0.033 (0.022)
Income category 7	–0.052* (0.022)
Income category 8	–0.061* (0.022)
Income category 9	–0.015 (0.024)
Education: some primary	0.031† (0.018)
Education: complete primary	0.068* (0.017)
Education: some secondary	0.086* (0.017)
Education: complete secondary	0.103* (0.017)
Education: some university	0.120* (0.019)
Education: university degree	0.155* (0.017)
City size: 2–5000	0.021† (0.011)
City size: 5–10000	–0.010 (0.012)
City size: 10–20000	0.042* (0.012)
City size: 20–50000	0.016 (0.011)
City size: 50–100000	0.053* (0.012)
City size: 100–500000	0.035* (0.010)
City size: > 500000	0.021* (0.010)
N	36375
Countries	33
Share of variance explained by country fixed effects.	0.72

Notes: * Statistically significant at 5 percent.

† Statistically significant at 10 percent.

Each regression includes country fixed effects and a set of interaction terms between GDP per capita and the 10 household income categories.

to the WVS question about willingness to pay higher prices, and zero otherwise. The table reports the coefficients on age, a female dummy, and income, education and city-size dummies. Not reported are coefficients on the interactions between per capita GDP and the income dummies, and a set of country fixed effects. Older respondents are significantly less likely to support protecting the environment. All else equal, a person 10 years older will be 1.7 percent less likely to agree to pay higher prices to protect the environment. Female respondents are about 2.5 percent more likely to support the environment. Support for the environment is generally greater for the higher-income respondents, though the trend in the income category coefficients is not uniformly positive. The negative coefficients imply that those in the top income category are more likely to agree to higher prices than those in the other income categories. And, support for the environment is consistently increasing with education, with respondents with a formal education more likely to support protecting the environment than those with no education. The coefficients on per capita GDP interacted with household income categories (not reported) are small, mostly statistically insignificant, and do not seem to follow any particular pattern.[12]

Figure 2.5 plots some country characteristics and regression coefficients against per capita GDP. Panel A of Figure 2.5 plots the average percent willing to pay higher prices to protect the environment, by country. Low-income countries display no particular pattern, while among mid- to high-income countries there may be a downward trend in the percent supporting the environment. Panel B of Figure 2.5 plots the fixed-effects coefficients from the regression in Table 2.2. After controlling for age, sex, household income, education, and city size, the same pattern persists: low-income countries display no pattern with respect to GDP, while willingness to pay appears to decline for high-income countries. This decline in MWTP for high-income countries is not inconsistent with any of the theoretical models, and is consistent with the "institutional constraints" story.

One reason MWTP may decline is that this question asks about a 20 percent increase in prices, obviously a relatively larger cost to high-spending households. If we have not successfully accounted for income with our demographic covariates and with the interactions between relative income categories and GDP, then the country fixed effects reflect in part the incomes of the respondents. Higher-income countries may exhibit lower MWTP because respondents are being asked to bear larger costs. In the original paper we examine the same results with three different dependent variables which indicate environmental support such as support for the statement "protecting the environment should be given priority, even if it causes slower economic growth." The dependent variable is one if the environment is the priority and zero if economic growth is the priority. The pattern of coefficients was similar with younger people, women, richer people, and more educated people more likely to agree that the environment should be a priority above growth. However, there is no apparent downward trend among mid- to high-income countries. This is open to (at least) two interpretations. It may be that the downward trend in MWTP in response to the price question is a spurious result of the fact that a price increase will cost higher-spending households more. Or, it

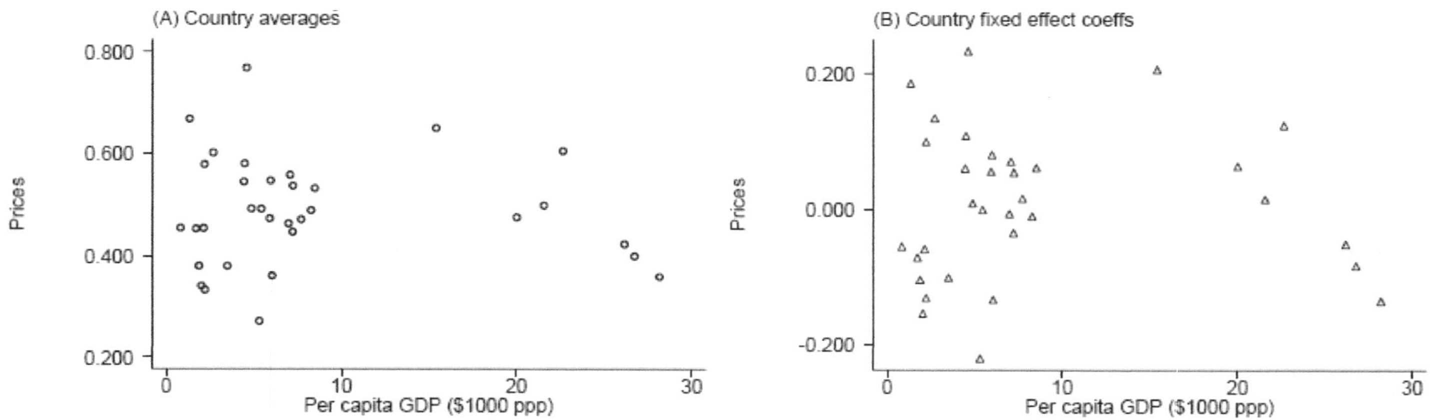

Figure 2.5 Country coefficients from Table 2.2

may be that the question about the environment being a priority is not interpreted by respondents as anything like a *marginal* willingness to pay.[13]

While MWTP does not appear either to increase or decrease with per capita GDP among the low-income countries, the country fixed effects do explain much of the variation in MWTP, and the estimated coefficients for the individual countries are generally statistically significant. This suggests that there may be country characteristics other than per capita GDP that affect the MWTP of respondents. In some cases there appear to be similarities among the MWTP of respondents in the same region. Among the Latin American countries, Venezuela, Brazil, Uruguay, and Mexico have similar estimated coefficients when examining the willingness to pay higher prices (although Chile, Peru, and the Dominican Republic are not very similar). However, there do not seem to be general patterns distinguishing the MWTP of low-income countries of one region from another.

The estimation technique presented here places no structure on the pattern of willingness to pay across countries. We have merely estimated linear probability models of the probability that people say "yes" in response to a question about the environment, and then plotted the coefficients on a set of country fixed effects. In addition to these results, we have also estimated linear probability models in the spline of per capita GDP, probit models and splines, and linear probabilities and probits of quadratic functions of per capita GDP. In those cases, we have included country characteristics including Gini coefficients, air pollution readings, and dummy variables for former Soviet bloc countries (transitional economies) and other low-income developing countries. We have also estimated these models with and without the sampling weights provided in the WVS. For none of the specifications, however, does a consistent pattern emerge for the low-income countries.

4 Conclusions

The various theories described in section 2 all aim to explain the observation that some pollutants worsen and then improve as countries' economies grow. Each theory has a different implication for the patterns of peoples' MWTP for improvements in environmental quality. Stokey's technological constraint explanation predicts that MWTP will increase with per capita GDP for countries with incomes below the level where their environments begin to improve. Jones and Manuelli's institutional constraint story predicts that MWTP will increase and then decrease with per capita GDP, with a peak at the point where countries' environments begin improving. And theories based on individual preferences, as well as the returns to scale explanation of Andreoni and Levinson, have no prediction about how MWTP will change as per capita GDP increases.

Using data from the WVS we do not find strong evidence that peoples' MWTP increases with per capita GDP among low-income countries. This may be because the technological and institutional constraint stories do not explain the inverse-U-shaped pollution–income path. Or, it may be because we have a poor measure of MWTP, from a deficient contingent valuation question, because we have poor controls for households' incomes, or because respondents are thinking about some environmental problem that does not follow an inverse U, or different environmental problems in different countries.

Finally, although we have not been able to discern a pattern in the relationship between MWTP for environmental improvements and national income, that is not to say that country-specific institutional explanations are not important. To the contrary, even though we have included ample demographic characteristics of respondents, the country fixed effects explain a large fraction of the variation in the responses. This suggests that country characteristics matter, though perhaps not in the stylized way suggested by the models in section 2.

Notes

1 The authors are grateful to Eli Berman, David Bloom, William Jack, John List, Gib Metcalf, Kerry Smith, and anonymous referees for helpful comments, to Sjamsu Rahardja for excellent research assistance, to the NBER for hosting and financing the Environmental Economics conference, and to the NSF for financial support (grant #SES-9905576).

2 This pattern has come to be called an "environmental Kuznets curve," after Simon Kuznets' observation that income inequality appears to follow a similar pattern, increasing and then decreasing with countries' incomes. See Carson (2010) for a recent examination of the empirical and theoretical literature in this area.

3 Bartlett (1994) wrote in the *Wall Street Journal* that "existing environmental regulation, by reducing economic growth, may actually be reducing environmental quality."

4 While a number of CV studies have examined how stated willingness to pay for environmental quality varies by household income within a country, both in industrialized and developing countries (Flores and Carson, 1997; Whittington, 1998), and some studies compare aggregate summaries of stated willingness to pay or support for the environment across countries (Bloom, 1995), our project is one of the first to use individual survey responses to compare how willingness to pay varies both across and within countries. Israel (2004) has a similar examination of these issues using a different data set with 15 countries. Since then, other authors have taken a similar approach, such as Owen and Videras (2006) utilizing the WVS from 2000–2001 using both country and individual-level characteristics to examine the relationship between civic cooperation and environmental support.

5 A second problem with the individual preferences explanation, and with Figure 2.1, is that it is not clear what the origin of the graph represents. If the linear "frontiers" represent tradeoffs between environmental quality and consumption, then a poor country is endowed with both low consumption and high pollution. A more realistic model would endow poor countries with clean environments, along with the ability to trade environmental quality for consumption.

6 Figure 2.2 is a reinterpretation of Figure 1 from Stokey (1998).

7 Note that if we switch one unit of resources (M) from abatement effort (E) to consumption (C), the change in pollution is $(1 - A_C + A_E)$. In the optimum, this has to be positive, otherwise we could get both more consumption and less pollution by making the switch, and the original situation could not have been optimal.

8 We are aware of the numerous critiques of the CV methodology (see Hausman, 2012). However, compared with alternative methodologies for calculating willingness to pay, such as travel costs, hedonics, or averting behavior, CV seems at least as likely to generate comparable values across countries. See Carson *et al.* (2000), and Smith (1997 and 2001), for defenses of CV methods.

9 The first wave of the data was conducted only for European countries. This third wave was the only wave available with numerous environmental questions at the time of this research project.

10 In theory, this leaves the survey open to strategic manipulation, with respondents concealing their true preferences in order to influence the ultimate outcome. In practice, we doubt this concern is relevant for these descriptive analyses.

11 Controlling for household income and other demographics, the proportion of respondents answering "yes" is *lower* for richer countries. If environmental quality is normal, this pattern only makes sense if the question is interpreted as a marginal increase in quality, and richer countries have cleaner environments.

12 We have also estimated the models in Table 2.2 without the interactive terms, with no significant effects on the other coefficients or on the pattern of country fixed effects coefficients.

13 Also in the original paper, two additional indicators of environmental support are examined: "have you chosen household products you think are better for the environment?" and "have you contributed to an environmental organization?" We believe that these last two questions reflect *total* rather than *marginal* willingness to pay. They do not ask about willingness to pay extra for an incremental improvement in environmental quality, but about whether the respondent already contributes in some way towards existing environmental quality. Furthermore, both poor households and rich households can purchase green products and contribute to green organizations at any level and still respond "yes" to this question. There is no sense in which this costs rich households more. In fact, if households buy products and contribute in proportion to their incomes, then poor households are paying *less* for the positive response to this question than are rich households. For both the raw responses to these questions and the country fixed effects coefficients, they exhibit an upward trend in the proportion saying "yes". This is consistent with the questions being interpreted as *total* willingness to pay, and hence inappropriate for examining the theoretical patterns described in section 2.

Appendix

Appendix Country averages from the World Values Survey

Countries ranked by per capita GDP	*Willing to pay higher prices to protect environment*[1]	*Per capita GDP (US$ for survey year)*[2]	*Number of observations*
Nigeria	0.454	0.82	1604
Bangladesh	0.667	1.34	1173
Ghana	0.452	1.71	42
India	0.379	1.87	1260
Azerbaijan	0.340	2.02	1561
Armenia	0.453	2.12	1621
Georgia*	0.578	2.20	2073
Moldova	0.332	2.20	900
China	0.600	2.68	1274
Ukraine	0.379	3.49	1687
Macedonia*	0.544	4.43	588
Peru	0.579	4.48	321
Dominic Rep	0.767	4.59	317
Bulgaria	0.492	4.86	653
Latvia*	0.271	5.30	1034
Belarus	0.491	5.42	1704
Croatia*	0.472	5.91	1084
Venezuela*	0.546	5.95	1069

Appendix Continued

Countries ranked by per capita GDP	*Willing to pay higher prices to protect environment*[1]	*Per capita GDP (US$ for survey year)*[2]	*Number of observations*
Lithuania	0.360	6.03	753
Estonia*	0.463	6.98	947
Brazil	0.557	7.06	1084
Russia	0.446	7.21	1690
Mexico	0.536	7.22	1022
Poland	0.470	7.71	976
Chile	0.488	8.28	897
Uruguay	0.531	8.49	880
Spain*	0.648	15.41	815
Finland	0.474	20.01	837
Australia	0.498	21.56	1712
Germany	0.604	22.65	1636
Switzerland*	0.422	26.18	909
Norway	0.399	26.76	1033
USA*	0.358	28.17	1219

Notes:
1 Authors' calculations from World Values Survey, Wave 3.
2 World Bank (2002), adjusted using purchasing power parity.
* Documentation available for household income brackets, used in table 3 and Figure 2.5.

References

Andreoni, James, and Arik Levinson. 2001. "The Simple Analytics of the Environmental Kuznets Curve." *Journal of Public Economics*. 80(2): 269–286.

Bartlett, Bruce. 1994. "The High Cost of Turning Green." *The Wall Street Journal*, September 14.

Bloom, David E. 1995. "International Public Opinion on the Environment." *Science*. 269: 354–358.

Carson, Richard T. 2010. "The Environmental Kuznets Curve: Seeking Empirical Regularity and Theoretical Structure." *Review of Environmental Economics and Policy*. 4(1): 3–23.

Carson, Richard T., Theodore Groves, and Mark J. Machina. 2000. "Incentive and Informational Properties of Preference Questions," mimeo, University of California San Diego.

Flores, Nicholas E., and Richard T. Carson. 1997. "The Relationship between the Income Elasticities of Demand and Willingness to Pay." *Journal of Environmental Economics and Management*. 33(3): 287–295.

Hausman, Jerry A. 2012. "Contingent Valuation: From Dubious to Hopeless." *Journal of Economic Perspectives*. 26(4): 43–56.

Israel, Debra K. 2004. "International support for environmental protection." *Environment and Development Economics*. 9: 757–780.

Israel, Debra and Arik Levinson. 2004. "Willingness to Pay for Environmental Quality: Testable Empirical Implications of the Growth and Environment Literature." *Contributions to Economic Analysis and Policy* (Berkeley Electronic Press), 3(1): article 2, http://www.bepress.com/bejeap/contributions/vol3/iss1/art2.

John, A. and R. Pecchenino. 1994. "An Overlapping Generations Model of Growth and the Environment." *The Economic Journal*. 104: 1393–1410.

Jones, Larry E. and Rodolfo E. Manuelli. 2001. "Endogenous Policy Choice: The Case of Pollution and Growth." *Review of Economic Dynamics*. 4(2): 369–405.

Owen, Ann L. and Julio Videras. 2006. "Civic Cooperation, Pro-Environment Attitudes, and Behavioral Intentions." *Ecological Economics*. 58: 814–829.

Smith, V. Kerry. 1997. "Pricing What is Priceless: A Status Report on Non-market Valuation of Environmental Resources." In Henk Folmer and Tom Tietenberg, eds., *International Yearbook of Environmental and Resource Economics 1997*. Cheltenham: Edward Elgar, pp. 156–204.

Smith, V. Kerry. 2001. "Fifty Years of Contingent Valuation," mimeo. North Carolina State University.

Stokey, Nancy L. 1998. "Are There Limits to Growth?" *International Economic Review*. 39(1): 1–31.

Whittington, Dale. 1998. "Administering Contingent Valuation Surveys in Developing Countries." *World Development*. 26: 21–30.

World Bank. 2002. *World Bank Development Indicators*. Washington DC.

3 The income elasticity of the impact of climate change

David Anthoff and Richard S.J. Tol

1 Introduction

Climate policy is an equity problem. Rich countries have emitted more greenhouse gases. Poor countries are generally believed to be more vulnerable to climate change than rich countries. Indeed, most people would argue that the relationship is causal. Poor economies are more exposed to weather and climate, for example because agriculture is more important, and poor societies have a lower adaptive capacity, for example because they lack in human capital. Poor countries also tend be in hotter places. At the same time, the global income distribution has changed dramatically over the last century, and will continue to change. Any assessment of the distributional implications of climate change will have to address how differential growth rates will affect relative vulnerabilities. This paper does exactly that.

Thomas Schelling wondered whether the best defense for poor societies against climate change impacts would be to develop (more) quickly, and whether this would be a more promising strategy for poor countries than to control greenhouse gas emissions (Schelling 1992). In this paper, we follow up on Anthoff and Tol (2012) and further test the Schelling Conjecture with the integrated assessment model FUND. Specifically, we estimate the income elasticity of climate change impacts. As in the previous paper, we find support for the Schelling Conjecture in very poor regions. That is, the income elasticity of climate change impacts is negative. Once regions have reached a certain level of development, however, further increases in development no longer reduce the impacts from climate change.

Among a number of otherwise similar models, FUND is unique in its rich representation of the interplay of economic development and climate change impacts. Most integrated assessment models assume functional forms for the impacts of climate change that mask any such effect. One example is the influential DICE model and its derivatives (Nordhaus and Boyer 2000, Nordhaus 2008). The damage function in DICE is a function of the global average temperature increase since pre-industrial times; it returns the welfare impact of climate change as a percentage of GDP. By assumption, therefore, damages from climate change always increase with GDP, and proportionally so.

Tol (1995) was the first to model vulnerability to climate change as an explicit function of development, breaking the ground for the analysis of the trade-off between development and climate policy (Tol and Dowlatabadi 2001, Tol 2005, Tol 2007, Tol, Ebi and Yohe 2007).

In a different strand of the literature, building on the work of Horowitz (2002), Hoel and Sterner (2007) suggest that the welfare impacts of climate change might be related to the consumption of other goods. As an example, they show that, with a constant elasticity of substitution utility function in consumption and environmental quality, the precise assumptions about the substitutability between consumption and environmental quality can make a significant impact on the *effective* discount rate to be used in an intertemporal setting. Sterner and Persson (2008) take this work a step further and replace the standard utility function in Nordhaus' DICE model with one of the form suggested in Hoel and Sterner (2007) and compute the optimal greenhouse gas mitigation paths under various parametric assumptions. Their results indicate clearly that relative prices matter, confirming the earlier conclusions of Hasselmann et al. (1997) and Yang (2003). Their numerical results, on the other hand, are not based on any empirical estimate of climate damages. They indicate that the interaction between consumption levels and environmental impacts can be an important aspect in the evaluation of climate impacts, but that further research would be required to quantify this effect. We here test the Sterner Conjecture that the impact of climate change is negative and a luxury good – that is, whether the income elasticity is greater than one.

Weitzman (2010) also investigates the functional form of the damage function from a theoretical point of view. He demonstrates how two different utility functions can lead to either a damage function like it is used in the DICE model or a damage function as investigated by Sterner and Persson.

FUND is the only integrated assessment model that specifies the relationship between temperature increases and income increases on human welfare in some detail. There are three features that make it suited to investigate the relationship between economic development and climate impacts. First, it has regionally disaggregated estimates of climate impacts. This allows for a differentiated view that takes into account different levels of development of different regions. Second, climate impacts in FUND are specified separately for a range of different impacts that affect human welfare. As such, structural differences between regions in the vulnerability to climate change impacts are accounted for: For example, FUND will have small (large) impacts from malaria in rich (poor) countries but with a high (low) value of the statistical life. Finally, different kinds of impacts react differently to development (income, urbanization, age structure, economic structure, technology) in the affected region.

This structure of the FUND model allows us to compute (rather than assume) the overall income elasticity of climate impacts for each region over time. Such an estimate will mainly depend on the income elasticities that have been estimated in previous work by the current authors or others for each individual impact and the share each of these impacts has in total impacts. An estimate of the income elasticity of impacts is a first attempt to answer the original question: Will an increase in wealth or development reduce or increase the impacts from climate change?

We present the precise methodology used in section 2 and a description of the integrated assessment model FUND in section 3. Section 4 presents and discusses results, and section 5 concludes and hints at further research topics.

2 Concepts

Income elasticities of climate change damages

We assess the income elasticities of climate change impacts along a business-as-usual path. We will first briefly repeat the standard definition of the income elasticity of damages and how we computed it with FUND and then point out why this is an interesting exercise with the FUND model, but not with a range of other, simpler models.

Let the impacts of climate change at a particular point in time in a particular region be given as

$$D_{tr} = D_{tr}(Y_{tr}, S_{tr}) \tag{1}$$

Here D_{tr} is the total impact in the unit of equivalent consumption, expressed in USD, in region r at time t. We assume that impacts depend on income Y_{tr} in the same region at the same time as well as on a vector of other variables S_{tr}.

Our definition of the income elasticity of the damages is just the standard one. First define

$$\Delta D_{tr} \equiv D_{tr}(Y_{tr} + \Delta Y, S_{tr}) - D_{tr}(Y_{tr}, S_{tr}) \tag{2}$$

to be the change in damages at time t in region r from the addition of a small extra amount of income ΔY. The income elasticity of impacts in region r at time t is then readily given by

$$\epsilon_{tr} = \frac{\Delta D_{tr}}{\Delta Y}\frac{Y_{tr}}{D_{tr}} \tag{3}$$

for a small change in income $\Delta Y < \delta$.

A classification

The interpretation of positive versus negative income elasticities of impacts changes with the sign of the total impacts. For beneficial impacts from climate change, a positive income elasticity means that those benefits increase with income, whereas a negative income elasticity implies that the beneficial impacts from climate change decrease with income. If climate change is harmful, a negative income elasticity means that rising incomes reduce those harmful impacts (as suggested by the Schelling Conjecture), whereas a positive income elasticity implies that an income rise increases the harmful impacts from climate change. This is set out in Table 3.1.

Table 3.1 The eight alternative cases for the effect of development on the damage by climate change.

	Elasticity < 0	Elasticity = 0	Elasticity < 1	Elasticity > 1
Damage < 0		absolute damage function		
Damage > 0	Schelling	absolute damage function		Sterner

Income elasticities larger than one (in absolute value) have a special significance: they suggest that the valuation of climate change impacts not only increases with an increase in income, but that the increase in valuation of the climate impact is even larger, in percentage terms, than the increase in income. Such cases are similar to "luxury goods" from standard economics, i.e. things that people care more about, the wealthier they get. This corresponds to the Sterner Conjecture.

Functional forms for damage functions

We next discuss two specific functional damage forms that have been used or discussed in the climate change economics literature, followed by an introduction to the damage function used by FUND.

The widely used DICE integrated model of climate change uses the following specific functional form for climate change impacts:

$$D_{tr}^{DICE}(Y) = Y - \frac{Y}{1+\psi T_{tr}^{2}}. \qquad (4)$$

Here D_{tr}^{DICE} is climate change impact at time t in region r, ψ is a parameter and T_{tr} is the assumed temperature increase at time t in region r of the underlying model. In this specification, the income elasticity is 1. Impacts are proportional to income. That is, DICE violates, by assumption, the Schelling and Sterner Conjectures.

Another possibility is that the damage function does not depend at all on income, i.e. that impacts from climate change are absolute and do not depend on economic development. In our framework this damage function would have the form

$$D_{tr}^{ABS}(Y) = F(T_{tr}). \qquad (5)$$

Here D_{tr}^{ABS} is climate change impact at time t in region r, $F(\cdot)$ is simply some function of the temperature that is assumed in the scenario for which climate damages are to be computed. We call this possibility an absolute damage function.

Again, computing the income elasticity for such a damage function is trivial: it is 0. Impacts are independent of income.

In the FUND model, damages have a much richer specification that does not allow for such a trivial computation of income elasticities. FUND's damages are the sum of individual damages functions for different types of impacts or sectors:

$$D_{tr}^{FUND}(Y) = \Sigma_s D_{trs}(Y). \tag{6}$$

$D_{trs}(\cdot)$ is the damage function for sector s in region r at time t, assuming a given temperature trajectory. The individual damage functions in FUND range from fairly simple functional forms – typically power functions or second-order polynomials – to complex sub-models of e.g. sea-level rise. For the purpose of this paper the main observation is that for each type of impact the income elasticity is different and calibrated to estimates from the impacts and valuation literature. As such, the income elasticity that we compute for a specific region and time will depend on the assumed income elasticities of the various damage categories that are accounted for in FUND and the shares of the various impact categories in the total impacts of a given region. The overall income elasticity is thus not assumed, but emerges, as does support (or lack thereof) for the Schelling and Sterner Conjectures.

3 The model

This paper uses version 3.8 of the *Climate Framework for Uncertainty, Negotiation and Distribution* (*FUND*).[1] Version 3.8 of *FUND* corresponds to version 1.6 (Tol 1999, Tol 2001, Tol 2002c) except for the impact module described in (Tol 2002a, Tol 2002b, Link and Tol 2004) and a series of smaller updates to parameters and specifications. A full list of papers, the source code, and the technical documentation for the model can be found online at www.fund-model.org.

In many ways, *FUND* is a standard integrated assessment model (Tol 1997, Tol 1999, Guo, Hepburn et al. 2006, Tol 2006). It has simple representations of the demography, economy, energy, emissions, and emission reduction policies for 16 regions (Table 3.2). It has simple representations of the cycles of greenhouse gases, radiative forcing, climate, and sea-level rise. In other ways, though, *FUND* is unique. It is alone in the detail of its representation of the impacts of climate change. Impacts on agriculture, forestry, water use, energy use, the coastal zone, hurricanes, ecosystems, and health are all modelled separately – both in "physical" units and their monetary value (Tol 2002a, Tol 2002b). Moreover, *FUND* allows vulnerability to climate change impacts to be an explicit function of the level and rate of regional development (Tol 2005, Tol, Ebi and Yohe 2007).

The climate impact module (Tol 2002a, Tol 2002b) includes the following categories: agriculture, forestry, sea-level rise, cardiovascular and respiratory disorders related to cold and heat stress, malaria, dengue fever, schistosomiasis, diarrhea, energy consumption, water resources, unmanaged ecosystems and tropical and extra tropical storms. All impacts are monetized.

Five scenarios are used in this analysis. The default socio-economic *FUND* scenario is based on the EMF14 Standardized Scenario, and lies somewhere in between the IS92a and IS92f scenarios (Leggett et al. 1992). The other four scenarios are the SRES scenarios A1B, A2, B1 and B2, as interpreted by the IMAGE model (IMAGE Team, 2001).

Table 3.2 FUND regions

Acronym	*Name*	*Countries*
USA	USA	United States of America
CAN	Canada	Canada
WEU	Western Europe	Andorra, Austria, Belgium, Cyprus, Denmark, Finland, France, Germany, Greece, Iceland, Ireland, Italy, Liechtenstein, Luxembourg, Malta, Monaco, Netherlands, Norway, Portugal, San Marino, Spain, Sweden, Switzerland, United Kingdom
JPK	Japan and South Korea	Japan, South Korea
ANZ	Australia and New Zealand	Australia, New Zealand
EEU	Central and Eastern Europe	Albania, Bosnia and Herzegovina, Bulgaria, Croatia, Czech Republic, Hungary, FYR Macedonia, Poland, Romania, Slovakia, Slovenia, Yugoslavia
FSU	Former Soviet Union	Armenia, Azerbaijan, Belarus, Estonia, Georgia, Kazakhstan, Kyrgyzstan, Latvia, Lithuania, Moldova, Russia, Tajikistan, Turkmenistan, Ukraine, Uzbekistan
MDE	Middle East	Bahrain, Iran, Iraq, Israel, Jordan, Kuwait, Lebanon, Oman, Qatar, Saudi Arabia, Syria, Turkey, United Arab Emirates, West Bank and Gaza, Yemen
CAM	Central America	Belize, Costa Rica, El Salvador, Guatemala, Honduras, Mexico, Nicaragua, Panama
SAM	South America	Argentina, Bolivia, Brazil, Chile, Colombia, French Guiana, Guyana, Paraguay, Peru, Suriname, Uruguay, Venezuela
SAS	South Asia	Afghanistan, Bangladesh, Bhutan, India, Nepal, Pakistan, Sri Lanka
SEA	Southeast Asia	Brunei, Cambodia, East Timor, Indonesia, Laos, Malaysia, Myanmar, Papua New Guinea, Philippines, Singapore, Taiwan, Thailand, Vietnam
CHI	China plus	China, Hong Kong, North Korea, Macau, Mongolia
NAF	North Africa	Algeria, Egypt, Libya, Morocco, Tunisia, Western Sahara
SSA	Sub-Saharan Africa	Angola, Benin, Botswana, Burkina Faso, Burundi, Cameroon, Cape Verde, Central African Republic, Chad, Congo-Brazzaville, Congo-Kinshasa, Cote d'Ivoire, Djibouti, Equatorial Guinea, Eritrea, Ethiopia, Gabon, Gambia, Ghana, Guinea, Guinea- Bissau, Kenya, Lesotho, Liberia, Madagascar, Malawi, Mauritania, Mozambique, Namibia, Niger, Nigeria, Rwanda, Senegal, Sierra Leone, Somalia, South Africa, Sudan, Swaziland, Tanzania, Togo, Uganda, Zambia, Zimbabwe
SIS	Small Island States	Antigua and Barbuda, Aruba, Bahamas, Barbados, Bermuda, Comoros, Cuba, Dominica, Dominican Republic, Fiji, French Polynesia, Grenada, Guadeloupe, Haiti, Jamaica, Kiribati, Maldives, Marshall Islands, Martinique, Mauritius, Micronesia, Nauru, Netherlands Antilles, New Caledonia, Palau, Puerto Rico, Reunion, Samoa, Sao Tome and Principe, Seychelles, Solomon Islands, St Kitts and Nevis, St Lucia, St Vincent and Grenadines, Tonga, Trinidad and Tobago, Tuvalu, Vanuatu, Virgin Islands

4 Results

Negative impacts

Tables 3.3 and 3.4 show the estimated income elasticities of climate change impacts for ten selected years and all 16 regions of the FUND model. The tables show both the mean across scenarios and the range of results. Table 3.2 shows the elasticities for regions and times with estimated net damages from climate change. Table 3.3 shows elasticities for regions and times with estimated net benefits from climate change.

We removed income elasticity estimates for time periods that are adjacent to a switch from beneficial to harmful impacts. These elasticities are estimated for impacts that are very close to zero and go through plus and minus infinity.

Income elasticities vary greatly between regions and change over time. They range from <–1 to >1, which suggests that depending on the circumstances of the society affected, additional income might reduce or increase impacts from climate change. This confirms earlier findings about climate change impacts: Impacts are highly heterogeneous across time and space and aggregated net world impact estimates hide a lot of the distributional consequences of climate impacts. The estimates also suggest that both the Schelling Conjecture and the Sterner Conjecture might be true for some regions in some time periods but not as a general feature of climate impacts.

If the income elasticity of impacts is greater than unity, absolute impacts and impacts relative to income rise with income. This is the Sterner Conjecture. Only the USA, Western Europe, the former Soviet Union (FSU), South Asia, North Africa (NAF) and sub-Saharan Africa (SSA) never have an income elasticity larger than 1 (for the period analyzed in this chapter). The reason is that the damage categories that have income elasticities larger than 1 in FUND – namely biodiversity loss, dryland loss, wetland loss and emigration and immigration due to sea-level rise – do not play a significant role in these regions. Sea-level rise is less of an issue in the former Soviet Union because most of its coast is uninhabited. In Africa, coastal protection rapidly expands with development. Sea-level-rise refugees would rarely move to any of these three regions. Biodiversity loss is valued less in poorer regions than is the case elsewhere, but biodiversity also contributes only a little to total impacts in richer regions.

In the regions with net damages that do have income elasticities larger than 1, the income elasticity falls over time and eventually drops below 1 (sometimes after 2100, not shown in Table 3.2). The main driver for this result is the shift in the composition of damages. As temperatures reach higher levels in later periods, the impacts in particular in the agricultural sector start to dominate the total damages. In FUND, it is assumed that the impacts from agriculture have an income elasticity <1 so that the growing importance of agriculture reduces the overall income elasticity of impacts. Furthermore, heat-related health impacts are important. The value of a statistical life is assumed to have an income elasticity of one, and the vulnerable population (elderly people in cities) increases with income.

Table 3.3 Estimated income elasticities when net climate change impacts are harmful. Shaded cells are consistent with the Schelling Conjecture; black cells with white text are consistent with the Sterner Conjecture; no cells are consistent with an absolute damage function

Region	*2010*	*2020*	*2030*	*2040*	*2050*	*2060*	*2070*	*2080*	*2090*	*2100*
ANZ										
CAM								1.1	0.9	0.8
								0.9–1.2	0.8–1.0	0.8–0.9
CAN									2.3	1.6
									1.4–3.3	1.2–1.8
CHI										1.0
										1.0–1.0
EEU					1.4	1.2	1.1	1.0	1.0	0.9
					1.3–1.7	1.2–1.2	1.1–1.1	1.0–1.0	0.9–1.0	0.9–0.9
FSU	−0.1	0.2	0.5	0.6	0.7	0.8	0.8	0.8	0.8	0.8
	−0.2–0.0	0.1–0.4	0.3–0.6	0.5–0.8	0.5–0.8	0.6–0.9	0.7–0.8	0.7–0.8	0.7–0.9	0.8–0.8
JPK										
LAM	−2.9	−0.7	0.4	0.6	0.8	0.8	0.9	0.9	0.9	0.9
	−10.4–10.4	−1.6–0.4	−0.4–1.1	−0.2–1.3	0.4–1.1	0.4–1.1	0.8–1.1	0.8–1.0	0.8–1.0	0.8–1.0
NAF	0.2	0.4	0.5	0.6	0.6	0.6	0.7	0.7	0.7	0.7
	0.0–0.3	0.2–0.6	0.4–0.7	0.3–0.7	0.5–0.7	0.5–0.8	0.7–0.8	0.7–0.8	0.6–0.8	0.7–0.8
MDE										1.4
										1.3–1.4
SAS								0.0	0.3	0.4
								−0.6–0.7	0.0–0.8	0.3–0.8
SEA				0.4	0.7	0.7	0.8	0.8	0.8	0.8
				−0.9–1.3	0.3–1.1	0.3–1.0	0.6–0.9	0.7–0.9	0.7–0.9	0.7–0.9
SIS										
SSA	−0.9	−0.7	−0.5	−0.3	−0.2	−0.1	0.1	0.2	0.2	0.3
	−1.0–−0.7	−0.8–−0.4	−0.6–−0.2	−0.7–0.1	−0.5–0.2	−0.5–0.3	−0.1–0.4	0.0–0.4	0.0–0.5	0.1–0.5

Table 3.3 Continued

Region	*2010*	*2020*	*2030*	*2040*	*2050*	*2060*	*2070*	*2080*	*2090*	*2100*
USA	–1.6	0.2	0.5	0.6	0.7	0.7	0.7	0.7	0.8	0.8
	–2.1––1.3	–0.2–0.4	0.2–0.6	0.4–0.7	0.5–0.8	0.6–0.8	0.6–0.8	0.6–0.8	0.7–0.8	0.7–0.8
WEU	–1.1	0.0	0.4	0.4	0.5	0.6	0.7	0.7	0.7	0.7
	–2.0––0.4	–0.7–0.4	–0.1–0.6	0.1–0.7	0.3–0.8	0.3–0.8	0.5–0.8	0.5–0.8	0.6–0.8	0.6–0.8

Table 3.4 Estimated income elasticities when net climate change impacts are beneficial; Schelling and Sterner disregards positive impacts; no cells are consistent with an absolute damage function.

Region	*2010*	*2020*	*2030*	*2040*	*2050*	*2060*	*2070*	*2080*	*2090*	*2100*
ANZ	0.5	0.5	0.5	0.5	0.5	0.4	0.4	0.2	–0.2	–1.4
	0.5–0.5	0.5–0.5	0.5–0.5	0.5–0.5	0.4–0.5	0.4–0.5	0.3–0.4	0.1–0.4	–0.9–0.2	–2.8––0.3
CAM	1.0	0.9	0.8	0.7	0.7	0.5				
	0.9–1.1	0.7–1.0	0.7–1.0	0.5–0.9	0.4–0.9	–0.3–1.0				
CAN	0.5	0.4	0.3	0.2	0.0	–0.5	–3.5	–3.5	–0.9	–1.8
	0.5–0.5	0.4–0.4	0.3–0.4	0.1–0.3	–0.2–0.1	–1.2––0.1	–11.9––0.2	–6.4––0.5	–0.9––0.9	–1.8––1.8
CHI	0.8	0.8	0.7	0.7	0.7	0.7	0.7	0.6	0.7	0.6
	0.8–0.8	0.7–0.8	0.7–0.8	0.7–0.8	0.7–0.8	0.7–0.8	0.6–0.7	0.5–0.7	0.5–0.7	0.4–0.7
EEU	0.6	0.3								
	0.6–0.7	0.1–0.5								
FSU										
JPK	0.7	0.7	0.7	0.7	0.7	0.7	0.7	0.6	0.6	0.4
	0.7–0.8	0.7–0.8	0.7–0.8	0.6–0.8	0.6–0.8	0.6–0.8	0.6–0.8	0.5–0.8	0.4–0.8	–0.3–0.8
LAM										
MAF										
MDE	0.8	0.8	0.7	0.7	0.7	0.7	0.6	0.5	0.2	0.6
	0.8–0.8	0.7–0.8	0.7–0.8	0.7–0.8	0.6–0.8	0.6–0.8	0.4–0.7	0.1–0.7	–1.2–0.7	0.5–0.6
SAS	1.6	1.4	1.3	1.5	1.6	3.0				
	1.2–2.0	0.9–2.0	0.9–2.0	0.9–2.1	0.9–2.4	0.8–5.4				
SEA	2.3									
	1.4–3.1									
SIS	0.9	1.1	0.9	1.0	1.0	1.0	0.9	1.0	1.0	1.1
	0.5–1.1	0.9–1.3	0.5–1.1	0.8–1.4	0.8–1.2	0.8–1.4	0.8–1.1	0.8–1.1	0.7–1.2	0.7–1.3
SSA										
USA										
WEU										

However, the rate of warming slows down over the century in all scenarios, so that acclimatization suppresses the impact.

If the income elasticity of impacts is negative, the Schelling Conjecture may hold. Development policy would reduce the impact of climate change, and may be preferred over greenhouse gas emission reduction. Among regions and times with net damages, only the USA, Western Europe, the former Soviet Union, Latin America, South Asia, Southeast Asia, and sub-Saharan Africa ever have negative income elasticities. This is often only present in the first few decades. In sub-Saharan Africa, it disappears in the second half of the century. Improvements in basic health care explain a large part of the negative income elasticity: both diarrhea and malaria deaths constitute a large portion of total damages in the early decades in poor regions and the incidence of these infectious diseases rapidly falls with economic growth. Once sub-Saharan Africa has left its extreme poverty (an assumption made in all of the commonly used socio-economic scenarios employed in climate change analysis), the further reduction in deaths from these diseases from an incremental increase in income is reduced.

Note that Table 3.3 shows that impacts vary with per capita income. We therefore find no support for an absolute damage function.

Positive impacts

So far, we have discussed the case of net damages of climate change. Climate change also has positive impacts, and these may dominate the negative effects in some periods and regions. In this case, the interpretation of the income elasticities, shown in Table 3.4, is different. The estimated income elasticities show a much more homogenous picture than for net damages. Most income elasticities in this case are between 0 and 1, suggesting that while *absolute* benefits from higher temperatures would increase with higher incomes, *relative* benefits fall. Income elasticities fall over time in almost all cases.

The main benefits are increased agricultural yield – CO_2 fertilization in all regions and a more beneficial climate in some – and reductions in heating costs. Heating benefits saturate over time: Once a region has reached a climate that does not require any winter heating at all, further temperature increases do not yield any further benefits. For both sectors, the income elasticities are between 0 and 1 and that explains why the overall income elasticities for regions and times with net benefits stay in the same range.

Like Table 3.3, Table 3.4 shows that impacts vary with per capita income. We therefore again find no support for an absolute damage function. Both the Schelling Conjecture and the Sterner Conjecture presume that impacts are negative.

5 Conclusion

We used the integrated assessment model FUND to compute the income elasticities of climate change impacts for different world regions over time. We find limited support both for the Schelling Conjecture that economic growth is always the best defense against climate change impacts and for the Sterner Conjecture that the impacts from climate change are always a "luxury good". We find no support for an absolute damage function, that is, an additive impact function, independent of the level of development.

For very poor societies, we find strong confirmation of the Schelling Conjecture. Impacts are dominated by health impacts in those regions and those are the kinds of impacts that rapidly disappear as societies develop and get richer. As a result, the distribution of the impacts of climate change will become less skewed. Climate change will become less pronounced as an equity problem. While we do not see this effect for more than a few decades, this result is most likely driven by strong, and maybe questionable, assumptions of the underlying socio-economic scenario. Almost all scenarios that are used in climate change analysis make strong assumptions about economic development. Today's very poor regions are assumed to develop quickly, and for all practical purposes no single region will be "left behind" or stay at an income level as seen today. This seems an area for future research: if some regions stay poor throughout the century, it is highly likely that even small increases in wealth might be the best way to lower the harmful impacts from climate change.

For wealthier regions we see that at least in the medium term, climate impacts show characteristics of a "luxury good," i.e. the valuation of a given temperature increase reacts more than proportionally to an increase in income – the Sterner Conjecture. But this effect wanes at later times, once agricultural impacts begin to dominate the total damage estimates and once warming slows down.

The conclusions we take from our results are twofold. First, we believe our results show that careful empirical analysis that takes into account regional and sectoral heterogeneities is required to answer bold questions such as whether climate change impacts are a luxury good (Sterner Conjecture), whether impacts are decoupled from development (absolute damage function), or whether development might be the best approach to lower climate impacts (Schelling Conjecture). Most likely, simple answers cannot be found, in many cases the answer will depend crucially on the circumstances. Our results rest on a large number of assumptions, but we believe the finding that income elasticities vary greatly between regions and time is a robust result. Second, we also believe that the few results on very poor regions (essentially sub-Saharan Africa for the first couple of decades of this century) make for a compelling argument along the Schelling Conjecture, namely that, especially for very poor regions, development is key to avoid the worst impacts from climate change.

Our results carry a long list of caveats with them. They are based on a single model, on a limited range of scenarios of economic development, they span time frames for which predictions of socio-economic development are highly difficult and the damage functions that are used are estimated on very limited data sets from a few geographical locations and are then extrapolated to the rest of the world. Our analysis ignores all aspects of uncertainty, in particular the potential for catastrophic but unlikely outcomes. The potential for catastrophes has been suggested as the real reason for concern about climate change (Weitzman 2009).

More research in this area, especially more original studies of climate change impacts, would certainly be most welcome.

Our results should be of interest for quite a large number of issues that have been discussed in the climate change economics literature in recent years. First, as Schelling has pointed out himself (Schelling 1999), there is a direct connection between discounting and distributional questions and the income elasticity of climate impacts. A marginal change in income will also change marginal utility of a region, and when a Ramsey framework is used, this will change the discount rate. It is the interaction of the effect on the discount rate and on the estimated damages that will determine how the net present value of impacts changes when income changes, the key measure that would drive today's policy decisions. Second, the income elasticities of impacts should also have an effect on risk adjustments to the computation of the net present value of expected damages, when uncertainty is introduced into a model like FUND. Future research on both questions would be most welcome.

Acknowledgements

We thank Robert Hahn, James Hammitt, an anonymous reviewer and participants of the workshop in honor of Thomas Schelling for helpful comments. All remaining errors are ours.

Note

1 The precise version used is FUND 3.8.1.

References

Anthoff, D. and R. S. J. Tol (2012). "Schelling's Conjecture on Climate and Development: A Test." In *Climate Change and Common Sense – Essays in Honour of Tom Schelling*, R. W. Hahn and A. M. Ulph (eds.). Oxford: Oxford University Press, pp. 260–274.

Guo, J., C. J. Hepburn, R. S. J. Tol and D. Anthoff (2006). "Discounting and the Social Cost of Carbon: A Closer Look at Uncertainty." *Environmental Science & Policy* **9**(3): 205–216.

Hasselmann, K., S. Hasselmann, R. Giering, V. Ocana and H. von Stoch (1997). "Sensitivity Study of Optimal CO2 Emission Paths Using a Simplified Structural Integrated Assessment Model (SIAM)." *Climatic Change* **37**(2): 345–386.

Hoel, M. and T. Sterner (2007). "Discounting and Relative Prices." *Climatic Change* **84**: 265–280.

Horowitz, J. K. (2002). "Preferences in the Future." *Environmental and Resource Economics* **21**: 241–259.

IMAGE Team (2001), *The IMAGE 2.2 Implementation of the SRES Scenarios: A Comprehensive Analysis of Emissions, Climate Change, and Impacts in the 21st Century*. National Institute for Public Health and the Environment, Bilthoven, 481508018.

Leggett, J., et al. (1992). "Emissions scenarios for the IPCC: an update." *Climate Change 1992 - The Supplementary Report to the IPCC Scientific Assessment*. J. T. Houghton, B. A. Callander and S. K. Varney (eds.). Cambridge, Cambridge University Press: 71–95.

Link, P. M. and R. S. J. Tol (2004). "Possible Economic Impacts of a Shutdown of the Thermohaline Circulation: An Application of FUND." *Portuguese Economic Journal* **3**(2): 99–114.

Nordhaus, W. (2008). *A Question of Balance: Weighing the Options on Global Warming Policies*. New Haven and London: Yale University Press.

Nordhaus, W. D. and J. Boyer (2000). *Warming the World: Economics Models of Global Warming*. Cambridge, MA: MIT Press.

Schelling, T. C. (1992). "Some Economics of Global Warming." *The American Economic Review* **82**(1): 1–14.

Schelling, T. C. (1999). Intergenerational Discounting. *Discounting and Intergenerational Equity*. P. R. Portney and J. P. Weyant. Washington, DC: Resources for the Future.

Sterner, T. and U. M. Persson (2008). "An even Sterner Review: Introducing Relative Prices into the Discounting Debate." *Review of Environmental Economics and Policy* **2**(1): 1–16.

Tol, R. S. J. (1995). "The Damage Costs of Climate Change: Toward More Comprehensive Calculations." *Environmental and Resource Economics* **5**(4): 353–374.

Tol, R. S. J. (1997). "On the Optimal Control of Carbon Dioxide Emissions – An Application of FUND." *Environmental Modelling and Assessment* **2**: 151–163.

Tol, R. S. J. (1999). "The Marginal Costs of Greenhouse Gas Emissions." *The Energy Journal* **20**(1): 61–81.

Tol, R. S. J. (2001). "Equitable Cost-benefit Analysis of Climate Change Policies." *Ecological Economics* **36**: 71–85.

Tol, R. S. J. (2002a). "Estimates of the Damage Costs of Climate Change. Part 1: Benchmark Estimates." *Environmental and Resource Economics* **21**(2): 47–73.

Tol, R. S. J. (2002b). "Estimates of the Damage Costs of Climate Change. Part 2: Dynamic Estimates." *Environmental and Resource Economics* **21**(2): 135–160.

Tol, R. S. J. (2002c). "Welfare Specifications and Optimal Control of Climate Change: An Application of FUND." *Energy Economics* **24**: 367–376.

Tol, R. S. J. (2005). "Emission Abatement versus Development as Strategies to Reduce Vulnerability to Climate Change: An Application of FUND." *Environment and Development Economics* **10**: 615–629.

Tol, R. S. J. (2006). "Multi-Gas Emission Reduction for Climate Change Policy: An Application of FUND." *Energy Journal* **27**: 235–250.

Tol, R. S. J. (2007). "The Double Trade-off between Adaptation and Mitigation for Sea Level Rise: An Application of FUND." *Mitigation and Adaptation Strategies for Global Change* **12**(5): 741–753.

Tol, R. S. J. and H. Dowlatabadi (2001). "Vector-Borne Diseases, Development and Climate Change." *Integrated Assessment* **2**(4): 173–181.

Tol, R. S. J., K. L. Ebi and G. W. Yohe (2007). "Infectious Disease, Development, and Climate Change: A Scenario Analysis." *Environment and Development Economics* **12**(5): 687–706.

Weitzman, M. L. (2009). "On Modeling and Interpreting the Economics of Catastrophic Climate Change." *The Review of Economics and Statistics* **91**(1): 1–19.

Weitzman, M. L. (2010). "What is the 'Damages Function' for Global Warming – and What Difference Might It Make?" *Climate Change Economics* **1**(1): 57–69.

Yang, Z. (2003). "Dual-rate Discounting in Dynamic Economic–Environmental Modeling." *Economic Modelling* **20**: 941–957.

Part II

The distributional incidence of benefits of environmental improvements

4 Environmental goods and the distribution of income

Udo Ebert

1 Introduction[1]

The literature in environmental economics is mainly concerned with (the correction of) market failure and the issue of allocation. The aim of this paper is to present a thorough (theoretical) investigation of the benefits from environmental commodities and of their effect on the income distribution. The article introduces an appropriate framework, discusses concepts for measuring and imputing benefits, offers a methodology for considering benefit incidence, and examines the determinants of progressivity/regressivity within this setup. Knowledge of the distributional effects of environmental goods is indispensable when the implications of environmental policy to the income distribution have to be derived (taking into account costs, as well).

We face at least two basic problems when environmental goods have to be evaluated. First, there are no markets on which these goods are traded. Therefore it is impossible to observe prices. Second, even if there were prices they would not reflect the consumers' marginal willingness to pay since demand for environmental goods is typically rationed. These goods have to be consumed in certain, fixed quantities which cannot be influenced by consumers. Insofar as environmental goods are comparable to other nonmarket goods like public goods. It is well known that the problem of revealing (marginal) willingness to pay for nonmarket goods has not yet been solved generally. On the other hand, the literature on the evaluation of nonmarket goods is voluminous. Mäler (1985), Freeman (1985), Johansson (1987) and Braden and Kolstad (1991) provide good surveys on the problems and methods employed. Therefore in practice often some methods can be used which allow us to evaluate nonmarket goods and to solve the problem of preference revelation in specific situations. This paper will not deal with this issue. It a priori assumes that the consumers' preference ordering is known. Thus its emphasis is on methodology and on recognizing the economic variables which determine benefit incidence.

Since we are not interested in the physical incidence of an environmental good, but in its benefit incidence, the benefits received from environmental goods have to be determined, i.e., have to be evaluated in monetary terms. Therefore we consider a typical consumer a first. Three measures of benefits are discussed: The equivalent variation, gross consumer surplus, and (total) willingness to pay for the environmental good in a market. The Hicksian measure reflects the total benefits enjoyed precisely. Gross consumer's surplus presents a simple approximation to it, also taking into account the marginal willingness to pay for the marginal and inframarginal units of the environmental good. The third measure evaluates the benefits by the amount the consumer would be willing to pay in a fictitious market. This income-equivalent equals the product of the respective marginal willingness to pay and the quantity of the environmental good. In this case value is used in the neoclassical sense of the marginal valuation put on a good. Then (net) consumer surplus is not taken into account. The concept follows early attempts at evaluating the benefits of public goods (cf. Aaron and McGuire (1971)). But here no particular assumptions – as e.g., separability of utility functions with respect to private and environmental goods – are made.

Having discussed the benefits received from an environmental good for a single consumer we consider their incidence. We assume that consumers posses the same preference ordering, but differ in income. There are several approaches to measure the distributional implications which depend on income. Is the distribution of benefits "pro-poor" or "pro-rich"? Early contributions (cf. Baumol (1974) and also Baumol and Oates (1988)) argue that the benefits are distributed progressively, i.e., they favor the rich. The basic argument is the following: environmental benefits increase with income or the income elasticity of demand for an environmental good is positive. Pearce (1980) reports about Freeman (1972) who "refers to income elasticities greater than zero as being evidence of a 'pro-rich' distribution since benefits rise with income." In the meantime it has become clear (cf. section 2 of Kristöm and Riera (1996)) that the income elasticity of *demand* is not the relevant variable, but that the income elasticity of willingness to pay for an environmental good is decisive. If it is e.g., greater than one the share of total benefits over income increases faster than income, i.e., benefits are distributed progressively.

In this paper we will follow up exactly this line: In accordance with the theory of tax incidence we will investigate whether the benefits from environmental goods, expressed as a fraction of income rise or fall with income. For a single environmental good it turns out that this fraction increases (decreases) if and only if the income elasticity of the benefit measure is greater (less) than one. Then benefits are distributed progressively, i.e., pro-rich (regressively or pro-poor).

For each benefit measure its income elasticity is the crucial variable when benefit incidence is under consideration. Closer inspection demonstrates that in any case the income elasticity of the *marginal* willingness to pay for the environmental good is important: When benefits are measured by price times quantity it is even equal to the income elasticity of total willingness to pay.

Thus the core of the paper is concerned with a discussion of the income elasticity of marginal willingness to pay when there is one environmental good. The elasticity obviously depends on the consumer's underlying preference ordering. In order to illuminate its relevance and to make it accessible to an empirical determination the elasticity is related to further economic variables characterizing the preference ordering. It turns out that it can be expressed by means of the income and own price elasticity of the (unconditional) demand for the environmental good. These elasticities cannot be observed directly, but can sometimes be inferred by some methods of evaluation. The result demonstrates that an income *and* a substitution effect play a role.

But the substitutability between the environmental good and the private goods is also relevant for benefit incidence: If e.g., there is a close (private) substitute to the environmental commodity consumers having higher incomes can more easily substitute the environmental by the respective private good. Therefore the price elasticities of the environmental good with respect to private goods play a role, too. This interpretation is strengthened by the fact that these price elasticities of demand can also be replaced by the Allen-Uzawa partial elasticities of substitution between the environmental good and the respective private good. The decomposition of the income elasticity of marginal willingness to pay which is obtained by the analysis can also be related to an earlier result proved for taxation of a public good according to the benefit principle (Kovenock and Sadka (1981); Snow and Warren (1983)).

Summing up, it is possible to present a number of characteristic variables and properties of the underlying preference ordering which influence and determine the income elasticity of marginal willingness to pay for an environmental good and thus its distributional impacts. It becomes (once again) clear that the income elasticity of *demand* for an environmental good is not sufficient to describe its distributional impacts. Normality of the environmental good (in its usual sense) only implies that the income elasticity of marginal willingness to pay is positive. It does not yield anything about progressivity or regressivity of the distribution of benefits.

Whenever there are several environmental goods which have to be taken into account things become much more complicated (see, Flores and Carson (1997)). Even if all environmental goods considered are normal and if the income elasticities of (unconditional) demand are strictly greater than one it is no longer guaranteed that the income elasticity of marginal willingness to pay is positive. The reason for this outcome is the fact that two goods can be e.g., Hicksian substitutes (complements) in the normal sense and Hicksian complements (substitutes) in the conditional framework (i.e., when the consumer can choose only private goods given the quantities of the environmental goods) at the same time. In this setup only few general conclusions about benefit incidence can be drawn.

In addition to the papers mentioned above there are further connections to the literature: In particular, three papers deal with topics which are formally related to the present one. Hanemann (1991) provides an explanation for the difference between WTP and WTA. He proves that not only an income effect but also a substitution effect is relevant. Flores and Carson (1997) consider the relationship between the income elasticities of demand and willingness to pay for environmental goods and discuss the elasticities and the Hicksian benefit measures. Finally, Carson, Flores, and Hanemann (1998) investigate the influence of sequencing on the evaluation of environmental goods. It must be stressed that the focus of the present paper is completely different: The aim is to develop a precise framework for an investigation of *benefit incidence*. The paper identifies the relevant properties of the underlying preference ordering and allows us to answer the question whether the distribution is pro-poor or pro-rich – given the information about preferences. Furthermore, the results are interpreted with respect to the distributional implications.

The organization of the paper is as follows: section 2 introduces the information about consumers and the consumers' preference ordering. In section 3 the general approach is described: the definition of benefit measures, the concept of benefit incidence, and the role of the income elasticity of marginal willingness to pay. Section 4 considers the determinants of this elasticity for a single and for several environmental goods. Section 5 offers some conclusions.

2 Consumers

In order to investigate the incidence of environmental benefits we have to choose an appropriate model. It has to comprise consumers having different incomes and to take into account the consumers' evaluation of the environment. Furthermore it should be simple. Therefore we use an "equal-preference" model; consumers possess the same preference ordering, but possibly differ with respect to income. This kind of model implies that there are no differences between poor and rich individuals as far as preferences are concerned. If the evaluation of an environmental good varies such differences are caused by differences in income. Therefore the framework allows us to borrow some concepts describing benefit incidence from public economics. They will be introduced in the next section. At first we give a more precise description of the underlying model.

We assume that there are m private market goods $X_1, \ldots, X_m$ and a nonmarket good G. The latter should be interpreted as a purely public commodity (like e.g., environmental quality measured appropriately) for the *population under consideration*. A typical consumer has a strictly convex preference ordering R over commodity bundles $(\mathbf{X}, G) = (X_1, \ldots, X_m, G)$. R is represented by an ordinal, twice differentiable direct utility function $U(\mathbf{X}, G)$ which is strictly quasi-concave and strictly increasing in each of its arguments; i.e., preferences are nonsatiated and the environmental good G is desired and not a "bad." M denotes a consumer's income. Then for simplicity the population is described by an interval $[\underline{M}, \overline{M}$ being the support of a continuous density function. The fact that the population is described by a continuum does not really restrict the following analysis. It facilitates the investigation of benefit incidence below.

We examine two different maximization problems. First, we investigate the problem actually faced by a consumer. Typically, a single consumer is not able to influence the quantity G. In her view it is fixed. Given the prices $\mathbf{p} = (p_1, \ldots, p_m)$ of market goods and her income M a consumer solves a conditional or constrained maximization problem:

$$\max U(\mathbf{X}, G)$$

$$s.t.\ \mathbf{pX} = M \text{ and } G \text{ fixed,where } \mathbf{pX} = \sum_{i=1}^{m} p_i X_i.$$

Its solution yields the observable conditional demand function $X_i(p_1, \ldots, p_m, G, M)$, $i = 1, \ldots, m$. They depend on the exogenous variable G. Inserting $X_i(\mathbf{p}, G, M)$ in the direct utility function U we obtain the conditional indirect utility function $V(\mathbf{p}, G, M)$ and the conditional expenditure function $E(\mathbf{p}, G, u)$. Given U, they are unique, but they cannot be recovered from the conditional demand system (cf. Ebert (1997, 1998)).

Second, though it is not realistic, we can, in principle, treat G also as market good. In this case we get a pseudo-choice problem whose solution turns out to be helpful. Then the consumer maximizes her utility given prices $\mathbf{p}$, p_G, and income $\hat{M}$:

$$\max U(\mathbf{X}, G)$$
$$s.t.\ \mathbf{pX} + p_G G = \hat{M}. \tag{1}$$

We get the ordinary (unconditional) Marshallian demand system as solution:

$$\hat{X}_i(\mathbf{p}, p_G, \hat{M}) \text{ for } i = 1, \ldots, m \text{ and } \hat{G}(\mathbf{p}, p_G, \hat{M}). \tag{2}$$

In the following all function related to problem (1) are designated by a hat ^. It should be stressed that the demand function $\hat{G}$ is not directly observable, but could be derived e.g., by means of contingent valuation surveys or other methods. The demand system can be employed to define the (unconditional) indirect utility function and the corresponding expenditure function $\hat{E}(\mathbf{p}, p_G, \hat{u})$. Using $\hat{E}$ we obtain the compensated demand functions

$$\hat{X}_i^c(\mathbf{p}, p_G, \hat{u}) = \partial \hat{E}(\mathbf{p}, p_G, \hat{u}) / \partial p_i, i = 1, \ldots, m \text{ and}$$
$$\hat{G}^c(\mathbf{p}, p_G, \hat{u}) = \partial \hat{E}(\mathbf{p}, p_G, \hat{u}) / \partial p_G \tag{3}$$

by Shepard's lemma. These functions, though hypothetical, will be used since they describe the underlying preference ordering: The systems (2) or (3) allow us to recover the underlying preference ordering.

Now we turn to the problem of evaluation and introduce the relevant concepts. Below the marginal willingness to pay for the environmental good will play a major role. If G is a market good consumers are willing to pay the market price p_G for a(nother) unit because of the assumption of utility maximization. When G is exogenously fixed (and the consumer is rationed) the marginal willingness to pay for G can be derived by an extension of Roy's identity from V:

$$w_G(\mathbf{p}, G, M) := \frac{\partial V(\mathbf{p}, G, M) / \partial G}{\partial V(\mathbf{p}, G, M) / \partial M}$$

and the compensated one from E:

$$w_G^c(\mathbf{p}, G, u) := -\partial E(\mathbf{p}, G, u) / G.$$

w_G and w_G^C, respectively, can be interpreted as virtual prices. Suppose that a consumer faces prices $p_1, \ldots, p_m$ for market goods, has income M, and that the quantity G is fixed. Then she chooses the commodity bundle $(X_i(\mathbf{p}, G, M), \ldots, X_m(\mathbf{p}, G, M))$. Now one can ask the question under which conditions the consumer would by $(X_1, \ldots, X_m, G)$ voluntarily. The answer is given by the virtual price and the virtual income. Assume that the market price p_G is equal to $w_G(\mathbf{p}, G, M)$ and let the consumer's (virtual) income be given by $\hat{M} = M + w_G(\mathbf{p}, G, M)G$. In this case she would buy the commodity bundle (**X**, G); i.e., we have

$$X_i(\mathbf{p}, G, M) = \hat{X}_i(\mathbf{p}, w_G(\mathbf{p}, G, M),\ M + w_G(\mathbf{p}, G, M)G) \text{ for } i = 1, \ldots, m$$

and

$$G = \hat{G}(\mathbf{p}, w_G(\mathbf{p}, G, M),\ M + w_G(\mathbf{p}, G, M)G) \tag{4}$$

These identities hold for all **p**, G, M. In other words, if M is increased by $w_G G$, the amount necessary to pay the bundle G at the virtual price $p_G = w_G(\mathbf{p}, G, M)$, the consumer is able to buy (**X**, G) and, indeed, chooses this bundle.[2] Thus virtual price and virtual income are helpful in connecting the unconditional demand system with the conditional demand system. Equation (4) is well-known in the theory of household behaviour under rationing (cf. equation (23) in Neary and Roberts (1980)).

This relationship can be exploited. (4) can be employed for an implicit definition w_G: It can be uniquely solved for $w_G = w_G(\mathbf{p}, G, M)$ (cf. the proof of Proposition 1 in Ebert (1998) and see section 4 below).

Finally, a general notation for elasticities is proposed. $\eta(x, y)$ denotes the elasticity of x with respect to y for the economic variables x and y, more precisely, if $x = x(y)$ we define

$$\eta(x, y) = \frac{dx}{x} / \frac{dy}{y} = \frac{dx}{dy}\frac{y}{x}.$$

In the following we will use e.g., $\eta(w_G, M)$, $\eta(\hat{M}, M)$, $\eta(\hat{G}, \hat{M})$ and $\eta(\hat{G}, p_G)$. They denote the income elasticity of marginal willingness to pay for G, of virtual income, of (unconditional) demand for G, and the own price elasticity of unconditional demand for G, respectively.

3 General approach

In this paper we assume that the environmental good is given (or provided) in the (fixed) quantity G which is the same for all consumers and which enters every consumer's utility function, i.e., there is no exclusion and no rivalness in consumption. We consider one period. Therefore time preference does not play a role. For an investigation of the distributional effects of an environmental good we have to solve two problems, namely: we have to measure the benefits enjoyed and to describe their incidence. The following subsections discuss the approach proposed.

3.1 Measures of benefits

Various benefit measure can be defined. Firstly, assuming that the consumer's preference ordering is known the total benefit enjoyed from consuming G can be measured by an appropriate (Hicksian) welfare measure (cf. Ebert (1993)). We introduce the equivalent variation

$$EV(\mathbf{p}, G, M) = E(\mathbf{p}, 0, u_G) - E(\mathbf{p}, 0, u_0)$$

where $V(\mathbf{p}, G, M)$ and $u_0 = V(\mathbf{p}, 0, M)$.

It measures the amount the consumer would be willing to pay in the situation when the environmental good is *not* provided (then the utility level u_0 is attained) in order to be as well off as in the present situation ($u_G = V(\mathbf{p}, G, M)$). The equivalent variation can also be defined implicitly by

$$V(\mathbf{p}, 0, M + EV) = V(\mathbf{p}, G, M).$$

Then $M + EV(\mathbf{p}, G, M)$ corresponds to the consumer's full income. EV reflects the corresponding benefits. The measure is in principle identical with Flores and Carson's (1977) definition of total willingness to pay if an appropriate utility level is used. We obtain in particular

$$EV(\mathbf{p}, G, M) = \int_0^G w_G^c(\mathbf{p}, \tilde{G}, u_G)\, d\tilde{G} \tag{5}$$

(their equation (11) for $u = u_G$).

These total benefits being based on the compensated marginal willingness to pay for G can, secondly, be approximated by gross consumer's surplus. The latter is defined by

$$CS(\mathbf{p}, G, M) = \int_0^G w_G(\mathbf{p}, \tilde{G}, M)\, d\tilde{G}, \tag{6}$$

i.e., by the amount the consumer would be willing to pay in a market *and* net consumer's surplus.

Finally we consider the amount of money the consumer would pay in a market. Since no market exists for the environmental good the market price is replaced directly by the marginal willingness to pay or Lindahl price. Then benefits enjoyed can be measure by

$$WTP(\mathbf{p}, G, M) := w_G(\mathbf{p}, G, M)G.$$

It is an income-equivalent of the benefits received from the consumption of the environmental good. $w_G G$ equals the amount the consumer would be willing to pay per unit times the total number of units consumed. Like every "income-equivalent" measure it neglects consumer surplus (cf. Brennan (1976)). The idea of imputing benefits from a nonmarket good in this way goes back at least to Aaron and McGuire (1970). They manage to make the concept operational by using a utility function which is separable between the private and the public good. In the present paper a priori no restrictions on the ordering are imposed.

The informational requirements of calculating *EV, CS* or *WTP* are different: For *EV* the entire preference must be known since the compensated marginal willingness to pay w_G^C can never be observed. It can be derived from $w_G(\mathbf{p}, G, M)$ by means of the expenditure function $w_G^C(\mathbf{p}, G, u) = w_G(\mathbf{p}, G, E(\mathbf{p}, G, u)))$. Furthermore, for *EV* and *CS* the marginal willingness to pay is used on the entire interval $[0, G]$, whereas for *WTP* only the marginal willingness to pay for G in the status quo is required. The formulation in (5) and (6) does not reveal the fact that sometimes the integrals considered do not exist. Whenever the environmental good is essential the integral tends to infinity when the lower bound approaches zero. Then also the expenditure function $E(\mathbf{p}, G, u)$ is not defined for $G = 0$. In such a case *EV* and *CS* cannot be employed, but *WTP* is, however, well defined.

At first sight the choice of a benefit measure seems to be difficult. We recommend to use the income-equivalent $WTP(\mathbf{p}, G, M)$, but, of course, the reader can choose *EV* or *CS*, instead. There are a number of arguments supporting our choice: We are interested in benefit incidence and have to "correct" M, the income observed, for the benefits received from consuming G. Income M equals the expenditure for and income necessary to buy the private goods consumed ($M = \sum p_i X_i$). The income-equivalent $WTP(\mathbf{p}, G, M) = w_G G$ is therefore measured in terms of income and in analogy to the evaluation of private goods. w_G corresponds to the Lindahl price of the environmental good in the same way as the price p_i of a private good corresponds to the marginal willingness to pay for it. Of course, the corresponding net consumer surplus is ignored, but "it is such neglect that necessitates discussion of the distribution of income as distinct from, say, the distribution of utilities" (Brennan (1976) p. 392. From a methodological viewpoint the environmental good is then treated like any public good in public economics (cf. Aaron and McGuire (1970)).

3.2 Benefit incidence

Using the general notation $B(\mathbf{p}, G, M)$ for the benefits enjoyed (it might be equal to *EV, CS*, or *WTP*) we are able to tackle the problem of benefit incidence. In accordance with the methods employed for taxes and benefits in public finance (cf. Lambert (2001)) we consider the (imputed) benefits from the environmental good, expressed as a fraction of income M: $b(\mathbf{p}, G, M) := B(\mathbf{p}, G, M)/M$. The rise or fall of the average benefit rate $b(\mathbf{p}, G, M)$ with income determines the incidence of benefits. Here the analysis is simplified by the assumption (presented above) that there is a continuum of consumers.

We introduce

Definition

Benefits are distributed

$$\left.\begin{matrix} progressively \\ proportionally \\ regressively \end{matrix}\right\} iff \frac{db(\mathbf{p},G,M)}{dM} \begin{matrix} > \\ = \\ < \end{matrix} 0.$$

If benefits increase faster than income their distribution is progressive or pro-rich. Otherwise benefits are distributed proportionally, i.e., they increase at the same pace as income, or average benefits decrease with income, their distribution is pro-poor. It should be obvious that the measure of benefit progression,[3] defined as db/dM, is a local measure; i.e., its sign can be positive or negative depending on the level of income M. Furthermore, it is implicitly assumed in the following that all incomes considered are feasible, i.e., $M \in [\underline{M}, \overline{M}]$.

Having clarified the notion of progression we are able to describe the relevant variable which determines the incidence of benefits. We directly obtain

$$Result\ 1: \frac{db(\mathbf{p},G,M)}{dM} = \frac{B(\mathbf{p},G,M)}{M^2}(\eta(B,\ M) - 1) \tag{R1}$$

The relevant factor is the income elasticity of benefits from G.

In the light of this result, $\eta(B, M) > 1$(or < 1) is a sufficient condition for overall progressivity (or regressivity). In this case benefits increase faster (slower) than income.

It is possible to relate average benefits to total income which is defined by

$$M^* = M + B(\mathbf{p},G,M), \tag{7}$$

i.e., the original income increased by the benefits received from the environmental good G. M^* is equal to the virtual income $\hat{M}$ introduced above if $B(\mathbf{p}, G, M) = WTP(\mathbf{p}, G, M) = w_G G$.

For given $\mathbf{p}$ and G income M and total income M^* are connected, i.e., we obtain $M^* = M^*(M)$ and $M = M(M^*)$ as well-defined functions as long as $1 + \partial B/\partial M > 0$. This condition is satisfied whenever G is normal or (not extremely) inferior. Given this relationship, the measure of benefit progression can be reinterpreted in another way. By definition we have

$$b(\mathbf{p},G,M) = \frac{M^*(M) - M}{M}$$

and therefore we get

$$Result\ 2: \frac{db(\mathbf{p},G,M)}{dM} = \frac{M^*}{M^2}(\eta(M^*,M) - 1. \tag{R2}$$

The measure of benefit progression depends on the elasticity of total income M^* with respect to original income M. If M^* and M increase in the same proportion benefits are proportionally distributed since $B = M^* - M$ or $\frac{B}{M} = \frac{M^*}{M} - 1$. Otherwise progression or regression is implied.

Combining (R1) and (R2) we are able to reveal a simple relationship between the elasticities involved:

$$\textit{Result 3}: \eta(B, M) - 1 = \frac{M^*}{B}(\eta(M^*, M) - 1). \tag{R3}$$

Both elasticities are linked closely which is not surprising in view of equation (7).

Another possibility is to consider benefit incidence with respect to *total* income M^*, i.e., to include benefits in the definition of income a priori. Then we have to define average benefits accordingly by

$$b^*(\mathbf{p}, G, M^*) = \frac{B(\mathbf{p}, G, M(M^*))}{M^*} = \frac{M^* - M(M^*)}{M^*}$$

Now the question arises how the change of b^* with respect to a change in total income is related to the incidence of benefits. At first we establish

$$\begin{aligned} \textit{Result 4}: \frac{db^*(\mathbf{p}, G, M^*)}{dM^*} &= \frac{M}{M^{*2}}(1 - \eta(M, M^*)) \\ &= \frac{M}{M^{*2}} \frac{\eta(M^*, M) - 1}{\eta(M^*, M)} \end{aligned} \tag{R4}$$

It is the analogue to result 2. Again the elasticity of total income with respect to original income (or its inverse $\eta(M, M^*)$) is the relevant variable. Inspection and comparison of (R2) and (R4) immediately demonstrate

$$\textit{Result 5}: \frac{db(\mathbf{p}, G, M)}{dM} \gtreqless 0 \Leftrightarrow \frac{db^*(\mathbf{p}, G, M^*)}{dM^*} \gtreqless 0. \tag{R5}$$

Both indicators are equivalent. It does not matter whether we choose M or M^* as point of reference. The reason for this outcome is simple: both are directly related by the benefits $B(\mathbf{p}, G, M)$ (see the discussion above).

Collecting these results and employing the definition of progression we get

Proposition 1

Assume that prices **p** *and the quantity G are fixed. Benefits are distributed progressively, proportionally, or regressively if and only if one of the following equivalent conditions is satisfied:*

(i) $\eta(B, M) = \eta(B(\mathbf{p}, G, M), M) \gtreqless 1$ *for all* $M \in [\overline{M}, \overline{\overline{M}}]$

(ii) $\eta(M^{*}, M) \gtreqless 1$ or $\eta(M, M^{*}) \gtreqless 1$ *for all* $M \in [\overline{M}, \overline{\overline{M}}]$

Obviously here the distribution of original incomes has to be taken into consideration.

3.3 Income elasticities

The analysis of the last subsection demonstrates that the income elasticity of the benefit measure is the crucial factor determining the incidence of benefits. The magnitude and computation of η (B, M) depends on the choice of the benefit measure. For $B = EV$ we obtain a complicated expression

$$\eta(EV, M) = \int_0^G \eta(w_G(\mathbf{p}, \tilde{G}, \tilde{M}), \tilde{M})|_{\tilde{M}=E(\mathbf{p},\tilde{G},u_G)}\, w_G^c(\mathbf{p}, \tilde{G}, u_G) \cdot \frac{\partial E(\mathbf{p}, \tilde{G}, u_G)}{\partial u_G} \frac{\partial V(\mathbf{p}, \tilde{G}, M)}{\partial M} d\tilde{G} / EV$$

Since the equivalent variation is based on the compensated marginal willingness $w_G^c(\mathbf{p}, \tilde{G}, V(p, G, M))$ to pay its income elasticity has to take into account the marginal change in the utility level. Flores and Carson call the factor $\frac{\partial E}{\partial u_G} \frac{\partial V}{\partial M}$ under the integral the utility adjustment factor (cf. their equation (13)). The income elasticity of consumer surplus is much simpler:

$$\eta(CS, M) = \int_0^G \eta(w_G(\mathbf{p}, \tilde{G}, M), M)\, w_G(\mathbf{p}, \tilde{G}, M) d\tilde{G} / CS$$

since the marginal willingness to pay w_G depends on income M directly. For the computation of both elasticities the income elasticity of the marginal willingness to pay plays a major role (for $\tilde{G}, \in [0, G]$). When benefits are measured by the income-equivalent *WTP* the elasticity is given by

$$\eta(WTP(\mathbf{p}, G, M), M) = \eta(w_G(\mathbf{p}, G, M), M),$$

i.e., directly by the income elasticity of marginal willingness to pay for G is fixed.

In any case the income elasticity $\eta(w_G, M)$ is important. The next section therefore provides a thorough investigation of the income elasticity of marginal willingness to pay for the environmental good.

4 Marginal willingness to pay

In view of the results derived in section 3 the income elasticity of marginal willingness to pay for G is the crucial determinant of benefit incidence when consumers' preferences are equal. Therefore, it seems reasonable to investigate the relationship between $\eta(w_G, M)$ and further variables or elasticities describing the underlying preference ordering R. If these elasticities can be determined empirically, it is possible to check benefit incidence. Whenever in the rest of the paper benefit incidence will be investigated *we assume that benefits enjoyed are measured by the total willingness to pay* $WTP(\mathbf{p}, G, M)$. In this case the income elasticities are identical ($\eta(WTP, M) = \eta(w_G, M)$) and total income M^* equals virtual income $\hat{M}$. The various forms of decomposition of $\eta(w_G, M)$ are, however, also helpful for a computation of $\eta(EV, M)$ and $\eta(CS, M)$.

The starting point of the analysis is the implicit definition of the virtual price $w_G = w_G(\mathbf{p}, G, M)$, for any prices $\mathbf{p}$, quantity G and income M:

$$G = \hat{G}(\mathbf{p}, w_G, M + w_G G). \tag{4}$$

The virtual price w_G guarantees by definition that the consumer buys the quantity G, given $\mathbf{p}$ and $M + w_G G$. This identity can already be found in Neary and Roberts (1980) and plays a role whenever virtual prices are considered.[4]

Using the implicit function theorem we obtain

$$\frac{dw_G}{dM} = -\frac{\dfrac{\partial \hat{G}}{\partial \hat{M}}}{\dfrac{\partial \hat{G}}{\partial w_G} + G\dfrac{\partial \hat{G}}{\partial \hat{M}}} \tag{8}$$

where $\hat{M} = M + w_G G$.

This equation is fundamental for the following investigation.

4.1 Income and substitution effect

Equation (8) demonstrates that the response of marginal willingness to pay for G to a change of income is closely related to the reaction of the demand for G when income or its price changes.

Extending and rewriting (8) we establish

Result 6:

$$\text{a)}\quad \eta(w_G, M) = -\frac{\eta(\hat{G}, \hat{M})}{\eta(\hat{G}, w_G) + \dfrac{w_G G}{M}\eta(\hat{G}, \hat{M})}\frac{M}{\hat{M}} \tag{R6a}$$

$$\text{b)}\quad \eta(w_G, M) = -\frac{\eta(\hat{G}, \hat{M})}{\eta(\hat{G}^c, w_G)}\frac{M}{\hat{M}} \tag{R6b}$$

(*Hanemann* (*1991*), *equation* (*16'*)*; Flores and Carson* (*1997*), *equation* (5) *as a generalization.*)

$$\text{c)}\quad \eta(w_G, M) = -\eta(w_G^c, G)\eta(\hat{G}, \hat{M})\frac{M}{\hat{M}} \tag{R6c}$$

(R6a) is another version of the fundamental equation (8). (R6b) is based on the Slutsky equation

$$\frac{\partial \hat{G}^c}{\partial w_G} = \frac{\partial \hat{G}}{\partial w_G} + G\frac{\partial \hat{G}}{\partial \hat{M}}$$

which leads to

$$\eta(\hat{G}^c, w_G) = \eta(\hat{G}, w_G) + \frac{w_G G}{\hat{M}}\eta(\hat{G}, \hat{M}) \text{ (see, also Hanemann (1991)).}$$

(R6c) is a direct consequence of (R6b) since

$$\frac{\partial \hat{G}^c}{\partial w_G} = 1/\frac{\partial w_G^c}{\partial G} \text{ (see, e.g., Ebert (1998)).}$$

Result 6 is interesting since the income elasticity of marginal willingness to pay for the environmental good is related to various elasticities. In (R6a) the (uncompensated) price and own income elasticity play a role. The denominator of the right-hand side in equation (R6a) can be replaced by the compensated price elasticity which in turn is identical to the inverse of the elasticity of (compensated) marginal willingness of pay with respect to the quantity of the environmental good.[5]

The meaning of (R6) is obvious: The income elasticity of marginal willingness to pay $\eta(w_G, M)$ depends on two factors: one characterizing an income effect and another one describing a substitution effect. The compensated own price elasticity $\eta(\hat{G}^c, w_G)$ is always negative. Therefore we have

$$sign\ (\eta(w_G, M)) = sign\ (\eta(\hat{G}, \hat{M})),$$

the sign of the income elasticity of w_G is the same as the sign of the income elasticity of $\hat{G}$. On the other hand their magnitudes may be different: $\eta(\hat{G}, \hat{M}) \gtreqless 1$ does not imply the magnitude of η (w_G, M) directly. All we know is that the income elasticity of marginal willingness to pay for G is positive (negative) if and only if G is a normal (inferior) good. But if the demand for G becomes more income elastic, the elasticity of marginal willingness to pay for G increases and therefore progression rises. If G is inferior the distribution of benefits is always pro-poor.

At first sight it is perhaps surprising that the own substitution effect is relevant for the income elasticity of marginal willingness to pay. But this fact can be explained nicely by interpreting (R6c). It is illustrated by means of Figure 4.1. Here prices **p** are fixed and M denotes a Hicksian composite commodity. Starting from

(M, G) (and point A) we examine the implications of an increase ΔM. Because of normality of the environmental good (which is assumed here) G increases by ΔG, the income effect depending on $\partial \hat{G}/\partial \hat{M}$. In order to derive the final impact on w_G we have to undo the change in G since the level of the environmental good is fixed. We have to move along the indifference curve from B to C, changing

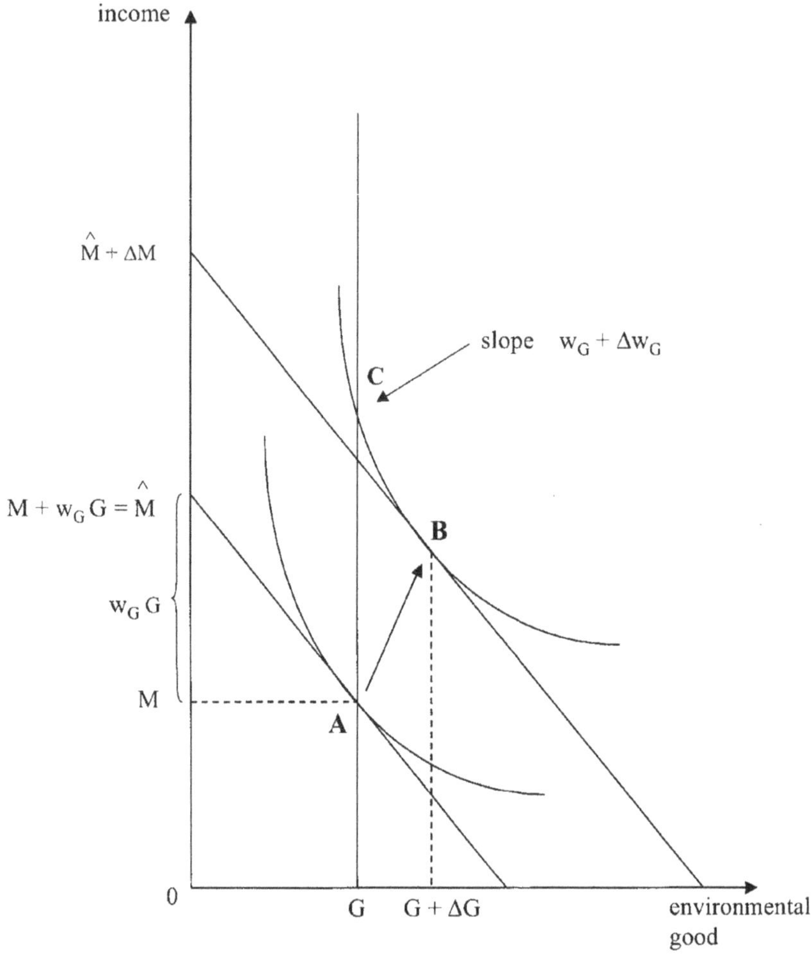

Figure 4.1 Income and substitution effect

$G + \Delta G$ to G. This operation (an inverse substitution effect) increases w_G by Δw_G. The outcome depends on $\partial w_G^c / \partial G$. Thus $\eta(w_G, M)$ can be decomposed into the product of the corresponding elasticities describing these effects.

The quantity elasticity of (compensated) marginal willingness to pay $\eta(w_G^c, G)$ is directly related to the curvature of the indifference curve: If the indifference curve is flat the elasticity is small. In this case the price effect is small as well; the distribution tends to be pro-poor. If the indifference curve is (almost) rectangular the compensated price increase is high (i.e., marginal willingness to pay increases fast). Then the distribution of benefits will be pro-rich. Thus the substitutability between the environmental good and the (aggregate of the) private goods is relevant. This aspect will be discussed in section 4.2.

We are also able to decompose the income elasticity of virtual income $\eta(\hat{M}, M)$.

$$Result\ 7\text{:}\ 1/\eta(\hat{M},M)=\eta(M,\hat{M})=\frac{w_G G}{M}\left(1+\frac{\eta(\hat{G},\hat{M})}{\eta(\hat{G},w_G)}\right)+1 \qquad \text{(R7)}$$

Proof:
Applying the implicit function theorem to equation (7) and using (8) we get

$$\frac{d\hat{M}}{dM}=1+G\frac{\partial w_G}{\partial M}=1+G\left(\frac{-\partial\hat{G}/\partial\hat{M}}{\partial\hat{G}/\partial w_G+G\partial\hat{G}/\partial\hat{M}}\right)$$

$$=\frac{\partial\hat{G}/\partial w_G}{\partial\hat{G}/\partial w_G+G\partial\hat{G}/\partial\hat{M}}$$

Inversion and extension yields

$$\frac{dM}{d\hat{M}}=1+\frac{w_G G}{\hat{M}}\frac{\eta(\hat{G},\hat{M})}{\eta(\hat{G},w_G)}$$

and

$$\eta(M,\hat{M})=\frac{M+w_G G}{M}+\frac{w_G G}{M}\frac{\eta(\hat{G},\hat{M})}{\eta(\hat{G},w_G)}=1+\frac{w_G G}{M}\left(1+\frac{\eta(\hat{G},\hat{M})}{\eta(\hat{G},w_G)}\right)$$

In view of (R3) and Proposition 1 (ii) this decomposition allows us to show that the progressivity of benefits depends on the magnitude of the ratio $-\eta(\hat{G}, \hat{M})/\eta(\hat{G}, w_G)$, i.e., on the ratio of the income to the price elasticity of demand for the environmental good. If it is greater (less) than one the benefits are distributed progressively (regressively). This result has been derived by Snow and Warren (1983) for a Lindahl model[6] in which a public good is provided *and* financed by benefit taxation. Then taxes are determined according to the (marginal) benefits consumers receive from the public good – as in our model based on virtual income.

Summing up, the (marginal) price and income effects determine the income elasticity of marginal willingness to pay. At first sight it seems that the elasticities involved are not observable: There is no market for the environmental good G. Therefore the price and income elasticity of the (ordinary) Marshallian demand function cannot be observed. A similar remark applies to $\eta(w_G^c, G)$. On the other hand these elasticities can sometimes be estimated (see section 5).

4.2 Substitutes

Up to now only the demand function for G and its response to a change in income and its own price have been used as determinants of the relevant elasticities. The private goods have not played any role. There is another possibility of decomposing the compensated own price elasticity $\eta(\hat{G}^c, w_G)$. Recalling that the compensated demand function $\hat{G}^c(p_1, \ldots p_m, w_G u)$ is homogeneous of degree zero with respect to prices, we are able to write down Euler's theorem

$$\sum_{i=1}^{m} p_i \frac{\partial \hat{G}^c}{\partial p_i} + w_G \frac{\partial \hat{G}^c}{\partial w_G} = 0$$

which yields

$$\eta(\hat{G}^c, w_G) = -\sum_{i=1}^{m} \eta(\hat{G}^c, p_i)$$

for the compensated own price elasticity. The elasticity we are interested in can be expressed by means of the (cross-) price elasticities of demand for G (with respect to the prices of the private goods).

We obtain

$$\textit{Result } 8 : \eta\left(w_G, M\right) = \frac{\eta(\hat{G}, \hat{M})}{\sum_{i=1}^{m} \eta(\hat{G}^c, p_i)} \frac{M}{\hat{M}}. \tag{R8}$$

Again it is clear that the denominator of the right hand side in (R8) is always positive. Thus G is a substitute for at least one private good. The (compensated) cross price elasticities describe the price (and substitution) effects. If there is a close substitute to the environmental good the respective price elasticity will be high and the income elasticity of marginal willingness to pay tends to be small: The distribution of benefits is more likely pro-poor (given that G is normal). This result is not surprising since in this case consumers having higher incomes can more easily substitute the environmental good by the respective private good. Therefore (marginal) willingness increases (relatively) slowly with income.

The elasticities $\eta(\hat{G}^c, p_i)$ are related to the respective partial elasticity of substitution $\sigma(\hat{X}, \hat{G})$ introduced by Allen and Uzawa. The elasticity of substitution between the environmental good and the private good equals the percentage change of the ratio of the quantity G to X_i arising from a percentage change in the price ratio p_i/w_G keeping utility unchanged (cf. Uzawa (1962)). Diewert (1974) provides the definition

$$\sigma(\hat{X}_i, \hat{G}) = \frac{\partial^2 \hat{E}(\mathbf{p}, w_G, u)}{\partial p_i \partial w_G} \frac{\hat{M}}{\hat{X}_i \hat{G}}.$$

Though the Allen-Uzawa elasticity of substitution plays a major role in production theory, it has also some meaning in consumer's theory:

Since $\dfrac{\partial^2 \hat{E}}{\partial p_i \partial w_G} = \dfrac{\partial \hat{G}^c}{\partial p_i}$ we obtain

$$\eta(\hat{G}^c, p_i) = \frac{\partial \hat{G}^c}{\partial p_i}\frac{p_i}{\hat{G}} = \frac{p_i \hat{X}_i}{\hat{M}}\sigma(X_i, G);$$

i.e., the compensated cross-price elasticity of demand equals the partial elasticity of substitution between the respective private good X_i and G, multiplied by the budget share $p_i\hat{X}_i$, $\hat{M}$. Thus $\sigma(\hat{X}_i, \hat{G})$ is the response of the compensated demand for the environmental good to a change in the price of private good i, appropriately normalized (see, Diewert (1974)).

Equation (9) and this relationship yield

$$\eta(\hat{G}^c, w_G) = -\sum_{i=1}^{m}\frac{p_i \hat{X}_i}{\hat{M}}\sigma(\hat{X}_i, \hat{G}).$$

This result can be employed to establish

Result 9:

$$\text{a) } \eta(w_G, M) = \frac{\eta(\hat{G}, \hat{M})}{\sum_{i=1}^{m}\frac{p_i X_i}{M}\sigma(\hat{X}_i, \hat{G})} \quad \text{(R9a)}$$

$$\text{b) } \textit{If } \sigma(\hat{X}_i, \hat{G}) = \sigma \textit{ for } i = 1, \ldots, m \quad \text{(R9b)}$$

$$\eta(w_G, M) = \frac{\eta(\hat{G}, \hat{M})}{\sigma}$$

The income elasticity $\eta(w_G, M)$ of marginal willingness to pay depends on the income elasticity of demand for $\hat{G}$ and the weighted sum of the partial elasticities of substitution between the private goods and $\hat{G}$. The weights reflect the respective budget share $p_i, X_i/M$ with respect to original income M and sum up to unity (R9a). If all partial elasticities of substitution are the same and equal to σ the right-had side simplifies (R9b).

Thus result 9 demonstrates that the income elasticity of marginal willingness to pay for G depends on the degree of substitutability between the environmental and the private goods. As discussed above the possibility of substitution favours consumers having high incomes.

The flatter is the indifference curve the higher is σ and the lower is the income elasticity of marginal willingness to pay w_G. Therefore the interpretation of this result is the same as for (R6). In particular for the preference ordering R represented by a utility function with $\sigma \equiv 1$ the income elasticity of marginal willingness to pay and the income elasticity of demand for G are identical!

A result similar to, but different from (R9b) is derived by Hanemann (1991). He defines the *aggregate* Allen-Uzawa elasticity of substitution between G and the Hicksian composite $X_0 = \sum_{i=1}^{m}\bar{p}_i X_i$ for given prices $\bar{p}_i, \ldots, \bar{p}_m$. Let it be denoted by σ_0. Then we obtain

Result 10: $\eta\left(w_G, M\right)\frac{\eta(\hat{G},\hat{M})}{\sigma_o}$ (R10)

(Hanemann (1991), equation (17)).

4.3 Progression and examples

The findings of this section have implications for a characterization of benefit incidence. Using (R6)–(R9) and proposition 1 we are able to establish

Proposition 2

Assume that prices **p** and the quantity G are fixed and that $B(\mathbf{p}, G, M) = WTP(\mathbf{p}, G, M)$. *Benefits are distributed progressively, proportionally, or regressively if and only if one of the following equivalent conditions is satisfied for all* $M \in [\overline{M}, \overline{\overline{M}}]$:

(i) $$-\frac{\eta(\hat{G},\hat{M})}{\eta(\hat{G},w_G)+\frac{w_G G}{M}\eta(\hat{G},\hat{M})}\frac{M}{\hat{M}} \gtreqless 1$$

(ii) $$-\frac{\eta(\hat{G},\hat{M})}{\eta(\hat{G}^c,w_G)}\frac{M}{\hat{M}} \gtreqless 1$$

(iii) $$-\eta(w_G^c,G)\eta(\hat{G},\hat{M})\frac{M}{\hat{M}} \gtreqless 1$$

(iv) $$-\frac{\eta(\hat{G},\hat{M})}{\eta(\hat{G},w_G)} \gtreqless 1$$

(v) $$\frac{\eta(\hat{G},\hat{M})}{\sum_{i=1}^{m}\eta(\hat{G}^c,p_i)} \gtreqless 1$$

(vi) $$\frac{\eta(\hat{G},\hat{M})}{\sum_{i=1}^{m}\frac{p_i X_i}{M}\sigma(\hat{X}_i,\hat{G})} \gtreqless 1$$

In other words, the relevant characteristics of the underlying preference ordering are the (un)compensated price elasticity and the income elasticity of demand for $\hat{G}$ and the partial elasticities of substitution between $\hat{G}$ and the private goods $\hat{X}_i$.

Finally some examples are presented:

1) Suppose that the direct utility $U(\mathbf{X}, G)$ function is given by a CES function

$$U(\mathbf{X},G)=\left(\sum_{i=1}^{m}a_i X_i^{-\rho}+a_{m+1}G^{-\rho}\right)^{-1/\rho} \quad \text{where } \sigma=\frac{1}{1+\rho}$$

Then the income elasticity of demand is equal to unity because of homotheticity and we obtain

$$\eta\left(w_G,M\right)=\frac{1}{\sigma}\overset{>}{\underset{<}{-}}1\Leftrightarrow\sigma\overset{<}{\underset{>}{-}}1$$

which was already derived by Kovenock and Sadka (1981) for the Lindahl model and $m = 1$. If $\sigma \equiv 1$, U is a Cobb-Douglas function and the distribution of benefits is proportional:

$$\eta\left(w_G,M\right)= 1.$$

2) Ebert (1997) considers the utility function

$$U(X_1,X_2,G)=(X_1+G)^{1/2}X_2^{1/2}G^{\varepsilon}$$

which is a generalization of a utility function Mäler (1971) used in the context of weakly complementary goods.

In this case

$$w_G(\mathbf{p},G,M)=p_1(1+\varepsilon)+\varepsilon M/G$$

and

$$\eta\left(w_G,M\right)=\frac{\varepsilon M}{p_1G(1+\varepsilon)+\varepsilon M}$$

For $\varepsilon = 0$ the private good 1 and the environmental good are perfect substitutes and therefore $w_G(\mathbf{p}, G, M) = p_1$. Then the distribution is pro-poor since the total willingness to pay for G is constant ($= p_iG$) and independent of income. The same result is obtained for any $\varepsilon > 0$ (since $\eta(w_G, M) < 1$).

3) Aaron and McGuire (1970) and Maital (19730 investigated specific separable utility functions. For a general separable function

$$U(\mathbf{X},G)=\overline{U}(\mathbf{X})+W\left(G\right) \tag{10}$$

one derives

$$V(\mathbf{p},G,M)=\overline{V}(\mathbf{p},M)+W\left(G\right)$$

and therefore

$$w_G(\mathbf{p},G,M)=W'\left(G\right)/(\partial\overline{V}(\mathbf{p},M)/\partial M)=W'\left(G\right)/\overline{V}_M(\mathbf{p},M)$$

where

$$\overline{V}_M = \partial\overline{V} / \partial M.$$

In this case the income elasticity of w_G is obviously given by $\eta(w_G, M) = -\eta(\overline{V}_M, M)$, i.e., by the negative income elasticity of the marginal utility of income[7] (for a fixed quantity of G).

Then,

$$\eta(w_G, M) \gtreqless 1 \Leftrightarrow \eta(\overline{V}_M, M) \lesseqgtr -1.$$

Examining the (net) fiscal incidence of the entire fiscal system in the United States in 1961 Maital (1973) argued that $\eta(\overline{V}_M, M)$ is equal to –1.5. Then of course benefits are distributed progressively.

4.4 General case

Thus far we have confined ourselves to considering only one environmental good G. In this subsection we assume that there are $n > 1$ environmental goods. The G, w_G etc. have to be replaced by vectors $\mathbf{G} = (G_1, \ldots, G_n)$, $\mathbf{w}_G = (w_{G_1}, \ldots, w_{G_n})$ etc. The analysis becomes more complex, but the reader will not have any problems extending the framework.

Benefits are defined as above[8] by $WTP(\mathbf{p}, \mathbf{G}, M)$: $\mathbf{w}_G\mathbf{G} = \sum_{i=1}^{n} w_{G_i} G_i$ and the average benefit rate by $b(\mathbf{p}, \mathbf{G}, M) = \mathbf{w}_G\mathbf{G}/M$. Result 1 (for $B = WTP$) can be generalized immediately to

$$\textit{Result 1} := \frac{db(\mathbf{p}, G, M)}{dM} = \sum_{i=1}^{n} \left(\frac{w_{G_j}, G_j}{M^2} (\eta(w_{G_j}, M) - 1) \right) \tag{R1'}$$

Similar changes have to be made to the rest of section 3.2.

It turns out that the income elasticities of the marginal willingness to pay for environmental goods are again the crucial determinants of benefit incidence. In order to relate them to other economic variables we now investigate a *system* of equations defining the marginal willingness to pay functions implicitly:

$$G_j = \hat{G}_j \left(\mathbf{p}, w_{G_1}, \ldots, w_{G_n}, M + \sum_{i=1}^{n} w_{G_j} G_j \right), j = 1, \ldots, n. \tag{4'}$$

Marginal willingness to pay $\mathbf{w}_G(\mathbf{p}, \mathbf{G}, M)$ is uniquely determined by (4') if the Jacobian matrix of the system of equation is invertible: This is a mild regularity condition which will be imposed in the following. The Jacobian matrix is equal to an $n \times n$ submatrix $\hat{S}_{GG} := (\hat{s}_{G_j G_k})$ of the Slutsky matrix, since differentiation of (4') yields

$$\frac{d\hat{G}_j}{dw_{G_k}} = \frac{\partial \hat{G}_j}{\partial w_{G_k}} + G_k \frac{\partial \hat{G}_j}{\partial M} = \frac{\partial \hat{G}_j^c}{\partial p_{G_k}} =: \hat{s}_{G_j G_k}.$$

Furthermore, it is well known that

$$\left(\frac{\partial \hat{G}_j^c}{\partial p_{G_k}}\right)^{-1} = \hat{S}_{GG}^{-1} = S_{GG} = \left(\frac{\partial w_{G_j}^c}{\partial G_k}\right)$$

where S_{GG} is an $n \times n$ submatrix of the Slutsky matrix belonging to the conditional framework in (1) (see, Neary and Roberts (1980) and Madden (1991)).

Now the implicit function theorem (cf. Berck and Sydsaeter (1993)) can be applied to derive

$$\textit{Result 11}: \eta\left(w_{G_j}, M\right) = -\sum_{k=1}^{n} \eta(w_{G_j}^c, G_k)\eta(\hat{G}_k, \hat{M})\frac{M}{\hat{M}} \qquad \text{(R11)}$$

for $j = 1, \ldots, n$.

It generalizes Result 6c. Again the income elasticity of marginal willingness to pay for an environmental good G_j is determined by substitution *and* income effects. But things are much more complicated than they are in the specific case $n = 1$. For $n > 1$ the possibilities of substitution between G_j and *all* environmental goods $G_k (k = 1, \ldots, n)$ play a role: $\eta(w_G^c, G_k)$ is the substitution elasticity between environmental good j and k. Furthermore the income elasticities of *all* environmental goods are relevant when the magnitude and sign of $\eta(w_G, M)$ are to be determined. Even if all environmental goods are normal the income elasticity of the marginal willingness to pay for good j is not necessarily positive!

The generalization of Result 6b is contained in Flores and Carson (1997) who consider the case $n = 2$. It is based on S_{GG}^{-1}.

For $n > 1$ the complementarily and substitutability of environmental goods is not easy to describe (cf. the discussion of this point in Madden (1991) and Ebert (1998)): G_j and G_k are called (Hicksian) substitutes (complements) in the conditional framework if $\partial w_{G_j}^c(\mathbf{p}, \mathbf{G}, u)/\partial G_k < 0 (> 0)$. On the other hand the signs of $\partial \hat{G}_j^c(\mathbf{p}, \mathbf{G}, u)/\partial w_{G_k}$ and $\partial w_{G_j}^c(\mathbf{p}, \mathbf{G}, u)/\partial G_k$ can be different. That means in particular that $\hat{G}_j$ and $\hat{G}_k$ may be (Hicksian) substitutes $\partial \hat{G}_j^c/\partial w_{G_k} > 0$ in the unconditional and complements in the conditional framework (and conversely). But there is one situation in which the classification of goods does not depend on the framework and in which the sign of the income elasticities $\eta(w_{G_j}, M)$ is unambiguous. If all environmental goods are (Hicksian) substitutes in the unconditional framework we obtain $S_{GG} < 0$ (see, Carson, Flores and Hanemann (1998), p. 319). Then we are able to establish by means of (R11):

Result 12:
Assume that all environmental goods are (Hicksian) substitutes in the unconditional framework (i.e., $\partial \hat{G}_j^c/\partial w_{G_k} > 0$ *for* $j \neq k$*) and normal. Then*

$$\eta(w_{G_j}, M) > 0 \textit{ for } j = 1, \ldots, n. \qquad \text{(R12)}$$

If all environmental goods are substitutes they can be interpreted as *one* good and the situation is similar to that investigated above. In this case the income elasticities $\eta(w_{G_j}, M)$ are positive, but, nevertheless, need not be greater than one (cf. section 4.1).

In view of this discussion it is not surprising that nothing general can be said about benefit incidence whenever there are two or more environmental goods. The interaction between the nonmarket goods leads to opposing effects which cannot be disentangled unambiguously.

5 Conclusion

This chapter has proposed a precise framework for an investigation of benefit incidence. Using a simple "equal-preference" model it is possible to describe the consumers' benefits received from environmental goods by the Hicksian equivalent variation, (gross) consumer surplus, or the total willingness to pay (in a market), i.e., the product of marginal willingness to pay and of the quantity of goods. In analogy to tax theory benefit incidence can be characterized by the (marginal) change of total benefits as a fraction of income with respect to a (marginal) change in income. It turns out that the crucial issue for progressivity or regressivity is the magnitude of the income elasticity of marginal willingness to pay for an environmental good. This elasticity can be related to a number of other variables: the own price and income elasticity of demand and to the Allen-Uzawa partial elasticities of substitution between the environmental good and the private commodities. Whenever several environmental goods have to be taken into account things become more complicated at the theoretical level since the substitutability and complementarity of the environmental goods involved can lead to opposing effects. Even normality of all (environmental) goods does not necessarily imply that the income elasticity of marginal willingness to pay is positive. Then benefit incidence can be examined only empirically. The same is true if the assumption of equal preferences is dropped. Applied valuation studies often find that individual characteristics other than income influence consumers' choices. In this case the above framework can be extended if there is a unique relationship between the other characteristics and income, or the analysis has to be made conditional on given types of consumers.

It has not been the objective of this paper to give a survey about the incidence of benefits of environmental goods. In practice we often face difficulties in determining the relevant variables of representative consumers' preference orderings. But there is some literature dealing with the incidence of governmental activities. Then the incidence of benefits as well as the incidence of taxation has to be considered. Important contributions to this area are Aaron and McGuire's (1970) article mentioned above and some papers using political processes to investigate the demand for public goods. E.g., Borcherding and Deacon (1972) and Bergstrom and Goodman (1973) employ such an approach.

Assuming that the median voter is the decisive voter they manage to determine the price and income elasticities of demand for (local) public goods. Their results on the demand for parks and recreation can be used for our purpose since parks can be interpreted as an environmental good G. The estimated values of the respective elasticities are presented by Table 1. E.g., Bergstrom and Goodman estimated[9] an income elasticity $\eta(\hat{G}, \hat{M}) = 1.32$ and a price elasticity $\eta(\hat{G}, w_G) = -0.19$ *for the median voter*. Therefore the ratio of the income to the price elasticity of demand for the environmental good $-\eta(\hat{G}, \hat{M}) / \eta(\hat{G}, w_G)$ is equal to 6.95 and the corresponding marginal change of benefits – measured as fraction of income – is therefore strictly positive:

$$\begin{aligned} sign\left(\frac{d\hat{b}(\mathbf{p}, G, M(\hat{M}))}{d\hat{M}}\right) &= sign\left(\frac{\eta(\hat{G}, \hat{M})}{\eta(\hat{G}, w_G)} - 1\right) \\ &= sign\left(-\frac{1.32}{-0.19} - 1\right) \\ &= sign(6.95 - 1) = sign(5.95). \end{aligned}$$

In this case total benefits received from consuming parks are unambiguously progressively distributed (as long as incomes levels close to the median voter's income are considered). Borcherding and Deacon's estimations also support this finding.

But this is not the only possible outcome. Höbky and Söderqvist (2003) investigate the demand for reduced eutrophication effects in the Baltic Sea using data from four Swedish contingent valuation studies. They estimate its price and income elasticities (see Table 4.1) and find that the income elasticity of marginal willingness to pay *for a representative consumer is* greater than zero, but less than unity. Then

$$sign\left(\frac{d\hat{b}(\mathbf{p}, G, M(\hat{M}))}{d\hat{M}}\right) = sign\left(-\frac{0.94}{-1.86} - 1\right) = sign(-0.49)$$

Thus benefits are (on average) regressively distributed.

Of course, these results cannot be generalized. The papers cited consider only the median and, respectively, representative income. On the other hand income elasticities depend on the level of income (see, e.g., Thompson and Tinsley (1978)). Besides that the outcome might be different if the quantity of the environmental good is varied (cf. also Kristöm and Riera (1996) for empirical results).

Table 4.1 Income and price elasticities of demand

Source	*G*	$\eta(\hat{G}, \hat{M})$	$\eta(\hat{G}, w_G)$	$-\frac{\eta(\hat{G}, \hat{M})}{\eta(\hat{G}, w_G)}$
Borcherding/Deacon (1972)	parks	2.74	–0.50	5.48
Table 3	and	0.49	–0.18	2.72
Bergstrom/Goodman	recreation	1.32	–0.19	6.95
Table 3				
Höbky/Söderqvist (2003)	reduced	0.94	–1.86	0.51
Table 5	eutrophication			

But the examples demonstrate that the model introduced and the decomposition of the relevant elasticity lend themselves to empirical application. The paper presents a framework for further empirical analysis: The question whether environmental benefits are regressively distributed more often than not can only be answered by an investigation of appropriate data.

Notes

1 I am grateful to Peter Lambert, Lutz Mommer, and two anonymous referees for helpful comments and suggestions.
2 See, Carson, Flores and Hanemann (1998) for a different, but equivalent characterization of virtual prices.
3 Cf. Ebert and Lambert (1999) for an investigation of tax-benefit systems.
4 See, Hanemann (1991)'s equation (11), and Flores and Carson (1997), p. 289. A slightly different, but essentially identical condition is employed in Madden (1991), p. 1498 and Carson, Flores, and Hanemann (1998), p. 316.
5 When compensated demand or willingness to pay functions are employed it is assumed that u equals the utility level attained: $V(\mathbf{p}, G, M)$.
6 See, e.g., Cullis and Jones (1992), Siebert (1992) for a thorough discussion of the Lindahl model.
7 Marginal utility of income is measured for the "canonical" form of the utility function (10). See also footnote 9 in Maital (1973).
8 The benefit measures EV and CS can, of course, also be generalized.
9 The model they base their estimates on can also be interpreted as Lindahl model.

References

Aaron, H. and M. McGuire (1970), 'Public Goods and Income Distribution', *Econometrica* **38**, 907–919.

Baumol, W. J. (1974), 'Environmental Protection and Income Distribution', in H. Hochman and G. Peterson, eds., *Redistribution through Social Choice*. New York: Columbia University Press.

Baumol, W. J. and W. E. Oates (1988), *The Theory of Environmental Policy*, second edition. Cambridge: Cambridge University Press.

Berck, P. and K. Sydsaeter (1993), *Economists' Mathematical Manual*, second edition. Berlin: Springer-Verlag.

Bergstrom, T. C. and R. P. Goodman, 'Private Demands for Public Goods', *American Economic Review* **63**, 280–296.

Borcherding, T. E. and R. T. Deacon (1972), 'The Demand for Services of Non Federal Governments', *American Economic Review* **62**, 891–901.

Braden, J. B. and C. D. Kolstad, eds. (1991), *Measuring the Demand for Environmental Quality*. Amsterdam: Elsevier Science Publishers B.V.

Brennan, G. (1976), 'The Distributional Implications of Public Goods', *Econometrica* **44**, 391–399.

Carson, R., N. E. Flores and W. M. Hanemann (1998), 'Sequencing and Valuing Public Goods', *Journal of Environmental Economics and Management* **36**, 314–323.

Cullis, J. and P. Jones (1992), *Public Finance and Public Choice*. London: Mc Graw Hill.

Diewert, W. E. (1974), 'A Note on Aggregation and Elasticities of Substitution', *Canadian Journal of Economics* **7**, 12–20.

Ebert, U. (1993), 'A Note on Willingness to Pay and Willingness to Accept', *Social Choice and Welfare* **10**, 363–370.

Ebert, U. (1997), 'Selecting Preferences for Nonmarket Goods, Possibilities and Limitations', *Public Finance* **52**, 301–317.

Ebert, U. (1998), 'Evaluation of Nonmarket Goods: Recovering Unconditional Preferences', *American Journal of Agricultural Economics* **80**, 241–254.

Ebert, U. and P. Lambert (1999), 'Combined Income Taxes and Tax-benefit Systems', *Economic Record* **75**, 397–404.

Flores, N. E. and R. T. Carson (1997), 'The Relationship between the Income Elasticities of Demand and Willingness to Pay', *Journal of Environmental Economics and Management* **33**, 287–295.

Freeman, A. M. (1972), 'The Distribution of Environmental Quality', in A. Kneese and B. Bower, eds., *Environmental Quality Analysis*. Baltimore: John Hopkins Press.

Freeman III, A. M. (1985), 'Methods for Assessing the Benefits of Environmental Programs', in A. V. Kneese and J. L. Sweeny, eds., *Handbook of Natural Resource and Energy Economics* **I** (6), 223–270. Amsterdam: Elsevier Science Publishers B.V.

Hanemann, W. M. (1991), 'Willingness to Pay and Willingness to Accept: How Much Can They Differ?', *American Economic Review* **81**, 635–647.

Höbky, S. and T. Söderqvist (2003), *Elasticities of Demand and Willingness to Pay for Environmental Services in Sweden*, forthcoming in: *Environmental and Resource Economics*.

Johannson, P.-O. (1987), *The Economic Theory and Measurement of Environmental Benefits*. Cambridge: Cambridge University Press.

Kovenock, D. and E. Sadka (1981), 'Progression under the Benefit Approach to the Theory of Taxation', *Economics Letters 8*, 95–99.

Kristöm, B. and P. Riera (1996), 'Is the Income Elasticity of Environmental Improvements Less Than One?', *Environmental and Resource Economics* **7**, 45–55.

Lambert, P. J. (2001), *The Distribution and Redistribution of Income*, third edition. Manchester: Manchester University Press.

Madden, P. (1991), 'A generalization of Hicksian q-substitutes and Complements with Application to Demand Rationing', *Econometrica* **59**, 1497–1508.

Maital, S. (1973), 'Public Goods and Income Distribution: Some Further Results', *Econometrica* **41**, 561–568.

Mäler, K.-G. (1985), 'Welfare Economics and the Environment', in A. V. Kneese and J. L. Sweeney, eds., *Handbook of Natural Resource and Energy Economics* **I** (1), 3–60. Amsterdam: Elsevier, Science Publishers B.V.

Neary, J. P. and K. W. S. Roberts (1980), 'The Theory of Household Behaviour under Rationing', *European Economic Review* **13**, 25–42.

Pearce, D. W. (1980), 'The Social Incidence of Environmental Costs and Benefits', in T. O'Riordan and K. Turner, eds., *Progress in Resource Management and Environmental Planning* **2**, John Wiley and Sons Ltd.

Siebert, H. (1992), *Economics of the Environment*, Berlin: Springer-Verlag.

Snow, A. and R. S. Warren (1983), 'Tax Progression in Lindahl Equilibrium', *Economics Letters* **12**, 319–326.

Thompson, C. St. and A. W. Tinsley (1978), 'Income Expenditure Elasticities for Recreation: Their Estimation and Relation to Demand for Recreation', *Journal of Leisure Research* **10**, 265–270.

Uzawa, H. (1962), 'Production Functions with Constant Elasticity of Substitution', *Review of Economic Studies* **29**, 291–299.

5 How much do we care about air quality improvements?

Evidence from Italian households

Chiara Martini and Silvia Tiezzi

1 Introduction

The value of improvements in air quality levels has been the subject of inquiry for many decades. How individuals, households or nations value improvements in air quality is crucial for policy planning and, in particular, for assessing the benefits of air quality improvements against their costs.

One of the most important drivers of the value of air quality improvements is income. The early environmental policy literature hypothesized a positive relationship between willingness to pay (WTP) for air quality improvements and income. This relationship is usually measured by the income elasticity of WTP, a very difficult to calculate yet crucial incidence measure. For example, how the net benefits of environmental improvements will be distributed by income levels is very important when evaluating reforms that will affect other countries or generations or different groups of citizens within a country. Depending upon the distribution of costs and benefits, air quality benefits may be pro-rich or pro-poor. They are pro-rich when they rise with income, and in this case they are said to be progressively distributed. They are pro-poor when they fall with income[1] and in this case they are regressively distributed. Even though the early environmental economics literature hypothesized air quality to be a luxury good (the demand for which increases more than proportionally with respect to income), more recent studies consider air quality as a normal good, implying that its income elasticity of demand is positive but not greater than one (Martini and Tiezzi, 2013).

Income, however, is not the only driver of air quality improvements and other factors may be relevant to guide public policy. Is there a change in preferences over time towards greater environmental quality? Are there diminishing returns to air quality improvements? How does the demand for air quality improvements vary by household location?

A better understanding of how these factors influence the WTP for air quality improvements is important to guide future air quality policy.

The purpose of this study is to explore the drivers of WTP for air quality improvements in Italy and to provide a tentative answer to the above questions. For this purpose we estimate the WTP for air quality improvements in Italy using a novel approach (Ebert, 2007) and a unique dataset.

The remainder of the paper is structured as follows. Section 2 summarises the main methods used in the literature to estimate WTP for air quality improvements and other environmental public goods. Section 3 explains the approach we adopt to estimate WTP for air quality improvements in Italy. In section 4 the demand system specification and the data used are presented. Section 5 comments on the results. Section 6 concludes.

2 Literature review

This section provides a literature review on the main methods available to estimate WTP for environmental quality improvements and their results. The different approaches will be briefly outlined, then the focus of a number empirical studies will be described, and the results – focusing in particular on drivers different from income – will be summarised.

Since the early 1970s different approaches have been adopted to estimate the demand for public goods and the WTP. The first was a collective choice approach based on the median voter theorem (Boercherding and Deacon, 1972; Bergstrom and Goodman, 1973). The assumption is that political decisions on the level of expenditure on public goods will be identical to the quantity demanded by the median voter. Champ *et al.* (2003), Freeman (2003), and Mäler and Vincent (2005) provide useful and broad overviews.

Since the seminal paper by Rosen (1974), the hedonic and location choice approaches have been widely used for measuring the value of environmental public goods, especially in the United States. The advantage of this approach is that observed behavior in the housing and labor markets is used to infer the value of non-market goods. The marginal WTP for public goods is measured, in this case, by their implicit prices as reflected in housing prices and wages. Recent methodological innovations can be found in Bajari and Benkard (2005), Ekeland *et al.* (2004), and Bayer *et al.* (2009).

Another important survey-based approach was introduced by Bergstrom *et al.* (1982), who fitted demand equations for local public services with data from a household survey supplied by the University of Michigan. This was followed by the flourishing of contingent valuation (CV) studies using stated preferences to estimate WTP for public goods, such as Kriström and Riera (1996), Alberini *et al.* (1997), Hökby and Söderqvist (2003), Schläpfer (2006), to cite a few.

Finally, averting behavior employs the demand for market goods as a proxy for environmental goods or services (Costa, 1997; Pereyra and Rossi, 1998; Ghalwash, 2006). Several studies used averting behavior to obtain WTP values for a reduction in exposure to air pollutants or in the symptoms that result from them. Berger *et al.* (1987), for example, derive WTP using both cost of illness and averting expenditures, including air conditioners. Differently, Dickie and Gerking (1991) adopt the household production approach to investigate the relationship between health and air quality, while Mansfield *et al.* (2006) combine stated preference and averting behavior to estimate WTP for a decrease in ozone pollution.

In general, income has emerged as a fundamental driver of WTP and it has been at the centre of many empirical studies devoted to estimating the WTP for different typologies of public goods. As a result, the income elasticity of WTP has been a widely used parameter,[2] and different approaches have produced heterogeneity in results. The most widely used approach uses data based on contingent valuation surveys (Kriström and Riera, 1997; Hökby and Söderqvist, 2003; Schläpfer, 2006). Studies based on this approach consistently find a very low income elasticity of WTP in the range 0.1–0.5. These elasticities contrast in magnitude with those calculated from collective choice-based studies for various public goods (Boercherding and Deacon, 1972; Bergstrom and Goodman, 1973) which are greater than one; and from averting-behavior approaches using the demand for market goods as a proxy for environmental goods or services (Costa, 1997; Pereyra and Rossi, 1998; Ghalwash, 2006).

A variety of environmental public goods have been analyzed in these contributions. Clearly, the corresponding WTP can have common drivers, but different drivers are likely to be relevant for different goods. In particular, biodiversity – and related variables, such as environmental services – has become the focus of several studies since the 1990s (Johansson, 1990; Riera, 1994; Li and Mattson, 1995) and at the same time climate change-related variables, such as air quality, have begun to be investigated (Berger *et al.*, 1987; Dickie and Gerking, 1991). The interest in these variables has grown later on (Carlsson and Johansson-Stenman, 2000; Léger, 2001; World Bank, 2002; Wang and Mullahy, 2006). The focus on renewable energy and other energy-related variables is more recent (Yoo and Kwak, 2009; Zografakis *et al.*, 2010; Mozumder *et al.*, 2011). Policies are more and more oriented towards the development of low-emissions energy sources as part of wider climate change mitigation strategies. In this respect, the WTP for air quality improvements and for energy-related variables may have more drivers in common than the WTP for biodiversity conservation.

In estimating the WTP for air quality improvements, income is a key driver but other variables are also important. In particular, health-related variables play a relevant role (Léger, 2001; Wang and Mullahy, 2006; Wang and Zhang, 2009), and the same is true for household location (Carlsson and Johansson-Stenman, 2000).

Carlsson and Johansson-Stenman (2000) estimate the WTP for reducing the concentration of harmful air pollutants by 50 percent in Sweden, concentrating on where beneficiaries both live and work. Reduced health impacts are the most important driver of WTP for slightly more than half of the sample. The living place also matters, with households in big cities having a slightly larger WTP. The authors estimate a two-step model for WTP, including a selection (Probit) and a structural equation. The estimated marginal effects for income and education are positive and significant in both equations, increasing both the probability of having a positive WTP, and the amount of WTP. Interestingly, men have a lower probability of a positive WTP than women, but they have a large maximum WTP. Having a serious disease and being involved in an environmental organization have a positive effect in the selection equation. By contrast, partner income, number of children, knowledge about pollution, retired status, and house ownership are significant in the structural equation.

Léger (2001) concentrates on the relationship between WTP for reducing ozone concentration in Montreal and health expenditures. The authors adopt a household production function approach (Gerking and Stanley, 1986) and use the time saved due to the reduced consumption of medical services for estimating WTP. Such an approach seeks to measure the trade-off between health expenditures and air quality, considering actual behavior and not survey responses. Socioeconomic variables such as age, sex, presence of kids, marital status, as well as labor-force participation are also included in the estimation, and they are all significant. WTP is relatively small when medical expenditures are limited to formal medical care (i.e. visits to physicians). When individuals rebuild their health stock, taking time off from work, WTP increases dramatically. Still, these estimates should be considered as lower bounds since they do not account for other medical expenses such as pharmaceuticals, nor they allow for individuals to value clean air per se.

World Bank (2002) examines the effects of reducing the concentration of different air pollutants in Mexico City, adopting different approaches, among which is the benefit transfer method. The study highlights that the value of health-risk avoidance depends on the type and magnitude of risk, and on income and cultural settings. Moreover, it is important to consider if the risk is experienced voluntarily or not, and the perception of its persistence. Consistently with Léger (2001), also in this case monetary estimates of health benefits are very likely to be a lower bound.

Afroz *et al.* (2005) compare the WTP values for reducing air pollution in Klang Valley, Malaysia obtained by different question formats. They also assess the significance of the WTP values by using explanatory factors such as socioeconomic variables and health variables, such as the duration of ill-health episodes or the number of symptoms. Gender, age, education, health conditions and income have a significant positive effect on WTP, education and income playing the most important role.

Wang and Mullahy (2006) develop a contingent valuation study in Chongqing, one of the largest cities in China. Based on these data and similarly to the two-step model developed by Carlsson and Johansson-Stenman (2000), they estimate the probability of finding a positive WTP, and then the WTP level. Age, gender, marital status, family size, education, income, employment, health condition, medical expenditures, household location, and pollution perception are used as explanatory variables. With respect to the determinants of the probability of positive WTP, age has a negative effect, while, not surprisingly, income has a positive one. As expected, people who believe that they live in a severely polluted area tend to have a higher probability of expressing a positive WTP. With respect to the determinants of WTP level, education and income show positive relationships with WTP, as well as living in more polluted areas. Unlike the results from the probability analysis, in this equation people from larger families tend to have higher WTP. Wang and Zhang (2009) use the same method to investigate WTP for air quality in the city of Ji'nan, in China. The same variables as in Wang and

Mullahy (2008) are used, adding also opinion about the correlation between pollution and health. Education, income, and medical expenditures are found to be significant for the probability of having a positive WTP. Surprisingly, factors such as gender, age, and household size are not significant. With respect to the factors affecting the amount of WTP, annual income, medical expenditures, and number of workers positively influence WTP. Both the probability of a positive WTP and the monetary amount are larger for men than for women.

Noonan (2011) analyses the variation in the benefits associated with air quality improvements by means of a meta-analysis. To this end, over 50 empirical analysis are collected, and the benefits estimates are converted to a common metric represented by WTP for air quality improvements. The studies analyzed employ different methods and data sources, and examine different scenarios. The meta-analysis is aimed at demonstrating how the benefits vary significantly across the sample, not only due to the differences mentioned above. As expected, income affects the benefits estimates. In particular, benefits are rising in income for wealthy nations but declining in income for developing countries. The amount of pollution reduction also substantively affects benefits estimates, due to diminishing returns of air quality improvements. This last trend is surveyed adopting two main approaches. First, a fixed-effects regression is used to check whether higher or lower baseline levels affect WTP, and finds no evidence of diminishing returns. The second approach estimates another fixed-effects regression to test for constancy in WTP, using the variation in air quality to explain the variation in WTP. A significant inverse relationship is found, confirming the expected decline in WTP for additional (larger) improvements.

When looking at studies of the WTP for energy-related variables, we find that drivers are partially similar to those already identified for air quality. Additional drivers become relevant in this case, such as energy prices (Mozumder *et al.*, 2011), environmental awareness, and the creation of new jobs (Ek, 2005; Zografakis *et al.*, 2010). Health variables appear to be less important in determining WTP for renewable energy.

Menegaki (2008) highlights that WTP for renewable energy is generally higher among individuals with high incomes (Wiser, 2007; Bergmann *et al.*, 2006). Individuals with lower incomes seem to assign a greater importance to job creation (Ek, 2005). Bergmann *et al.* (2006) and Zografakis *et al.* (2010) also find that WTP is sensitive to the creation of additional jobs. WTP is higher among younger people, those who do not rent their home, do not have children and are highly educated (Wiser, 2007; Ek, 2005). Also, attitudinal factors positively affect WTP, such as having family and friends supporting renewable energy use (Wiser, 2007) and having an interest in environmental issues (Ek, 2005).

Yoo and Kwak (2009) find that age and education are not statistically significant when estimating the WTP for renewable energy development, in contrast with Zografakis *et al.* (2010), who find a positive effect of having a high family income and a large house, and access to more environmental information. Both studies adopt a contingent valuation approach, respectively applied to Korea and Greece. Applying the same approach to New Mexico, Mozumder *et al.* (2011)

show that energy prices positively influence WTP for renewable energy development. Environmental concerns also have a positive influence, as well as the share of income donated to environmental causes. Consistent with earlier findings (Kotchen and Moore, 2007; Ito *et al.*, 2010), the level of education has a negative impact on WTP, which is a contrasting result with other studies available on this topic (for example, Carlsson and Johansson-Stenman, 2000; Wang and Mullahy, 2006).

The WTP for energy efficiency is a very seldom investigated variable. Galarraga *et al.* (2011) propose a combined approach for estimating WTP for improving the energy efficiency of home appliances in Spain, using the results of the hedonic approach together with the Quantity Based Demand System model. Own and cross-price elasticities for substitute goods are provided, in particular having low and high energy efficiency. Introducing demographic-related variables such as household composition or location – as in, for example, Ghalwash (2008) – could provide useful insights into the determinants of the demand for energy-efficient appliances.

Studies estimating the WTP for other environmental public goods confirm the importance of location as a driver of WTP (Basili *et al.*, 2006), and this driver becomes even more relevant, due to the greater connection with non-global environmental public goods.

Ghalwash (2008) investigates the demand for environmental services by means of demand-system estimation. In the model, translating intercepts are included for household size and composition and also for the place of residence, enabling the author to obtain demand elasticities for different regions.

Broberg (2010) estimates the WTP for biodiversity, in particular concentrating on the predator policy (i.e. policies aimed to protect wolves) in Sweden. He finds that the place of residence plays a relevant role, living inside or near wolf territories having a negative effect on the WTP for predator policy. The likelihood of supporting the policy increases with income, but this effect is not significant. The author considers the number of household members a budget-related factor having both a direct effect on preferences for environmental quality and an indirect one through the budget constraint.

Travisi *et al.* (2004) perform a meta-analysis to analyze the variation in the estimated WTP associated with the impacts of pesticide risk. They find that WTP is influenced by the perception of risk and the information available, by socio-demographic characteristics, and by geographic location. These findings highlight that differences in WTP might be caused by non-income differences, for example in terms of whether the household lives in a rural or urban location (Lindhjem, 2007).

In general, although income is often considered a relevant covariate in WTP estimation, recent meta-analyses have focused on the determinants of income effects (Schläpfer, 2006; Jacobsen and Hanley, 2009). Schläpfer (2006) finds that income effects tend to be much smaller when developing a CV approach than in collective-choice models. If the cost distribution is well defined and existing institutions are envisaged to provide the public good, the author finds that the probability of a significant income effect is lower. Other variables are relevant in such cases, for example demographic-related or location variables.

Jacobsen and Hanley (2009) investigate a sample of 145 WTP estimates, where only 56 reported a significant income effect, 39 reported an insignificant income effect and 50 did not report any information. The likelihood of observing a significant income effect decreases with the income level and is lower for preserving existing biodiversity than for increasing biodiversity.

To summarize, although income plays a central role in many studies, other variables are relevant WTP drivers. Household composition, in terms of both age and employment status of the members, and household geographical location are examples. In the following empirical analysis we emphasize the role played by these additional drivers.

3 Household production and demand analysis

To estimate the WTP for improvements in air quality in Italy we use a new methodological approach, proposed by Ebert (2007). This is based on the following assumptions: (i) a complete (conditional) demand system for market goods, which may depend on environmental goods, can be observed; (ii) a household production function, combining market and environmental goods according to a given technology, is known; (iii) the environmental goods considered do not enter the utility function directly. Using these assumptions Ebert shows that one can derive the marginal WTP functions for the non-market goods which augment the conditional demand system. Then one has to investigate the integrability of the mixed demand system consisting of the demand functions for market goods and the inverse demand functions for the non-market goods. If the integrability conditions are satisfied a unique preference ordering can be recovered and the WTP can be obtained, as well as relevant derived parameters, like the income elasticity of WTP.

To implement this approach we consider household production of the level of internal air quality chosen by the household and assume that households combine a market good, air conditioning, with a non-market good, the level of external air quality, in order to produce the desired level of internal air quality according to a given technology. Since the household production function implicitly describes the marginal rate of substitution between air quality and air conditioning, we can compute the marginal WTP for marginal improvements in air quality. The bundle of air pollutants considered in our air quality index is known to have strong health effects in terms of respiratory diseases (WHO, 2005) but is not correlated with higher temperature levels. Then it can be assumed that a high concentration of these pollutants is mainly associated with a demand for ventilation and internal air quality. Consequently bad air quality conditions are very likely to be correlated with expenditure on air conditioners, which are an input in producing the level of air quality preferred by the household.

The data set we use is obtained by merging data on Italian households' monthly current expenditure and unique information on a bundle of air pollutant concentrations. We show that the resulting (mixed) demand system is integrable and we compute the marginal WTP for a marginal increase in the index of air quality.[3]

4 Empirical strategy

4.1 A Conditional Censored Almost Ideal Demand (CCAID) System

Conditional demand functions can be used to deal with non-market goods, such as environmental goods or bads. The level of, for example, air quality provided without charge to the user may affect the individual's consumption of goods available in the market. Since consumption of air quality is fixed, it is the conditional demand functions which are appropriate for the analysis of an individual demand for goods and services in the short run (Pollack, 1969). The functional form chosen to specify our model is the Almost Ideal Demand System (AIDS, Deaton and Muellbauer, 1980b). To obtain the system of conditional uncompensated shares equations we use a logarithmic *conditional* cost function, for household h, which implies PIGLOG preferences (Pollack and Wales, 1992):

$$ln\, C(u, p, d^h, q) = ln\, a(p, d^h, q) + u\, b(p) \tag{1}$$

where $a(p, d^h, q)$ and $b(p)$ are functions of the market price vector p, ln indicates the natural logarithm, d^h are demographic variables and q is the fixed quantity of the non-market good, air quality in this case. $a(p, d^h, q)$ is increasing and homogenous of degree one in p and $b(p)$ is increasing and homogenous of degree zero in p. $C(u, p, d^h, q)$ is the *conditional cost function*, i.e. the minimum cost necessary to achieve utility level u, given the price vector p, given demographics d^h and when the quantity q of the non-market good is given. The corresponding system of conditional Marshallian demand functions for household h and goods $i = 1, \ldots, n$ expressed as expenditure shares is given by:

$$w_i^h = \alpha_i + \sum_j c_{ij}\, ln\, p_j + b_i\, ln\left[\frac{y^h}{P^h}\right] + \sum_i (\alpha_i + \alpha_{ik} d_k^h + g_i q)\, ln\, p_i \tag{2}$$

where y^h is total expenditure of household h; the parameters c_{ij} are defined as $c_{ij} = \frac{1}{2}(c_{ij}^* + c_{ji}^*) = c_{ji}$; α_{ik} are the coefficients of the translating intercepts $d^h = d_1^h \ldots d_k^h$, which in this model include household types, household locations and an annual time trend and P^h is a Translog price index specified as:

$$P^h = \alpha_0 + \sum_i (\alpha_i + g_i q + \alpha_{ik} d_k^h)\, ln\, p_i + \frac{1}{2} \sum_i \sum_j c_{ij}^*\, ln\, p_i\, ln\, p_j \tag{3}$$

Demand functions (3) satisfy integrability, i.e. are consistent with utility maximization, when the following parametric restrictions hold: $\sum_i \alpha_i = 1, \sum_i b_i = \sum_j c_{ij}^* = 0, \sum_i \alpha_{ik} = 0\, \forall k$(Adding-up);$\sum_j c_{ij} = 0$(Homogeneity); $c_{ij} = c_{ji}$ for all i, j (Symmetry).

The presence of zeros in the dependent variables is quite important for our specific sample. To deal with this problem we use the two-step estimator proposed by Shonkwiler and Yen (1999), which involves probit estimation in the first step and a selectivity-augmented equation system in the second step.[4] The system of equations (3) is thus estimated in the following form:

$$s_i = \Phi(z_i^{'}\tau_i)w_i(p, y;\theta) + \delta_i\varphi(z_i^{'}\tau_i) + \xi_i \qquad (4)$$

where s_i is the observed expenditure share for good i; z_i is a vector of exogenous variables; τ_i is a parameter vector; θ is a vector containing all parameters (α_i, α_{ik}, b_i, g_i end c_{ij}) in the demand system, $\xi_i = s_i - E(s_i)$ and where $\phi(\cdot)$ and $\Phi(\cdot)$ are the standard normal probability density (pdf) and distribution (cdf) functions, respectively. The system of equations (4) is estimated in two steps: (i) we obtain Maximum Likelihood (ML) probit estimates $\hat{\tau}_i$ of τ_i using the binary outcome $s_i = 0$ and $s_i > 0$; (ii) we calculate $\Phi(z_i' \hat{\tau}_i)$, $\phi(z_i' \hat{\tau}_i)$ for all i and estimate θ, δ_1, δ_2, …, δ_n in the augmented system (4) by ML. Such a two-step estimator is consistent, but the error terms are heteroscedastic, thus the estimated elements of the second-step conventional covariance matrix are inefficient. For simplicity, we empirically calculate the standard errors of WTP and elasticities using bootstrapping and running 500 replications. This ensures that the standard errors of these derived parameters are correct.

Differentiation of equation (4) gives demand elasticities for the first $n - 1$ goods. Elasticities for the nth good are obtained exploiting the Cournot and Engel restrictions (Deaton and Muellbauer, 1980a, p. 16). Denoting the Marshallian, Hicksian and expenditure elasticities for good i as σ_{ij}^h, σ_{ij}^{*h} and σ_i^h, respectively, then σ_{nj}^h, σ_{nj}^{*h} and σ_n^h can be calculated using the Cournot restriction $\sum_{i=1}^{n} w_i^h \sigma_{ij}^h + w_j^h = 0$ and the Engel restriction $\sum_{j=1}^{n} \sigma_{ij}^h + \sigma_i^h = 0$.

Exogenous variables used in the first-step probit estimates are: total expenditure, dummies indicating household location, whether the household resides in a big town, seasonality, and the annual time trend in logarithms. The dependent variable in the first-step probit estimates is the binary outcome defined by the expenditure in each good. The proportion of consuming households for Food, Housing and Communication all exceed 95 percent, which prevents reliable probit estimates. Thus, probit is estimated only for the remaining commodities, for which the predicted pdf and cdf are included in the second step of the procedure (see Yen, Lin and Smallwood, 2003, p. 464). In all the estimates we impose homogeneity and symmetry. Economic theory also requires the matrix of the substitution effects to be negative semi-definite. Such a requirement is satisfied by adopting a Cholesky decomposition procedure of the price coefficients. Finally, we drop the "other goods and services" equation to accommodate adding up.

4.2 Household production and WTP for air quality improvements

To specify the WTP function for improvements in air quality we choose the class of household production functions:

$$Z = F_{\varepsilon}(Y, q) = (Y^{1/2} + 1)\, q^{\varepsilon} \qquad (5)$$

for $\varepsilon \in (0, 1/2)$ proposed by Ebert (2007, p. 285). Y is the quantity of air conditioners used as an input into the household production of Z, the internal level of air quality chosen by the household, and q is our index of air quality. In this household production function Y is a non-essential good.[5] This class of household production functions implies the cost functions:

$$C_{\epsilon}(p_Y, q, Z) = \begin{cases} 0 \; for \; Z \leq q^{\epsilon} \\ p_Y \left(\dfrac{z}{q^{\varepsilon}} - 1 \right)^2 \; for \; Z > q^{\epsilon} \end{cases} \qquad (6)$$

The corresponding WTP function is:

$$w_q(p, q, y) = 2\varepsilon p_Y (Y^{1/2} + 1)\, Y^{1/2}/q \qquad (7)$$

We consider three values of ε: $\varepsilon = 0.1$, $\varepsilon = 0.35$ and $\varepsilon = 0.5$ and we test whether the WTP function (7) is integrable by checking whether the integrability conditions are satisfied. Ebert (2007, p. 283) sets out the necessary and sufficient conditions for integrability of this conditional demand system supplemented by a WTP function. The first three conditions are symmetry conditions of the Slutsky matrix for the augmented demand system:

$$s_{xY} = \frac{\delta x}{\delta p_Y} + Y \frac{\delta x}{\delta y} = \frac{\delta Y}{\delta p_x} + X \frac{\delta Y}{\delta y} = s_{Yx} \qquad (8)$$

$$s_{xq} = \frac{\delta x}{\delta q} - w_q \frac{\delta x}{\delta y} = -\left(\frac{\delta w_q}{\delta p_x} + x \frac{\delta w_q}{\delta y} \right) = -s_{qx} \qquad (9)$$

$$s_{Yq} = \frac{\delta Y}{\delta q} - w_q \frac{\delta Y}{\delta y} = -\left(\frac{\delta w_q}{\delta p_Y} + Y \frac{\delta w_q}{\delta y} \right) = -s_{qY} \qquad (10)$$

where s_{xY} are the conventional Slutsky substitution effects for market goods x and Y, i.e. they measure the change in the quantity demanded of each element in vector x following a change in the price of good Y, whereas s_{xq} is the change in the quantity demanded of each element in x following a change in the price (WTP) of q. Condition (8) is satisfied by assumption, because x and Y form a conditional demand system, but conditions (9) and (10) have to be checked. In addition the Slutsky matrix of substitution effects for the market goods x and Y must be negative semidefinite. Finally, the change in the quantity demanded of good q following a change in its price (WTP) must be negative:

$$s_{qq} = \frac{\delta w_q}{\delta q} - w_q \frac{\delta w_q}{\delta y} < 0 \qquad (11)$$

When conditions (8) to (11) are satisfied the mixed demand system with household production defined by (4), (5) and (7) is integrable. This approach does not require further assumptions and it provides a useful and operational basis for recovering preferences. Its starting points are the "observed" demand functions for market goods and the household production functions. Conditions like weak complementarity or the essentiality of inputs are not required, nor is required the imposition of the Willig condition to derive exact welfare measures (see Ebert, 2007, p. 278 for a discussion of this point).

4.3 Data

We use monthly cross-sections, from January 2002 to December 2006, of individual Italian households' current expenditures collected by the National Institute of Statistics (ISTAT) through a specific and routinely repeated survey[6] called "Indagine sui Consumi delle Famiglie." In this survey, current expenditures are classified into about two hundred elementary goods and services, with the exact number changing from year to year, due to minor adjustments in the list of items.[7] Also included is detailed information on the household structure, such as regional location, number of household members, ownership of air conditioners. All annual samples are independently drawn according to a two-stage design.[8]

A sub-sample of 10,671 observations has been selected, considering households owning air conditioners[9] and living in eight regions of Italy: Friuli-Venezia Giulia, Trentino Alto Adige, Liguria, Lombardia, Toscana, Lazio, Sardegna and Sicilia representing four macro-regions: North East (NE), North West (NW), Centre (CE), South and the Islands (SI). We estimate a ten-commodities demand system: (1) Food and beverages; (2) Housing excluding rent; (3) Air conditioners; (4) Clothing; (5) Health care; (6) Transport; (7) Communication; (8) Recreation; (9) Alcohol and tobacco; (10) Other goods and services.[10] Each commodity has been obtained as an aggregate of detailed current expenditures on more than two hundred elementary goods and services.[11] The list of commodities has been chosen according to availability of monthly and regional consumption price indices, also supplied by ISTAT, which are included in the data set. These prices have been extracted from the Consumer Price Index (1998=100), also published by ISTAT. Specifically, we use the Consumer Price Index for the whole nation (NIC), which monitors sales prices every month in all Italian provinces. NIC is divided into 12 expenditure categories entered into the national index with a specific weight reflecting the relative importance of the concerned good on total consumption. Many of these categories coincide with the commodities in our demand system. Some of them have been aggregated to correspond to the remaining goods in our demand system. In addition, we consider expenditures on air conditioning and the corresponding elementary price index also supplied by ISTAT. To summarize, the sample used in our estimations consists of 10,671 household observations collected for eight regions over 12 months for five years. Using r to indicate the region, m the month and y the year, the data have been organized by lining up monthly data ($m = 1 - 12$) on each macro-region ($r = 1 - 4$) for each year ($y = 1 - 5$) in a vector of 10,671 observations.

A set of dummy variables is included to account for the macro-area in which the household lives (NW, NE, CE, SI) and for the likely seasonality in air conditioning expenditure (SEASON) equal to 1 for the warmest months of the year: June, July, August and September. We also add a categoric variable (LOC) for whether the household lives in a town with more than 50,000 inhabitants (1), fewer than 50,000 inhabitants (2) or in a small village (3) and a logarithmic annual time trend.

We combine these data with information on air concentrations of three pollutants: Ozone (O_3), Particulate (PM_{10}) and Nitrogen Dioxide (NO_2). These have been used to compute a categorically continuous index of air quality (IQA), a standardized indicator of air quality in a given location. Following the definition given by the National Agency for the Protection of the Environment (APAT) according to European guidelines, the index is constructed as a weighted average of data on hourly concentrations of three air pollutants supplied by APAT.[12] The weights were provided by each of the regional agencies in charge of calculating air quality indices on a regional basis.

Data on hourly concentrations of Ozone (O_3), Particulate (PM_{10}) and Nitrogen Dioxide (NO_2) were available from 1 January 2002 to 31 December 2006. For each Italian region hourly pollutant concentrations have been collected from a very large number of stations located in a Traffic, Industrial or Background area. We consider concentrations from traffic and background stations only in order to merge them with consumption expenditures of households in urban or background areas. Due to missing data over the investigation period, only eight Italian regions have been considered: Lombardia, Liguria, Friuli Venezia Giulia, Trentino Alto Adige, Lazio, Toscana, Sicilia and Sardegna.

Starting from a total of 1,596,938 hourly observations, a daily regional IQA_d has been obtained as: $IQA_d = \frac{I_1 + I_2}{2}$ where the subscript d indicates the day; $I_1 = \left(\frac{PM_{10}}{\overline{PM_{10}}} \right) \times 100$ is a sub-index where PM_{10} is the mean daily particulate concentration and $\overline{PM}_{10}$ is the threshold value for particulate concentrations admitted by the Italian law[13] ($50 \mu g/m^3$). The second sub-index, I_2, is simply the highest between Nitrogen Dioxide and Ozone concentrations: $I_2 = max(NO_2, O_3)$. Threshold values for NO_2 and O_3 concentrations are, respectively, 200 $\mu g/m^3$ and 120 $\mu g/m^3$.

Daily IQAs have been averaged over each month to obtain monthly indices. As a result, our regional IQA is given by a sample of 960 observations (12 months × 5 years × 16 areas). These monthly indices have then been used to construct a categoric variable (LQ) varying between 1 (low air quality) and 7 (high air quality) used in estimation.

Summary statistics of the data are shown in Table 5.1 (NO = North West; NE = North East; CE = Centre; SI = South and Islands). Figures 5.1 and 5.2 show the pattern over time of the national and regional monthly IQA.

5 Results

Table 5.2 shows first-step probit estimates along with their asymptotic standard errors. Many of the variables included are significant at the 5 percent level in

Table 5.1 The data (no. of households = 10,671)

Current expenditures (euros/month)	*mean*	*std dev*	*min*	*max*
Total expenditure	1,784.705	1,063.757	250.019	6,958.370
Food from stores	485.747	283.304	0.000	2,374.739
Alcohol and tobacco	44.466	58.495	0.000	551.480
Clothing	190.509	285.023	0.000	4,387.530
Household operation	210.760	154.237	0.000	3,501.580
Air conditioners	12.315	82.999	0.000	1028.930
Health	112.068	278.392	0.000	5,228.750
Transport	162.021	129.441	0.000	1,042.620
Communication	64.838	50.950	0.000	652.949
Recreation	52.934	85.197	0.000	1,597.560
Other goods and services	458.282	530.354	0.000	5,228.920
Price indices (1998=1)				
Food from stores	1.135	0.034	0.826	1.337
Alcohol and tobacco	1.247	0.115	0.826	1.436
Clothing	1.127	0.040	0.824	1.364
Housing	1.145	0.053	0.821	1.365
Air conditioners	0.964	0.040	0.869	1.074
Health	1.095	0.034	0.816	1.365
Transport	1.190	0.068	0.815	1.392
Communication	0.842	0.083	0.701	1.393
Recreation	1.101	0.030	0.813	1.393
Other goods and services	1.185	0.052	0.809	1.393
Other exogenous variables				
IQA	5.630	1.232	1.000	7.000
NW	0.279	0.448	0.000	1.000
NE	0.108	0.311	0.000	1.000
CE	0.219	0.414	0.000	1.000
SI	0.393	0.488	0.000	1.000
LOC	1.158	0.446	1.000	3.000
SEASON	0.346	0.476	0.000	1.000
Annual time trend	3.183	1.378	1.000	5.000

each expenditure share equation. Income plays a positive role in explaining the budget share of all goods. Seasonality and the annual time trend also play a significant role in the probability of consuming many of the commodities. The index of air quality (*LQ* variable) is also significant in explaining the decision to purchase air conditioners and has the expected negative sign.[14] Going from a big to a small town (*LOC* variable) has a negative role in determining purchase of air conditioners, probably because big cities are more polluted. Going from a big to a small town also plays a positive and significant role in explaining Transport and Alcohol/Tobacco choices, but has a negative and significant role, as expected, in explaining recreation choices. Hicksian (compensated) elasticities, based on parameters of the second-step,[15] are computed at the sample mean as: $\sigma_{ij}^{*h} = \sigma_{ij}^{h} + \sigma_{i}^{h} w_{j}^{h}$ where σ_{ij}^{h} is the uncompensated price elasticity of good *i* with respect to price *j* and σ_{i}^{h} is the expenditure elasticity of good *i*.

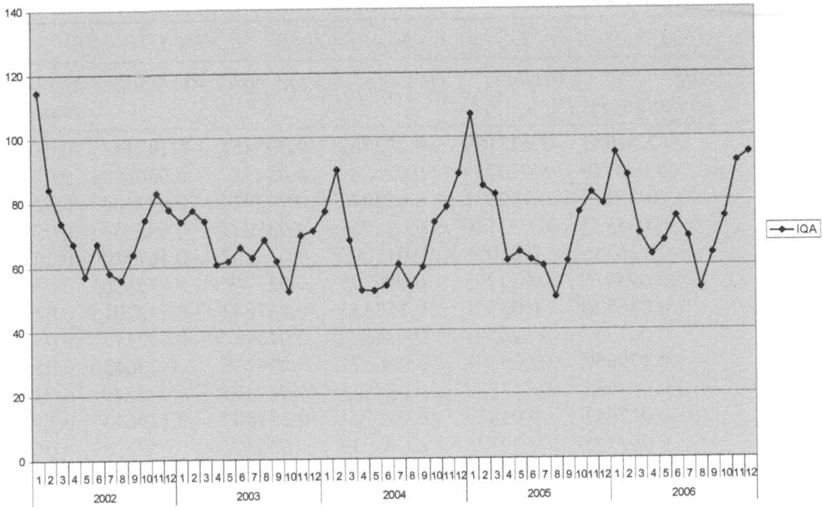

Figure 5.1 Index of air quality 2002–2006

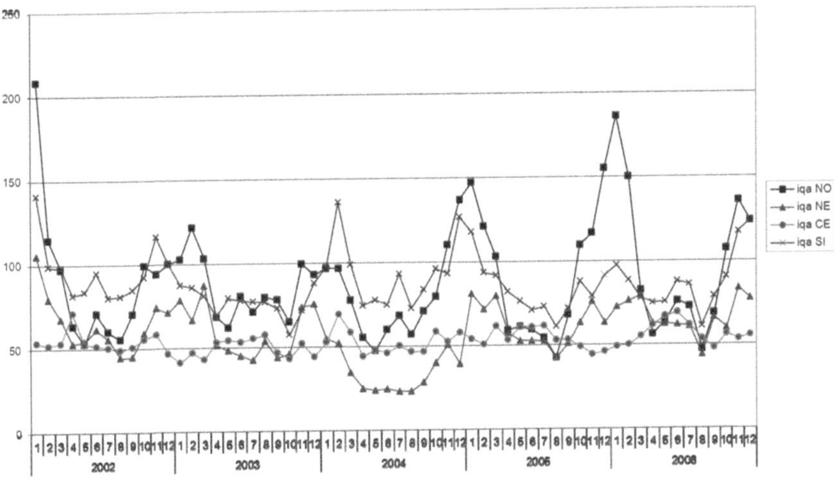

Figure 5.2 Index of air quality by region 2002–2006

These elasticities are shown in Table 5.3 along with expenditure elasticities for all goods and the estimated budget shares. All expenditure elasticities are significantly different from zero. Air conditioning appears to be a luxury good, with an income elasticity equal to 1.30.[16] As to the budget shares, Food, Housing, Transport and Clothing are the consumption categories to which the largest

Table 5.2 First-step probit estimates

n. obs. = 10,671	*i = 3*	*i = 4*	*i = 5*	*i = 6*	*i = 8*	*i = 9*
	Air conditioners	*Clothing*	*Housing*	*Transport*	*Recreation*	*Alcohol/ tobacco*
Constant	**–2.31089**	**–2.223189**	**–0.273782**	**0.305451**	**–0.10744**	0.036938
	0.052149	*0.030557*	*0.026787*	*0.034357*	*0.030894*	*0.026971*
Income	**0.35108**	**0.985871**	**0.624047**	**0.949924**	**0.897164**	**0.524992**
	0.035823	*0.032160*	*0.024951*	*0.038235*	*0.032454*	*0.025117*
NE	–0.136346	0.01096	0.011092	–0.013062	**–0.167920**	**–0.201669**
	0.095070	*0.054493*	*0.049739*	*0.059706*	*0.055830*	*0.050095*
NW	–0.046520	0.03251	**0.159532**	**–0.137643**	–0.042201	0.022482
	0.067357	*0.040594*	*0.036888*	*0.046737*	*0.042147*	*0.037690*
SI	**–0.279650**	0.005593	–0.056621	**0.294275**	**–0.29642**	0.056652
	0.073988	*0.041384*	*0.037855*	*0.049493*	*0.042240*	*0.039231*
LOC	–0.017661	–0.01439	–0.027704	**0.279807**	**–0.129643**	**0.130386**
	0.091733	*0.052728*	*0.048059*	*0.066572*	*0.052518*	*0.050459*
SEASON	**0.404687**	**–0.100387**	–0.128067	–0.02515	**–0.139139**	**0.064412**
	0.050421	*0.029482*	*0.027122*	*0.034511*	*0.029847*	*0.028129*
LTrend	–0.069255	**–0.074566**	0.013046	**–0.06303**	**–0.122640**	**–0.004166**
	0.046642	*0.025875*	*0.023626*	*0.030016*	*0.026298*	*0.024221*
LQ	**–0.215504**	–0.009866	–0.066255	0.063225	**–0.153797**	**–0.078265**
	0.066753	*0.038757*	*0.035390*	*0.043823*	*0.039883*	*0.036113*
mean of dep. Var.	0.032	0.746	0.627	0.862	0.763	0.703
Log Likelihood	–1401.06	–5418.99	–6630.24	–3822.81	–5260.13	–6216.29
Scaled R-Squared	0.182	0.117	0.077	0.085	0.109	0.051
Predicted Power	0.968	0.756	0.666	0.862	0.770	0.705

Note: Standard errors in italics below coefficients. Bold entries correspond to rejection of $H_0 : e = 0$ at the 5 percent significance level for a two-tailed test.

part of the monthly expenditure is allocated. This is in line with similar works on Italian household consumption (Moschini and Rizzi, 1997; Balli and Tiezzi, 2010). All the compensated own price elasticities, calculated at the sample means of variables, have the correct sign and are statistically significant. Air conditioning displays a very high and significant compensated own price elasticity (1.80), but none of the cross-price elasticities are significant. Some of the other compensated own price elasticities are greater than one: Food, Clothing, Health, Transport and Communication.

The conditional demand system (4) and the WTP function (7) are integrable if and only if the integrability conditions are satisfied. These integrability conditions, calculated at the sample mean for $\varepsilon = 0.5$ are all satisfied, therefore the mixed demand system with household production is integrable.

Household marginal WTPs for improvements in air quality in euros/month for five income groups are shown in Table 5.4 for three values of ε. All standard errors

Table 5.3 Mean household budget shares, w_j, expenditure elasticities, e_j and Hicksian elasticities e^*_{ij}

	j = 1	*j = 2*	*j = 3*	*j = 4*	*j = 5*	*j = 6*	*j = 7*	*j = 8*	*j = 9*	*j = 10*
	Food	*Housing*	*Air conditioners*	*Clothing*	*Health*	*Transport*	*Recreation*	*Communication*	*Alcohol/tobacco*	*Other goods*
w_j	0.300	0.137	0.006	0.093	0.054	0.095	0.042	0.027	0.026	0.219
e_j	**0.731**	**0.495**	**1.334**	**1.860**	**0.575**	**1.438**	**0.534**	**1.619**	**1.004**	**1.235**
	0.006	*0.010*	*0.256*	*0.065*	*0.134*	*0.056*	*0.012*	*0.085*	*0.107*	*0.036*
e^*_{1j}	**–1.439**	–0.137	0.064	**0.362**	**0.543**	0.003	**–0.172**	**0.479**	0.037	0.260
	0.252	*0.115*	*0.056*	*0.190*	*0.155*	*0.139*	*0.042*	*0.099*	*0.077*	*0.243*
e^*_{2j}	–0.301	**–0.675**	–0.0461	0.078	0.783	**0.341**	**0.139**	**0.335**	–0.011	**–0.645**
	0.254	*0.189*	*0.048*	*0.172*	*0.178*	*0.138*	*0.053*	*0.115*	*0.072*	*0.209*
e^*_{3j}	2.569	–0.649	**–1.796**	–0.377	0.511	0.840	0.663	–0.226	–0.050	–1.486
	2.018	*0.839*	*0.604*	*0.676*	*1.065*	*0.638*	*0.455*	*0.255*	*0.376*	*1.460*
e^*_{4j}	**0.982**	0.186	–0.016	**–1.050**	–0.255	**0.230**	**0.141**	–0.137	0.025	–0.167
	0.435	*0.181*	*0.041*	*0.225*	*0.247*	*0.128*	*0.078*	*0.145*	*0.050*	*0.229*
e^*_{5j}	**2.093**	**1.341**	0.053	–0.318	**–1.612**	–0.312	–0.125	–1.215	–0.001	0.097
	0.606	*0.341*	*0.115*	*0.441*	*0.712*	*0.313*	*0.136*	*0.218*	*0.189*	*0.618*
e^*_{6j}	0.193	**0.468**	0.052	0.200	–0.188	**–1.442**	–0.062	–0.001	0.055	0.725
	0.306	*0.146*	*0.038*	*0.117*	*0.177*	*0.173*	*0.059*	*0.120*	*0.046*	*0.244*
e^*_{7j}	**–1.222**	**0.456**	0.120	0.347	–0.195	–0.317	**–0.392**	0.199	0.057	**0.946**
	0.299	*0.181*	*0.088*	*0.256*	*0.251*	*0.201*	*0.106*	*0.153*	*0.104*	*0.299*
e^*_{8j}	**3.871**	**1.293**	–0.043	–0.496	**–2.442**	0.045	0.247	**–2.477**	**0.001**	0.000
	0.777	*0.400*	*0.137*	*0.528*	*0.449*	*0.396*	*0.176*	*0.475*	*0.209*	*0.622*
e^*_{9j}	0.421	0.026	–0.012	0.047	0.010	0.179	0.084	–0.008	**–0.641**	–0.109
	0.614	*0.264*	*0.053*	*0.178*	*0.386*	*0.163*	*0.116*	*0.214*	*0.175*	*0.382*
e^*_{10j}	**0.779**	–0.235	–0.057	–0.109	–0.320	**0.375**	**0.162**	–0.233	–0.012	–0.350
	0.269	*0.124*	*0.055*	*0.153*	*0.178*	*0.143*	*0.051*	*0.111*	*0.073*	*0.324*

Note: Standard errors in italics below coefficients. Bold entries correspond to rejection of $H_0 : e = 0$ at the 5 percent significance level for a two tailed test.

Table 5.4 WTP for air quality improvements (euros/month)

Income Level	*ε = 0.15*	*ε = 0.35*	*ε = 0.5*
Overall sample mean	**0.687**	**1.602**	**2.290**
(10,671)	*0.025*	*0.062*	*0.087*
$y \leq 800$	**0.141**	**0.329**	**0.470**
(1,016)	*0.018*	*0.044*	*0.062*
$y \leq 2000$	**0.475**	**1.108**	**1.582**
(4,993)	*0.022*	*0.049*	*0.070*
$y \leq 4000$	**1.476**	**3.444**	**4.920**
(2,808)	*0.059*	*0.140*	*0.194*
$y \leq 6000$	**2.260**	**6.207**	**8.867**
(401)	*0.253*	*0.587*	*0.870*
$y > 6000$	**2.296**	**5.357**	**7.652**
(72)	*0.484*	*1.071*	*1.568*

Notes: Standard errors in italics below coefficients. Bold entries correspond to rejection of $H_0 : e = 0$ at the 5% significance level for a two tailed test.
y = household disposable income proxied by total current expenditure.

have been obtained using bootstrapping and 500 replications. WTP is smaller than €10 for most households, in particular a value around €3 has a very high frequency. Changing the value of ε from 0.5 to 0.1 implies a very small impact on the WTP distribution. The WTP is positively correlated to household income, revealing that rich households value air quality improvements more highly than do poor ones. Nevertheless, when expressed as a fraction of household income WTP increases only slightly with income for any value of ε. For higher income levels WTP as a fraction of income decreases from 0.25 percent for $y \leq 6000$ to 0.13 percent for $y > 6000$. The fact that households in lower-income groups have a relatively higher WTP for air quality improvements is consistent with findings by Kriström and Riera (1996) and Hökby and Söderqvist (2003). This may be because higher-income households live on average in areas with relatively low levels of air pollution and they therefore experience a less relevant physical improvement (e.g. air quality changes from good to very good) in air quality in comparison with low-income households. A lower WTP for richer households may also be explained by a larger set of substitution possibilities.

5.1 WTP by household location

Table 5.5 shows how WTP varies across four geographical areas of Italy. Intuition suggests that certain areas, where big metropolitan areas are located, may be more likely to exhibit larger values due to their longer experience of air quality problems. This pattern is confirmed by the results of our empirical analysis, showing higher WTP values for the North West and the Centre, the macro-regions where the big metropolitan areas are located.

Noonan (2011) also tests the hypothesis according to which the WTP is lower for higher starting levels of air quality. In our study, the value of WTP is highest for the North West, the macro-region having the worst air quality, as shown in Figure 5.2. The South and the Islands are the next macro-region in terms of IQA value, which on average is particularly high, although not the worst. This pattern is not mirrored by the WTP value, which in this case is the lowest. By contrast, the WTP for a marginal improvement in air quality is high for the Centre, which has the best IQA performance. The fact that the Centre has a higher WTP than the North East shows that the hypothesis described in Noonan (2011) is not sustained in our analysis, which is consistent with the first approach in the meta-analysis developed by the author. This issue will be further investigated in the next paragraph, in particular with respect to the second approach adopted by Noonan (2011) to test the hypothesis of decreasing returns.

Table 5.5 clearly indicates the presence of other relevant drivers of WTP, different from the baseline level of air quality. Income plays a key role, with the North West being the richest macro-region, followed by the Centre. As described in the literature review, other drivers are very likely to influence WTP, such as the perception of pollution and its effects, and the education level. Moreover, the production specialization of the macro-region examined, i.e. the prevailing sector among energy-intensive industries, agriculture or services, could turn out to be relevant.

5.2 WTP is declining as the level of air quality improves and over time

Does the WTP for additional improvements in air quality decline with increasing air quality levels? The possibility that the benefits of further improvements fade away as our air gets cleaner and that the benefits are rising over time is crucial for designing efficient air policies. The existing literature shows that WTP for air quality improvements is declining as the level of air quality improves (Noonan, 2011).

Our study confirms this result. In Table 5.6 we report the rate of change of WTP with respect to our index of air quality (Q_WTP). This result is in contrast with the

Table 5.5 WTP by household location (euros/month)

Location	*WTP (mean)*
North West	**4.047**
(2,483)	*0.349*
North East	**2.620**
(1,017)	*0.357*
Centre	**3.009**
(1,462)	*0.131*
South and Islands	**1.755**
(3,763)	*0.209*

Notes: Standard errors in italics below coefficients. Bold entries correspond to rejection of $H_0 : e = 0$ at the 5 percent significance level for a two-tailed test.
Number of observations in parentheses below location. Number of observations does not match the full sample due to the missing values in estimated WTP.

Table 5.6 Rate of change of WTP over time and with respect to the index of air quality

	Rate of change
Q_WTP	–1.188
	(0.206)
T_WTP	–0.001
	(0.151)

Note: Standard errors in parentheses.

pattern described in Section 5.1 according, to which WTP is related only partially to the baseline levels of air quality. Such a finding is nevertheless consistent with the general results of other literature studies, showing an important role played by other drivers, besides income such as education, household composition, and labor status.

Whether the value of air quality improvements increases or decreases over time is another important issue. Even though air quality standards should be set and implemented irrespective of the costs of doing so, the level of public support for those standards is certainly important in deciding the level of environmental protection. If there is a time trend in environmental values reflecting a change in individual preferences towards environmental public goods, then the sum of benefits may change over time, affecting cost-benefit analysis. In Table 5.6 we also compute the rate of change of WTP with respect to our time trend (T_WTP). This rate of growth turns out to be negative and around –1 percent per year, but it is not statistically significant. Studies introducing a time trend as an explanatory variable in regressions investigating factors affecting WTP for improvements in air quality also find a negative time trend (Noonan, 2011).

6 Final remarks

This paper makes three contributions to the literature. First, it operationalizes the approach developed by Ebert (2007) for recovering the underlying preference ordering from observed behavior when non-market goods are employed in household production. Second, it uses a unique dataset, where household consumption data are combined with an index of air quality, to estimate the marginal WTP for air quality improvements in Italy. Third, it studies how WTP is affected by households' location, by the initial level of air quality and how WTP changes over time.

The results are consistent with other studies investigating WTP for marginal improvements in air quality, and in particular with the meta-analysis developed by Noonan (2011).

According to our results, WTP appears to be:

- very sensitive to the geographical location of the household
- not related to the baseline level of air quality, but displaying decreasing returns
- decreasing over time (although the coefficient is not statistically significant).

Household production combined with demand analysis has a number of advantages over other approaches. First, it is not exposed to the biases of stated preferences methods because only choice-based data are used. Second, it is operational and could be used, at a low cost, in any country where micro-data on household consumption are available. In addition, the availability of demographic characteristics would allow accounting for heterogeneity of households in WTP such as location, number of household members and gender. Third, it allows flexibility both in the specification of the demand system and in the specification of the household production function. Different classes of household production functions could and should be explored. Different environmental goods could be considered and included in the demand system.

Notes

1 Turning to environmental costs, rather than benefits, they will be progressively (pro-poor) distributed when they rise with income and regressively (pro-rich) distributed when they fall with income.
2 The main problem in estimating the income elasticity of WTP is that individual demand and prices for a public good cannot be directly observed. Since the quantity of most environmental goods is rationed, the income elasticity of WTP for a fixed quantity of the public good rather than the income elasticity of demand is the relevant parameter for measuring benefit incidence.
3 The data set and estimation approach are the same as those used by Martini and Tiezzi (2013). However the two papers differ in how they use the demand system estimates. The present paper focuses on WTP drivers other than income, whereas Martini and Tiezzi (2013) focuses exclusively on the income elasticity of willingness to pay.
4 Shonkwiler and Yen (1999), Yen, Lin and Smallwood (2003) and Yen and Lin (2006) provide useful literature review on estimation procedures for censored demand systems.
5 That is to say that Y is not necessarily required to produce Z given q. See Ebert (2007, fn11), for an interpretation of this property.
6 A different sample of households is interviewed each month; the item list also includes non-current expenditures, with a total of about 280 goods and services.
7 We implicitly assume strong separability in consumers' preferences between current and other expenditures.
8 Details on the sampling procedure used to collect these data can be found in ISTAT, *Indagine sui Consumi delle Famiglie. File standard. Manuale d'uso. Anni 1997–2006.*
9 This choice is explained by the fact that air conditioners are an input in the household production function to produce the household level of air quality (see section 4.2 for a description of the household production function).
10 The rationale for choosing to include home-related expenditures (aggregate (3)) is that a substitution relationship is likely to exist between air conditioning and other goods and services purchased by the household (by way of example, the need for air conditioning is likely to diminish in better-insulated houses).
11 Aggregation is possible, assuming, as is usually done, that goods within each group are consistent with the Hicks and Leontief Composite Commodity Theorem (Deaton and Muellbauer, 1980a, pp. 120–121).
12 Data on air pollutant concentrations are freely downloadable at www.apat.it. The same data are available from the European Air Quality Database of the European Environmental Agency.
13 D.M. 60/02.
14 We expect a negative sign, since the IQA is computed in such a way that higher values are associated with better air quality conditions.

15 Second-step parameters are not reported, to save space, but are available from the authors upon request.

16 It is worth mentioning that the income elasticity associated with air conditioning, as well as the price elasticities, are all short-term elasticities. Since the stock of air conditioners is built up over time, and such a process is likely to be incomplete in some regions, the income elasticity of WTP is also to be interpreted as valid in the short term.

References

Afroz, R., M.N. Hassan, M. Awang and N.A. Ibrahim (2005) Willingness to Pay for Air Quality Improvements in Klang Valley Malaysia, *American Journal of Environmental Sciences*, 1, pp. 194–201.

Alberini, A., M. Cropper, T. Fu, A. Krupnick, J. Liu, D. Shaw and W. Harrington (1997) Valuing Health Effects of Air Pollution in Developing Countries: The Case of Taiwan, *Journal of Environmental Economics and Management*, 34, pp. 107–126.

Bajari, P. and L. Benkard (2005) Demand Estimation with Heterogeneous Consumers and Unobserved Product Characteristics: A Hedonic Approach, *Journal of Political Economy*, 113 (6), pp. 1239–1276.

Balli, F. and S. Tiezzi (2010) Equivalence Scales, the Cost of Children and Household Consumption Patterns in Italy, *Review of Economics of the Household*, 8, pp. 551–552.

Basili, M., M. Di Matteo and S. Ferrini (2006) Analysing Demand for Environmental Quality: A Willingness to Pay/Accept Study in the Province of Siena (Italy), *Waste Management*, 26, pp. 209–219.

Bayer, P., N. Keohane and C. Timmins (2009) Migration and Hedonic Valuation: The Case of Air Quality, *Journal Environmental Economics and Management* 58, pp. 1–14.

Berger, M.C., G.C. Blomquist, D. Kenkel and G.S. Tolley (1987) Valuing Changes in Health Risk: A Comparison of Alternative Measures, *Southern Economic Journal*, 53, pp. 967–983.

Bergmann, A., N. Hanley and R. Wright (2006) Valuing the Attributes of Renewable Energy Investments, *Energy Policy*, 34, pp. 1004–1014.

Bergstrom, T.C. and R. Goodman (1973) Private Demands for Public Goods, *American Economic Review*, 63, pp. 280–296.

Bergstrom, T.C., D.L. Rubinfeld and P. Shapiro (1982) Micro-based Estimates of Demand Functions for Local School Expenditures, *Econometrica*, 50, pp. 1183–1205.

Boercherding, T.E. and R.T. Deacon (1972) The Demand for the Services of Nonfederal Governments, *American Economic Review*, 62, pp. 891–901.

Broberg, T. (2010) Income Treatment Effects in Contingent Valuation: The Case of the Swedish Predator Policy, *Environmental and Resource Economics*, 46, pp. 1–17.

Carlsson, F. and O. Johansson-Stenman (2000) Willingness to Pay for Improved Air Quality in Sweden, *Applied Economics*, 32, pp. 661–669.

Champ, P.A., K.J. Boyle and T.C. Brow (2003) *A Primer on Non-Market Valuation*. Dordrecht, Netherlands: Kluwer Academic Publishers.

Costa, D. (1997) Less of a Luxury: The Rise of Recreation Since 1888, NBER Working Paper n. 6054.

Deaton, A. and J. Muellbauer (1980a) *Economics and Consumer Behaviour*. Cambridge: Cambridge University Press.

Deaton, A. and J. Muellbauer (1980b) An Almost Ideal Demand System, *American Economic Review*, 70, pp. 312–336.

Dickie, M. and S. Gerking (1991) Valuing Reduced Morbidity: A Household Production Approach, *Southern Economic Journal*, 57, pp. 690–702.

Ebert, U. (2007) Revealed Preferences and Household Production, *Journal of Environmental Economics and Management*, 53, pp. 276–289.

Ek, K. (2005) Public and Private Attitudes towards "Green" Electricity: The Case of Swedish Wind Power, *Energy Policy*, 33, pp. 1677–1689.

Ekeland, I., J. Heckman and L. Nesheim (2004) Identification and Estimation of Hedonic Models, *Journal of Political Economy*, 112(1.2), pp. S60–S109.

Freeman III, A.M. (2003) *The Measurement of Environmental and Resource Values*. Washington, DC: Resources for the Future.

Galarraga, I., M. González-Eguino and A. Markandya (2011) Willingness to Pay and Price Elasticities of Demand for Energy-Efficient Appliances: Combining the Hedonic Approach and Demand Systems, *Energy Economics*, 33, pp. S66–S74.

Gerking, S. and L.R. Stanley (1986) An Economic Analysis of Air Pollution and Health: The Case of St. Louis, *Review of Economics and Statistics*, 68, pp. 115–121.

Ghalwash, T. (PhD dissertation) (2006) Demand for Environmental Quality: An Empirical Analysis of Consumer Behavior in Sweden. Department of Economics, Umea, Sweden.

Ghalwash, T. M. (2008) Demand for Environmental Quality: An Empirical Analysis of Consumer Behavior in Sweden, *Environmental and Resource Economics*, 41, pp. 71–87.

Hökby, S. and T. Söderqvist (2003) Elasticities of Demand and Willingness to Pay for Environmental Services in Sweden, *Environmental and Resource Economics*, 26, pp. 361–382.

ISTAT, Indagine sui Consumi delle Famiglie. Istituto Nazionale di Statistica (ISTAT), Roma, (various years).

Ito, N., K. Takeuchi, T. Tsuge and A. Kishimoto (2010) Applying Threshold Models to Donations to a Renewable Electricity Fund, *Energy Policy*, 38, pp. 1819–1825.

Jacobsen, J.B. and N. Hanley (2009) Are there Income Effects on Global Willingness to Pay for Biodiversity Conservation? *Environmental and Resource Economics*, 43, pp. 137–160.

Johansson, P.O. (1990) Willingness to Pay Measures and Expectations: An Experiment, *Applied Economics*, 22, pp. 313–329.

Kotchen, M.J. and M.R. Moore (2007) Private Provision of Environmental Public Goods: Household Participation in Renewable-Electricity Programs, *Journal of Environmental Economics and Management*, 53, pp. 1–16.

Kriström, B. and P. Riera (1996) Is the Income Elasticity of Environmental Improvements less than One? *Environmental and Resource Economics*, 7, pp. 45–55.

Léger, P.T. (2001) Willingness to Pay for Improvements in Air Quality, Cahier de recherche n. IEA-01-02.

Li, C.-Z. and L. Mattson (1995) Discrete Choice under Preference Uncertainty: An Improved Structural Model for Contingent Valuation, *Journal of Environmental Economics and Management*, 28, pp. 256–269.

Lindhjem, H. (2007) 20 Years of Stated Preference Valuation of Non-Timber Benefits from Fennoscandian Forests: A Meta-Analysis, *Journal of Forest Economics*, 12, pp. 251–277.

Mäler, K.G. and J.R. Vincent (2005) *Handbook of Environmental Economics, Vol. II: Valuing Environmental Changes*. Amsterdam: Elsevier.

Mansfield, C., F.R. Johnson and G. van Houtven (2006) The Missing Piece: Valuing Averting Behavior for Children's Ozone Exposures, *Resource and Energy Economics*, 28, pp. 215–228.

Martini, C. and S. Tiezzi (2013) Is the Environment a Luxury? An Empirical Investigation using Revealed Preferences and Household Production, Forthcoming Resource and Energy Economics. DOI: 10.106/j.reseneeco.2013.11.014..

Menegaki, A. (2008) Valuation for Renewable Energy: A Comparative Review, *Renewable and Sustainable Energy Review*, 12, pp. 2422–2437.

Moschini, G. and P.L. Rizzi (1997) La struttura dei consumi delle famiglie in Italia, *Rivista Internazionale di Scienze Sociali*, 105, pp. 449–471.

Mozumder, P., F. William, W. F. Vásquez and A. Marathe (2011) Consumers' Preference for Renewable Energy in the Southwest USA, *Energy Economics*, 33, pp. 1119–1126.

Noonan, D.S. (2011) How Much Do We Care about the Air? Evidence on the Value of Air Quality Improvements, AEI (American Enterprise Institute) Working Paper 2011–07.

Pereyra, A. and M. Rossi (1999) Are Environmental Goods a Luxury? *Revista de la Escuela de Economca y Negocios* 1, 3.

Pollack, R.A. (1969) Conditional Demand Functions and Consumption Theory, *The Quarterly Journal of Economics*, 83(1), pp. 60–78.

Pollack, R.A. and T.J. Wales (1992) *Demand System Specification and Estimation.* New York: Oxford University Press.

Riera, P. (1994) The Social Value of Areas of Special Environmental Interest in Mediterranean Countries, in *Environmental and land use issues: an economic perspective*, Proceedings of the 34th EAAE Seminar held in the Mediterranean Agronomic Institute of Zaragoza, Spain, edited by L.M. Albisu and C. Romero, pp. 351–360.

Rosen, S. (1974) Hedonic Prices and Implicit Markets: Product Differentiation in Pure Competition, *Journal of Political Economy*, 82, pp. 34–55.

Schläpfer, F. (2006) Survey Protocol and Income Effects in the Contingent Valuation of Public Goods: A Meta-analysis, *Ecological Economics*, 57 (3), pp. 415–429.

Shonkwiler, J.S. and S. Yen (1999) Two-step Estimation of a Censored System of Equations, *American Journal of Agricultural Economics*, 81, pp. 972–982.

Travisi, C.M., R.J.G.M. Florax and P. Nijkamp (2004) A Meta-Analysis of the Willingness to Pay for Reductions in Pesticide Risk Exposure, FEEM Nota di Lavoro 101.

Wang, H. and J. Mullahy (2006) Willingness to Pay for Reducing Fatal Risk by Improving Air Quality: A Contingent Valuation Study in Chongqing, China, *Science of the Total Environment*, 367, pp. 50–57.

Wang, Y. and Y. Zhang (2009) Air Quality Assessment by Contingent Valuation in Ji'nan, China, *Journal of Environmental Management*, 90, pp. 1022–1029.

Wiser, R. (2007) Using contingent valuation to explore willingness to pay for renewable energy: a comparison of collective and voluntary payment vehicles, *Ecological Economics*, 62, pp. 419–32.

World Bank (2002) Improving air quality in metropolitan Mexico City: An Economic Valuation, Policy Research Working Paper 2785.

Yen, S.T. and B. Lin (2006) A Sample Selection Approach to Censored Demand Systems, *American Journal of Agricultural Economics*, 88 (3), pp. 742–749.

Yen, S.T., B. Lin and D. Smallwood (2003) Quasi- and Simulated-likelihood Approaches to Censored Demand Systems: Food Consumption by Food Stamp Recipients in the United States, *American Journal of Agricultural Economics*, 85 (2), pp. 458–478.

Yoo, S. and S. Kwak (2009) Willingness to pay for renewable electricity in Korea: a contingent valuation study, *Energy Policy*, 37, pp. 5408–5416.

Zografakis, N., E. Sifaki, M. Pagalou, G. Nikitaki and V. Psarakis (2010) Assessment of public acceptance and willingness to pay for renewable energy sources in Crete, *Renewable and Sustainable Energy Review*, 14, pp. 1088–1095.

Part III

The distributional incidence of the costs of environmental policies

The case of carbon/energy taxes

6 Household-level studies on the distributional impact of carbon/energy taxes

Chiara Martini

1 Introduction

The scientific research has shown how the rising concentration of greenhouse gases (GHG) is very likely to be associated with changes in world climate (IPCC, 2007). A relevant role in determining the level of greenhouse gases (GHG) in the atmosphere is represented by CO_2 emissions from fuel combustion (IEA, 2012). For this reason, in order to minimise the negative effects of climate change, the relative cost of the various types of energy sources should reflect their carbon content and not only the cost of the associated energy technology. In order to introduce such a cost structure government intervention is needed, and reorienting energy taxation represents a potentially effective policy strategy (OECD, 2010; OECD, 2011). The taxation of energy products is in fact not necessarily in line with the environmental consequences – CO_2 emissions in particular – of energy use. Ecological (or environmental-oriented) Tax Reforms (ETR) aim at implementing the changes needed to reorient energy taxation, and they are mainly represented by the introduction of carbon taxation, or by its gradual increase. This paper is devoted to the study of the distributional implications of ETRs, concentrating on low- and middle-income households which may be disproportionately affected by carbon tax.

Energy use has a central role in individual consumption, and in recent years the taxation of energy has gained much attention within the political debate. This phenomenon has a variety of explanations. First, energy use contributes to significant environmental concerns such as climate change, air pollution and natural resource depletion. Taxation affects the relative prices of different energy sources and uses, and therefore the pattern of total energy consumption. The tax setting should be aimed at favoring clean energy sources and technologies. In doing so, distributional effects may arise, since energy taxation affects people's net incomes and therefore has significant welfare implications. The other main reason for taxing energy is to raise revenue. In fact, the demand for energy products is relatively inelastic, and thus government revenue is relatively stable. Again, the impact on household budgets of higher energy taxes is potentially a cause of concern.

Two main criteria for taxing energy can be identified, an externality-based criterion and a revenue-based one. They may appear to be contrasting, since the first assumes a responsiveness in energy consumption and production patterns, whereas the second is based on the hypothesis of low elasticity of the demand for energy products The first criterion is more based on substitution effects among energy products (i.e. their cross-price elasticities), while the second is based on the own-price elasticity of each product. Both mechanisms operate in the long and in the short run. OECD (2006) highlights that the short-run price elasticity of energy as a whole is relatively low, ranging between –0.13 and –0.26. By contrast, elasticity is considerably higher in the long run, in the range of –0.37 to –0.46. Looking at gasoline, elasticity estimations are lower (–0.15 to –0.28) in the short term, but higher (–0.51 to –1.07) in the long term. Such a differentiation of short- and long run elasticities implies that if the price signal persists, the behavior of firms and individuals will change. Therefore, in the long run energy taxes can have a significant impact on energy demand and its composition (OECD, 2001, 2006). Energy or carbon taxation influences final consumer prices in two ways: a direct effect, when energy consumption is concerned, and an indirect effect, shown by increases in other goods the production of which has entailed energy use (Speck, 1999). The level of reactivity to price changes induced by the tax differs greatly between products, countries, time spans and income groups (Dahl, 2012).

In many countries, the reform of energy taxes and the introduction of carbon taxation has been the subject of lively debate. One of the main reasons for this is the concern about the distributional effects on socially weak or low income groups. Although they are certainly worthy of consideration, potentially adverse distributional issues need to be addressed without sacrificing the economic signals sent by the environmental-oriented tax reforms (OECD, 2006). This paper will be structured as follows: section 2 describes some experiences of energy and carbon taxation, section 3 deals with different approaches for the investigation of taxation distributional effects, section 4 reviews the literature contributions of each approach, and section 5 concludes.

2 The taxation of energy products

Already in 2006, the OECD confirmed the high potential for governments to introduce ETRs and recommended reducing existing exemptions in energy taxation, which risk undermining its environmental effectiveness. Restoring the role of energy taxation in achieving environmental objectives could imply negative effects on income distribution. In fact, due to the relative importance of energy products in the consumption bundle of households in different income classes, energy taxation could have the potential to affect poorer households more. Moreover, because of the widespread fear that energy taxation could affect industrial competitiveness, exemptions or refunds are often designed to protect certain sectors, such as energy-intensive industries. As a result, the tax burden falls for the most part on the transport and residential sectors, embedding potential regressive effects. In particular, Vehmas (2005) investigates how differentiated taxation practices – which may be introduced to achieve other policy goals, such as distributional concerns – make environmental-oriented taxation less effective.

Tax departures – defined as exceptions from an ideal environmental tax – can be structured in different ways: referring to the tax base, exempting some fuels or uses from tax; or to the tax level, taxing specific users at lower rates. In this section several approaches to energy and carbon taxation will be described, with a particular focus on EU member states.

The Nordic countries can be described as forerunners in energy taxation in the European Union. At the annual Nordic Council meeting in Helsinki in 1997 – in the middle of the debate on the proposal for a European carbon tax – members of parliament from five Nordic countries made a unanimous recommendation to their governments to harmonise energy taxes across the region.

Despite of their geographical proximity, a "Nordic model" for CO_2 taxation does not exist: taxes differ widely with respect to rates, tax base and exemptions, trying to adapt to specific national features (Speck et al., 2006). Even so, several common characteristics can be identified: first, ETRs are often put into place gradually; second, exemptions for energy-intensive sectors are widely used in order to protect national competitiveness; and third, a special treatment is often reserved for electricity. With regard to excise rates, sometimes revenue objectives prevail over environmental ones, so that gasoline and other transport fuels are more heavily taxed (in relation to coal), having a low price elasticity and allowing for an easy increase in tax revenue. In what follows, carbon and energy taxation will be examined, trying to focus on tax departures, in particular those relevant to easing the adverse distributional impacts on specific households.

Finland in 1990 was the first country in Europe to impose a CO_2 tax, levied on fossil fuels depending on their carbon content. All energy products began to be taxed according to both the energy and carbon content. In contrast to other Nordic countries, Finland does not differentiate between tax rates for private users and industrial users. Many tax departures exist, for example relative to peat and natural gas, which are mainly used by households. The taxation of transport fuels has a long tradition in Finland, as is the case in other Nordic countries. However, environmental issues did not enter into the justification of excise taxes on transport fuels until 1987, when the Finnish authorities introduced differentiated tax rates on gasoline according to the lead content (Finnish Economic Council, 2000). The total tax burden levied on transport fuels doubled between 1990 and 2000, but has increased by only around 5 percent since 2000.

Energy policy in Sweden became particularly relevant in conjunction with the oil crisis in the early 1970s, in reaction to the fear of an oil shortage. In the 1980s, the motivation for policy intervention switched to environmental concerns, and later on the double-dividend started to constitute a relevant issue in the political debate (Johansson, 2000). The tax rates on electricity are set based on geographical considerations: since 1981 the municipalities of northern Sweden have been charged a lower electricity tax, for reasons of climate. In 1998, the electricity tax scheme was further refined and the tax rates were differentiated according to the consumption level, applying a higher tax rate to large consumers.

Also in the Netherlands, small energy consumers are exempt from tax. Distributional reasons similarly inspired the structure of taxation in Norway, where the taxation of fuels used for residential heating is lower than for other uses. Expenditure on this energy service is considered a necessary good which all households should be able to afford.

In Germany special exemptions in excise duties applied to energy products are also aimed to promote more efficient energy production processes. For this reason, the heat supplied via district heating systems and electricity produced from natural gas or renewable energy are exempted from tax.

In 1999, the German Bundestag passed the "Law Introducing the Environmental Fiscal Reform," which increased the excise taxes on several energy products according to their carbon content. Energy products for heating (light fuel oil and natural gas) are taxed almost one order of magnitude less than transport fuels (Kohlhaas, 2000). In addition to this differentiation, special treatment is provided according to the sector using the energy. Private households, the transport sector and services pay the standard tax rates on electricity and heating fuels, whereas reduced rates are paid by other sectors, such as manufacturing industry, in order to ensure that the ETR does not impair international competitiveness. In this case it is obvious that the impact on residential consumers is more relevant than that on industrial consumers, and the potential presence of adverse distributional effects deserves further investigation.

In United Kingdom the Climate Change Programme was launched in November 2000, and the Climate Change Levy was imposed on all non-residential energy bills, typically raising them by 8–10 percent, with the aim of providing an incentive to increase energy efficiency and reduce CO_2 emissions. The structure of the levy aims at protecting poorer households from a disproportionate impact on their budgets (OECD, 2005). Clearly, imposing a tax also on residential energy consumption would have provided a wider price signal, directed to all economic agents, and in consequence more environmentally effective results. The British case is an extreme example of the outcome of distributional concerns when implementing environmental-oriented tax reforms.

In Italy concerns about potential regressivity have been one of the main reasons why the implementation of a planned ETR was halted. With the Budget Law for 1999 the Italian government introduced a carbon tax by means of a gradual increase in excise duties over a period of five years. The reform was very significant, since Italy was the second-largest European economy, after Germany, to introduce an ETR. In addition, Italy was the first country in southern Europe to introduce CO_2 taxation, already implemented in several northern states. The package re-modulated the excises levied on different energy products, used both as transport and heating fuels, in order to better reflect their carbon content. Specific measures were introduced, such as a lower excise on heating products for industrial users than for households, and a lower excise on natural gas tax in some areas of southern Italy.

The higher excise rates affected transport and heating fuels and then, for the most part, households. The Italian ETR also introduced a tax reduction for industries because of the revenue re-utilisation through a reduction of social contributions. The ETR has been the subject of great debate since its introduction, because of the potential negative effects on economic growth and income distribution. The gradual increases in the excise duties were halted only one year after their introduction, due also to the increase in crude oil market prices. It is worth mentioning that the carbon tax had a marginal impact on the overall excise on energy products, similar to the ETR introduced in the Netherlands in 1996. In the United Kingdom the excise duties on fuels were increased by 6 percent per year starting from 1997, a rate well above the Italian annual excise increase.

In general, the examples of national experiences provided above show that countries differ markedly in the way they tax energy. Differences are observed in the range of products taxed, in tax base definitions and in tax rate levels and rebates. Nonetheless, some common trends may be identified (OECD, 2013). Transport fuels are generally taxed more heavily than heating fuels, and road fuels tend to have the highest tax rates. As for heating fuels, large differences arise between countries. Aside from the absence of many of the externalities associated with road use, low tax levels may relate in part to concerns about the distributional impacts, as is the case for residential heating. Electricity is very often taxed and constitutes a good largely consumed by households.

In Europe, a relatively broad range of products is taxed according to EU Directive 2003/96 (Energy Taxation Directive – European Council 2003). Moreover, a general tendency to higher tax rates relative to many non-European countries can be detected, although rates are generally not explicitly set with regard to carbon content. According to the taxation approach in the EU Directive, most fossil fuels for heating use are taxed, and the consumption of electricity is also taxed. Some countries, such as Belgium, Hungary, Poland and Portugal exempt (or tax at a very low level) several product uses, particularly within the heating category.

Inspired partly by approaches adopted in some Nordic countries, in June 2011 the European Commission proposed amending the Energy Tax Directive by splitting the minimum tax rates – currently based only on the energy content of products – into two separate components (European Commission 2011). The first would be based on CO_2 emissions and the second on energy content, and the coverage and rates would expand gradually. As highlighted in Weisbach (2011), this reform process would imply an overall increase in energy taxation, and the impacts on households would deserve further investigation with respect to their distributional consequences.

3 The distributional impacts of carbon taxation

The environmental benefits associated with reorienting energy taxation and implementing ETRs may be counteracted by adverse consequences on specific income or social brackets. Such a phenomenon may impede the introduction of ecological tax reforms, complicating their political acceptability.

Distributional impacts of energy and carbon taxation generally refer to the risk that poorer households or social groups are more impacted in terms of tax payments and decreases in disposable income. The distribution of environmental benefits at household level is rarely taken into account in distributional analysis (Kriström, 2006). Aspects that instead are usually dealt with are represented by:

1 the differentiation in the consumption of energy products and services
2 the differentiation in income and price elasticities
3 the direct and indirect effects of taxation on emissions and prices
4 revenue recycling.

As highlighted by Ekins et al. (2011), the impacts of taxes on the household use of energy are very often regressive, whereas transport taxes tend not to be, although the impacts differ between urban and rural households. The relative importance of energy products and services in the consumption bundle of different households may depend on a range of demographical variables, such as the number and age of members. The same is true for the estimation of income and price elasticities. Moreover, energy and carbon taxation can be analyzed also by considering their price effects in relation to direct emissions from energy products and to indirect emissions from products which required the use of energy for their production. Finally, the net distributional impact is often less regressive, or not regressive at all, once the wider distributional effects are taken into account. Energy and carbon taxation have more indirect effects, associated with revenue recycling. Potential regressive effects can be removed by further adjustments in the tax or benefits system, aimed at compensating more impacted households.

Different partial equilibrium methods can be chosen for studying the impacts associated with environmental reforms in energy taxation. According to the analytical approach adopted, four main categories can be distinguished:

1 demand system estimation
2 Input-Output (I-O) matrices analysis
3 computation of measures or indices, such as Gini or Suits index
4 other approaches, based on other micro-simulation models.

It is worth specifying that such a classification may not be the only alternative for grouping studies of the distributional effect of energy and carbon taxation. Demand system estimation is by far the most extensively used approach. Starting from a utility function representing rational preferences, the maximisation problem is modeled and the equations for expenditure shares on different goods are derived. The coefficients obtained from the estimation can be used to compute demand elasticities, and also welfare measures such as equivalent or compensating variation.

I-O matrices analysis can be usefully employed to compute the price increase associated with carbon taxation of direct and indirect energy consumption. With respect to indirect effects, two kinds of coefficients can be computed for each sector based on I-O matrices. The first type of coefficient would allow for the calculation of direct energy consumption as an intermediate good, the second type for the calculation of indirect energy consumption, referring to the use of energy as an input for producing other intermediate goods used in the production process. In this way the price effects of energy or carbon taxation on all final goods can be evaluated, referring to intermediate energy and non-energy consumption, and applied to the consumption bundles of different households.

The distributional impacts of environmental-oriented tax reforms can also be assessed through the computation of measures reflecting the changes in income for households belonging to different brackets. In particular, indices are widely used. As for the Gini coefficient, it is represented by the ratio of the area that lies between the Lorenz curve, which plots the cumulative percentage of population (x-axis) against the corresponding proportion of total income (y-axis), and a diagonal line representing perfect equality of incomes. An increase after a tax reform would indicate a tax effect that increases inequality in income distribution, whereas a reduction would be associated with an opposite tax effect. The Suits index (Suits, 1977) is similar to the Gini index, but refers to a space formed by the cumulated percentages of total income and of total tax burden, where a 45-degree line represents the line of tax proportionality and every curve below (above) is a tax progressivity (regressivity) curve. The index varies between –1 and 1 and in the case of a regressive tax, when members of the lowest income bracket pay a greater share of their income as tax, the Suits index is negative. Other measures can be computed, and in general this approach has the important advantage of being directly comparable among different tax reforms or countries.

The last category consists mainly in other micro-simulation models, focused on additional information related to household consumption. In the case of carbon and energy taxes, they are represented by vehicle utilisation and ownership, other vehicles' characteristics and, in few cases, benefits from reduced fuel use. The studies in such a category allow investigation of the components through which short- and long-run behavioral responses are determined, although demand elasticities for energy goods are rarely estimated. For example, this kind of micro-simulation approach is able to show the decrease in kilometers driven or the changes in vehicle ownership associated with gasoline taxation. In this category, analyses of distributional characteristics may also potentially be included. In fact, such analyses use micro-data and estimate the marginal effects of taxation based on a ranking of goods. When developing a distributional characteristic approach behavioral responses are rarely estimated, and the marginal effects of taxation are usually computed by assuming that the ranking of goods remains unaffected.

These categories have different abilities in assessing the relevant issues in distributional analysis identified above. For example, demand system estimation is particularly well suited for examining the differentiation in the consumption of energy products and services, and in income and price elasticities. By contrast, direct and indirect effects on emissions and prices may be better identified by employing I-O matrices. Clearly, the approaches differ also in the variables that they need for assessing the distributional impacts. Demand system estimation, as well as distributional characteristics analysis, uses micro-data on household expenditures, which are usually associated with data on household composition and location. On the other hand, data included in I-O matrices mirror the structure of the whole economy of a country, together with the material flows needed to produce the economic output of each sector. The price effects estimated through I-O data could be combined with household expenditure patterns in order to estimate tax incidence.[1] Finally, also the computation of measures and indices generally needs data at household level. Current income, lifetime income, reflecting the expected flow of earnings during people's lifetime, or total expenditure may be used as inputs to compute measures and indices. All these variables have some disadvantage. Current income and total expenditure do not reflect the fact that households in the lowest income or expenditure groups could be investing in human capital (e.g. graduate students), or disposing of extensive savings (e.g. retired people). Lifetime income relies on strong assumptions about household consumption decisions, assuming that they are based on a complete knowledge of future income flows. Energy and carbon taxes in general look considerably less regressive with lifetime income measures than with annual income measures.

4 Review of literature

Energy and carbon taxation are widely used options among environmental policy tools. This explains why, due to representativeness and economic relevance criteria, they have been the focus of many studies in the literature assessing distributional impacts. Findings from different contributions are not always unanimous, since they may measure incidence and household welfare differently, for example considering or not behavioral responses to policy-induced price changes. This section will show how different methods investigate different variables and, more importantly, often imply different results. The aim of this literature review is (more than being accurately exhaustive) to provide a criterion for classifying partial equilibrium studies and to draw a picture of the implications of the different methods. The review will be conducted in chronological order, and will try to adopt a critical point of view.

Demand system

Demand system estimation has a long tradition in the analysis of distributional effects and it is certainly characterised by a high potential in terms of both variables and types of impacts which can be taken into account. Useful insights can be obtained by comparing different distributional measures computed using the coefficients estimated by the demand system, distinguishing for demographical and locational characteristics.

Revenue raised can also be calculated, together with different recycling scenarios. The limitations of this approach can be eased by combination with other methodologies, as will be shown in the following.

Symons et al. (1994) combine demand system estimation – in particular, the AIDS model – with the I-O matrices approach and the computation of indices and measures of distributional impacts. Different scenarios for ETR in the UK are simulated, and it turns out that how the reform is structured, in particular the combination of carbon taxation with a reduction in existing excise duties, affects the potential for regressive distributional impacts. Moreover, regressivity is decreased when different revenue reutilisation options are introduced, represented by indirect taxes reductions, compensation through the direct tax system and equity-based transfers. Such a mix of different approaches allows the development of deeper and wider considerations of the distributional impacts of ETR, showing the relevance of the fiscal system structure and revenue recycling in shaping them.

In the same vein, Labandeira and Labeaga (1999) examine the effects of a tax levied on Spanish CO_2 emissions. The empirical analysis proceeds in two stages: an I-O model is employed to calculate the indirect price changes after the introduction of carbon taxation, then a demand system with Spanish household microdata is simulated. A similar combination of I-O analysis and micro-simulation of demand responses is used also by Cornwell and Creedy (1996). In particular, the authors estimate a Quadratic Almost Ideal Demand System (QAIDS; Banks et al., 1997), and the elasticities provided by the model are used to compute the tax burden. The short-run reaction to the carbon tax is limited, and the tax burden by decile of expenditure appears to be proportionally distributed. Also, this approach provides the possibility of investigating variables different from income, such as demographic variables. An analysis of sub-samples distinguishing by the age and number of household members shows that differences in the tax payments are not significant. In any case, it is important to have the possibility of checking for the impact of such variables, which other contributions will describe as particularly relevant.

Brännlund and Nordström (2004) show instead the high potential of applying a unique approach – demand system estimation – for studying in depth the distributional effects, investigating the role of different household characteristics and revenue recycling options. They analyze carbon taxation in Sweden by means of a two-stage budgeting model which combines micro and macro data to assess the separability between labor supply and demand for non-durable goods. Adopting the QAIDS specification, the differences in consumption patterns between different households are modeled by adding intercepts and slope parameters in the budget share equations. The household characteristics taken into account are represented by the number of children under and over 18 years old, number of household components and their employment status, age of the head of household and locational variables. The authors consider two different scenarios: a 100 percent increase of the CO_2 tax combined with a lowering of general VAT and a 100 percent increase of the CO_2 tax associated to a lower VAT on public transport. The tax is regressive in both scenarios, although less regressive in the second. Doubling the CO_2 tax implies a clear disadvantage for inhabitants of rural regions, who have a higher energy demand (Speck et al., 2006), for example because they have to travel further and have less access to public transportation. The results obtained by Brännlund and Nordström (2004) are not consistent with other studies, according to which carbon taxes are progressive because they affect the portion of the population who own cars and not the poorer brackets, who generally do not (Ekins and Dresner, 2004; Bach et al., 2002; Smith, 2000). This divergence in results allows one to say that the variables and household characteristics taken into account could be highly relevant in shaping the taxation impacts. Car ownership is rarely included in demand system estimation, and this is surprising, given that carbon taxation greatly affects transport fuel prices. The importance of behavioral responses, locational variables and country-specific characteristics is confirmed by EEA (2011), which highlights how distributional impacts can be eased by less-pronounced differences between urban and rural households, as is the case in Switzerland, thanks to a more extensive public transport system.

West and Williams (2004), differently from the studies described above, examine the sensitivity of distributional impacts to the incidence measure adopted and mainly focus on the role of income. They model an increase in gasoline taxation, using total expenditure as a proxy for lifetime income and estimating a demand system distinguishing for expenditure class and household type. Different incidence measures are computed: equivalent variation, allowing for cross-price and income effects, and assuming a constant-elasticity demand curve (see, among others, Cornwell and Creedy, 1997; Brännlund and Nordström, 2004); an approximation of the consumer surplus change, not considering cross-price effects but using elasticities that vary by quintile; another approximation of the consumer surplus change, assuming constant own-price demand elasticities among households; the difference between expenditure levels before and after the tax plus the income change resulting from the policy. Incidence could be overestimated or underestimated by the third measure, depending on the number of households with relatively elastic or inelastic demand. Since low-income households may fall into both categories – they could be more responsive to gasoline price changes, due to their low budgets, or less responsive, due to fewer transportation alternatives in the long run – it is key to estimate own-price elasticities by expenditure level. The last incidence measure, used also by Poterba (1991), Metcalf (1999) and West (2004), will tend to overstate the burden of tax increases, since it ignores consumers' shift away from the taxed good. The results show that the differences among equivalent variations computed by expenditure level – and the first consumer surplus measure – are not significant. Comparing the two consumer surplus measures points out that assuming constant demand elasticities across quintiles makes the gasoline tax look more regressive, upper-income quintiles being less price-responsive than lower-income ones.[2] Regressivity is reduced when tax revenue is returned through an equal percentage reduction in the marginal tax rate on labor income, labor income being a greater fraction of total income for low-income households. The main finding of this study confirms the significance of household income for the distributional impacts, as well as their high sensitivity to the incidence measure adopted.

Similar results are obtained by Bento et al. (2005), who simulate an increase in the gasoline tax under two different scenarios, according to which revenue is rebated to households in proportion to income or to their gasoline tax payments. Again, the household income level is key in shaping the results, since, with income-based recycling, low-income households are penalised more than high-income households, whereas with tax-based recycling the impact of the tax across income groups is close to proportional.

Tiezzi (2005) simulates the ex-ante effects of introducing carbon taxation in Italy, as was set with the Budget Law for 1999, then affecting mainly transport fuels, and heating fuels relatively less. Based on the estimates from an AIDS, compensating variations are computed for different household types and expenditure levels. They do not allow supporting the regressivity of carbon taxation: contrary to what has been found by similar studies (Brännlund and Nordström, 2004; West and Williams, 2004), the tax burden is progressively distributed across households. As Smith (2000) pointed out for the UK, the progressivity result might be due to the fact that households in the lowest levels of expenditure do not own a car. In fact, in the British study the distributional effect is reversed and carbon taxation is found to be regressive when only car-owning households are taken into consideration. It has been already highlighted how controlling for car ownership is a rarely adopted estimation strategy; nevertheless, it is very likely to affect the distributional effects, for example the results obtained for Italy.

With regard to the inclusion of demographic variables, another example is provided by Labandeira et al. (2006), who estimate an AIDS demand system using different sub-samples to capture how carbon taxation impacts vary according to household characteristics. A significant impact is found between the expenditure level on different energy goods and household composition, work status (active or retired) and the place of residence (rural, intermediate and urban). Both income and price elasticities vary when computed by household type, in particular with regard to the place of residence. For example, when the size of the municipality increases there is a greater substitution of transport fuels with public transport. Transport fuels and public transport turn out to be luxury goods, whereas all the other energy goods are normal goods. Income is a relevant variable for distributional effects – consistent with the findings from other contributions – since poorer households are more responsive to changes in energy prices, likely due to a larger share of energy in total expenditure.

Creedy and Sleeman (2006) examine the effects of imposing a carbon tax in New Zealand, distinguishing for different characteristics related to household composition. Another interesting feature is using information on the industrial use of fossil fuels and the carbon intensity of each good, so that indirect emissions can be taken into account. This strategy allows overcoming the limitation of demand system estimation, which is able to provide the effects of taxation only on energy goods, which are taxed explicitly. Households with relatively low total expenditure levels spend a proportionately greater amount on taxed goods such as gasoline and heating fuels, but also on carbon-intensive commodities such as electricity. The estimation of a Linear Expenditure System (LES; Stone, 1954) allows computation of welfare effects and also a summary measure of inequality for each demographic group and for all groups combined. For the majority of household types, the tax burden does not vary monotonically with total expenditure, producing a very small redistributional effect, which may easily be compensated by revenue recycling. It seems that the value added of considering industrial use of fossil fuels and carbon intensity could be better exploited, for example by examining the sensitivity of distributional impacts to different taxation scenarios.

Demand system estimation can also be usefully complemented by integrating it with a computable general equilibrium (CGE) model, as in Labandeira et al. (2009). The CGE model is used to evaluate both the efficiency and sectoral impacts of an ETR in Spain, while the demand system is employed to assess the distributional effects on households. The result from QAIDS estimation show once again the importance of considering demographic variables, for instance related to household location in rural areas, where there is limited access to energy commodities and services, such as public transport. A relationship between household composition and energy consumption was also found, as, for instance, households with a retired component spend a smaller proportion on transport fuels, since they benefit from public transport subsidies. Significant income effects are observed, with respect both to the choice of energy commodities, for example LPG is preferred by low-income households, representing a cheap substitute for natural gas, and to consumption patterns, since transport fuels are consumed more by high-income households, being associated with car ownership.

Martini (2010) compares two demand systems (QAIDS and AIDS) for estimating the distributional impacts associated with the introduction of carbon taxation in Italy. Demographic variables, such as household composition and the age of its members, and locational variables are taken into account and imply a relevant differentiation in elasticities estimates. On the basis of equivalent and compensating variation, the carbon tax is not regressive. By contrast, when the tax is applied only to transport fuels it is regressive, while it continues not to be regressive when it is imposed only on heating fuels. As highlighted for other studies, this result could potentially be due to ownership patterns: in Italy heating devices are still not widespread and are in several cases centralised (so that consumption is not fully responsive at the individual level), whereas the motorisation rate is among the highest for EU member states. Also, in this case there could be a problem of omitted variables in the estimation, the inclusion of which could affect the overall distributional effect. Finally, the revenue raised in northen, southern and central Italy is computed, showing how demand system estimation can be exploited also to develop public finance projections, basing them on the behavioral responses of different household types.

Besides the contributions previously described – all based on demand system estimation – behavioral responses to price changes induced by carbon taxation can be estimated by adopting relatively simpler approaches. For example, Cornwell and Creedy (1997) follow the theoretical framework of a Linear Expenditure System (LES) but estimate elasticities by means of the Frisch parameter. Such an approach is easier to implement, but as a consequence its results are less rich in their content and potentially also less realistic. In this case, carbon taxation turns out to be regressive: calculated on the basis of annual income, both compensating and equivalent variation fall as income rises.

To summarise, the analysis of this first methodological approach has shown the high potential of demand system estimation, which has been used by a wide range of contributions. Although they have in common the theoretical approach, the results obtained differ widely, due to differences in the functional form employed, the choice to combine with other approaches and the variables they control.

Price and income elasticities

When examining the results of demand system estimation, it seems appropriate to focus on the results in terms of elasticity. In fact, they are a key parameter in determining the overall incidence of ETRs. In the following, the results from meta-analyses devoted to the elasticity – both income and own-price – of transport fuels will be summarised. Their findings can be somehow referred to the relevant elasticities of other energy goods. It is important to note that the high importance of variables different from income, in particular demographic and locational, is confirmed also by an analysis of price and income elasticity. The meta-analyses described here also show the relevance of the method chosen for estimating elasticities and then the effect on distributional impacts.

Espey (1998) developed a meta-analysis to determine if there are factors that systematically affect price and income elasticity of gasoline. They turn out to be represented by: the assumptions in the demand model; the explanatory variables chosen; the countries included and the time frame of the data; the econometric estimation technique. In particular, excluding variables modeling vehicle ownership and its characteristics positively biases the estimates, providing more income-elastic gasoline demand.

A similar analysis is developed by Goodwin et al. (2004), finding that price elasticities are negatively related to income, and in general tend to fall over time when the income level is increasing. According to the authors, in the long-run the demand responses are more significant, due to the wider set of alternatives. Johansson and Shipper (1997) support this result, asserting that in the long run the behavioral response to increases in fuel prices comes from changes in car fuel efficiency rather than from driving less.

Also, Basso and Oum (2007) attempt to synthesise the information on automobile fuel demand. Studies using disaggregated data show that the demographic profile plays a major role in determining fuel consumption. When demographic variables are not included in the demand model, the associated effects are only partially captured by the income elasticity.

It is worth considering that the elasticities of different energy goods are very likely to differ. Gasoline is an energy product for which a high share of total consumption can be attributed to households, whereas only about two-fifths of electricity sales are to households. Electricity is an intermediate good widely used by industries in their production processes, and this specificity highlights the value added of investigating the distributional impacts of tax reforms by an approach such as I-O matrices, able to capture the economy-wide connections. For this reason, allowing for increases in prices of final goods indirectly affected by energy or carbon taxation is particularly important when investigating distributional impacts.

Input-output matrices analysis

The review of the contributions that develop I-O matrices analysis confirms the usefulness of combining different approaches, which appears particularly significant for the I-O approach. In particular, I-O matrices allow disentangling the dependence of production patterns on energy goods and CO_2 emissions, and a common assumption is represented by the full translation of taxation, resulting in higher prices for final products relative to their energy and carbon content. Both household direct emissions, obtained by applying emission factors to the energy goods consumed, and indirect emissions, derived from intermediate use of energy goods in the production processes as represented in I-O matrices, can be considered. With I-O methodology, demographic and locational variables can also be taken into account in the estimation.

Already the first contributions show the importance of the assumptions and the variables chosen to measure the distributional impacts. Casler and Rafiqui (1993) compute the price effects of gasoline taxation on 89 final goods consumed by households, using I-O tables. They assume that the tax is fully passed on to consumers, and that firms' intermediate consumption and household consumption are fixed. Both hypotheses constitute a limit of the use of I-O matrices, and the second one can be removed with the estimation of a demand system. When income is measured on an annual basis, the tax is far less regressive than direct expenditure data indicate. Rural consumers are adversely affected, but the tax burden to income ratio for the lowest quintile is only slightly higher than for the top quintile.

Bull et al. (1994) use a similar approach to compare a carbon tax constituted by an indirect and a direct component, respectively based on energy and carbon content. Differently from Casler and Rafiqui (1993), the authors focus on the sensitivity of distributional impacts with regard to a broad range of household income variables, including annual income, annual total consumption and lifetime income. On the basis of annual income, the carbon tax appears regressive with regard to both its direct and indirect component, with the first more distributionally adverse than the second. Instead, on the basis of lifetime income, the direct component remains regressive, but the indirect component becomes mildly progressive.

Labandeira and Labeaga (1999) combine I-O matrices with demand system estimation, and in this way they are allowed to consider behavioral responses. They assume a full shifting on output prices of carbon taxation imposed on intermediate goods, which could imply an overestimation of indirect effects. Relative to the supply side, it is assumed that no substitution takes place in the production process, therefore the results should be taken only as a short-term approximation for carbon taxation indirect effects. In distributional terms, the tax turns out to be proportionally distributed.

Unlike other studies that consider reforms that introduce carbon taxation, Wier et al. (2005) examine the existing CO_2 tax in Denmark. The authors explore the potential of I-O matrices in many ways, namely the consideration of direct and indirect effects, the comparison of different incidence measures and reform scenarios. Locational variables appear to be significant. In particular, the direct tax burden is heavier on rural households – who have higher transport and heating needs – but it is partly offset by their lower indirect tax payments related to non-energy goods. The study also confirms that the regressivity depends on the way income is measured. The tax is strongly regressive on the basis of annual income, the direct component of the tax accounting for most of the adverse impact, while regressivity is greatly reduced using total expenditure. With respect to reform scenarios, shifting the taxation from energy-intensive products (CO_2 tax) to food products (GHG tax) leads to a more equal distribution of the tax burden across income groups. Removing the hypothesis according to which carbon taxation is fully passed on to consumers and exploring different scenarios for passing on would further enrich the analysis.

Bandyopadhyay et al. (2007) investigate the impact of a hypothetical carbon tax imposed in the US in a revenue-neutral context. The adoption of an I-O approach allows computing the tax paid as a combination of both an explicit and implicit tax, paid respectively on household direct and indirect emissions, the last component being associated to non-energy goods and transferred by the producers to their prices. The tax is weakly regressive in the US context, consistent with the findings of Tiezzi (2005), according to which ETRs are either neutral or weakly progressive or regressive, depending on the relative proportion of energy expenditures on the total. Metcalf (2007) also uses an I-O matrix to investigate the potential impacts of a carbon tax in the US, and the tax burden appears to be weakly regressive. When different hypotheses of tax credits are investigated, the relevance of revenue reutilisation in mitigating adverse impacts is clearly shown. Both contributions show the useful property of I-O methodology, which allows obtaining the indirect emission content of each good and then estimating the impacts of carbon taxation on the whole consumption bundle of the household. This clearly enriches the results also when different revenue recycling scenarios are compared.

Kerkhof et al. (2008) adopt an approach similar to Bandyopadhyay et al. (2007) in order to compare the distribution of the tax burden of a GHG tax and a CO_2 tax imposed on industry and households. Direct and indirect tax payments of Dutch households in different income groups are calculated by applying the price change of final products to household expenditures. The GHG tax distributes the tax burden more equally across income groups than does the CO_2 tax, consistent with what was already found by Wier et al. (2005). Such a result is likely to be due to the fact that the difference in the share of expenditure on food between low- and high-income households is lower than the difference in their share of electricity and gas.[3] Interestingly, the authors recognise that their study, as every I-O analysis, does not consider behavioral responses after the tax-induced price changes, being based on fixed I-O coefficients and exogenously determined final demand. The inclusion of behavioral responses, also at the level of goods supply, will certainly affect the final effect on product prices and then the overall distributional impacts.

Many advantages are associated with linking I-O matrices with CGE models, and one of the most relevant is represented by being able to remove the hypothesis of full shift of carbon taxation onto final consumer prices. To this end, Metcalf et al. (2008) use the results from the EPPA model (Paltsev et al., 2007) as input in the I-O matrices. The reductions in carbon emissions are also used to predict the revenue raised by carbon taxation. Assuming full forward shifting, the carbon tax results are highly regressive, with regard to both its direct and indirect component. The regressivity can be offset with a lump-sum rebate of the carbon tax revenue. By changing the incidence of the tax-induced price increase on the basis of the results from the EPPA model, the authors find that a lower level of passing-on for the tax burden may significantly dampen the regressivity of a carbon tax.

As is clear from some of the contributions examined in this subsection (Wier et al., 2005; Bandyopadhyay et al., 2007; Kerkhof et al., 2008), I-O matrices analyses always use expenditure data to determine the distributional effects. Nevertheless, behavioral responses are almost never taken into account, affecting the final results in terms of the amount and direction of distributional impacts. In fact, if low-income households had fewer substitution possibilities than high-income households, then potential regressive results would be exacerbated. Also, the consideration of demographic and locational variables is rare in I-O analyses, and this is likely to be a relevant omission.

Computation of measures and indices

Several distributional analyses are based on the computation of measures and indices, and very often they compare the impacts, measuring them with different indicators, and also investigate different scenarios for revenue recycling. At the same time, this methodological approach implies many limitations, the most relevant ones being the exclusion of behavioral responses and the complications associated with including demographic and locational variables.

Poterba (1989) is among the first contributions emphasising the quantitative significance of different income measures for the degree of regressivity of gasoline taxation in the US. In particular, annual income makes the tax look consistently more regressive than lifetime income, proxied by annual consumption expenditure.

Another early and comprehensive study was undertaken by Smith (1992), who analyzed carbon taxation in several EU countries. The interesting feature of this contribution is that an ad hoc regressivity measure is developed, expressed as the ratio between the share of tax payments on total household expenditure of the poorest quartile over the same share of the richest quartile. Since a falling ratio with rising income is observed, the carbon tax is weakly regressive for most countries, more strongly regressive for the UK and Ireland. Including a comparison with other measures of distributional impacts would certainly have enriched the study and its results.

Metcalf (1999) examines the effects in the US of a package of environmental taxes, including a carbon tax. Although the overall package disproportionately affects low-income groups, the reform can be made distributionally neutral – under a range of different income measures – through income and payroll tax reductions.

This study highlights the potential of the computation of measures for comparing different revenue recycling scenarios. Consistent with Poterba (1989), it is found that choosing lifetime income sharpens the regressivity effects.

As was already highlighted for other approaches, the combination of different methods allows going beyond the limitations associated with their single application. Symons et al. (2002) examine the impact of carbon taxation on a sample of European countries, and to do this combine I-O analysis with the computation of measures and indices. The results shows that the tax burden faced by consumers varies significantly across the income distribution, very likely reflecting a different proportion of total expenditure allocated to the taxed goods. This suggests that variables different from income, for example related to household composition or location, could have relevance in shaping consumption patterns of the taxed goods. To further confirm this intuition, different patterns emerge according to the country examined: the tax looks regressive in Germany, France and, to a lesser extent, Spain, whereas this is not the case for the UK and Italy. The inclusion of demographic and locational variables could have provided useful information to explain this differentiation.

Jacobsen et al. (2003) investigate the distributional impact in Denmark of carbon, energy and transport-related taxation.[4] The distributional impact is examined by computing the share of the tax payments by decile relative to disposable income or to consumption expenditure (as a proxy of lifetime income). In this study the investigation of two different indicators is associated with common results. Transport-related taxes turn out to be progressive, whereas a regressive effect is associated to carbon and energy taxes. Such impacts differ from what is found by Martini (2010), whereas they are consistent with Sterner (2012), and also with Speck (1999) and Symons et al. (2000),[5] showing that the results can show common patterns even when obtained by different methodological approaches. Focusing on the approach given by the computation of measures, the results are consistent with other contributions (Poterba, 1989; Metcalf, 1999), since the adverse distributional effect appears to be eased when the share is computed using household expenditure. This pattern is confirmed also when the distributional impact is evaluated based on the marginal change in Gini index as a result of additional tax collection: positive changes indicate a regressive tax burden, and vice versa. Transport-related taxes reduce inequality and then can be considered progressive, whereas energy and carbon taxes turn out to increase inequality, likely due to a consumption of taxed goods more biased towards low-income groups than the average. It is worth noting that this contribution takes into account demographic variables, observing that the groups traditionally perceived as the most vulnerable, such as the unemployed or retired, are not those suffering the largest tax burden.

The study by Wier et al. (2005), described in previous subsection, also computes the Gini index, estimating it relative to disposable income as well as total expenditure. Together with the Suits index, the two indicators are computed, assessing the total effect of CO_2 taxation and also decomposing its direct and indirect effects, the last ones computed by means of I-O matrices. Using disposable income, the direct component of CO_2 taxation is more regressive than the indirect, both referring to the Gini and Suits index. Interestingly, using total expenditure significantly affects the results: the direct component, as well as the total effects of CO_2 tax, is still regressive, but the indirect component appears progressive. This contribution shows that the computation of indices can be usefully combined with I-O, allowing assessment of the effect on indices of direct and indirect tax components.

Sterner (2012) investigates the impact of carbon taxation in several European countries, employing different variables for measuring income and on this basis computing the Suits index. The evidence of regressivity is very weak. Also in this contribution the income variable chosen for measuring incidence and the country examined have important consequences on the results. Using current income, carbon taxation is found to be weakly regressive in most European countries, with very small impacts. By contrast, the use of total expenditure as a proxy of lifetime income reverses the results and neutral or proportional distributional effects are observed.

The overview provided in this subsection confirms the advantages associated with the combination of different approaches, in particular when measures and indices are computed based on price changes obtained from I-O matrices. A limitation is that, as was already highlighted for the I-O approach, also with the computation of measures and indices, the household consumption pattern is generally assumed to be left unchanged by the tax change, not including any information about behavioral responses.

Other approaches

In this subsection different approaches will be described, sometimes having substantial differences in their characteristics. In particular, some more "technology-oriented" micro-simulation models will first be described, and then the computation of distributional characteristics will be briefly mentioned. It should be considered that these approaches are "less standard" than the others described in previous subsections, and for this reason they allow the capture of different features which are more specific and, in a sense, novel.

Nichele and Robin (1995) investigate the introduction of carbon taxation in France, developing an econometric approach for matching individual cross-sections and aggregated time-series and estimating price and income effects on household consumption. The tax burden appears to be regressively distributed and strong substitution effects are found relative to heating and electricity, which are reflected in the revenue raised.

Bach et al. (2002) performed an ex-ante impact assessment of the German ETR on households in different income brackets. In particular, they combine the "Postdam" consumer model alternatively with an econometric macroeconomic model or a general equilibrium model. This approach is particularly interesting, since different scenarios are provided by the two economy-wide models, and their implications can be included as input in the partial equilibrium (consumer) model. As in other studies, this approach also allows consideration of both demographic variables and different recycling scenarios. The total net burden decreases with disposable income, and increases with family size. However, distributional effects appear rather moderate, confirming the results from other studies, such as Sterner (2012), and they become even less pronounced when revenue recycling is introduced. Similar results are obtained by Bork (2006), who uses the same micro-simulation model to perform an ex-post evaluation of the German ETR. When different tax components are investigated separately, energy taxation has a decreasing burden with regard to income, whereas transport fuel taxation has an inverted U-shaped pattern in income, i.e. first increasing, then decreasing with income.

West (2004) concentrates on motor vehicle taxation, in particular simulating a tax on vehicle size, a mileage tax and a subsidy to vehicle "newness," and integrates behavioral responses into the incidence analysis. The novelty of this contribution is related both to the possibility to investigate very specific types of taxes and to the modeling approach, which infers gasoline demand from automobile purchase decisions and miles traveled. The results show that households in lower income deciles have more elastic demands for miles traveled. When tax payments as a share of lifetime income (proxied by annual consumption) are computed using household-specific elasticities the tax appears less regressive than when behavioral responses are not taken into account or are assumed to be constant across income groups. Also, the consumer surplus change as a share of income becomes larger from the lowest decile to the middle deciles, and then drops sharply for the top decile. Some of this impact is due to the fact that low-income households do not own a vehicle: tax regressivity becomes greater when only households owning motor vehicles are considered. The value added of this study is certainly to provide a comparison among the results obtained from different modeling hypothesis for behavioral responses and incidence measures.

Callan et al. (2008) use the SWITCH micro-simulation model to assess the impact of carbon taxation in Ireland. Investigating the uses of energy for heating, electricity and motor fuels, the tax burden is slightly heavier for rural and small households. Revenue recycling to increase social welfare payments and decrease income taxes is also modeled, showing that a modest increase in welfare payments would offset the negative impacts of a carbon tax in the lower half of the income distribution. The advantage of using micro-simulation models is in general allowing for the consideration of demographic and locational variables, and at the same time for the simulation of public finance scenarios for revenue recycling.

A few other micro-simulation models will be outlined in the following, many of them focusing on car ownership and distribution of benefits from reducing car use. Asensio et al. (2002) focus on the distributional effects of gasoline taxation on car ownership in Spain, controlling also for the city size. The possibility of computing income elasticities of gasoline expenditure both conditional and unconditional on the level of car ownership is associated with useful insights into distributional impacts. In fact, non-conditional elasticities are lower for higher-income households and for those living in rural areas or small cities. On the other hand, if car ownership levels are taken as fixed, the corresponding elasticity is around one half the value of the non-conditional one. Household expenditure is used as a proxy of lifetime income, and the changes of the average rate of gasoline taxation have a progressive effect in the lowest income levels. This effect, however, vanishes when a certain income level is reached, and the threshold is lower in smaller cities. The impacts on vertical inequality in income distribution are measured by the Reynolds–Smolensky index, defined as the marginal change in the Gini index. In the largest municipalities, gasoline taxation reduces inequality, although very slightly, while in the smallest ones the opposite effect is observed. This distributional analysis provides an example of completeness, since many different issues are considered, namely specific behavioral responses, demographical and locational variables, an incidence measure and also an inequality index.

In an analysis of gasoline taxation in the US by Bento et al. (2005), households are grouped by income, family size and employment status, and the cost of the policy relative to income is highest for those not retired and with children. Two options for revenue recycling are considered, tax based and income based, respectively proportional to tax payments or income. Under the first option, gasoline taxation is close to proportional, with a small effect of relative price changes on vehicle ownership choices, whereas with the second one poorest households are more heavily affected. A large heterogeneity in distributional impacts is also associated with employment status and car ownership. In the same vein, but going further in the modeling both of demographic variables and revenue recycling scenarios, Bento et al. (2009) estimate the effects of gasoline taxation on the market for new and used cars, controlling for cars[6] and household heterogeneity, in the latter case with regard to vehicle ownership and distance travelled. Additional demographic variables are represented by the region of residence and ethnic background. Different revenue recycling options are also considered, namely income based, flat (in equal amounts to every household) and VMT based (vehicle-miles travelled). The authors estimate elasticities for different household types with regard to gasoline price and also operating costs. Flat recycling implies a welfare improvement, whereas income-based recycling benefits only the very rich. VMT-based recycling implies an almost flat pattern of impacts across the income distribution, although the welfare losses are greater for higher-income households who drive relatively less fuel-efficient vehicles.

Bureau (2011) investigates alternative scenarios of carbon taxation in France, focusing on the role of car ownership and, more interestingly, on the distribution of benefits associated with reduced car congestion. The increases in the cost of driving induced by taxation, and the corresponding effects on kilometers travelled, are modeled, allowing for different household behavioral responses. The price elasticity of driving by income bracket is then incorporated as a consumer surplus measure of tax burden. Peri-urban and rural households suffer welfare losses even when revenue recycling is considered, based on household size or on income. These welfare losses are mitigated by taking into account the benefits from congestion reduction. Beyond the inclusion of demographic characteristics and revenue recycling scenarios, a very important value added of this contribution is the focus on benefits distribution, which is often disregarded, implying a potential overestimating of fuel taxation regressivity.

Even if the computation of distributional characteristics has been never applied to energy or carbon taxes, it appears to have a high potential and to be well suited for such analyses. Santoro (2005) described this approach in more detail, showing that in order to perform a distributional characteristics analysis, the relative importance of different goods in the consumption bundle of households in different income brackets should be evaluated, and goods ranked in decreasing order of importance. The ranking is obtained for different values of the inequality aversion parameter in the social welfare function. Then, the effects of marginal tax reforms can be assessed with regard to the different rankings. Distributional characteristics analysis has been widely applied to investigate marginal changes in other taxes (among others, Newbery, 1995; Liberati, 2001; Mayeres and Proost, 2001).

Main findings

The studies analyzed allow the highlighting of several important elements of distributional analyses of carbon taxation, represented by the consideration of behavioral responses, demographic and locational variables, indirect price effects, different incidence and inequality measures, and revenue recycling options. Some issues for further research can also be identified, of which several examples are provided in the following.

With regard to demand system estimation, most of the contributions use the same demand system and vary the incidence measure. It might be interesting for future research to compare the results of alternative demand systems, based on different theoretical assumptions and functional forms, keeping the incidence measure fixed.

Demand system estimation is not able to consider the indirect price effects of taxation, which can be estimated by I-O matrices. On the other hand, when I-O analyses are developed, energy or carbon tax is often calculated without accounting for behavioral responses: such an assumption implies several distortions, for example with regard to the amount of raised revenue available for compensating adversely impacted households.

This seems to constitute an important issue to support the combination of different approaches in order to obtain more complete evaluations. However, this strategy would also suffer of several limitations. For example, with regard to both demand system and I-O analyses, the widely adopted hypothesis according to which firms fully pass on in prices the higher costs resulting from carbon and energy taxes would need to be removed. Allowing for different scenarios for tax passing-on would in fact allow obtaining a range of more reliable estimates of distributional impacts, not overestimating potential regressive impacts. Moreover, also the substitution possibilities in production processes are missing in both demand system and I-O analyses, implying different types of distortions in the estimates. In fact, substitution possibilities are likely to decrease the carbon or energy intensity of production processes, particularly in the long term, and then they would also reduce the incidence of carbon and energy taxes on final prices, easing potential adverse distributional effects.

Also, the approaches based on computation of measures and indices would need more often to be complemented with other approaches, allowing the impact on household income and expenditure to be obtained in a more reliable way. Finally, the different models outlined as other approaches appear to be particularly promising to assess specific issues which are rarely investigated by more traditional modeling strategies, such as the effects on benefit distribution or car ownership.

5 Conclusions

As was highlighted in section 2, energy can be taxed in different ways, and exemptions and other specific provisions may be designed that aim to address distributional concerns. Carbon taxation is in force or planned to be introduced in an increasing number of countries. In this case also the tax structure may reflect distributional concerns.

With or without special provisions, the approach chosen to tax energy goods, and the potential implementation of environment-oriented tax reforms, may potentially be associated with adverse distributional implications. Section 4 has provided a review of the research contributions studying the impacts on households of different choices of energy and carbon taxation, and the evidence for regressivity of ETRs appears not to be unanimous. Different research approaches imply different results, and none of them is comprehensive of all interactions and potential effects of carbon and energy taxation.

Household income or expenditure seem not be the only relevant variables for assessing potential regressive impacts. In fact, other demographic variables, such as household composition, age and employment status of its members, car and other energy-related goods ownership variables, although not widely investigated, turn out to be relevant in distributional effects analysis. The same is true for locational variables, for example the urban or rural context, the size of municipality, the availability of public transport. These variables influence the distributional impact in a direction and amount which depends on the type of taxation modeled, and to some extent on more macroeconomic characteristics of the country examined. This is not only true for demand system estimation, but is also relevant when examining the impacts on the Gini coefficient or on emissions and prices by means of an I-O matrix. For example, as highlighted in Ekins et al. (2011), the proportion of car ownership is lower in low-income households, and households without cars are not directly affected by motor fuel taxes. The effects are also influenced by region-specific factors, such as energy supply structure, energy-efficiency characteristics of domestic fuel use and reliance on car transport. Some of these variables are taken into account by studies belonging to the category of "other approaches", and it seems that linking such methods with more traditional ones could be a promising research strategy.

The inclusion of revenue raised in distributional analysis seems to be a key issue, since it allows assessment of different options for recycling, and their ability to compensate potential adverse distributional effects. This is particularly relevant considering the high risk of losing in environmental effectiveness that arises when tax departures are introduced in carbon and energy tax structure, highlighted among others by Vehmas (2005). Easing negative distributional effects by modifying the tax structure and introducing special provisions does not seem, in this sense, a fruitful policy strategy. Distributional concerns may be better dealt with outside the taxation system itself, with specific revenue recycling and compensation measures (Heine et al., 2012; OECD, 2010).

Given the high importance that environment-oriented tax reforms are assuming in national and international political debate, it appears particularly important to devote further research to these issues, in an attempt to solve some of the drawbacks highlighted in this literature review. The availability of different methodological approaches could represent a significant value added in this direction.

Notes

1 This approach is a macroeconomic approach, somewhat close to general equilibrium models, since it takes into account the interconnections among the different sectors operating in the economy examined. Nevertheless, in distributional analysis it is used only to estimate price effects, and occupational effects or international trade changes are not taken into account. For this reasons it is classified with partial equilibrium studies and dealt with in this contribution.
2 The authors estimate short-run elasticities, which implies that households do not respond to gasoline price increases by, for example, buying more fuel-efficient cars.
3 In both cases, low-income households spend a higher share of the income than do high-income households.
4 Carbon taxation belongs to a category called "green taxes," within which it is by far the largest component. Energy and transport taxation refer, respectively, to electricity and fuels used for heating purposes, and to gasoline.
5 According to the last study, carbon and energy taxes are more regressive in northern than in southern Europe.
6 To give an idea, 350 different car models are taken into account.

References

Asensio, J., A. Matas, and J. Raymond (2002), "Petrol expenditure and redistributive effects of its taxation in Spain," *Transportation Research*, 37, 49–69

Bach, S., M. Kohlhaas, B. Meyer, B. Praetorius, and H. Welsch (2002), "The effects of environmental fiscal reform in Germany: a simulation study," *Energy Policy*, 30, 803–811.

Bandyopadhyay, G., F. Bagheri, and M. Mann (2007), "Reduction of fossil fuel emissions in the USA: a holistic approach towards policy formulation," *Energy Policy*, 35, 950–965.

Banks, J., R. Blundell, and A. Lewbel (1997), "Quadratic Engel Curves and consumer demand," *The Review of Economics and Statistics*, 4, 527–539.

Basso, L. J. and T. H. Oum (2007), "Automobile fuel demand: a critical assessment of empirical methodologies," *Transport Reviews*, 27, 449 – 484.

Bento, A., L. Goulder, E. Henry, M. Jacobsen, and R. von Haefen (2005), "Distributional and efficiency impacts of gasoline taxes: an econometrically-based multi-market study," *American Economic Review*, 95, 282–287.

Bento, A. M., L. H. Goulder, M. R. Jacobsen, and R. H. von Haefen (2009) "Distributional and efficiency impacts of increased US gasoline taxes," *American Economic Review*, 99, 667–699.

Bork, C. (2006), "Distributional effects of the ecological tax reform in Germany: an evaluation with a microsimulation model," in *The Distributional Effects of Environmental Policy*, edited by Y. Serret and N. Johnstone, Empirical Policy Analysis Unit, OECD Environment Directorate.

Brännlund, R. and J. Nordström (2004), "Carbon tax simulations using a household demand model," *European Economic Review*, 48, 211–233.

Bull, N., K. Hassett, and G. Metcalf (1994), "Who pays broad-based energy taxes? Computing lifetime and regional incidence," *Energy Journal*, 15, 145–164.

Bureau, B. (2011), "Distributional effects of a carbon tax on car fuels in France," *Energy Economics*, 33, 121–130

Callan, T., S. Lyons, S. Scott, R. S. J. Tol, and S. Verde (2008), "The distributional implications of a carbon tax in Ireland," ESRI Working Paper No. 250.

Casler, S. D. and A. Rafiqui (1993), "Evaluating fuel tax equity: direct and indirect distributional effects," *National Tax Journal*, 46, 197–205.

Cornwell, A. and J. Creedy (1996), "Carbon taxation, prices and inequality in Australia," *Fiscal Studies*, 17, 21–38.

Cornwell, A. and J. Creedy (1997), "Measuring the welfare effects of tax changes using the LES: an application to a carbon tax," *Empirical Economics*, 22, 589–613.

Creedy, J. and C. Sleeman (2006), "Carbon taxation, prices and welfare in New Zealand," *Ecological Economics*, 57, 333–345.

Dahl, C. (2012), "Measuring global gasoline and diesel price and income elasticities," *Energy Policy*, 41, 2–13.

EEA (European Environment Agency) (2011), "Environmental tax reform in Europe: implications for income distribution," EEA Technical Report No. 16/2011, Copenhagen. Available at: www.eea.europa.eu/publications/environmental-tax-reform-in-europe.

Ekins, P. and S. Dresner (2004), *Reducing the impact of 'green' taxes and charges on low income* households, York: Joseph Rowntree Foundation.

Ekins, P., H. Pollitt, J. Barton, and D. Blobel (2011), "The implications for households of environmental tax reform (ETR) in Europe," *Ecological Economics*, 70, 2472–2485.

Espey, M. (1998), "Gasoline demand revisited: an international meta-analysis of elasticities," *Energy Economics*, 20, 273–295.

European Commission (2011), "Proposal for a Revision of the EU Energy Tax Directive," COM(2011)169. Available at: http://ec.europa.eu/taxation_customs/resources/documents/taxation/com_2011_169_en.pdf.

European Council (2003), Directive 2003/96/EC of 27 October 2003 restructuring the Community framework for the taxation of energy products and electricity.

Finnish Economic Council (2000), *Environmental and Energy Taxation in Finland – Preparing for the Kyoto Challenge*, Prime Minister's Office Publication Series 2000/4.

Goodwin, P., J. Dargay, and M. Hanly (2004), "Elasticities of road traffic and fuel consumption with respect to price and income: a review," *Transport Reviews*, 24, 275–292.

IEA (International Energy Agency) (2012), *CO_2 Emissions from Fuel Combustion*, Paris: OECD.

Heine, D., J. Norregaard, and I. W. H. Parry (2012), "Environmental tax reform: principles from theory and practice to date," *IMF Working Paper*, Washington, DC: International Monetary Fund. Available at: www.imf.org/external/pubs/ft/wp/2012/wp12180.pdf.

IPCC (Intergovernmental Panel on Climate Change) (2007), *Fourth assessment report, Working Group III: Mitigation of Climate Change: Contribution of Working Group III to the Fourth Assessment Report of the Intergovernmental Panel on Climate Change*, eds B. Metz, O. Davidson, P. Bosch, R. Dave, and L. Meyer, Cambridge and New York: Cambridge University Press.

Jacobsen, H. K., K. Birr-Pedersen, and M. Wier (2003), "Distributional implications of environmental taxation in Denmark," *Fiscal Studies*, 24, 477–499.

Johansson, B. (2000) "Economic instruments in practice 1: carbon taxes in Sweden," Swedish Environmental Protection Agency.

Johansson, O. and L. Shipper (1997), "Measuring the long-run fuel demand of cars: separate estimations of vehicle stock, mean fuel intensity and mean annual driving distance," *Journal of Transport Economics and Policy*, 31, 277–292.

Kerkhof, A. C., H. C. Moll, E. Drissen, and H. C. Wilting (2008) "Taxation of multiple greenhouse gases and the effects on income distribution: a case study of the Netherlands," *Ecological Economics*, 67, 318–326.

Kohlhaas, M. (2000), "Ecological tax reform in Germany: from theory to policy," *Economic Studies Program Series*, 6, American Institute for Contemporary German Studies, Johns Hopkins University.

Kriström, B. (2006), "Framework for assessing the distribution of financial effects of environmental policy," in "*The Distributional Effects Of Environmental Policy*," edited by Y. Serret and N. Johnstone, Empirical Policy Analysis Unit, OECD Environment Directorate, Paris: OECD.

Labandeira, X. and J. M. Labeaga (1999), "Combining input–output analysis and micro-simulation to assess the effects of carbon taxation on Spanish households," *Fiscal Studies*, 20, 305–320.

Labandeira, X., J. M. Labeaga, and M. Rodríguez (2006), "A residential energy demand system for Spain," *Energy Journal*, 27, 87–111.

Labandeira, X., J. M. Labeaga, and M. Rodríguez (2009), "An integrated economic and distributional analysis of energy policies," *Energy Policy*, 37, 5776–5786.

Liberati, P. (2001), "The distributional effects of indirect tax changes in Italy," *International Tax and Public Finance*, 8, 27–51.

Martini, C. (2010), "The distributive effects of carbon taxation in Italy," in *Critical Issues in Environmental Taxation Volume VIII*, edited by C. Dias Soares, J. Milne, H. Ashiabor, K. Deketelaere and L. Kreiser, Oxford: Oxford University Press.

Mayeres, I. and S. Proost (2001) "Marginal tax reform, externalities and income distribution," *Journal of Public Economics*, 79, 343–363

Metcalf, G. E. (1999), "A distributional analysis of green tax reforms," *National Tax Journal*, 52, 665–681.

Metcalf, G. E. (2007) "A proposal for a U. S. carbon tax swap: an equitable tax reform to address global climate change," Washington, DC: The Hamilton Project, Brookings Institution. Available at: www.brookings.edu/~/media/research/files/papers/2007/10/carbontax%20metcalf/10_carbontax_metcalf.pdf.

Metcalf, G. E., S. Paltsev, J. Reilly, H. Jacoby, and J. Holak (2008) "Analysis of a carbon tax to reduce U.S. greenhouse gas emissions," Cambridge, MA: MIT Joint Program on the Science and Policy of Global Change Report No. 160. Available at: http://mit.edu/globalchange/www/MITJPSPGC_Rpt160.pdf.

Newbery, D. M. (1995), "The distributional impact of price changes in Hungary and the United Kingdom," *Economic Journal*, 105, 847–863.

Nichele, V. and J. Robin (1995), "Simulation of indirect tax reforms using pooled micro and macro French data," *Journal of Public Economics*, 56, 225–244.

OECD (Organisation for Economic Co-operation and Development) (2001), *Environmentally Related Taxes in OECD Countries: Issues and Strategies*, Paris: OECD.

OECD (2005), "The United Kingdom Climate Change Levy: a study in political economy," Paris: OECD. Available at: www.oecd.org/LongAbstract/0,3425,en_2649_34281_34508471_1_1_1_1,00.html.

OECD (2006), *The Political Economy of Environmentally Related Taxes*, OECD, Paris.

OECD (2010), *Taxation, Innovation and the Environment*, Paris: OECD. Available at: www.oecd.org/env/taxes/innovation.

OECD (2011), *Towards Green Growth*, Paris: OECD. Available at: www.oecd.org/dataoecd/37/34/48224539.pdf.

OECD (2013), *Taxing Energy Use*, Paris: OECD. Available at: www.oecd.org/tax/tax-policy/taxingenergyuse.htm.

Paltsev, S., J. Reilly, H. Jacoby, A. Gurgel, G. Metcalf, A. Sokolov and J. Holak (2007), "Assessment of U.S. cap-and-trade proposals," MIT Joint Program on the Science and Policy of Global Change, Report 146. Available at: http://web.mit.edu/globalchange/www/MITJPSPGC_Rpt146.pdf.

Poterba, J. M. (1989), "Lifetime incidence and the distributional burden of excise taxes," *American Economic Review*, 79, 325–330.

Poterba, J. (1991), "Is the gasoline tax regressive?" in *Tax Policy and the Economy*, edited by D. Bradford, Vol. 5, Cambridge, MA: MIT Press.

Santoro, A. (2005), "Marginal commodity tax reforms: a survey," SIEP Working Paper No. 414, Pavia: Società Italiana di Economia Pubblica.

Smith, S. (1992), "The distributional consequences of taxes on energy and the carbon content of fuels," *European Economy*, Special Edition No. 1/1992, 241–68.

Smith, Z. (2000), "The petrol tax debate," Briefing Note n. 10/2000, London: Institute for Fiscal Studies.

Speck, S. (1999), "Energy and carbon taxes and their distributional implications," *Energy Policy*, 27, 659–667.

Speck, S., M. S. Andersen, H. Ø. Nielsen, A. V. Ryelund, and C. Smith (2006), "The use of economic instruments in Nordic and Baltic environmental policy 2001–2005," Nordic Council of Ministers, TemaNord 2006:525.

Sterner, T. (2012), "Distributional effects of taxing transport fuel," *Energy Policy*, 41, 75–83.

Stone, J. R. N. (1954), "Linear expenditure systems and demand analysis: an application to the pattern of British demand," *Economic Journal* 64, 511–527.

Suits, D. B. (1977), "Measurement of tax progressivity," *American Economic Review*, 67, 747–752.

Symons, E., J. Proops, and P. Gay (1994), "Carbon taxes, consumer demand and carbon dioxide emissions: a simulation analysis for the UK," *Fiscal Studies*, 15, 19–43.

Symons, E., S. Speck, and J. Proops (2000), "The effects of pollution and energy taxes across the European income distribution," Keele Department of Economics Discussion Papers 2000/05, University of Keele.

Symons, E., S. Speck, and J. Proops (2002) "The distributional effects of carbon and energy taxes: the cases of France, Spain, Italy, Germany and UK," *European Environment*, 12, 203–212.

Tiezzi, S. (2005) "The welfare effects and the distributive impact of carbon taxation on Italian households," *Energy Policy*, 33, 1597–1612.

Vehmas, J. (2005) "Energy-related taxation as an environmental policy tool – the Finnish experience 1990–2003," *Energy Policy*, 33, 2175–2182.

Weisbach, D. A. (2011), "Carbon taxation in the EU: expanding EU carbon price," Working Paper 11/15Oxford University Centre for Business Taxation,.

West, S. E. (2004), "Distributional effects of alternative vehicle pollution control policies," *Journal of Public Economics*, 88, 735–757.

West, S. E. and R. C. Williams III (2004), "Estimates from a consumer demand system: implications for the incidence of environmental taxes," *Journal of Environmental Economics and Management*, 47, 535–558.

Wier, M., K. Birr-Pedersen, H. K. Jacobsen, and J. Klok (2005), "Are CO_2 taxes regressive? Evidence from the Danish experience," *Ecological Economics*, 52, 239–251.

7 Carbon pricing and distributional effects on firms

A methodological survey

Rossella Bardazzi and Maria Grazia Pazienza

Introduction

European climate strategy aims at fixing a unique price for carbon so as to implement the 'polluter pays principle' and signal the real cost of releasing greenhouse gases. The ultimate goal is, of course, to cut down on emissions and combat climate change. The price signal is designed to induce consumers and firms to change their energy mix towards new products and inputs with a lower environmental impact. Pursuing this ambitious goal involves the use of an enormous amount of resources[1] and, at the same time, a significant change in consumers and firms' habits and behaviour, which environmental policy should stimulate with all the available instruments. An evaluation of the distributional impact of these policies appears vital, not just from a fair distribution standpoint, but also so as to consider the political feasibility of climate policy.

In this chapter we focus on the side of the firm, considering the modelling tools available for an empirical estimation of the distributional impact of carbon pricing policy. After a brief discussion of the main economic instruments and carbon pricing policies (section 2), section 3 focuses on clarifying the impact on firms in terms of profits and competitiveness, reviewing the ample and heterogeneous set of indexes employed in the economic literature. In section 4 the available economic models are analysed, considering the advantages and disadvantages of different techniques in assessing distributional analysis. The potential for combining different modelling tools is investigated in section 5. Section 6 contains our conclusions.

1 Carbon pricing and market-based instruments

The debate on the choice of the optimal environmental policy is still an open question since several trade-offs may arise if competing evaluation criteria are considered. Instruments rank differently according to whether efficacy, cost-effectiveness, dynamic efficiency, distributional impact, political feasibility or the degree of uncertainty, among others, are used as the evaluation criteria. A very broad and well-known classification of policy instruments divides them into 'command and control' and 'market-based' instruments. In the case of command and control (such as technology standards, non-marketable quotas, prohibition) the policy target and agents' behaviour are generally well specified and the policy target is achieved by imposing mandatory obligations or restrictions on agents' behaviour. On the contrary, market-based instruments (taxes, fees, marketable quotas, subsidies, liability systems) operate by creating incentives to change behaviour, since they modify the relative prices that consumers and firms face.[2] Market-based instruments rely on a price signal and therefore do not specify how agents should behave so as to comply with the policy target, as opposed to regulatory (or mandatory) instruments.

In the context of energy use, the goal of emissions reduction can be achieved by restrictions on inputs or outputs, the requirement to use specific filters (or carbon sequestration technology) or by altering the relative price on the basis of the emission or carbon content of inputs or products. In the case of the price signal policies, carbon/energy taxes and emission trading schemes – the effects of which are theoretically identical[3] – are, by far, the most important instruments.

Positive and negative aspects of market-based instruments

Market-based (or incentive-based) instruments are generally suggested as the main policy tool to be used, due to their cost-effectiveness[4] (the optimal solution is reached at the minimum total cost) and therefore to the higher degree of neutrality, as compared to agents' choices.[5] This neutrality ensures that each agent chooses the quantity (to be produced or consumed) and the technologies which best adapt to his/her particular situation and characteristics. Moreover, if the price signal (the carbon price) is equal to the external cost of carbon emission (as in Pigouvian taxation), the social optimum can be restored if pollution externalities are the only deviations from the optimality.[6] Lastly, the use of a carbon price may be favourably accepted as a fair policy because it matches the polluter pays principle, according to which the burden of the external cost should be put on the agent causing the pollution.[7]

Notwithstanding these important characteristics, market-based instruments are questioned for their easily identifiable impact on prices – which in turn leads to political opposition – and the potential unfairness of the distributional impact among agents. It is worth stressing that all environmental policy instruments cause costs to economic agents directly or indirectly. These costs may be visible or hidden, invariant in time or sporadic, easy to shift or not, collectively or privately borne; nevertheless they are present in all cases. In the case of a standard regulation, for instance, the investment cost needed to comply with a new emission filter device might be difficult to detect for the public but, despite this opacity, may be passed on to prices. As carbon emissions are mainly linked to fossil fuel use, the carbon price signal – which is supposed to induce agents to change their energy mix towards carbon-free fuels –spreads rapidly, depending on the energy use of consumers and firms. If carbon-free products are not available or the elasticity of input substitution is low, the carbon pricing policy increases costs and the general price level in the short run, which in turn reduces real wages and attractiveness of exports.

Is carbon pricing increasing or reducing welfare?

This pessimistic view of the effect of environmental policy has been challenged by the widely discussed Porter hypothesis and, with regard to carbon taxation, by the double dividend hypothesis. In Porter's view,[8] a stringent environmental policy is potentially beneficial to firms because it gives a powerful stimulus to innovate production routines (technological or process innovation) in order to increase efficiency, discover new input combinations or new marketable products.[9] This is due to the fact that in the real world x-inefficiency (also due to governance and information ineffectiveness) and bounded rationality hamper the exploitation of all production and market opportunities. However, in order to produce a significant change in the pattern of growth and opportunities, the innovation process should be as free as possible, and not constrained by the technological choices of policy makers. Relative to this point, as previously stressed, market-based instruments are neutral because they give only a monetary incentive to find substitutes for polluting inputs and products. Establishing a single price on all CO_2 emissions has proved to be the most promising policy for encouraging innovation and the adoption of emission-saving technologies.

In addition, the optimistic view asserts that the negative effects of market-based instruments can easily be minimised by an efficient use of the revenues collected by taxing the carbon content or by auctioning permits in an emission trading scheme. It is worth stressing that according to the Pigouvian framework for environmental taxes, the revenue raised by the tax is, in principle, a side-effect and the use of the resources is not relevant to the policy. Indeed, earmarking funds or lump sum direct compensatory measures have been used to mitigate the adverse economic effects of the carbon pricing policy. However, these uses of the revenues have been considered as a way of decreasing the price signal and the polluter pays principle: they may cause inefficient public spending and rent-seeking behaviour.[10]

Under the 'double dividend' hypothesis,[11] the revenue raised by environmental taxation might be employed to cut other existing distortionary taxes (such as labour and income taxes), thereby obtaining an environmental gain and a decrease in the inefficiency of the existing tax system. The possibility that carbon pricing can improve the efficiency of the overall tax system has been questioned by several authors and depends on the magnitude of the existing distortion and of the distortion caused by the carbon pricing policy. As an example, Bovenberg and de Mooji (1994) demonstrate that, even in the presence of pre-existing distorting taxes, the optimal pollution tax may lie below the Pigouvian tax, which fully internalises the marginal social damage from pollution, as specific Pigouvian taxes may in some cases exacerbate existing distortions. Even if the final effect of environmental taxes on welfare cannot be assessed in a definitive way, the idea of a double dividend has been a powerful stimulus to the use of green taxes and market-based instruments in general. Starting from the second half of the 1990s, a number of fiscal reforms have been designed as Environmental Tax Reforms (ETR), focusing on an increase of environmentally related taxes and a decrease in income taxes or social security contributions.

Whatever the idea of a net gain for the overall welfare of the economy, the distributive impact of environmental taxes or carbon pricing is not negligible and must be carefully evaluated before implementing compensatory measures or designing a comprehensive ETR. These distributional impacts have indeed significant implications not only for distributive justice but also for political feasibility.

3 Distributional issues

An effective environmental policy achieves the goal of changing consumption and production patterns and therefore it distributes benefit and costs unevenly, creating *winners* and *losers* among the economy's households and firms. However, considering households and firms as two separate types of agents potentially affected by the environmental policy is partially misleading, as all the economic impacts reaching firms will sooner or later have an effect on households as well. In addition to price and employment reactions, the impacts of which on households are obvious, it is important to remember that the ultimate owners of firms are households, and therefore changes in distributed profits will have an impact on disposable income.

There is a large and well-established empirical literature on the distributional impact on households and consumers, as shown elsewhere in this book. Carbon pricing effects are generally analysed by comparing the net income distribution of families and individuals under different policy scenarios and through the well-established apparatus of inter-deciles distribution and Gini-type indexes.

The logical corresponding indicator for firms would be net profit, as it automatically considers cost and turnover variations. However, profits appear to be a partial and inadequate indicator of the overall impact. On the one hand, profits are strongly influenced by the economic cycle; on the other hand, policy maker's interest is in the ability of firms to cope with international competition, to innovate and to increase employment. In this wider perspective, the definition of a redistributive impact among firms basically matches the broader idea of an effect on competitiveness, but the methodology for evaluating this effect is far from established, as competitiveness at the national, sector or firm level is still a controversial and multi-faceted notion.

Historically, competitiveness was analysed as a country's share of the world market for its products. Currently, the most common characterisation of competitiveness has a broader and longer-term meaning which looks at society as a whole. According to the European Commission Competitiveness Report (European Commission, 2004), competitiveness requires 'high and rising standards of living of a nation with the lowest possible unemployment',[12] whereas for the OECD it may be defined as 'the degree to which a country can, under free and fair market conditions, produce goods and services which meet the test of international markets, while simultaneously maintaining and expanding the real incomes of its people over the long term'.[13] However, this very general national goal of increasing living standards – which may in principle be evaluated by looking at GDP growth, GDP per capita and income inequality – can be only indirectly linked to environmental policy and carbon pricing, as several policies and concurrent factors affect the aggregate output. Such an indicator appears useful for assessing the long-run impact of the policy on growth or on the relative position of countries,[14] but does not appear suitable for measuring the distributional impact on different sectors or firms within a given country.

A first key issue to be solved is the first-level impact between polluting or energy-intensive industries and other agents within the economic system (non-polluting and non-energy-intensive industries, consumers, taxpayers, workers). It is worth stressing that the tax-shifting and price pass-through literatures have clarified that the final economic burden of a carbon pricing policy is not necessarily borne by the formal taxpayer and therefore the ‘polluter pays principle’ might remain only an abstract principle. Firms’ ability to offset carbon taxes or increasing costs of regulation depends on the characteristics of the market (competition, elasticities and openness to international trade) and the burden of carbon pricing may be totally or partially shifted to other sectors of society, through a price increase or a consistent decrease in demand. The higher the ability to shift carbon cost burden, the smaller will be the impact on profits and other competitiveness index.

Distribution analysis among firms: main indicators

As discussed in the following paragraphs, the relative burden of the policy among different agents can be estimated with a macro aggregated model or calculated as a result of a disaggregated model, such as multisectoral, CGE or micro-simulation models. Moreover, different models imply also different data and therefore different kind of indices are available. Table 7.1 shows different indicators which may be added to profits to assess impacts of carbon policies on firms, considering macro and micro approaches.

From the most aggregated perspective, when the impacts are evaluated at country level, GDP, being a composition of income wages and profits, can signal if the carbon price policy is affecting the standard of living of a country. Exchange rates and international trade flows can be added to gain a general idea of the economic activity reaction. International industrial sector competitiveness has been traditionally viewed as an industry’s ability to increase or maintain its market share, winning the competition with foreign firms in the same sector. In this case, the sector’s export shares and foreign investment flows are taken into account: if a business sector experiences lower exports after a carbon pricing policy which increases energy prices, this may be interpreted as an indication that this policy has reduced its competitiveness.

However, a good performance on foreign markets does not necessarily indicate success in the long run or a sustainable growth path, because the external constraint may force firms to internalise energy cost increases through wage stagnation[15] and a decrease in profits. Moreover, the attention to export performance precludes an assessment of the effect on competition in domestic markets. A profitability loss will in turn undermine investments and innovative capacity.

Table 7.1 Measure of climate policy impact on firms and indicators by level of analysis

	Level of analysis	*Measure of impact*	*Indicator*
Macro	International/ national: aggregated indicators	Prosperity/standard of living	GDP (growth and per capita)
		International trade	Real exchange rate; international trade flows
		Productivity	Productivity growth
	International/ national/regional: industrial sectors (MESO)	Market and financial performance, international trade	Gross operating surplus; export share
		Investment, productivity. innovation	Investment flow, direct foreign investment, total factor productivity, R&D and patents
	International/ national/regional: firm and plant level	Market and financial performance, efficiency, international trade	Turnover, ROI, ROS, cash flow, estimated cost functions
Micro		Investment, productivity. innovation	Investment, direct foreign investment, productivity, R&D and patents
		Reputation and market value	Reputation indices, stock market value
		Survival	Birth and mortality indicator, networking, changes in governance

Source: This table is a modified version of a table in Iraldo et al. (2011), where a survey of the main empirical papers on environmental policy and competitiveness can be found.

The second tier of Table 7.1 shows that competitiveness at the industry level is generally evaluated through current performance indicators (profits as measured by industry's gross operating surplus, export shares, inward or outward foreign direct investment (FDI), productivity) or the ability to determine future performance (investments, R&D expenditure, patents), but both types of indicators should be jointly considered. An outward FDI, for example, may be interpreted as a signal of the strength of the sector but may also be a signal of carbon leakage: the carbon pricing policy may have promoted delocalisation of national industries through the acquisition of foreign plants.

An industrial sector is often very heterogeneous in what it produces, in how it produces it and to whom it sells. Production and cost functions vary greatly among regions and firm sizes, because different regions may, for example, have different energy tax rates (in the case of fiscal decentralisation) and energy prices are frequently differentiated among firms.[16] Therefore, analysing the impact of carbon pricing policies at the firm or plant level may add important information (bottom tier of Table 7.1). Balance sheet data at firm level enable the calculation of several profit indexes (return on sales, return on equity, return on investment), the financial structure and the role of investment and assets. Indeed, in addition to the aforementioned measures of competitiveness, analysis at the micro level may consider the effect on reputation and market value and the impact on firms' demography. The idea that firms can be both 'green and competitive' or, in other words, that 'it pays to be green' comes directly from the Porter hypothesis and underlines the fact that after a new environmental policy regulation, various abatement opportunities maybe exploited and profits, reputation and market value may benefit from this stimulus.[17] At the firm level, firms' reputation and stock market valuation may be analysed as case studies or as a new characteristic of larger datasets and models. Finally, a carbon pricing policy may have important implications for firms' demography in each sector of activity. The cost increase due to carbon pricing may drive some firms out of the market or may imply considerable restructuring of the governance, employment, geographical localisation or production network. Even a steady GDP growth or sector profit can conceal a turbulent firm's demography if some firms gain economic rents (as may occur in the case of the free allocation of emission permits) and others are thrown out of the market.

4 Energy/environmental models for firms: a taxonomy

Over the last two decades there has been a plethora of studies on the impact of environmental taxation on the economy. Applied research which analyses the economic and environmental effects of this policy on firms is based on the use of economic models, and different approaches may be followed. For the purpose of this survey, a taxonomy of modelling tools can be designed according to some characteristics of the models with regard to (i) the level of economic activity aggregation, (ii) the theoretical approach, (iii) the integration between energy/environment/economy and (iv) the geographic coverage. Although other modelling features could be identified to further differentiate modelling approaches, we consider these as the key aspects influencing the questions and answers each model is able to provide.

Official statistics on firms are usually available at the macro level, at most disaggregated by sectors of economic activity. However, more recently microdata have become increasingly available either from limited ad hoc surveys conducted by research institutes or within large-scale projects involving national statistical institutes. We can therefore firstly distinguish between macro models based on time series data and micro-simulation models which use longitudinal firm-level statistical information capturing the heterogeneity within a sector of economic activity. This microeconomic approach allows investigation of issues of competitiveness – such as those mentioned in the previous section – with detailed information on profitability indexes and firms demography. Macroeconomic models can be further disaggregated at the sectoral level, becoming multisectoral tools. This level of analysis can be defined as mesoeconomic, as it refers to the sectoral detail of the economy, and this feature is particularly useful for fully capturing the complex interrelations between the economy and the environment and also for simulating the detailed aspects of a policy which is often tailored to specific economic sectors.

Borrowing from West's classification of models for regional analysis (1995), we can further distinguish macro models for environmental/energy policy evaluation into three categories: conventional input-output energy models, input-output +

econometric models, and computable general equilibrium (CGE) models. While the basic input-output (IO) energy model is static, with fixed technological coefficients and without price effects, macro-econometric and CGE models can be dynamic but differ deeply in several characteristics such as the use of econometric estimation, the economic theory underlying agents' behaviour, the time horizon of the simulation exercises. In general, these models evaluate the economic and environmental effects of policies on the economic system as a whole, including households and firms, but they are also able to consider the on-going interactions between final demand, intermediate inputs and sectoral production and therefore those economic activities gaining or losing from the introduction of a carbon tax can be clearly identified.

The level of integration between the economic system and the energy/environmental sides of the model is highly relevant for qualifying the effects of an environmental policy evaluated with a model. The causation linkage – providing feedback effects between the economy, the energy market and environmental emissions – is a valuable characteristic allowing a better understanding of the interactions. In this case, the production of industries or the final consumer demand influences energy demand and, vice versa, the expenditure for energy consumption has a direct influence on macroeconomic variables. Conversely, models can be built without any kind of feedback, being energy/environmental models or economic models only, where a tax policy is applied but without any impact on the energy demand and supply. Otherwise there might be a one-way causation linkage: an energy sub-model is linked to the main economic model but the direction of effects is only from the first to the second and no feedback is implemented.

Finally, the geographic coverage may be global when a multi-country approach is adopted in view of the fact that an ETR is implemented at a national level but impacts on other countries via international trade. However, models can cover a set of countries belonging to a specific region – such as the European Union – where a specific policy concerning carbon taxation and tradeable permits could be implemented. Country models may also play a role in explaining the effects on the national economy produced by a unilateral environmental policy, as has often happened in the past decades.

All these characteristics affect the ability of each model to assess impacts of environmental policies in terms of indicators as summarised in Table 7.1. As we will see in the following, multisectoral macro-econometric models can benefit from the industry disaggregation to evaluate the distributive effects of policies on different economic activities and to derive profitability and competitiveness indicators at the sectoral level as regards gross operating surplus, employment, productivity and investments. If the model is open to international trade, export shares and international competitiveness dynamics can be estimated as well. More detailed profitability indexes can be produced with micro-simulation models, although dynamic interactions with the overall economic system are underrated unless these models are linked to a macromodel. Distributional effects at the micro level are estimated as first-round impact produced by policies concerning tax rates, incentives, exemptions and compensative measures.

Input-output models

A large body of literature may be cited to demonstrate the ability of IO analysis to support the evaluation of economic and environmental impact on firms. One recent example is in the *Handbook of Input-Output Economics in Industrial Ecology* (Suh, 2009), which followed two special issues of the official journal of the International Input-Output Association in 1998 and 2005.[18] Formulated by Wassily Leontief in the 1930s, IO analysis has been used ever since in countless applications including energy and environmental analysis. Leontief himself pioneered the extension of the IO model to incorporate externalities – such as pollution – into the traditional IO framework (Leontief, 1970; Leontief and Ford, 1972) and many other authors followed his approach. In fact the IO model describes interactions between economic sectors and, specifically, an energy extension of this model simply takes into account the total amount of energy required to deliver a product to final demand, both directly and indirectly. Indeed during the production process energy inputs are directly used (direct energy requirements) but there is also a consumption of energy which is embodied in non-energy inputs (indirect energy requirements). The sum of both components comprises the total energy requirement for the production of a specific good.[19] The same methodology can be used to consider the interactions between the economic system and the environment. In this case, an environmentally extended IO framework is able to assess the direct and indirect environmental flows triggered by a given final demand and this feature has attracted the attention of researchers and practitioners for decades.

An extended IO model is particularly well suited for simulating the introduction of a carbon/energy tax, thus combining the tradition of using IO models to evaluate fiscal policies from a multisectoral perspective with the development of energy and environmental extensions of the original model. One of the first applications of an energy tax within a US IO model was developed by Bullard and Herendeen (1975). In the 1970s considerable attention was paid to energy use given supply shortages following OPEC embargoes,[20] and these authors simulated the introduction of an energy tax as a tool for encouraging energy conservation and for raising the revenue needed to solve energy-related problems. In their application the tax is assumed to be passed on to the consumer through a price increase. In general this traditional IO approach shows the advantage of taking economic interdependencies into account, but suffers from some limits as well. In fact a fixed production technology and constant relative prices are usually assumed; the possibility for an industry to change the energy mix as a result of a carbon tax is therefore ruled out. However, the simplicity and immediacy of the approach makes it widely used even today for a variety of studies. In fact, the hypothesis of constant input coefficients might be less problematic in the case of fossil fuels because demand is relatively inelastic in the short run, due to the relative absence of substitution possibilities. These models can therefore still be used to evaluate economic and environmental impact in the short term. Distributional effects are estimated at a 'mesoeconomic' level – concerning the industrial classification of the IO table – as the effects on sectoral gross operating surplus, changes in employment by industry and effects on domestic and international competitiveness. As regards international trade, a common hypothesis of this modelling approach concerns imports and the geographical dimensions of models: in a single-region model imported goods purchased as inputs by domestic firms are considered as produced with the same domestic technology, although imports from non-policy-constrained areas are expected to be more carbon intensive. On the other hand, multi-regional IO models overcome the import assumption as each country's technology and energy input structure is considered.

Finally, further developments set the constant coefficients hypothesis aside and define IO coefficients as a function of relative prices, such as in the Hudson-Jorgenson model (Hudson and Jorgenson, 1974). The combination of the IO modelling framework with econometric analysis is one of the most promising developments of this approach and gives rise to the second category of models according to the classification by West (1995).

Energy econometric macromodels

This modelling approach is characterised by econometrically estimated parameters based on time series analysis. Macroeconomic models can be built at an aggregate level or with very limited sector classification – such as agriculture, industry, services – and thus they aim at studying policy impact on macro variables such as GDP, inflation, aggregate household consumption, the unemployment rate, etc. In the case of energy/environmental policies, the sectoral approach and inter-industry interdependencies are needed to evaluate the effects on specific economic activities since issues are sector specific and policies are often targeted at sectors (with different tax rates, exemptions, etc.). We will therefore limit our analysis below to models presenting this multisectoral perspective.

Most of these models have a core of IO data and relations embedded in a complete macroeconomic framework. Because the structural econometric equations have a dynamic structure, a temporal distribution of the effects produced by external shocks can be studied. As a result, both the short- and long-term effects of policies can be analysed. The economy is represented with a disaggregated industry detail and, hopefully, each economic sector is modelled individually while macroeconomic total variables are calculated through aggregation (bottom-up approach), thus incorporating intersectoral interdependencies into the analysis.[21] The effects of carbon taxes on industry prices are explicitly modelled in the cost structure of each industry: as the cost of energy inputs rises, each industry can pass on a portion of these costs to the output prices, which may lead to a reduction of domestic and international competitiveness. This effect may be captured through an international trade model, if available, and the environmental impact can be estimated as well, if energy and emission modules are implemented with the economic macro model. The impact of tax rates on the industry cost structure may induce price-dependent substitution between energy carriers. In these models the effects of an ETR can be analysed: if distortionary taxes are reduced – such as labour taxes so that the *double dividend* may arise – employment increases if the elasticity of labour demand is significantly higher than one. Therefore the form of revenue recycling and the magnitude of parameters play a crucial role in the overall economic effects on firms.

Some early examples of this approach are represented by the Interindustry Forecasting Project (INFORUM) modelling family (Almon, 1991), founded in 1967 and internationally developed with a group of country models based on a common structure and software, linked through an international bilateral trade model. This project is still very active nowadays[22] and some national partners have developed energy-environmental modules to be used for climate mitigation policy analysis. The Italian INFORUM model (INTIMO, Interindustry Italian Model) has been used to estimate the short-term effects on the national economy of a unilateral introduction of a carbon tax according to the 1992 EC directive, with several simulation scenarios regarding tax rates and compensating measures (Bardazzi and Piacentino, 1993; Bardazzi, Grassini, Piacentino, 1994). The economic model has been extended to include an energy satellite model but it does not allow for any substitution towards the less carbon-intensive fuels and it has no feedback on the main economic model.

More recently, other models of the same family have been developed further to allow a thorough analysis of the same topic.[23] PANTA RHEI is an environmentally extended version of the macro-econometric INFORUM-type model INFORGE of the German economy (Lutz, 2011) which includes an economic core with structural equations at 59 sectors and an energy-emission module fully integrated into the main model and has been used for the simulation of several policies, including an environmental tax reform in Germany (Bach et al., 2002). GINFORS (Global INterindustry FORecasting System) is a global model covering all EU27 member states and other trade partners for a total of 50 countries, developed by the same research group (Meyer and Lutz, 2007; Lutz et al., 2010).[24] The countries' economies are either modelled with IO models or aggregate macro models, while import demand and export prices are endogenous to each country. Energy and emission modules for all countries are included, based on the energy balances of the International Energy Agency. A bilateral trade model links the country models at the economic activity level: the imports of one country are the exports of another. Nearly all behavioural parameters are derived from econometric-statistical analysis, assuming bounded rationality of agents with myopic foresight, which means that the system of factor demand functions and consumption functions cannot be explicitly derived from production and utility functions. Prices are explained by the mark-up hypothesis, which is typical in oligopolistic markets. GINFORS has recently been used – along with the E3ME model described below – to model a large-scale environmental tax reform (Ekins and Speck, 2011).

E3ME is a dynamic, large-scale econometric model of Europe's economies, energy systems, and environment (hence three Es). The model has been developed as part of the EC research framework programme in the tradition of the Cambridge Econometrics' Multi-Sectoral Dynamic Model for the UK (Barker and Peterson, 1987). The model is multisectoral (69 economic sectors), multicountry (33 countries: EU27, Norway, Switzerland and four candidate countries) and dynamic, thus providing a long-term equilibrium solution.[25] This model, which can be classed in the same tradition as the INFORUM modelling approach (Barker et al., 2009a; Almon, 1991), contains around 30 sets of econometrically estimated equations which give the model empirical grounding on the basis of IO tables and national accounts data. Two-way linkages between the economy, energy demand/supply and the environment are incorporated, thus considering interactions and feedback effects. The model has been used in several European projects concerning energy/environmental policies with ex-ante simulations of hypothetical ETR and ex-post evaluation of applied reforms in European countries[26] and is described in several contributions (Barker, 1998; Barker, 1999; Barker et al. 2009a, 2009b, 2011a, 2011b).

The general structure of GINFORS and E3ME is very similar although some differences concern geographical and sectoral coverage, the treatment of technical progress and international trade, and the econometric methods used.[27] However, both models are described by their authors as not being CGE models, stressing the differences between the macro-econometric modelling approach and the CGE modelling framework.[28] In these macro models parameters for behavioural relationships are derived empirically using econometric methods applied to historical time series datasets. This makes it possible to work without some of the assumptions common to CGE models, such as perfect competition or rational expectations. Moreover, as these models do not assume equilibrium in the short or long run, if there is a disequilibrium with unemployment and underutilisation of capacity, appropriate policies can be effective both in increasing employment and in improving the environmental impact (Barker, 2004). Dynamic macro models econometrically estimated on time series data can represent the transitional path in response to policy changes. However, the estimation of effects in the very long run can be problematic, as economic structures are expected to change significantly – in part due to technological change – and more assumptions are required.

As the models are solved on an annual basis, distributional effects on firms not only have a sector-specific dimension but also show a distinctive dynamic path. Sectors show significantly different behavioural responses, which are reflected in their performance in terms of profits and employment. Revenue recycling is usually related to labour cost reduction and these models can show whether these measures create additional employment or drive up wages. Indicators in terms of export shares and international competitiveness can be effectively estimated as well.

In Ekins and Speck (2011) GINFORS and E3ME macro models are used to simulate the implementation of ETR in Europe. In line with other studies, as surveyed in Hoerner and Bosquet (2001) and, more recently, in Dannenberg et al. (2008) results show either a limited increase (E3ME) or a limited decrease (GINFORS) of GDP in all scenarios, but both models produce an increase of employment at the aggregate level. There is a general, moderate loss of competitiveness, but trends are dissimilar at the sector level, where, not unexpectedly, the main sectors that lose out from the reform are the more energy intensive, while those gaining most are the more labour intensive, which benefit from the revenue recycling measures. These sector differences are an indicator that economic activity and firms' heterogeneity matter.

To fully understand the differences in the simulation results produced by different modelling assumptions, we shall now turn to the CGE models.

Computable general equilibrium models

CGE models rely heavily on neoclassical general equilibrium theory and market equilibrium assumptions. Firms are profit maximisers or cost minimisers, and households are represented as utility maximisers. Explicit specifications about the forms of utility functions, producers' production functions and market clearing conditions are included. Some authors claim that these solid micro-foundations are the key characteristics making CGE models preferable to other approaches (Borges, 1986; Zhang, 2008; Pissarides, 2008). The central core of the database is usually a set of IO data and a SAM – Social Accounting Matrix – for a single given year which, however, is used only as a representation of the flows between industries, households, governments, importers and exporters. CGE models can be dynamic: in this case, investment spending turns into capital – either at an aggregate level and then allocated to sectors or directly at the sector level – and the productive capacity of the sector is increased. Moreover, the utility function is taken to be separable across time, thus the present value of utility is maximised subject to 'inter-temporal' budget constraints. These dynamic models are far more challenging to design, maintain and solve and consequently comparative-static models are by far the most common class of CGE models.[29]

CGE models do not rely on the econometric approach to estimate equation parameters. In contrast to macro-econometric models previously described, behavioural and technological parameters are chosen by the modeller through a procedure called calibration. This method consists of assigning values to equation parameters (elasticities of substitution, income elasticities of demand, supply elasticities, etc.)[30] on the basis of information drawn from various empirical studies in the literature and specific databases. In other words, econometric studies based on different countries, time periods and data are 'imported' in the CGE model to define suitable parameters so that the resulting equations are numerically consistent with the available data at the base year. An example of a CGE database is the GTAP (Global Trade Analysis Project), which includes a specific behavioural parameters file which enters directly into the GTAP Data Base along with an Energy Data Base. In some cases, the data on which the model is based may have to be adjusted so that consistency with the initial equilibrium of the model is achieved (since the real world is typically in disequilibrium, whereas the neoclassical model is not). In general these models are not validated against historical data. In some cases, in an attempt to strengthen their empirical foundations, parameters are revised (in line with new estimates from the literature) to reproduce the variability of the distribution of observed key variables through a stochastic simulation approach.[31] Macro modellers argue that aggregate behaviour is not necessarily consistent with optimising individual behaviour relationships and, moreover, they criticise the poor use of historical data which are manipulated to fit the calibrated parameters and the theoretical model.[32] On the other hand, CGE modellers emphasise the theoretical underpinnings of their models – which incidentally are not absent in macro models – and dismiss the importance of time series data. In fact, this modelling approach has been successfully applied in developing countries where data are neither available nor appropriate for standard econometric analysis, while it is hard to understand the need to manipulate historical statistics for European economies.[33] As stated by Ahmed and O'Donoghue (2007), given their main assumptions and characteristics, CGE models should not be regarded as forecasting tools, but as an instrument for detecting underlying long-run tendencies, although the treatment of technological change as exogenous may be problematic in this regard. It is hard to think of CGE as the best tool to estimate distributive effects on firms: as zero profits are generally assumed, it is not possible to compare effects on profitability indexes in the two equilibrium positions, before and after the environmental policy. Through the calibrated elasticities, behavioural responses among different agents can be captured, including inter-fuel and inter-factor substitution in the firm production structure given by the relative price changes of energy types. In general, CGE models consider a pass-through effect of a tax on domestic and international prices, thus implying price variations and behavioural responses both of firms and of households. Effect in terms of GDP variation is assessed, although results on sectoral output are detailed at a rather aggregate level of industry disaggregation. Finally, export share changes are estimated as a result of international competitiveness variation.

Besides the general econometric critique of CGE, there is also a specific critique of these models as tools used for climate change mitigation and sustainability analysis (Barker, 2004; Scrieciu, 2007). The theoretical assumption that the economy is at an optimal equilibrium implies that the introduction of a carbon tax to reduce CO_2 emissions is, by definition, costly. Therefore, 'the models cannot adequately assess win-win development policies that both improve the economy and the environment' (Barker, 2004, p. 8).

Examples of CGE models which cover the interactions between the economy, the energy system and the environment and are designed to evaluate environmental policies include GEM-E3 (Capros et al., 1997), GTAP-E (Burniaux and Truong, 2002; McDougall and Golub, 2007), OECD ENV-Linkages Model (Burniaux and Château, 2008) and AIM/CGE (Kainuma et al., 1999). All these models are based on the GTAP database, albeit modified and integrated with other data sources depending on the geographic coverage and the aim of the analysis. They have all been extensively used for alternative policy simulations (as examples for GEM-E3, see Conrad and Schmidt, 1998 and Kouvaritakis et al., 2005; for OECD ENV: OECD, 2008; for AIM/CGE: Matsumoto and Masui, 2011). In particular, GTAP-E has been used for studying several energy-related issues and for climate mitigation policies on a medium-term horizon[34] (Nijkamp et al., 2005; Kemfert et al., 2006). In some cases the model has been taken as a starting point and modified by the users (for a recent example see Antimiani et al., 2013)), as the main practical advantage of this model is well expressed by Beckman, Hertel and Tyner (2011): 'the beauty of using this model is that it is readily accessible on the web, it has been widely used by others, and results based on this model have been published in several journals' (p. 800). A carbon/energy tax is implemented as an increase of prices; then, through the general equilibrium demand elasticities, there is a resulting change in the aggregate quantity demanded. Purchases of energy intermediate inputs by firms are the dominant contributor to this effect on demand, therefore inter-fuel substitution is the key to the price responsiveness of firms' demand for energy as well as the elasticity between energy and other production factors such as capital and labour. Indeed, as shown by Beckman, Hertel and Tyner (2011), results of GTAP-E are very sensitive to these values, which are calibrated by using elasticities from the related literature.[35] In fact the authors aim at correcting the original model, which appears invalid because it is unable to reproduce the observed energy price volatility in the years 2001–2006, due to a set of overly large elasticities incorporated into the model. Obviously, high price elasticities enable policy makers to obtain a reduction of energy consumption and greenhouse gas emissions through a modest increase in energy taxes and therefore environmental tax reforms are less costly. After a revision of these parameters taken from more recent (econometrically estimated) values in the literature, the results are closer to the historical observations and all users are advised to change the set of elasticities of substitution in their GTAP database.

As in the case of macroeconomic models, CGE-based studies also consider that a weak double dividend may occur after implementing an environmental tax reform. A positive impact on employment can be explained by revenue recycling measures in favour of labour, but the introduction of labour market imperfections to the model increases the double-dividend effect (Dannenberg et al, 2008). In CGE models, predicted macroeconomic costs tend to be smaller because of the modelling assumption toward an efficient equilibrium solution.

Micro-simulation models

A micro-simulation model is a partial equilibrium model which focuses on one side of the market and takes micro-level units (generally households and firms) as the basic units of analysis. Within this kind of model each unit is described by several attributes (e.g. income, family and employment status for households; sector of activity, dimension and profits for firms) and therefore an *image* of the heterogeneity of the phenomenon under scrutiny is represented. The method was devised and developed by Orcutt in the USA in the late 1950s but spread only over the last two decades, when computing power and large datasets became available.

The vast majority of micro-simulation models are household models, assessing the effect of public policies (mainly taxes, health and pension schemes) on families' income, consumption and labour supply. Micro-simulation models on firms, on the contrary, are extremely rare, and this is probably due to the unavailability of firm-level data and to the difficulty of estimating stable behavioural functions.

Whatever the unit of analysis, micro-simulation models can be classified according to several characteristics. One of the key ways of making a distinction is to look at *static* versus *dynamic* techniques.[36] *Static* models represent a sort of snapshot: they use cross-sectional data and are able to reproduce the budget set (or the main items of a balance sheet) for households and firms. After a policy stimulus, impacts can be calculated by comparing the initial state to the post-policy state in terms of changes in income, profits, distribution or, more in general, winners and losers. They are also known as *arithmetic* models. Dynamic models allow for a change in some state variables, such as a change of demographic status of households and firms (such as dying, marrying, giving birth, or opening, closing and merging for firms). The relevant characteristics are calculated in each period through transition probabilities at each period in time, which permits a movement of the micro units forward through time (ageing procedure).[37]

Both static and dynamic models can also be split into *behavioural* and *non-behavioural* models. The latter do not allow a change in behaviour of the unit of analysis and can estimate the first-round effect of the policy reform. Behavioural models, on the contrary, enclose a behavioural or reaction rule – mainly elasticity – and are able to simulate the single unit's response to a policy change (supply and demand of labour and consumption goods, energy input mix).

Although in principle a dynamic and behavioural model may offer the most exhaustive representation of an impact analysis, this kind of compound modelling instrument may be data and computing demanding; moreover, such a complex model is also very sensitive to ageing and behavioural assumptions and is therefore usually built only for a specific analysis purpose.[38] This is even more so for firms, where birth and death rates are more complex to estimate and purely static models or static behavioural models are generally employed.

In the case of highly detailed data at a local level, the technique is known as *spatial micro-simulation.* In order to obtain representative units at a local level, census data are combined with ad hoc survey data. These models are employed especially for local planning (industrial and housing) and travel mode choices.

Micro-simulation at firm level

In the case of firms, the structure of a micro-simulation model is generally less stable than in the case of households. As discussed before, a micro-simulation model is an attempt to represent a population, with its heterogeneity and behavioural reactions, considering that the main characteristics may be considered fixed for a certain time period. In the case of firms, this assumption is frequently unsatisfactory, as important characteristics (legal status, governance, localisation, price policies, energy mix) may easily change during a time span and some important phenomena (such as formal and informal multinational groups or networks) are very difficult to investigate. The available datasets are usually specialised in specific phenomena (balance sheets, employment, patents and R&D, demography) and in medium-large corporations.[39] Due to the highly unstable characteristics of firms, the matching procedure of heterogeneous data sources is usually difficult. Therefore micro-simulation models for firms tend to be even more specialised than household models and mainly focused on medium and large corporations.[40]

Data on environmental phenomena are even harder to find and to merge than other data. Due to the scarcity of environmental data, environmentally related micro-simulation models or even empirical estimations are rare and only recently, as an effect of the growing interest in climate policies, have the analyses increased in number and scope. Among the relevant variables, energy use, waste produced, investment in environmentally friendly devices and ETS (Emissions Trading Scheme) permit trading position are collected for some countries but the heterogeneity of the sources hampers the merging process with other general datasets. Greenhouse gas emission data at a firm level are not available, but can be estimated if a reliable set of proxies – such as energy use and sector of activity – is accessible.

To our knowledge, the only example of a firm-level micro-simulation model considering environmental and other important variables in a structural way is the Diecofis model, representing employment structure, balance sheets and environmentally related characteristics of Italian firms. In this model, social contributions, taxes on profits and excise taxes are modelled for several years and frequently updated. The dataset used is a multi-source business data bank based on micro-data created at the Italian National Statistical Office[41] which covers large corporations as well as small, unincorporated firms. In the model, direct (corporation taxes, social contributions) and indirect taxes (social contributions, energy taxes) are modelled on the basis of information on the legal status, sector of activity, balance-sheet data, exports, employment structures and energy input mix at firm level. Greenhouse gas emissions are estimated at firm level on the basis of energy inputs and sector of activity. It is worth noting that this particular dataset allows for the computation and use of firm-level energy tax rates: this is particularly important as energy-related taxes vary widely according to energy use and characteristics of the user.[42] The same applies for exemptions and revenue recycling measures, which are tailored on specific characteristics: these features are very significant for estimating distributional effects on firms as they allow identifying precisely which firms are affected by policies and to what extent profit distribution changes. Indicators such as the profitability and international competitiveness indexes can be computed, as well as effects on employment, energy demand and exports.

The model is also dynamic because data can potentially be updated each year: as a result, behavioural functions can be estimated using the time and the cross-sectional dimension. This particular tool permits the estimation of policies considering a double-dividend approach or compensating measures focused directly on firms. In Bardazzi et al. (2004) an assessment of a carbon tax scheme designed by the Italian government in 1998 is performed: the scheme involved an increase in energy taxes and a decrease in firms' social contributions, introduced as a compensatory measure. In this case an ex-ante and static assessment of the impact of the energy tax reform was run, highlighting that compensatory measures were adequate for balancing the burden of the reformed energy taxation, though winner and loser positions in terms of profitability emerged.[43] In more recent papers, the Diecofis model has been used to test the behavioural reaction to a policy stimulus:

looking at the panel structure, firms' own and cross-price elasticities have been estimated for several energy inputs, stressing the difference among sectors and between large and small firms.[44]

Although not organised in a structural model, several interesting firm-level estimations have been run on environmental issues. Using firm-level cross-country data, Commins et al. (2009) tested the effect of energy and carbon taxes on several measures of corporate performance (investment, employment, total factor productivity and profitability) during the period 1996–2007. The panel estimation shows a significant impact of energy taxes (computed as sectoral tax rate) and a remarkable heterogeneity among sectors, not only in terms of size, but also in the direction of the effect. The general result of the estimation enhances the credibility of the Porter hypothesis and, in particular, found an average positive relation between energy taxes investments and profitability. Martin et al. (2011) analysed the impact of the Climate Change Levy package[45] on energy intensity, profitability and employment of the British business sector. They built a plant-level dataset considering an annual production survey, energy use and participation in the Climate Change Agreement. By comparing energy intensity in time and among firms (participating or not participating in the Climate Change Agreement), the authors find a strong negative effect of the tax on electricity and energy use, whereas no significant impact on employment, survival and Total Factor Productivity can be traced.

A new strand of micro-level estimations uses new and detailed information coming from the implementation of the European ETS. Abrell et al. (2011) built a dataset of 2,100 firms by combining balance-sheet data from Bureau Van Dick and permit allocation and emissions coming from the EU-ETS registry and found a very limited influence of being a firm subjected to ETS on profitability, even though some variation among sectors can be identified. Martin et al. (2012), as another example, built a firm-level dataset by combining balance-sheet data, survey data and CO2 emissions coming from the EU-ETS registry with the aim of analysing corporate reactions to environmental policy and the compensation scheme linked to ETS.

5 Integrating micro and macro models

Policy instruments targeted at changing the costs of energy consumption include energy taxes, tradable permits, subsidies and efficiency standards. The relative efficacy and effectiveness of these instruments may differ substantially at the microeconomic (individual firm) level. Therefore, from this point of view, firms' heterogeneity can be effectively treated with firm-level information and methodological tools built on this data, that is to say a micro-simulation model. As previously discussed, however, this approach is generally static and its results are limited to investigating the instantaneous first-round effects of policy changes. The behavioural and dynamic effects on firms can be estimated if the micro-simulation model becomes dynamic and behavioural equations are introduced. This evolution requires that micro-data are not limited to a one-year cross-section but that either repeated cross-sections or panel data are available. The advantage of such models in evaluating the distributional effects on firms is that they can estimate critical parameters – such as the elasticities of production factors and inter-fuel substitution – on very large survey data, allowing for differentiation between firms grouped according to different characteristics. However, their main drawback is that they do not endogenise relative prices and they do not consider the overall efficiency effects of public policies because they lack an economy-wide perspective. Finally, tracing the impact of carbon pricing instruments is complicated by the fact that these are levied on intermediate inputs, and therefore indirect effects can accumulate and produce a larger impact on final goods prices. On the other hand, macro models can offer both a set of relationships for the economic system as a whole and medium-/long-run effects of policy changes, also including effects in secondary markets. We can conclude that these two perspectives are somewhat complementary.

The idea of combining micro and macro models is not new, as it dates back to Orcutt (1967), who suggested linking multiple models through 'adaptors and key variables used as intermediaries' (p. 120). However, the number of researchers developing micro-macroeconomic models is still very small worldwide, notwithstanding the progress in computational and econometric methods. Several types of integration can be envisaged (Baekgaard, 1995). The simplest approach is a sequential ('layered') procedure where the two separated models can be linked via common variables but there are no feedback effects between them. This sequential approach can be top down or bottom up (Peichl, 2009). In the first case macroeconomic variables are computed in the macro model and are then used as input for the micro-simulation model, which is adjusted to match the exogenous macro aggregate. Conversely, in the bottom-up approach information from the micro-simulation level is fed to the macro model, which is calibrated to these values. An alternative type of integration consists in an iterative linkage between the two models where information is exchanged at each iteration until convergence is achieved. In this case bi-directional interactions are considered. While this approach is the most appealing, it is also the most challenging and difficult to implement.

A growing interest in this field has produced some examples of integrated macro-micro-simulation models with a focus on households and income distribution effects. Some surveys on this issue have been produced (Ahmed and O'Donoghue, 2007; Davies, 2009; a special issue of the *International Journal of Micro-simulation* edited by Bussolo and Cockburn, 2010), other studies are applications of integrated models to specific public policy issues (e.g. Peichl, 2009) and, in particular, distributional effects on households of energy policies (Labandeira, Labeaga and Rodriguez, 2009; Buddelmeyer et al., 2012). Cameron and Ezzedin (2000) propose the integration between an IO model and a micro-simulation model for households to endogenise disposable income and personal consumption, while Labandeira and Labeaga (1999) follow a similar approach to estimate the impact of carbon taxation on Spanish households.

Applied literature on integrated models for firms is very scarce, mainly due to the rarity of micro-simulation models for firms. A recent example is presented by Ghezzi and Sciclone (2009), where two micro-simulation models (a tax-benefit model for Italian households and a micro model for firms to simulate fiscal policies impact) and an IO demand-driven macro model for an Italian region are linked. In this model when taxes on business activity are changed, profits and dividends may vary, thereby affecting investment and household disposable income – and consumption – respectively. These aggregate demand changes are passed on to the macro model and the necessary production variation is the feedback effect to the firms' micro model.

In the case of carbon pricing – and any revenue recycling measures – we can expect that a micro-simulation model of firms could compute the 'morning after' distributional effects in terms of competitiveness by exploiting the heterogeneity of enterprises with regard to their input structure. When an energy-environmental module is implemented, these impacts can be very disaggregated both as regards energy carriers and emissions. This first-round effect on production costs could be passed on to the macro model, where interactions among sectors are considered and indirect effects can be estimated. Industrial and consumer price equations can then be computed and affect final demand. Other transmission channels through investments (and technological progress if endogenous) can be envisaged. Structural changes can be induced by permanent increases in energy costs, especially if prices of different energy inputs do not vary by the same amount. A model should therefore be able to capture these effects at the sectoral level because they affect the overall economy. Therefore distributional effects on firms would benefit the heterogeneous information at the micro level and include also the dynamic second-order effects of the macro model through relative price changes and interactions among economic actors in the economy.

6 Conclusions

A cornerstone of modern European environmental policy is the idea of getting the right price for carbon through several instruments, among which carbon taxes and permit exchange mechanisms are the most relevant. However, a policy altering the relative prices of inputs and products raises several concerns about fairness, equity competitiveness and long-run growth implications. Fairness is usually linked to the idea that the polluting agent pays for the negative externality; unfortunately the question of who really bears the economic cost of market-based instruments is far from being unquestionably resolved. The tax-shifting and price pass-through literature has clarified that the final economic cost of a carbon pricing policy is not necessarily borne by the formal taxpayer and therefore the 'polluter pays' principle may remain only an abstract principle. Depending on the agent's ability to offset increasing costs, the burden of carbon pricing can be totally or partially shifted to other sectors of society, through a price increase or a consistent decrease in demand.

As discussed in this paper, the relative burden of the policy among different agents can be estimated with a macro aggregated model or calculated as a result of a CGE or a multisectoral econometric model. In both cases, after estimating the relative incidence of the policy among agents, a detailed distributional impact analysis can be performed among consumers and/or among firms by using micro-simulation models.

There is a broad and well-established empirical literature on distributional impact on households and consumers. On the other hand, distributional analyses for firms have been performed mainly at sector level because energy and environmental data on individual firms are much rarer and more recent, but they are nevertheless strategic, as the heterogeneity among firms is even higher than household heterogeneity. As a very general finding, the empirical literature identifies positive signals for environmental policies: fuel and factor elasticities are non-negligible and the profitability and competitiveness impacts – with a high heterogeneity by sector and firm dimension – appear non-prohibitive, especially in the cases where a double dividend can be identified.

However, impact estimations are strongly model dependent, not only with regard to the ability to implement policy details and to identify various aspects of policy effects and feedbacks, but also for the underlying theoretical hypotheses. Intentionally, in this paper a hierarchy of these methodological approaches is not proposed: their key characteristics have been described and therefore their strong and weak points in the analysis of climate mitigation policies can be easily identified. With regard to climate policy evaluation, in this work we have focused particularly on the structural characteristics of the models concerning key parameters (elasticities of substitution) and the time path to the new equilibrium. These features are particularly important for the issue at stake, given its long-term nature. Another key assumption concerns technological progress: it is difficult to prevent an overly short-sighted or overly optimistic assumption of the future evolution of technologies from seriously influencing the estimation of policy effects on the economy, particularly on firms' costs and competitiveness (Söderholm, 2012). The use of empirical results of modelling studies should therefore be very cautious and, in general, different model approaches, when compared, should be regarded as complementary rather than as substitutes. The limitations and shortcomings of applied analysis do not mean that it is useless. Economic models are sometimes the only tool for identifying the main driving forces behind the costs of a policy as well as the main uncertainties involved in the policy design. We believe that some of the limitations concerning firms' substitution analysis – concerning both production factors and energy inputs – could be overcome by increasing the level of disaggregation, thus taking energy products and firms' heterogeneity into account. The integration of the micro-simulation with the macroeconomic approach follows this line of reasoning, permitting the estimation of very specific parameters and simultaneously considering all major interactions at the general equilibrium level.

Notes

1 See Dannenberg et al. (2008) for a survey of economic costs. Focusing on public resources, see Galeotti et al. (2011).

2 The classification of environmental instruments is more far-reaching and complex than presented. According to some authors, institutional devices (to facilitate a Coase approach resolution) or voluntary programmes (voluntary agreement, labelling) may even constitute separate categories. See the Perman et al. (2011) classification.

3 Although a number of conditions must be met to make environmental taxes and tradeable emission permit systems equivalent, in this paper we consider the two policy instruments as fully equivalent. This assumption also implies that emission permits are not allocated *for free* and a certain amount of public resources are raised in both cases.

4 The economic efficiency of market-based instruments is a key factor for guaranteeing the feasibility of policy intervention: an environmental policy should be undertaken only if it assures a net welfare gain. In other words, the welfare gain from pollution abatement must exceed the cost borne by polluters and economic agents in general.

5 See European Commission (2007), OECD (2006).

6 Dixit (1985) defined this result the 'targeting' principle': the externality problem should be resolved by directly targeting its source. In the more general second-best framework, with multiple market failures (or unavailability of some instruments) the prescriptions of optimal taxation theory are strongly assumption dependent.

7 As for the political acceptability of price signals, this fairness characteristic emerges only in the case of emission trading or special pollution taxes, when the identification of the polluter coincides with big firms or specific behaviour. In the case of carbon taxes on fuels, on the contrary, political acceptability is very low.

8 The main references for the Porter Hypothesis are Porter (1991) and Porter and van der Linde (1995). Porter's call for a positive role of environmental regulation has been classified into three definitions, namely the weak, strong and narrow hypothesis (Jaffe and Palmer, 1997). According to the weak definition, environmental regulation enhances innovation, whereas the strong definition says that environmental regulation often improves firms' competitiveness by producing innovation which may more than compensate regulatory compliance costs. The narrow formulation stresses the role of market-based instruments as the best tools for promoting innovation.

9 Literature on the Porter Hypothesis is particularly abundant. The empirical literature, however, has not yet reached conclusive results on the relevance of the link between environmental regulation and innovation and growth. For a recent survey see Ambec et al. (2010).

10 In the case of earmarking, revenue resources are set aside to pay for a specific environmental project: this way earmarking fixes the use of tax revenue in advance and makes such expenditure programmes difficult to change, a principle conflicting with the unitary principle of public budget. However, it has been proved that earmarking increases the public acceptability of environmental taxes (Kallbekken and Sælen, 2011).

11 Goulder (1995) distinguishes a *weak* double dividend as the case with a positive welfare gain from using revenues to reduce distortionary taxes and a *strong* double dividend as the case where cutting inefficient taxes reduces the overall distortionary costs of taxation.

12 European Commission (2004).

13 OECD (1992).

14 The concept of competitiveness at a national level has been severely questioned by Krugman as dangerous and leading to distorting domestic economic policy: 'competitiveness is a meaningless word when applied to national economies. And the obsession with competitiveness is both wrong and dangerous' (Krugman, 1994, p. 44).

15 Unit labour costs are frequently employed as a proxy for competitiveness, with an increase being a signal of a competitivity loss and a decline as a sign of improvement. However, an upward trend may also indicate the leading role of a country in international competition and the goal of higher labour earnings to fulfil the general idea of nations' competitiveness discussed above. See also Andersen (2009).

16 The variation in energy prices faced by heterogeneous firms is shown in Bardazzi, Oropallo and Pazienza (2009).

17 Several studies provide evidence that higher environmental performance is associated with better financial performance. However, the significant correlation found by most papers does not demonstrate the causality direction, and the link between environmental and financial performance remains unclear (see Telle, 2006).

18 See Forssell and Polenske (1998), Suh and Kugawa (2005). An older review of environmental IO studies can be found in Forsund (1985).

19 For a formal representation of this basic energy IO model see Miller and Blair (2009), chapter 9.

20 Manne, Richels and Weyant (1979) examine works on energy modelling and issues relevant at that time.

21 Alternatively, top-down sectoral results can be obtained if the model computes the macrovariables at the first step and then these totals are split among sectors (top-down approach). In classifying modelling approaches for climate policy, 'top-down' and 'bottom-up' may have a different – more common – meaning. Bottom-up models consider the energy sector in detail and do not include a complete representation of the overall economic system, with a greater emphasis on technologies. Top-down models are aggregate models of the entire economy including energy and environmental variables in their framework to assess climate policy impacts. In this sense, all models considered here belong to the latter group (Söderholm, 2012).

22 For recent reports, publications and conferences see the website http://inforumweb.umd.edu/.

23 Two other INFORUM country models – the LIFT model of the US economy and the Mudan model of the Chinese economy – have been enhanced with energy modules to simulate the impact of several energy policies, including carbon taxes (see Meade and Nyhus, 2009).

24 This global model has been constructed based on previous experience with COMPASS (Comprehensive Model of Policy Assessment). COMPASS shared the same philosophy as GINFORS but was based on a different software, a more limited database and a restricted number of sectors. However, this older version of the global model was used for simulating the impact of a hypothetical carbon tax in G7 countries (Meyer and Lutz, 2002). GINFORS has been linked to the large-scale INFORGE model to measure the feedback effect via international trade (Meyer et al., 2007).

25 This detail refers to version 5.5 of E3ME revised in 2012. For further updates and model documentation see the website www.camecon.com/AnalysisTraining/suite_economic_models/E3ME.aspx.

26 See for example the COMETR research (The Competitiveness Effects of Environmental Tax Reform), founded by the European Commission, and the PETRE project (Productivity and Environmental Tax Reform in Europe), founded by the Anglo-German Foundation.

27 For a detailed comparison of these technical modelling aspects see Barker et al. (2011b).

28 The emphasis placed on this difference can be captured in Barker et al. (2011b), p. 178.

29 Standard CGE models assume competitive markets and flexible prices to clear all markets. However, it is possible to allow for imperfect competition, non-market clearing, heterogeneous agents and other variations. However, the most common class of CGE models consists of comparative-static models where the economy is studied at two different points in time: the benchmark equilibrium and the future counterfactual equilibrium. The transition path toward the future equilibrium where the economy converges is not explicitly modelled (Peichl, 2009). Even the dynamic models cannot tell us about the time it takes to reach the new equilibrium, as the *number of periods* can be known but not *the length of each period* along the transition.

30 This practice is very different from the use of econometric methods as in a macro-

econometric model where parameters are fitted to the data of the country or region considered using econometric techniques instead of calibration.

31 Beckman, Hertel and Tyner (2011) propose a similar validation procedure for GTAP-E.

32 For a detailed analysis of several criticisms of this modelling approach see Barker (2004), Grassini (2007) and Scrieciu (2007).

33 In fact, in the accompanying documentation, the GTAP database is described as not being a repository of IO tables because the original data is modified in order 'to facilitate the operation of economic simulation models assuring users a consistent set of economic facts' (www.gtap.agecon.purdue.edu/databases/v7/).

34 GTAP-E is declared as not ideal for long-term (i.e. 50-year) climate policy analysis because it is a static model and this characteristic imposes a medium-run (3–5 years) time horizon.

35 The debate on inter-fuel elasticities of substitution is widespread and several problematic issues arise with regard to the time horizon, the types of energy considered, the units of analysis. Alternative definitions of elasticities are examined in the literature (cross-price elasticities, Allen elasticities and Morishima elasticities) which have different characteristics; it has been noted that empirical results about the substitutability of inputs – and then on the overall distributive impacts – may depend on the measures of substitution used (Bardazzi, Oropallo, Pazienza, 2012).

36 Other important characteristics which may be useful for classifying dynamic models are the possibility to include new agents (open/closed models) and the use of continuous or discrete time intervals to run the model (annual transitional matrix versus survival function). For a methodological survey see O'Donoghue (2001), Harding, Williamson and Zaidi (2009), Bourguignon and Spadaro (2006).

37 Static models can also be used to simulate a policy impact in a period subsequent to that in which the data was collected. In this case the original survey data is re-weighted or the monetary values are inflated with price indexes.

38 As discussed by Mitton, Sutherland and Weeks (2000), all the processes needed to build a micro-simulation model involve some degree of approximation. As adding behavioural responses introduces further uncertainty linked to estimation parameters, an evaluation of efficiency between a more comprehensive model and a higher uncertainty is necessary.

39 Wherever the role of small and unincorporated firms is relevant, such as in Italy, Belgium and Spain, a large part of the economic system is usually ignored by modelling, due to the difficulties of finding reliable data.

40 Among the pioneering models on firms, the Inland Revenue in the UK developed a micro-simulation model based on tax return data in the 1970s with the aim of revenue estimation. Currently, firm micro-simulation models aimed at forecasting corporation tax revenue are employed in UK, Canada and Italy. See Ahmed (2006) for a survey.

41 The integrated and systematised information system on enterprises is the result of an integration process of different administrative sources. All of the above ISTAT surveys are based on common EUROSTAT standards and classifications.

42 See OECD (2013) for a cross-country analysis of energy-related effective tax rates.

43 In Bardazzi et al. (2004), heterogeneity in competitiveness among firms is analysed through several indexes (profitability, labour productivity and export intensity). Using a specific decomposition of the Gini index, a composite performance indicator which combined the three indexes allowed a comparative analysis of a multifaceted definition of performance.

44 As shown by Bardazzi et al. (2009, 2012), small firms generally exhibit lower individual and cross-price elasticities than medium and large ones. This means that market-based instruments are expected to have greater efficacy among larger firms. The current relative inflexibility of the SME energy mix indicates that in order to obtain a switch toward greener energy inputs, important investments are needed.

45 The Climate Change Levy is a unit tax on energy used by non-domestic users intro-

duced in the United Kingdom in 2001. Two different kinds of compensatory measures were introduced: on the one hand a share of total revenue was recycled to finance a decrease in National Insurance contributions; on the other hand, firms adopting a binding emission reduction target (regulated by specific environmental agreements) can obtain a substantial reduction in the tax.

References

Abrell, J., Ndoye Faye, A. and Zachmann, G. (2011), 'Assessing the Impact of the EU ETS Using Firm Level Data', *Bruegel Working Paper*, 2011/08.

Ahmed, S. (2006), 'Corporate Tax Models: A Review', Bank of Pakistan Working Paper Series No. 13.

Ahmed, V. and O'Donoghue, C. (2007), 'CGE-Microsimulation Modelling: A Survey', MPRA Paper No. 9307.

Almon, C. (1991), 'The INFORUM Approach to Interindustry Modeling', *Economic Systems Research*, 3(1), 1–7.

Andersen, M. (2009), 'Carbon-energy Taxation, Revenue Recycling and Competitiveness', in M. Andersen and P. Ekins (editors) *Carbon-energy taxation: Lessons from Europe*, Oxford University Press, pp. 3–23.

Antimiani, A., Costantini, V., Martini, C., Palma, A. and Tommasino, E.C. (2013), 'The GTAP-E: Model Description and Improvements', in V. Costantini and M. Mazzanti (eds) *The Dynamics of Environmental and Economic Systems: Innovation, Environmental Policy and Competitiveness*, Springer, pp. 3–24.

Bach, S., Kohlhaas, M., Meyer, B., Praetorius, B. and Welsch, H. (2002), 'The Effects of Environmental Fiscal Reform in Germany: A Simulation Study', *Energy Policy*, 9, 803–811.

Baekgaard, H. (1995) 'Integrating Micro and Macro Models: Mutual Benefits', in *International Congress on Modelling and Simulation Proceedings*, 4, 253–8.

Bardazzi, R. and Piacentino, D. (1993), 'The Effects of a Carbon Tax: Simulations for Italy in a Multisectoral Model', paper presented at the First Meeting of Italian Environmental Economists', Pavia, 18 March 1993.

Bardazzi, R., Grassini, M. and Piacentino, D. (1994), 'Politica dell'ambiente e attività produttiva: gli effetti settoriali dell'introduzione di un'imposta sul carbonio in Italia', in *Ricerche quantitative per la politica economica 1993*, Banca d'Italia, pp. 487–513.

Bardazzi, R., Oropallo, F. and Pazienza, M.G. (2004), 'Accise energetiche e competitività delle imprese: un'applicazione sull'esperimento della Carbon Tax', *Economia delle Fonti di Energia e dell'Ambiente*, no. 3, 2004.

Bardazzi, R., Oropallo, F. and Pazienza, M.G. (2009), 'Is It Time for a Revival of ETR in Italy? Energy Elasticities and Factor Substitutability for Manufacturing Firms', *Rivista di Politica Economica*, July–September, 205–240,

Bardazzi, R., Oropallo, F. and Pazienza, M.G. (2012), 'Firms' Energy Demand and the Role of Energy Taxes: Elasticities Estimation of Industrial Firms in Italy', in *9th International Conference on the European Energy Market (EEM)*, 1–8, IEEE.

Barker, T. (1998), 'The Effects on Competitiveness of Coordinated versus Unilateral Fiscal Policies Reducing GHG Emissions in the EU: An Assessment of a 10% Reduction by 2010 using the E3ME model', *Energy Policy*, 26(14), 1083–1098.

Barker, T. (1999), 'Achieving a 10% Cut in Europe's Carbon Dioxide Emissions Using Additional Excise Duties: Coordinated, Uncoordinated and Unilateral Action Using the Econometric Model E3ME', *Economic Systems Research*, 11(4), 401–421.

Barker, T. (2004), 'Economic Theory and the Transition to Sustainability: A Comparison Of General-Equilibrium and Space-Time-Economics Approaches', Tyndall Centre Working Paper 62.

Barker, T. and Peterson, W. (1987), *The Cambridge Multisectoral Dynamic Model of the British Economy*, Cambridge, UK: Cambridge University Press.

Barker, T., Junankar, S., Pollit, H. and Summerton, P. (2009a), 'The Effects of Environmental Tax Reform on International Competitiveness in the European Union: Modelling with E3ME', in M.S. Andersen and P. Ekins (eds) *Carbon Energy Taxation. Lessons from Europe*, Oxford University Press, pp. 147–214.

Barker, T., Junankar, S., Pollitt, H. and Summerton, P. (2009b), 'The Macroeconomic Effect of Unilateral Environmental Tax Reforms in Europe, 1995 to 2012', in J. Cottrell, J.E. Milne, H. Ashiabor, K. Deketelaere and L. Kreiser (eds) *Critical Issues in Environmental Taxation*, Volume VI, Oxford University Press, pp. 73–100.

Barker, T., Lutz, C., Meyer, B., Pollitt, H. and Speck, S. (2011a), 'Modelling an ETR for Europe', in P. Ekins, and S. Speck (eds) *Environmental Tax Reform (ETR) – A Policy for Green Growth*, Oxford University Press, pp. 204–235.

Barker, T., Lutz, C., Meyer, B. and Pollitt, H. (2011b), 'Models for Projecting the Impacts of ETR', in P. Ekins, and S. Speck (eds) *Environmental Tax Reform (ETR) – A Policy for Green Growth*, Oxford University Press, pp. 175–203.

Beckman, J., Hertel, T. and Tyner, W. (2011), 'Validating Energy-Oriented CGE Models', *Energy Economics*, 33(5), 799–806.

Borges, A.M. (1986), 'Applied General Equilibrium Models: An Assessment of their Usefulness for Policy Analysis', OECD Economic Studies No. 7.

Bourguignon, F. and Spadaro, A. (2006), 'Microsimulation as a Tool for Evaluating Redistribution Policies', Ecineq Working Paper No. 20

Bovenberg, A. L. and R., de Mooji (1994), 'Environmental Levies and Distortionary Taxation', *The American Economic Review*, 84(4), 1085–1089.

Buddelmeyer, H., Hérault, N., Kalb, G. and de Jong, M.V.Z. (2012), 'Linking a Microsimulation Model to a Dynamic CGE Model: Climate Change Mitigation Policies and Income Distribution in Australia', *International Journal of Microsimulation*, 5(2), 40–58.

Bullard, C.W. III and Herendeen, R.A. (1975), 'Energy Impact of Consumption Decisions', *Proceedings of the IEEE*, 63(3), 484–493.

Burniaux, J. M. and Château, J. (2008), *An Overview of the OECD ENV-Linkages Model* (No. 653), OECD Publishing.

Burniaux, J. and Truong, T. (2002), 'GTAP-E: An Energy-Environmental Version of the GTAP Model', GTAP Technical Paper No. 16, Purdue University.

Bussolo, M. and Cockburn, J. (eds) (2010), 'Macro-Micro Analytics: A Guide to Combining Computable General Equilibrium and Microsimulation Modelling Frameworks', *International Journal of Microsimulation*, special issue, 3(1).

Cameron, G. and Ezzeddin, R. (2000), 'Assessing the Direct and Indirect Effects of Social Policy: Integrating Input-Output and Tax Microsimulation Models at Statistics Canada', in L. Mitton, H. Sutherland and M. Weeks (eds), *Microsimulation Modelling for Policy Analysis*, Cambridge, UK, Cambridge University Press.

Capros, P., Georgakopoulos, T., Van Regemorter, D., Proost, S., Schmidt, T.F.N. and Conrad, K. (1997), 'European Union: The GEM-E3 General Equilibrium Model', *Economic & Financial Modelling*, special double issue, 4(2–3), 51–160.

Commins, N., Lyons, S., Schiffbauer, M. and Tol, R.S.J. (2009), 'Climate Policy And Corporate Behavior', ESRI working paper, No. 329, http://hdl.handle.net/10419/50043.

Conrad, K. and Schmidt, T.F.N. (1998), 'Economic Effects of an Uncoordinated Versus a

Coordinated Carbon Dioxide Policy in the European Union: An Applied General Equilibrium Analysis', *Economic Systems Research*, 10(2), 161–182.

Dannenberg, A., Mennel, T. and Moslener, U. (2008), 'What Does Europe Pay for Clean Energy? Review of Macroeconomic Simulation Studies', *Energy Policy*, 36(4), 1318–1330.

Davies, J.B. (2009), 'Combining Microsimulation with CGE and Macro Modelling for Distributional Analysis in Developing and Transition Countries', *International Journal of Microsimulation*, 2(1), 49–65.

Dixit, A. (1985), 'Tax Policy in Open Economies', in M. Feldstein and A.J. Auerbach (eds) *Handbook of Public Economics*, 1, Amsterdam: North Holland, pp. 313–374.

Ekins, P. and Speck, S. (eds) (2011), *Environmental Tax Reform (ETR) – A Policy for Green Growth*, Oxford University Press.

European Commission (2004), *European Competitiveness Report, Competitiveness and Benchmarking*, Brussels: European Commission.

European Commission (2007), Green Paper on Market Based Instruments for Environment and Related Policy Purposes (COM(2007) 140), Brussels: European Commission.

Forssell, O. and Polenske, K.R. (1998), 'Introduction: Input–Output and the Environment', *Economic Systems Research*, 10, 91–97.

Forsund, F.R. (1985), 'Input-output Models, National Economic Models, and the Environment', in A.V. Kneese and J.L. Sweeney (eds) *Handbook of Natural Resource and Energy Economics*, Vol. 1, Amsterdam: Elsevier, pp. 325–341.

Galeotti, M., Glachant, M., Olmos, L., Pazienza, M.G., Ranci, P., Ruester, S. and Sartori M. (2011), 'The Impact of Climate and Energy Policies on the Public Budget of EU Member States' www.eui.eu/Projects/THINK/Documents/THINKPublicBudgetReport.pdf.

Ghezzi, L. and Sciclone, N. (2009) 'A Micro-macro Model for Fiscal Policy Simulations', *Politica Economica*, 25(2), 185–210.

Goulder, L.H. (1995), 'Environmental Taxation and the "Double Dividend": A Reader's Guide,' *International Tax and Public Finance*, 2, 157–184.

Grassini, M. (2007), 'Rowing along the Computable General Equilibrium Modelling Mainstream', *Studi e Note di Economia*, 12(3), 315–343.

Harding A., Williamson, P. and Zaidi, A. (2009), *New Frontiers in Microsimulation Modelling*, Ashgate.

Hoerner A. and Bosquet, B. (2001), 'Environmental Tax Reform: The European Experience', Washington, DC: Center for a Sustainable Economy, (February).

Hudson, E.A. and Jorgenson, D.W. (1974), 'U.S. Energy Policy and Economic Growth, 1975–2000', *The Bell Journal of Economics and Management Science*, 5(2), 461–514.

Iraldo, F., Testa, F., Melis, M. and Frey, M. (2011), 'A Literature Review on the Links between Environmental Regulation and Competitiveness', *Environmental Policy and Governance*, 21, 210–222.

Jaffe, A. and Palmer, K. (1997), 'Environmental Regulation and Innovation: A Panel Data Study,' *The Review of Economics and Statistics*, MIT Press, 79(4), 610–619.

Kainuma, M., Matsuoka, Y. and Morita, T. (1999), 'Analysis of Post-Kyoto Scenarios: The Asian-Pacific Integrated Model', *The Energy Journal*, special issue, 207–220.

Kallbekken, S. and Sælen, H. (2011), 'Public Acceptance for Environmental Taxes: Self-interest, Environmental and Distributional Concerns', *Energy Policy*, 39, 2966–2733.

Kemfert, C., Kohlhass, M., Truong, T. and Protsenko, A. (2006) 'The Environmental and Economic Effects of European Emissions Trading', *Climate Policy*, 6, 441–455.

Kouvaritakis, N., Stroblos, N., Paroussos, L., Revesz, T., Zalai, E. and van Regemorter, D. (2005), 'Impacts of Energy Taxation in the Enlarged European Union, Evaluation with

GEM-E3 Europe', study for the European Commission DG TAXUD, final report, July 2005.

Krugman, P. (1994), 'Competitiveness: A Dangerous Obsession', *Foreign Affairs*, 73(2), 28–44.

Labandeira, X. and Labeaga, J.M. (1999), 'Combining Input-Output Analysis and Micro-simulation to Assess the Effects of Carbon Taxation on Spanish Households', *Fiscal Studies*, 20(3), 305–320.

Labandeira, X., Labeaga, J.M. and Rodriguez, M. (2009), 'An Integrated Economic and Distributional Analysis of Energy Policies', *Energy Policy*, 37, 5776–5786.

Leontief, W. (1970), 'Environmental Repercussions and the Economic Structure: An Input–Output Approach', *The Review of Economics and Statistics*, 52(3), 262–271.

Leontief, W. and Ford, D. (1972) 'Air pollution and the economic structure: Empirical results of input-output computations', *Input-output Techniques*, 9–30.

Lutz, C. (2011), 'Energy Scenarios for Germany: Simulations with the Model PANTA RHEI', in D. Mullins, J. Viljoen and H. Leeuwner (eds) *Interindustry Based Analysis of Macroeconomic Forecasting*, South Africa: STN Printers, pp. 203–224.

Lutz, C., Meyer, B. and Wolter, M.I. (2010), 'The Global Multisector/Multicountry 3E-Model GINFORS. A Description of the Model and a Baseline Forecast for Global Energy Demand and CO_2-Emissions', *International Journal of Global Environmental Issues*, 10(1–2), 25–45.

Manne, A.S., Richels, R.G. and Weyant, J.P. (1979), 'Energy Policy Modeling: A Survey', *Operations Research*, 27(1), 1–36.

Martin, R., de Preux, L.B. and Wagner, U.J. (2011), 'The Impacts of the Climate Change Levy on Manufacturing: Evidence from Microdata', NBER Working Paper No. 17446.

Martin, R., Muûls, M., de Preux, L.B. and Wagner, U.J. (2012), 'Industry Compensation under Relocation Risk: A Firm-Level Analysis of the EU Emissions Trading Scheme', CEP Discussion Paper No. 1150,

Matsumoto, K. and Masui, T. (2011), 'Analyzing Long-Term Impacts of Carbon Tax Based on the Imputed Price, Applying the AIM/CGE Model', *Management of Environmental Quality: An International Journal*, 22(1), 33–47.

McDougall R. and Golub, A. (2007), 'GTAP-E: A Revised Energy-Environmental Version of the GTAP Model', GTAP Research Memorandum No. 15.

Meade, D.S. and Nyhus, D.E. (2009), 'Using the Inforum LIFT and Mudan Models to Investigate the Impacts of Cap and Trade Legislation on International Leakages', in R. Bardazzi, and M. Grassini (eds) *Energy Policy and International Competitiveness*, Firenze University Press, pp. 3–28.

Meyer, B. and Lutz, C. (2002), 'Carbon Tax and Labour Compensation – a Simulation for G7', in K. Uno (ed.) *Economy-Energy-Environment Simulation: Beyond the Kyoto Protocol*, Dordrecht, Boston, London: Springer, pp. 185–190.

Meyer, B. and Lutz, C. (2007), 'The GINFORS Model. Model Overview and Evaluation', Petre Working Paper, Osnabrück, www.petre.org.uk/papers.htm.

Meyer, B., Lutz, C., Schnur, P. and Zika, G. (2007), 'Economic Policy Simulations with Global Interdependencies: A Sensitivity Analysis for Germany', *Economic Systems Research*, 19(1), 37–55.

Miller, R.E. and Blair, P.D. (2009). *Input-Output Analysis. Foundations and Extensions*. Second ed. Cambridge University Press.

Mitton, L., Sutherland, H. and Weeks, M. (2000), *Microsimulation Modelling for Policy Analysis*, Cambridge University Press.

Nijkamp, P., Wang, S. and Kramers, H. (2005), 'Modeling the Impacts of International

Climate Change Policies in a CGE Context: The Use of the GTAP-E Model', *Economic Modelling*, 22, 955–974.

O'Donoghue, C. (2001), 'Dynamic Microsimulation: A Survey', *Brazilian Electronic Journal of Economics*.

OECD (1992), *Technology and the Economy: The Key Relationships*, OECD Publishing.

OECD (2006), *The Political Economy of Environmentally Related Taxes*, OECD Publishing.

OECD (2008), *OECD Environmental Outlook to 2030*, OECD Publishing.

OECD (2013), *Taxing Energy Use. A Graphical Analysis*, OECD Publishing.

Orcutt, G H. (1967), 'Microeconomic Analysis for Prediction of National Accounts', in H. Wold, G.H. Orcutt, E.A. Robinson, D. Suits and P. de Wolff (eds), *Forecasting on a Scientific Basis – Proceedings of an International Summer Institute*, Lisbon: Gulbenkian Foundation, pp. 67–127.

Peichl, A. (2009), 'The Benefits and Problems of Linking Micro and Macro Models. Evidence from a Flat Tax Analysis', *Journal of Applied Economics*, 12(2), 301–329.

Perman, R., Ma, Y., Common, M., Maddison, D. and McGilvray, J. (2011) *Natural Resource and Environmental Economics*, 4th edition, Addison Wesley.

Pissarides, C. (2008), 'Assessment of Macro Economic Transmission Mechanisms of Carbon Constraints through the UK economy', A Report for the Committee on Climate Change.

Porter, M. (1991), 'America's Green Strategy', *Scientific American*, 264(4), 168.

Porter, M. and van der Linde, C. (1995), 'Toward a New Conception of the Environment–Competitiveness Relationship', *The Journal of Economic Perspectives*, 9(4), 97–118.

Scrieciu, S. (2007), 'The Inherent Dangers of Using Computable General Equilibrium Models as a Single Integrated Modelling Framework for Sustainability Impact Assessment. A Critical Note on Böringer and Löschel (2006)', *Ecological Economics*, 60, 678–684.

Söderholm, P. (2012), 'Modeling the Economic Costs of Climate Policy: An Overview', *American Journal of Climate Change*, 1(1), 14–32.

Suh, S. (ed.) (2009), *Handbook of Input-Output Economics in Industrial Ecology*, Amsterdam: Springer.

Suh, S. and Kagawa, S. (2005), 'Industrial Ecology and Input-output Economics: An Introduction', *Economic Systems Research*, 17(4), 349–364.

Telle, K. (2006), 'It Pays to be Green' – A Premature Conclusion?', *Environmental and Resource Economics*, 35(3), 195–220.

West, G.R. (1995), 'Comparison of Input–Output, Input–Output+ Econometric and Computable General Equilibrium Impact Models at the Regional Level', *Economic Systems Research*, 7(2), 209–227.

Zhang, Z. (2008), 'Macro-Economic and Sectoral Effects of Carbon Taxes: A General Equilibrium Analysis for China', *Economic Systems Research*, 10(2), 135–159.

8 Distributional effects of carbon pricing in Ireland

A computational general equilibrium approach

Stefano Verde[1]

1 Introduction

In December 2009, the Irish government introduced carbon taxation. The tax on fossil fuels was originally set at €15 per tonne of carbon dioxide (€15/tCO_2) and then raised to €20, two years later. Both coal and peat (the second is an important local energy source) were initially exempt, but as of 2013 the tax applies to all fossil fuels without exceptions. The sectors already regulated by the EU Emissions Trading Scheme (EU ETS) are not subject to the tax, however, as emissions would simply 'move' somewhere else in the EU – the tax within the EU ETS would be environmentally ineffective (Conefrey *et al.* 2008).[2]

After previous attempts, the carbon tax was brought in thanks to the determination of the Greens (who were at the time in government) and the occurrence of a severe crisis of public finances. The need to raise extra fiscal revenues also explains why the tax, contrary to what had been set forth originally, is not revenue neutral. That is, its yield is not returned to the economy ("recycled") in the form of lower taxes or higher public spending, to counter the side-effects of carbon pricing, notably the deterioration of firms' competitiveness and the regressive impact on households. These issues, competitiveness and regressiveness, should not be overlooked, however. Ireland has indeed a very open economy and, certainly in the short term, the tax without revenue recycling can only be regressive (e.g., Callan *et al.* 2009, Verde and Tol 2009).

While already a few empirical works assess the short-term distributional effects of carbon taxation in Ireland, this is the first to extend the analysis to the medium term. In that sense, this study is not only the first application to Irish data, but also one of few in the international literature. Using Computational General Equilibrium (CGE) analysis, we simulate the adoption of a \$20/tCO_2 carbon tax in Ireland. A \$20/tCO_2 tax, with no exemptions and distinction between EU ETS and non-EU ETS sectors, is not very far from describing the existing regime. It is not our aim, however, to simulate the existing Irish carbon tax. More generally, we investigate the medium-term impact of moderate carbon pricing on the Irish economy, with a special focus on income distribution.[3] The analysis is one of comparative statics, in which the variables of interest change relative to a baseline 'no-carbon tax' scenario. The characteristics of the model are such that these changes are best interpreted as effects unfolding over a period of three to five years, approximately (Beckman *et al.* 2011).

The first question we wish to answer is whether carbon pricing is regressive in the medium term. The time horizon over which the distributional effects of carbon pricing are assessed has implications for the methods that should be used and, potentially, for the results and the ensuing conclusions. The vast majority of the international literature considers only the impact on households' income occurring though consumption: higher energy prices and, thus, the losses in purchasing power and welfare. As energy is a necessity good, carbon pricing is typically regressive. However, while limiting the analysis to the cost of living may be appropriate to appreciate short-term effects, the same does not hold for the longer horizon. Over time, firms respond to changes in relative prices and in the demand for their products by modifying their own demand for production factors. At the same time, workers may be discouraged from supplying labour and capital may flow out of the economy. Changes in the remuneration and employment of primary factors determine additional distributional effects, for different households rely in different proportion on labour, capital and transfers as income sources. It is therefore necessary to take account of both the uses as well as the sources of income to capture distributional effects beyond the short term.

The second question we deal with is revenue recycling. In particular, we consider five alternative ways in which the yield of the carbon tax could be used: (a) household transfers, and lower taxes, respectively, on (b) consumption, (c) labour, (d) labour income and (e) capital income. In contrasting the results of the five scenarios, we look at a number of variables, but focus on GDP and distributional effects across households. Since it includes revenue recycling, the work intersects the 'double dividend' literature, which is concerned with the question of whether both lower emissions and greater welfare can be achieved through carbon pricing and lower distortionary taxes. In our model, however, labour supply is fixed, which precludes the emergence of a double dividend from the labour market – the typical case.

A variant of the popular Global Trade Analysis Project (GTAP) model, G-EMH, has been developed expressly for this study. G-EMH combines two versions of the standard GTAP model, namely GTAP-E (Burniaux and Truong 2002, McDougall and Golub 2007) and GTAP-MH (Gotor and Tsigas 2011). The first links together energy-related CO_2 emissions and the economy, while the second allows for multiple representative households. The household sector is partitioned into groups and each of these is represented by a virtual household assumed to behave as the mean of the group. In our application, the household groups correspond to the deciles of the income distribution.

G-EMH was obtained by merging two models, but some additional features have been introduced. Of these, the most important are (a) renewables in the electricity sector, and (b) the distinction between resident and non-resident households – particularly relevant for the Irish case. The GTAP database provides the information needed to operate the model. Only, the breakdown by income decile both of household incomes and expenditures is based on micro-data from the Irish Household Budget Survey (HBS).

The study is organized as follows. Section 2 reviews the relevant literature. Section 3 presents the G-EMH model. Section 4 illustrates the data. Section 5 describes the scenarios. Section 6 discusses the results. Section 7 concludes.

2 Literature review

A sizeable literature on the economic effects of carbon taxes has been produced over the last couple of decades. Two main strands can be identified. One of them addresses the question of whether revenue-neutral carbon taxes may induce not only an environmental benefit but an economic one too, what is called a double dividend.[4] This typically comes about as an efficiency gain for the economy when the green levy substitutes other more distortionary, pre-existing taxes. The other bulk of research is concerned with distributional effects of carbon taxes across households.[5] With only a few exceptions, there have been no intersections between these two strands.

In the double dividend literature, economy-wide models are needed because the interest lies in the impact of the environmental tax reform on the economy as a whole. By contrast, partial equilibrium analysis is the standard approach in the literature of distributional effects. Often, however, input-output or CGE models are used in a first stage to determine the impact of the tax on consumer prices; the price changes thus derived are then fed into a micro-simulation model of the household sector. The downside of such an approach is that it ignores feedback and general equilibrium effects, including changes in wages, rents, transfers and employment.

Only in recent years, with the exception of Jorgenson *et al.* (1992), economy-wide models with multiple households have been used to analyse efficiency and equity effects of carbon pricing simultaneously. This is perhaps surprising, as the literature in which economy-wide and micro-simulation models are used in combination is far from scant.[6] More information and greater model sophistication, however, are needed to analyse the effects of carbon pricing than, say, trade liberalization. Nonetheless, there is common ground between the two types of literature as to how the macro and the micro frameworks are linked. In the CGE literature, Bourguignon and Savard (2008) identify three approaches: (a) the CGE micro-simulation sequential approach, (b) the representative household approach, and (c) the integrated multi-household approach. The first effectively corresponds to what has been previously referred to as a partial equilibrium approach. With the second, the population of households is partitioned into groups and each group is represented by a virtual household assumed to behave as the mean of the group.[7] G-EMH, our model, belongs to this category. The third approach is an extension of the second, in that it includes as many households as those in the survey. This approach is the most powerful, but implementation may be difficult: solving the model may be challenging because of its size and the reconciliation of aggregate and micro-data may be problematic.

The first part of this section gives an account of the few studies, in the international literature, that use economy-wide models with multiple households to analyse efficiency and equity implications of carbon pricing in the same framework. Given the lack of similar applications for Ireland, the second part recalls those which are nonetheless relevant and provide evidence against which the findings of this study can be contrasted.

International literature

Jorgenson *et al.* (1992) are the first to analyse the distributional impact of carbon pricing using an economy-wide model. A dynamic CGE model of the US economy, IGEM, is used to estimate the economic effects of adopting a sequence of carbon taxes that holds US CO_2 emissions constant at the 1990 level. Over 16,000 household types are tracked, classified by demographic characteristics and income level. Revenue neutrality is enforced by making the average tax rate on labour income endogenous. Equivalent variations in wealth throughout lifetime are calculated for each household type and combined in a single indicator via a social welfare function. The impact of carbon taxation on growth is found to be negative, but modest (less than 0.5 per cent in real GNP, in 2020). The impact on welfare is found to be mildly regressive. However, if equality is measured in absolute terms and the social welfare function reflects high inequality aversion, the effect becomes mildly progressive.

Jorgenson *et al.* (2010) extend Jorgenson *et al.* (1992), update it with new data and apply it to different scenarios. The main methodological innovation concerns the inclusion of leisure in the measure of household welfare. The simulated policies are caps on all greenhouse gas emissions in the US, which would bring them to 50 per cent and 80 per cent below the 1990 level, over the period 2012–50. As the price of goods rises relative to leisure, households substitute toward the latter and reduce labour supply. Real GDP falls substantially, by just over 2 per cent and 4 per cent in the less and more stringent scenarios, respectively. Private consumption falls by almost half as much. Yet, the welfare impact is regressive but modest (substantially less than 1 per cent for all of the 244 household types), as the increase in leisure partially offsets the reduction in consumption.

Roson (2003) constructs a dynamic CGE model of the Italian economy to assess the efficiency and equity effects of carbon taxation with revenue recycling in that country. The constraint imposed on emissions reflects the national Kyoto target and the carbon tax rate is endogenously determined. The carbon tax revenue is recycled by lowering either labour taxes or taxes on capital income. Six representative households, classified by income level, and ten time periods are considered. The tax is introduced in the third period. Households maximize utility over an infinite horizon and anticipate the policy shock. A modest double dividend appears only with lower taxes on capital. Surprisingly, the double dividend is progressively distributed. This is explained by the distribution of capital income, which is quite even across households, and the assumptions of symmetric changes in employment levels and equal access to international capital markets for all households.

Van Heerden *et al.* (2006) use a CGE model similar to ORANI-G to investigate the potential for a double or even triple dividend in South Africa. Forty-eight household types (four race groups, twelve income groups) are represented. Cuts in four different energy-related taxes, notably on emissions, fuels, electricity and energy, are considered, in combination with three revenue-recycling schemes: lower direct taxes, indirect taxes and taxes on food consumption. The focus is on poverty rather than the whole income distribution. They find that a triple dividend can be achieved, in the form of lower emissions, higher GDP and less poverty, if any of the four taxes is recycled through a reduction in food prices. However, depending on which tax is reduced, the relative weight of the three dividends changes.

Yusuf and Resosudarmo (2007) analyse the impact of carbon taxation on household income distribution in Indonesia. A modified version of ORANI-G is deployed, with two hundred household categories. These correspond to the income centiles of urban and rural households. In contrast with most studies from industrialized countries, carbon taxation without revenue recycling is found to be progressive. The change in the use of primary factors following carbon taxation is to the advantage of lower-income households. In addition, the expenditure of lower-income households, especially in rural areas, is less sensitive to the prices of energy-related commodities. However, neither of the two simulated recycling schemes – a cut of the sales tax rate and a lump-sum transfer to all households – delivers a double dividend.

Oladosu and Rose (2007) use their own CGE model to simulate the impact of carbon taxation on the economy of the Susquehanna River Basin, a geographical region of the US. The household sector is disaggregated into nine income brackets. The study is interesting for at least three reasons. First, it applies to a sub-national region and, what is more, a geographical region. Secondly, the authors distinguish between short- and long-run horizons and results vary in consequence. Third, in contrast with most of the literature applied to industrialized economies, carbon taxation turns out to be mildly progressive. No evidence of a double dividend is found for either of the two recycling schemes envisaged. As expected, transfers enhance progressivity more than cuts in income taxes.

Rausch *et al.* (2011a) develop USREP, a CGE model of the US economy which comprises eleven sub-regions and, for each of these, eight household income groups. This first application of USREP involves the simulation of a \$15/tCO_2-eq carbon price which is determined via a cap-and-trade scheme. With allowance auctioning, revenues are recycled via transfers, labour and income taxes. With free allowances, they are returned to households in proportion to capital income. Under none of the scenarios does economic growth benefits from carbon pricing. Moreover, free allowance schemes are found to be highly regressive, while an efficiency–equity trade-off emerges with allowance auctioning, where transfers and income taxes are at opposite ends.

Rausch *et al.* (2011a) has subsequently been extended in two different directions. Rausch *et al.* (2010) apply a recursive dynamic version of USREP to compare three alternative cap-and-trade schemes for the US. These are based on the US Congress bills Waxman-Markey, Kerry-Lieberman and Cantwell-Collins. All proposals seek similar overall cuts in emissions by 2050, but differ in how allowances and auction revenues would be distributed. There is no trace of a double dividend, as either the allowance revenue is mostly used to make up for the budget deficit (induced by restrictions on emissions and subsequently reduced economic activity) or labour and capital taxes are actually increased to enforce revenue neutrality. The three schemes have similar aggregate costs, but these are greater if labour and capital taxes go up. As for the distributional effects, the authors emphasize the following two results. First, sources-side (of income) effects dominate uses-side effects; a point which is reinforced by the finding that carbon pricing without revenue recycling is neutral to modestly progressive. Secondly, they find there is an efficiency gain to distributing value to wealthier households because less is spent on energy and more goes into savings and investment. This is an additional explanation for the equity–efficiency trade-off, which is usually justified by the distortionary effects of taxes.

Rausch *et al.* (2011b) extends Rausch *et al.* (2011a) by incorporating 15,588 households from the US CEX survey data as individual agents. This is as yet the only work to use what we have previously referred to as the integrated multi-household approach. To solve such a large model, an algorithm borrowed from Rutherford and Tarr (2008) is used. The algorithm decomposes the numerical problem into two sub-problems and finds the equilibrium by an iterative procedure between those.[8] On the whole, the results confirm the findings of Rausch *et al.* (2011a), but also show how variation of impacts within household subgroups can swamp variation across groups.

Rose *et al.* (2012) analyse the distributional effects of California's forthcoming (2012–20) cap-and-trade scheme for alternative combinations of allowance allocation and revenue recycling. These involve free allocation of allowances with 0 or 100 per cent pass-through of opportunity costs onto consumers, and full auctioning with revenue recycling via lower personal income taxes or household transfers. A detailed macroeconometric model, REMI PI$^+$, is adapted to enable distributional analysis. The household sector is subdivided by ten income brackets. The direct costs or savings of the policies are taken from another study (CARB 2010) and referred to as the baseline scenario. The economy grows in all four scenarios: the most with free allowances and 0 per cent opportunity costs pass-through, the least with 100 per cent pass-through. Differences are not large, however. As regards the distributional implications, a clear efficiency–equity trade-off emerges between systems for allowance allocation (free versus auctioned), but the two recycling options are virtually equivalent.

Irish literature

There are no studies estimating the impact of carbon pricing both on economic growth and income distribution (together) in Ireland. Thus, we first review those which focus on growth and then turn to the set of works on distributional implications.

Using HERMES, a macroeconometric model of the Irish economy, Bergin *et al.* (2004) examine the effects of a €20/tCO_2 carbon tax. A number of revenue-recycling options are considered and contrasted against a ten-year no-tax baseline scenario. With lower taxes on labour, it is found, a double dividend would be achieved.[9] Though the effect would be smaller, the same is true for a reduction in VAT. This results in lower nominal wages to the point that it offsets the adverse impact on competitiveness. Though not modelled, a cut in VAT is generally progressive.

Wissema and Dellink (2007) construct a CGE model for Ireland, based on 1998 data. They find that a carbon tax just above €10/tCO_2 could reduce emissions by some 25 per cent, with little impact on overall welfare (less than 1 per cent for a €30/tCO_2 tax). Substitution between capital and energy is indicated as a critical factor. Wissema (2007) augments the same model by allowing for unemployment and endogenous labour supply and pairs carbon taxation with revenue recycling. She finds lower indirect taxes bring about only a 'weak double dividend',[10] whereas a strong negative welfare result is associated with lower labour taxes. This result is due to the loss in households' leisure, which in a context of almost full employment is necessary to meet higher labour demand.

Conefrey *et al.* (2008) again use HERMES, but in a different way this time. They consider a €20/tCO_2 tax, but instead of using a dynamic no-tax baseline scenario, they maintain the economic structure fixed at its 2005 level. This way, they can isolate the equilibrium effects of the tax from any other unrelated changes in the economy – effectively, more a CGE type of exercise. Two recycling options are considered, namely household transfers and lower income taxes. Only with the latter, a double dividend is likely. International competitiveness of manufacturing and services is the main channel through which the hypothesized tax reforms affect the economy. The impact on emissions turns out to be very limited: a reduction of around 2 per cent at most.

Turning to the works focused on distributional implications, Scott (1992) finds that the first-round effects of a carbon tax would be markedly regressive.[11] This conclusion is based on the pattern of fuel consumption across household income deciles as it emerges from the 1987 HBS. Scott and Eakins (2004) repeat the work with more recent data and obtain similar results. O'Donoghue (1997), in addition, captures the indirect impact of the tax (through the higher cost of living, not only fuel prices) combining HBS data and input-output analysis. As in other similar studies, the tax burden is borne more equally by households once the indirect impact is taken into account. Callan *et al.* (2009) and Verde and Tol (2009) are in the spirit of Scott and Eakins (2004) and O'Donoghue (1997), respectively. However, though the approach remains partial equilibrium, they add revenue recycling. This is done by using a micro-simulation tax-benefit model, SWITCH. The two studies, which draw on the same data, conclude that the most equitable way to compensate households is through a modest increase in a mix of welfare payments.

Finally, a few other applied works are partially related to the literature just recalled. Among these, Healy (2003) and Scott *et al.* (2008), who deal with fuel poverty – an issue of concern in Ireland; Leahy *et al.* (2009), who look at the spatial incidence of carbon taxation; Boyle (2000) and a study of Indecon (2002), which focus on the impact of carbon taxation across industries.

3 The G-EMH model

The GTAP model is a most popular multi-regional CGE model of the global economy. Originally created to analyse the economic effects of trade liberalization, it is operated with data compiled by a team of researchers with base at Purdue University.[12] With reference to a given year, the GTAP database collects input-output tables, bilateral trade data and tariff data for most countries in the world; it also provides values for all of the model's parameters as well as data on greenhouse gas emissions. In its most recent version, which refers to 2007, the GTAP database comprises 129 regions, 57 production sectors, or goods (each sector only produces one good), and five primary factors.[13]

A number of adaptations of the GTAP model have been developed over the years in order to better address specific issues. Among these are GTAP-E (Burniaux and Truong 2002; McDougall and Golub 2007), which was created to analyse the effects of energy and climate policies, and GTAP-MH (Gotor and Tsigas 2011), which introduces multiple households. G-EMH is a new variant that has been developed expressly for this study precisely by merging GTAP-E and GTAP-MH. It is therefore the first to allow distributional analyses of energy and climate policies.

In this section, G-EMH is presented. As both GTAP-E and GTAP-MH are already illustrated in the respective papers, the focus here is on the features that characterise G-EMH relative to the two original models.

'E': energy

The GTAP-E model modifies the production structure of the standard GTAP model so as to more closely mimic the ability of firms to substitute among alternative fuels and between primary factors and energy. It also incorporates CO_2 emissions from the combustion of fossil fuels as well as mechanisms to model regional carbon taxes and international emissions trading. Figure 8.1a shows GTAP-E's multi-tier Constant Elasticity of Substitution (CES) production function. Each nest is identified by one parameter, σ, which represents the elasticity of substitution between pairs of inputs.[14,15] The CES reduces to the Leontief and Cobb-Douglas functions if the elasticity of substitution is equal to 0 and 1, respectively. Thus, in GTAP-E, primary factors and energy, on the one hand, and intermediate inputs, on the other, combine in fixed proportions (Leontief). By contrast, some degree of substitutability is allowed at all other levels (Burniaux and Truong 2002). These elasticities can vary across both sectors and regions.[16]

G-EMH keeps GTAP-E's production structure as just described, but adds some detail to the electricity nest. As Figure 8.1b shows, two levels are added to the CES structure in order to allow for different types of electricity technologies. Specifically, wind and hydro are separated from all other sources (fossil fuels, nuclear, other renewables, etc.) to isolate the positive impact carbon pricing is expected to have on the former.[17] While a more detailed disaggregation of the electricity sector would be feasible and desirable in certain applications, it would not make the results of this study much more interesting. This is because the sum of wind and hydro already makes up most of total renewable electricity in Ireland (93 per cent, in 2004). At the same time, adding technologies requires a considerable amount of extra work because, for each technology, specific estimates of production functions (i.e., the shares of capital, labour, services, etc., in total costs) and unit production costs ($/kWh) are needed.[18] For wind and hydro, these estimates were found in Bosello *et al.* (2011). The values therein were thus used, together with electricity output data published by the International Energy Agency. Figure 8.2 shows the production functions (as shares of total costs) of wind and hydro, derived specifically for Ireland. Moreover, each nest needs its own elasticity of substitution. The values 2 and 0.5, between 'non-intermittent' and wind, and between hydro and 'other electricity', respectively, were taken from Bosello *et al.* (2011) too. They reflect the idea that wind more than hydro has the potential to expand if relative prices are tilted by carbon pricing. At the same time, 2 is a sufficiently low value to prevent unrealistic responses of the wind sector.[19]

The same representation of electricity applies to household and government demand functions, which are identical (Figure 8.3). This is not the case in GTAP-E or standard GTAP, where household demand is governed by the Constant Difference of Elasticities (CDE) function. One nice property of the CDE function is that it is non-homothetic. That is, the budget shares change with income level. To keep the CDE function, however, we would have had to recalibrate it for each household to the respective elasticities (to be estimated, in turn, in a previous stage). We thus preferred to use the simpler CES functional form for household demand too.

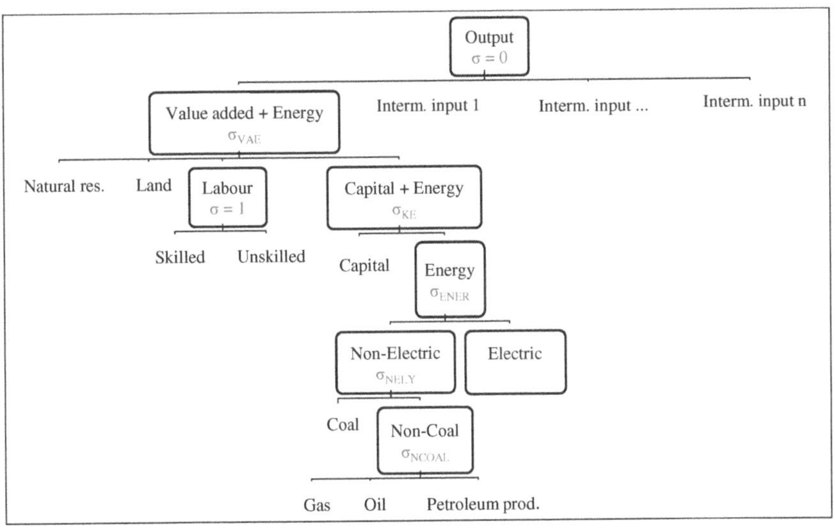

Figure 8.1a Industries' demand in GTAP-E

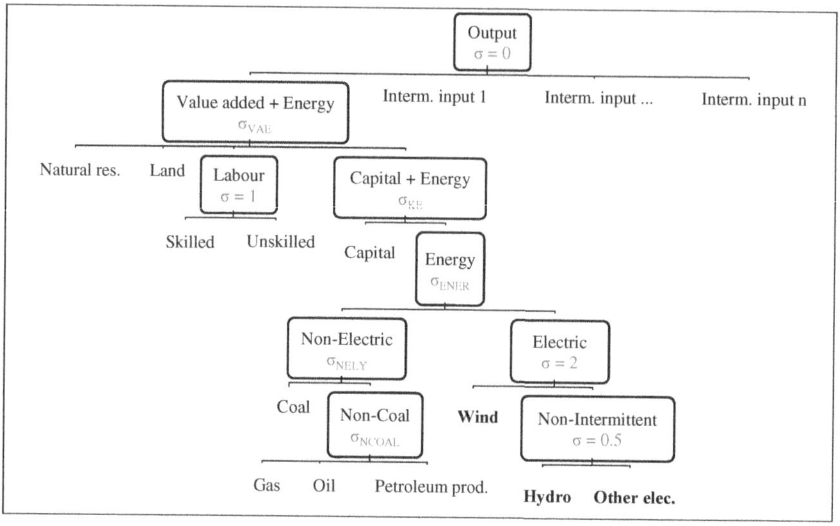

Figure 8.1b Industries' demand in G-EMH

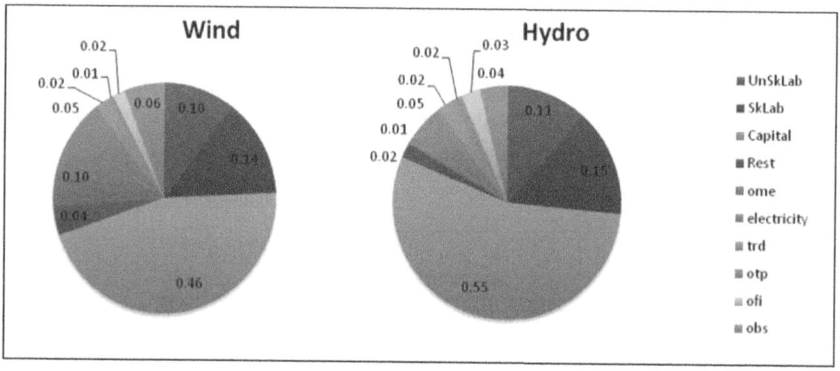

Figure 8.2 Wind and hydro's production functions

Legend: (1) *UnSkLab* – Unskilled labour; (2) *SkLab* – Skilled labour; (3) Capital; (4) Rest; (5) *ome* – Other machinery and equipment; (6) Electricity; (7) *trd* – Trade; (8) *otp* – Land transport; (9) *ofi* – Financial services; (10) *obs* – Business services.

'MH': multiple households

The standard GTAP model only has one representative household. Therefore, distributional analysis is not viable. Gotor and Tsigas (2011) introduce multiple households. Effectively, they keep the theoretical structure of the standard GTAP model (McDougall 2003) and replicate it by the number of households. Regional flows are partitioned accordingly, but totals are preserved so that more information and rebalancing of the GTAP input-output table are not needed.

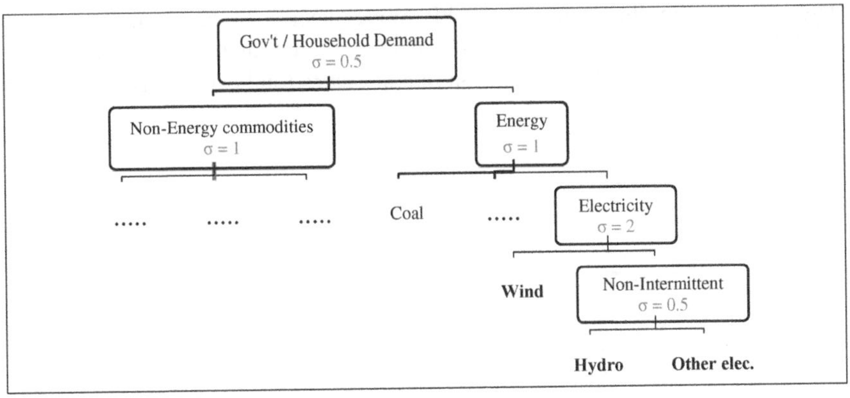

Figure 8.3 Government and household demand in G-EMH

Some fundamental equations

The income identity is central to the model, as it establishes the duality of households as consumers and income recipients. Each household has its own sources of income, which consist of net returns to primary factors, *EVOA*,[20] and 'net tax transfers', *NetTaxTr*. On the uses side, incomes are fully allocated to private commodities, *PRIVEXP*, government services, *GOVEXP*, and savings, *SAVE*. In GTAP notation,

$$\sum_{e \in ENDW} EVOA_{er}^{h} - VDEP_{r}^{h} + NetTaxTr_{r}^{h} \equiv Y_{r}^{h}$$

$$\equiv \sum_{i \in TRAD} PRIVEXP_{ir}^{h} + GOVEXP_{ir}^{h} + SAVE_{r}^{h} \qquad [1]$$

$$\forall h \in HH, \forall r \in REG$$

where *ENDW* is the set of primary factors; *TRAD* is the set of tradable goods; *HH* is the set of households; *REG* is the set of regions; *VDEP* is capital depreciation; *h* and *r* denote the household and region, respectively.

The sums over households of *GOVEXP* and *SAVE* correspond to 'government spending' and 'gross domestic savings' in national accounts.[21] The sum of households' incomes, *Y*, is equal to 'net domestic product' (GDP net of capital depreciation). In operational terms, private expenditure and earned income can be ascribed to households based on national household surveys. As for *GOVEXP* and *SAVE*, we imputed the first in equal amounts and the second in proportion to households' income.

The sum of net tax transfers, *NetTaxTr*, which are given by the difference between total income and net factor income, equals the sum of all tax revenues.

These, which in the standard GTAP model accrue to regional income, in GTAP-MH accrue to households in different, fixed shares, *NetTaxTrSh*. We illustrate this point with the equation that allocates total carbon tax revenues to households:

$$CTAX_r^h = NetTaxTrSh_r^h \times \left[\left(\sum_{h \in HH} \sum_{i \in TRAD} DPCTAX_{ir}^h + IPCTAX_{ir}^h + DGCTAX_{ir}^h + IGCTAX_{ir}^h \right) + \left(\sum_{i \in TRAD} \sum_{j \in PROD} DFCTAX_{ir}^j + IFCTAX_{ir}^j \right) \right] \quad [2]$$

$$\forall h \in HH, \forall r \in REG$$

where the total yield of the carbon tax (the sum in square brackets) stems from households' (*P*), government's (*G*) and firms'(*F*) consumption both of domestic produce (*D*) and imports (*I*).

Another fundamental equation is the one that determines the percentage change in each household's income, y^h. This is how it looks (small letters denote percentage change variables, capital letters indicate level variables):

$$y_r^h = \begin{bmatrix} FY_r^h \times fy_r^h + \\ 100 \times Y_r^h \times del\_inctaxr_r^h + INCTAX_r^h \times y_r^h + \\ 100 \times Y_r^h \times del\_indtaxr_r^h + INDTAX_r^h \times y_r^h + \\ 100 \times Y_r^h \times del\_co2taxr_r^h + CTAX_r^h \times y_r^h + \\ Y_r^h \times incomeslack_r^h \end{bmatrix} / Y_r^h \quad [3]$$

$$\forall h \in HH, \forall r \in REG$$

where the first four lines in brackets are, in this order, (a) the change in total net factor income, and the changes in revenues from (b) income taxes, (c) indirect taxes and (d) carbon taxation; *del_inctaxr*, *del_indtaxr* and *del_co2taxr* are the changes (non-percentage) in the respective revenue-to-income ratios, and *Y* is the income level.

Income distribution is altered whenever percentage income changes are not identical for all households. Differences across households in the relative importance of different income sources, including household transfers, are therefore at the root of endogenous variations in income distribution. For example, for a given increase in the return on capital, households who rely on capital income relatively more than others will benefit in greater proportion too. It follows that the accuracy of simulation results critically depends on how well the breakdown of income data, by household and source, approximates the actual distribution.

The last fundamental equation we look at is the clearing condition for the labour market. In our simulations, we adopt the standard assumption of GTAP whereby labour supply is fixed.[22] The clearing condition implies that labour is perfectly mobile across sectors. The same is true for capital. We thus have:

$$\sum_{h \in HH} RESSHARE_{er}^{h} \times qoe_{er}^{h} = \sum_{j \in PROD} SHREM_{ejr} \times qfe_{ejr} + endwslack_{er} \qquad [4]$$

$$\forall e \in ENDWM, \forall r \in REG$$

where $RESSHARE_{er}^{h}$ is the share of endowment e supplied by h; qoe_{er}^{h} is the percentage change in h's supply of e; $SHREM_{ejr}$ is the share of e employed by sector j; qfe_{ejr} is the percentage change in j's demand for e; $ENDWM$ is the set of mobile endowments (i.e., unskilled labour, skilled labour and capital).

The non-resident household

As pointed out just above, the accuracy of simulation results critically depends on how well the breakdown of income, by household and source, approximates the actual distribution. The large number of multinationals operating in Ireland means a significant share of capital income is earned by non-residents. In 2004, the base year in this application, Ireland's GNP was about 14 per cent smaller than GDP. Ignoring this fact would affect the simulation results, as a consequence of the fact that the derived income shares would not reflect the actual composition of households' income. We therefore address this issue by adding a fictional household, 'HHNR', whose sole function is to absorb the share of capital income earned by non-residents. This expedient, not used in previous applications of GTAP-MH, is neutral to the structure of the model. That is, it does not require any alteration of the model's equations.

4 Data

Regions, sectors and primary factors

Version 7 of the GTAP database (Narayanan and Walmsley 2008), which depicts the global economy in 2004, is used in this study. Five regions, 25 sectors and five primary factors are considered. Both the sectoral and regional aggregations reflect the fact that the study is centred on Ireland. As the UK, Europe and North America are Ireland's main trading partners, each of them constitutes a separate region in the model – Ireland and 'Rest of the World' being the remaining two. Similarly, the sectoral aggregation is based on Ireland's most energy-intensive and export-oriented industries. As regards the endowments, or primary factors, these are land, unskilled labour, skilled labour, capital and natural resources. Table 8.1 shows the aggregation of regions, sectors and primary factors used in our application.

To help anticipate the incidence of carbon pricing across the sectors – although, for space reasons, sectoral effects are not addressed in the results section – Figures

Table 8.1 Aggregation of sectors, regions and primary factors

Sectors	*Regions*	*Factors*
Fishing	Ireland	Land
Coal	UK	Unskilled labour
Oil	Rest of Europe	Skilled labour
Gas	North America	Capital
Mining	Rest of the world	Natural resources
Dairy products		
Other food products		
Petroleum, coal products		
Chemical, rubber, plastic products		
Manufacture of non-metallic mineral products		
Manufacture of non-ferrous metals		
Electronic equipment		
Other machinery and equipment		
Electricity – hydro		
Electricity – wind		
Electricity – other		
Trade		
Land transport		
Water transport		
Air transport		
Financial services		
Insurance		
Business services		
Public administration and defence, health, education		
Rest		

Note: See Narayanan and Walmsley (2008, ch. 2) for details on the GTAP database.

8.4a–8.4c show the respective (a) CO_2 emissions, (b) emissions intensity and (c) the share of electricity in total costs, as they appear in the GTAP database. Emissions correspond to the direct use of fossil fuels, but sectors for which electricity is an important production factor are also vulnerable to carbon pricing, to the extent that the latter impacts on electricity prices. To identify which sectors will suffer the biggest increases in production costs through this channel, Figure 8.4c shows the shares of electricity in total costs. Furthermore, Table 8.2 shows the breakdown, by fuel, of Irish industries' and households' CO_2 emissions. Three-fourths of them are caused by industries, one fourth by households.

Households

Each region comprises eleven households. The number is the same in all regions only for practical convenience.[23] For Ireland, they represent the income deciles and the eleventh, HHNR, acts for the non-resident population. For all other regions, the breakdown of the household sector is only fictional, in the sense that the eleven households are identical. This by no means affects the simulation results pertaining

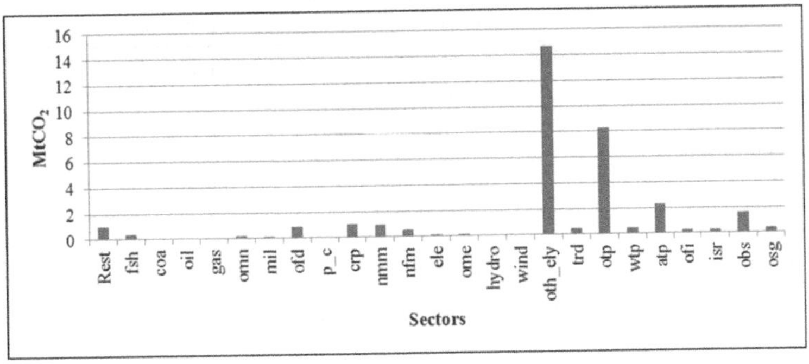

Figure 8.4a Irish industries' emissions; $MtCO_2$

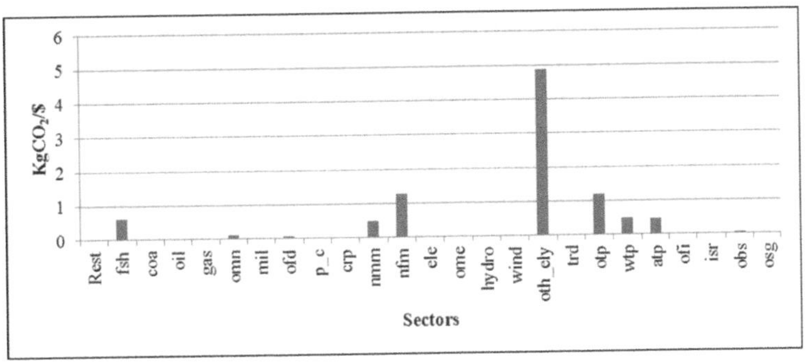

Figure 8.4b Irish industries' emissions intensities; $KgCO_2$/$

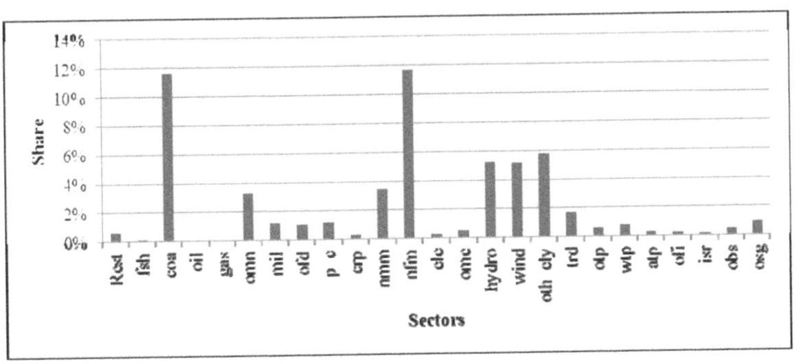

Figure 8.4c Share of electricity in total costs of Irish industries; per cent

Legend: fsh – Fishing; *coa* – Coal; *oil* – Oil; *gas* – Gas; *omn* – Mining; *mil* – Dairy production; *ofd* – Other food; *p_c* – Petroleum, coal production; *crp* – Chemical, rubber, plastic production; *nmm* – Manufacture of non-metallic mineral prod.; *nfm* – Manufacture of non-ferrous metals; *ele* – Electronic equipment; *ome* – Other machinery and equipment; *hydro* – Hydro; *wind* – Wind; *oth_ely* – Other electricity; *trd* – Trade; *otp* – Land transport; *wtp* – Water transport; *atp* – Air transport; *ofi* – Financial services; *isr* – Insurance; *obs* – Business services; *osg* – Public administration and defence, Health, Educ.; *Rest*.

Table 8.2 Emissions by user and fuel; $MtCO_2$

Fuel	*Industries*	*Households*	*Total*
Coal	6.9	1.7	8.6
Oil	0.0	0.0	0.0
Gas	7.4	1.7	9.1
Petroleum products	19.7	8.2	27.9
Total	33.9	11.6	45.6

to Ireland, nor aggregate ones of the other regions. If all of a region's households are identical, aggregate results are the same as if there was only one representative household.[24]

Uses and sources of income

In order to split Ireland's GTAP data by household income decile, income sources and consumption items of the 2004–5 HBS were first mapped to GTAP's factor and commodity classifications. Expenditure and income flows were then disaggregated by decile by applying the respective shares. On the sources side of income, labour income was classified by skill level (skilled, unskilled) according to the profession of the head of household.[25] Capital income was determined by subtracting total labour income from total earned income, as the difference is largely self-employed income and asset income. Rents from land and natural resources were imputed using capital income shares, as the survey contains too little information on those. All sources of income that are not tied to a factor, such as pension payments or household transfers, fall in 'net tax transfers', *NetTaxTr*.

In the absence of suitable statistics from national accounts, the amount of capital income allocated to the non-resident household was determined as follows. In the HBS, which contemplates only residents, capital income earned by all households is a third of labour income. Then, assuming labour income in GTAP is earned entirely by residents, a third of that amount is the capital income that can be attributed to those. This meant 26 per cent of capital income was imputed to resident households, while the rest, 74 per cent, went to the non-resident household.[26]

Table 8.3 reports Ireland's shares of earned income by factor, as found in the GTAP database. Table 8.4 shows the distribution of earned income, by factor and household, as we derived it based on the HBS.

Table 8.3 Earned income by factor; per cent

Factor	*Share of earned income*
Land	0.6
Unskilled labour	25.2
Skilled labour	18.4
Capital	55.6
Natural resources	0.2
Total	100.0

Table 8.4 Distribution of earned income by factor and household; per cent

Factor	*HH1*	*HH2*	*HH3*	*HH4*	*HH5*	*HH6*	*HH7*	*HH8*	*HH9*	*HH10*	*HHNR*	*Total*
Land	0.6	0.4	0.8	1.6	2.2	2.2	3.1	3.3	3.8	7.9	74.0	100.0
Unskilled labour	1.1	1.2	2.9	7.0	9.5	13.0	13.9	16.8	17.9	16.7	0.0	100.0
Skilled labour	0.2	0.3	1.0	2.2	5.6	6.3	11.5	14.2	19.7	38.9	0.0	100.0
Capital	0.6	0.4	0.8	1.6	2.2	2.2	3.1	3.3	3.8	7.9	74.0	100.0
Natural resources	0.6	0.4	0.8	1.6	2.2	2.2	3.1	3.3	3.8	7.9	74.0	100.0

Table 8.5, instead, shows the breakdown of GDP, by household and source. These shares indicate the relative importance of different income sources, for different households. For example, a given increase in the return to capital income is for the richest decile almost twice as important as for the ninth decile, and nine times as important as for the first decile. By the same token, a given change in net tax transfers (non-factor income) is for the first decile almost three times as important as for the tenth decile.

On the uses side of income, as the HBS does not specify the origin of the items purchased, it was assumed that if, for instance, the sixth decile counted for 12 per cent of total household demand for dairy products, the same share applied equally to imported and domestically produced dairy products. Government expenditure and savings, as already said, were distributed in equal amounts and in proportion to income, respectively.[27]

5 Model closure and simulation scenarios

In CGE jargon, the 'closure' refers to the choice of which variables are exogenous to the model and which are endogenous – all the others. The one or more variables that are 'shocked' to simulate a given scenario must be exogenous; all other exogenous variables remain unchanged throughout the simulation.[28] As the model's equations represent an economic system, the closure is intended to reflect economic reasoning. We adopt the standard closure of the GTAP model, whereby primary factors, policy variables, technical change variables and population are exogenous; prices, quantities of commodities and incomes are endogenous.[29]

The five scenarios we simulate have in common the introduction of a \$20/tCO_2 carbon tax in Ireland, applied to all emissions with no exemptions for any fuel or sector. The scenarios only differ one from another with respect to revenue recycling. In the first, the total yield of the carbon tax is returned to households in the form of transfer payments. Such a scheme is aimed at offsetting the regressive impact of carbon taxation. In the other four scenarios, the carbon tax is accompanied by a reduction in one (only) of the existing taxes. In theory, the more distortionary the tax (that is cut) is, the greater the positive effect on GDP will be. At the same time, the given tax cut will impact on income distribution depending on its specific incidence on households' sources and uses of income. The tax breaks we considered recur in the double dividend literature and, specifically, regard: (a) final consumption, (b) labour, (c) labour income and (d) capital income. All of them are endogenously determined, under the constraint of revenue neutrality.[30] More information on the different scenarios is given below.

Household transfers, 'TRANSF'

In the first scenario, the total yield of the carbon tax is fully redistributed to households via transfer payments. Different households receive transfers in different amounts, which correspond to the *NetTaxTrSh* shares.[31] The scheme is not strictly

Table 8.5 Distribution of income sources (GDP) by household; per cent

Source	*HH1*	*HH2*	*HH3*	*HH4*	*HH5*	*HH6*	*HH7*	*HH8*	*HH9*	*HH10*	*HHNR*
Net tax transfers	0.95	0.95	0.90	0.81	0.74	0.69	0.63	0.58	0.52	0.32	0.00
Land	0.00	0.00	0.00	0.00	0.00	0.00	0.00	0.00	0.00	0.00	0.00
Unskilled labour	0.02	0.02	0.05	0.11	0.13	0.18	0.17	0.20	0.21	0.18	0.00
Skilled labour	0.00	0.00	0.01	0.02	0.06	0.06	0.10	0.12	0.17	0.30	0.00
Capital	0.03	0.03	0.05	0.08	0.10	0.10	0.12	0.13	0.14	0.27	1.00
Natural resources	0.00	0.00	0.00	0.00	0.00	0.00	0.00	0.00	0.00	0.00	0.00
Total	1.00	1.00	1.00	1.00	1.00	1.00	1.00	1.00	1.00	1.00	1.00

revenue neutral, because the share of total tax revenues in GDP can change in the new equilibrium.[32] As low-income households rely on transfer income relatively more than better-off ones, this scheme should mitigate, at the least, the likely regressive impact of the tax. Indeed, this will be the case if the share of total revenues in GDP – revenues that are redistributed – rises; vice versa, it will exacerbate regressiveness. The first outcome is deemed more likely because the reform is merely redistributive and does not include measures that clearly favour economic growth.

Private consumption, 'VAT'

In this scenario, the total yield of the carbon tax is fully used to finance a uniform cut in the tax on private consumption. This tax reform, on the one hand, affects the demand for CO_2-related energy; on the other, it incentivizes consumption. Because the carbon tax poses an incentive to substitute non-energy commodities for energy commodities, as well as renewable electricity for conventional electricity, and since fossil fuels are largely imported, it is conceivable that this reform may have a limited or even a positive impact on the economy. As regards distributional effects, the tax cut, similar to one in VAT, should mitigate the impact of carbon pricing on the cost of living. However, as energy still gets more expensive, the net impact may well remain regressive.

Cost of labour, 'LABFACT'

In this scenario, the total yield of the carbon tax is fully used to finance a uniform cut in the tax on labour. Thus, this reform reduces the cost of labour as a production factor. While it will not be sufficient to fully compensate energy-intensive industries for the extra cost of the carbon tax, labour-intensive sectors may reap a net benefit. This reform incentivizes labour demand, but, crucially, labour supply is fixed in our model. As a result, the reduction in labour taxes does not affect employment, but only raises nominal wages. Under these circumstances, we have no reason to expect an increase in GDP. Households who earn greater shares of their income from labour will benefit more than others, in relative terms.

Labour income, 'LABINC'

In this scenario, the total yield of the carbon tax is fully used to finance a uniform cut in the tax on labour income. Microeconomic theory tells us that a reduction in the tax of labour income should induce an expansion on labour supply. In our model, however, labour supply is fixed. Therefore, 'by construction' no gain, in the form of greater employment, can be achieved. As in the previous scenario, households who earn greater shares of their income from labour will benefit more than others, in relative terms. Only, this time not because wages are pushed up by higher labour demand, but as a result of lower direct taxation. This and the previous scenario mainly differ with respect to sectoral effects: in *LABFACT*, the tax cut favours labour intensive sectors and then translates into higher wages; in *LABINC*, the tax cut simply means higher net wages.

Capital income, 'CAPINC'

In the final scenario, the total yield of the carbon tax is entirely used to finance a uniform cut in the tax on capital income. All the rest staying the same, a cut in the tax of capital income raises the return on capital and it thus attracts investment, both domestic and from overseas. If the capital inflow is sufficiently large, a double dividend in the form of greater GDP may arise. In any case, households who rely on capital income relatively more than others will get proportionally greater benefits in this scenario. The majority of capital income, however, does not accrue to the resident population.

6 Simulation results

This section presents the results, for Ireland, of the five scenarios just described. Given the sizeable amount of output, the analysis is focused on a few variables of interest. Emissions abatement and macroeconomic effects are first examined. We then turn our attention to distributional effects.

Emissions abatement and macroeconomic effects

The simulated carbon tax is environmentally effective, as the fall in CO_2 emissions ranges from 10.9 per cent to 11.1 per cent across the five scenarios. Accordingly, the yield of tax in the new equilibrium, which is negatively related to emissions reduction (emissions are the base of the carbon tax), ranges between $811.2m and $809.3m.[33] These results and the others discussed in this paragraph are found in Table 8.6.

Table 8.6 Macroeconomic effects and emissions abatement

Variables *% change if not differently specified*	*Scenarios* *TRANSF*	 *VAT*	 *LABFACT*	 *LABINC*	 *CAPINC*
Real GDP	–0.22	–0.18	–0.22	–0.21	–0.11
Nominal GDP	0.06	–0.30	0.06	0.10	0.20
GPD deflator	0.28	–0.12	0.28	0.31	0.31
Gini coefficient	–0.92	0.02	0.04	0.06	0.01
CO_2 emissions	–11.1	–10.9	–11.1	–11.0	–11.1
Carbon tax revenue ($m)	809.5	811.2	809.5	810.6	809.3
Nominal wage, unskilled	–0.08	–0.07	0.59	–0.02	–0.01
Nominal wage, skilled	0.04	–0.03	0.71	0.14	0.05
Investment	–1.14	–1.09	–1.14	–1.15	0.69
Current return on capital	–0.80	–0.76	–0.80	–0.81	0.49
Exports' volume	–0.14	–0.18	–0.14	–0.25	–0.26
Trade balance, change ($m)	297.3	87.0	286.9	85.9	–76.3
Imports value, change ($m)	–453.0	–301.3	–447.1	–381.0	–237.5
Exports value, change ($m)	–155.7	–214.4	–160.2	–295.1	–313.8

Note: In the calculation of the Gini coefficient, the non-resident household was not considered.

Higher economic growth – and, thus, a double dividend – is not achieved under any of the five scenarios. On the whole, the deterioration of international competitiveness prevails on the effects of the measures accompanying the carbon tax. This result, however, strongly depends on the specific structure of the model, which critically assumes full employment. The full employment assumption is acceptable for 2004 Ireland, but not for today's Ireland.[34] Moreover, it ignores the fact that, historically, Ireland's labour force is very elastic through migration (Bergin and Kearney 2007, Conefrey *et al.* 2008).

The most favourable outcomes for real GDP are obtained by lowering taxes on capital income (–0.11%) and private consumption (–0.18%), respectively; to follow, the GDP impacts are virtually the same under *TRANSF* (–0.22%), *LABFACT* (–0.22%) and *LABINC* (–0.21%). *CAPINC* comes on top because the rate of return on capital rises (0.49%) and thereby attracts substantial investment (0.69%). The positive effect of the reform, however, largely goes to the advantage of the non-resident. Besides, international competitiveness deteriorates the most under *CAPINC*, as the fall in exports' volume shows (–0.26%). As regards the labour market, because labour supply is fixed, changes in labour demand are fully absorbed through wages. Wage increases, both for skilled and unskilled labour, stand out in the *LABFACT* scenario. Moreover, in all the scenarios wage changes for skilled labour are more favourable than those for unskilled labour. This is because less CO_2 intensive productions, notably renewable electricity, require skilled labour more than unskilled labour.

The percentage change in the Gini coefficient measures the impact on income distribution. The coefficient itself (in levels) ranges between 0 and 1, the two values representing perfect equality and perfect concentration, respectively. Therefore, a negative variation indicates a move towards a more even distribution; vice versa, it indicates greater inequality. In the calculation of the Gini coefficient, the non-resident household was not considered; that is, the coefficient measures income dispersion over the resident population.[35] It turns out that only in one case, under the *TRANSF* scenario, the distribution of income becomes more even (–0.92%). This is because the yield of the carbon tax adds to the resources redistributed to households and low-income households rely on non-factor income relatively more than others. In the other scenarios, the change in the Gini coefficient is positive, but very small. This is because the tax breaks directly (*LABINC*, *CAPINC*) or indirectly (*VAT*, *LABFACT*) favour labour or capital income, the importance of which increases with income level. The Gini coefficient, however, measures the impact on the distribution of nominal income, while carbon pricing affects the cost of living in the first place. In the next paragraph, we thus take account of differences in the composition of consumption, which in turn determine different impacts in real terms.

Distributional effects

Figure 8.5 shows, for the five scenarios, the percentage changes in household income across the ten households (resident) representative of the income deciles.

A positively inclined curve indicates that the impact of the reform is regressive; vice versa, the impact is progressive. The results for nominal GDP and the Gini coefficient, in Table 8.6, reflect the position (height) and the slope, respectively, of these curves.[36] What this graph does not tell us is the impact of carbon pricing on the cost of living. We captured this by constructing household-specific consumer price indices (part of the model), which reflect the composition, or pattern, of consumption. The percentage variations in these price indices, under the five scenarios, are shown in Table 8.7.[37] When deflating household nominal income using these indices, Figure 8.5 completely changes.[38] When a carbon tax is introduced, low-income households face higher inflation than richer ones do, because consumption by the first is more carbon intensive (Verde and Tol 2009). As a result, all the five curves in Figure 8.5 rotate upwards. The incidence of carbon pricing from virtually neutral becomes regressive; only, in the *TRANSF* scenario,

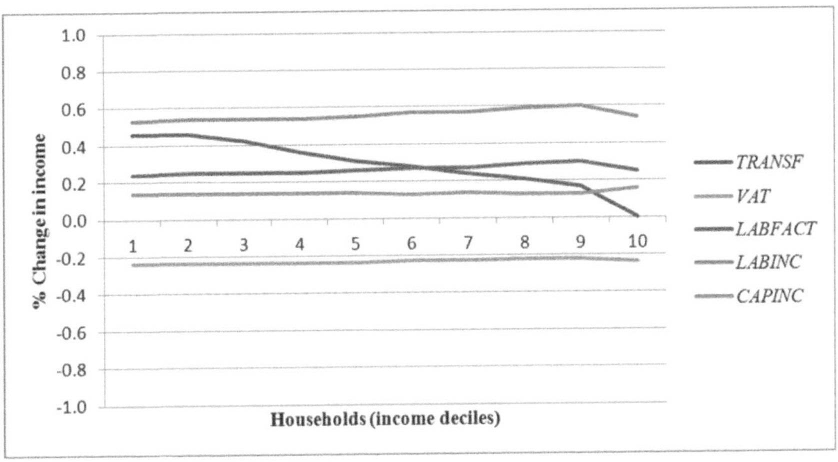

Figure 8.5 Impacts on nominal income across income distribution

Table 8.7 Consumer price index by income decile, per cent changes

Household	*Scenarios*				
	TRANSF	*VAT*	*LABFACT*	*LABINC*	*CAPINC*
1	0.74	–0.30	0.74	0.75	0.75
2	0.74	–0.29	0.74	0.76	0.76
3	0.69	–0.35	0.69	0.70	0.70
4	0.64	–0.40	0.64	0.65	0.65
5	0.60	–0.43	0.60	0.62	0.62
6	0.59	–0.44	0.59	0.61	0.61
7	0.54	–0.50	0.54	0.56	0.55
8	0.50	–0.53	0.50	0.52	0.52
9	0.50	–0.53	0.50	0.52	0.52
10	0.44	–0.60	0.44	0.46	0.46

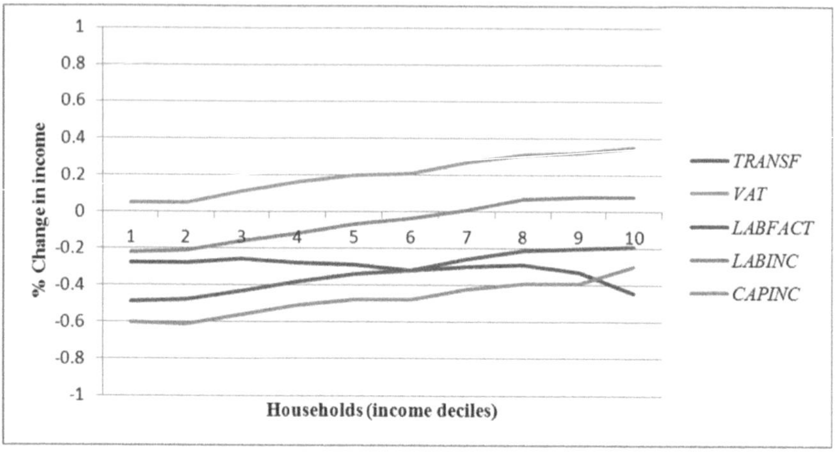

Figure 8.6 Impacts on real income (CPI adjusted nominal income) across income distribution

from clearly progressive it becomes almost neutral. At the same time, the positions (heights) of the curves change too, highlighting the difference between variations in nominal and real income.

Some conclusions can be drawn on the basis of this evidence. First, the answer to our original research question, as to whether carbon pricing without revenue recycling is regressive in the medium term, would be 'yes'. Indeed, only if the proceeds of carbon pricing are redistributed to households through transfer payments – only in that case – the overall impact on real incomes is virtually neutral on income distribution. Without redistribution, the overall impact would be regressive. Second, pairing the carbon tax with a lower tax rate on private consumption would make all households (resident) better off than under any of the other scenarios – the *VAT* curve, in Figure 8.6, lies entirely above the others. In a policy maker's perspective, the always controversial question of trade-off between efficiency and equity would not really arise. Whether the policy maker implicitly adopted a Utilitarian or a Rawlsian social welfare function, in either case *VAT* would be the most preferable scheme among those we considered.

7 Conclusions

Using CGE analysis, we simulated the medium-term impact of a \$20/tCO_2 carbon tax on the Irish economy, under five different revenue-recycling scenarios. Two main research questions have been addressed, namely (a) whether carbon pricing, without revenue recycling, is regressive, and (b) how the recycling schemes considered compare with respect to their impacts on economic growth and income distribution.

The work adds to a still limited literature in which economy-wide models are used for distributional analyses of energy and climate policies. In this sense, it is the first application to Irish data. A CGE model with multiple representative households, combining two different versions of the GTAP model (Hertel 1997), GTAP-E (Burniaux and Truong 2002; McDougall and Golub 2007) and GTAP-MH (Gotor and Tsigas 2011), was expressly created for this study. Thus, part of its contribution is also a new tool, the applicability of which is vast, considering the growing interest in the field as well as the popularity and the flexibility of GTAP.

In response to the first research question, we found that the impact of carbon pricing, in Ireland, is regressive over the medium term. Only if the proceeds of the carbon tax are redistributed to households through progressive transfers is the impact on real incomes virtually neutral. Without redistribution, the overall impact is regressive. In the medium term as well, the distributional impact of carbon pricing thus remains an issue to be addressed. For that, revenue recycling offers a number of options.

We have considered five alternatives for revenue recycling: (a) progressive household transfers, and lower taxes on (b) consumption, (c) labour, (d) labour income and (e) capital income. The carbon tax per se proved to be environmentally effective, as CO_2 emissions fell by 10.7 per cent to 11.1 per cent across the five scenarios. None of the recycling schemes, however, produced the second dividend, intended as a positive effect on real GDP. The least negative impact on GDP was achieved by reducing the tax on capital income (–0.11%); to follow, a cut of the tax on consumption (–0.18%), and then the three remaining schemes, which were virtually equivalent (–0.21%, –0.22%). In relation to these results, two remarks are in order. First, a lower tax on capital income attracts investment, but a large part of the benefit is not reaped by resident households. Second, the two schemes whereby taxes on labour and labour income are cut are neutralised by the fact that labour supply, in the model, is fixed. Thus, 'by construction', they cannot possibly induce higher employment, but instead they determine higher net wages. They effectively act as transfer payments to the benefit of those who already have a job.

The four recycling schemes which involve tax cuts turned out to be virtually equivalent in terms of the degree of regressiveness, or relative effects across income distribution. They did differ, though, in the magnitude and even the sign of those effects. In principle, a higher GDP results in a higher level of household income. In the scenario where the tax on capital income is lowered, however, a large part of the benefit does not end to the resident, as was previously pointed out. As a result, the average impact on households across income distribution was in fact more adverse than in all other scenarios. By contrast, a lower tax on consumption turned out to make all households across income distribution better off than under any of the other scenarios.

These results are of course contingent, at least in some measure, both on the data and on the model that produced them. A number of improvements of the model can be thought of, but two of them seem particularly desirable for this type of analysis. First, endogenising labour supply. This is needed to allow for typical double dividend scenarios, where labour supply responds to environmental tax reform according to the labour-leisure choice model. Second, making the model dynamic. We have made the point that a higher GDP may not result in better-off households, if capital is largely owned by non-residents. The model we used, however, is static, in that new investment does not become productive. If it did, as it does in dynamic models, investment may benefit resident households through higher labour demand.

Appendix

Table A1 CES elasticities in production structure

Sector	*Elasticities of substitution*						
	VAE	*KE*	*ENER*	*NELY*	*NCOAL*	*ESUBD*	*ESUBM*
Rest	1.17	0.5	1	0.5	1	2.58	6.3
fsh	0.2	0.5	1	0.5	1	1.25	2.5
coa	0.2	0	0	0	0	3.05	6.1
oil	0.2	0	0	0	0	5.2	10.4
gas	0.65	0	0	0	0	10.77	32.49
omn	0.2	0.5	1	0.5	1	0.9	1.8
mil	1.12	0.5	1	0.5	1	3.65	7.3
ofd	1.12	0.5	1	0.5	1	2	4
p_c	1.26	0	0	0	0	2.1	4.2
crp	1.26	0.5	1	0.5	1	3.3	6.6
nmm	1.26	0.5	1	0.5	1	2.9	5.8
nfm	1.26	0.5	1	0.5	1	4.2	8.4
ele	1.26	0.5	1	0.5	1	4.4	8.8
ome	1.26	0.5	1	0.5	1	4.05	8.1
hydro	1.26	0.5	1	0.5	1	2.8	5.6
wind	1.26	0.5	1	0.5	1	2.8	5.6
oth_ely	1.26	0.5	1	0.5	1	2.8	5.6
trd	1.68	0.5	1	0.5	1	1.9	3.8
otp	1.68	0.5	1	0.5	1	1.9	3.8
wtp	1.68	0.5	1	0.5	1	1.9	3.8
atp	1.68	0.5	1	0.5	1	1.9	3.8
ofi	1.26	0.5	1	0.5	1	1.9	3.8
isr	1.26	0.5	1	0.5	1	1.9	3.8
obs	1.26	0.5	1	0.5	1	1.9	3.8
osg	1.26	0.5	1	0.5	1	1.9	3.8

Note: *VAE*: CES primary factors; *KE*: CES capital – energy; *ENER*: CES non-electricity – electricity; *NELY*: CES coal – non-coal; *NCOAL*: CES gas, oil and petroleum production; *ESUBD*: CES domestic – import (Armington); *ESUBM*: CES import – import (Armington).

Legend: *fsh* – Fishing; *coa* – Coal; *oil* – Oil; *gas* – Gas; *omn* – Mining; *mil* – Dairy production; *ofd* – Other food; *p_c* – Petroleum, coal production; *crp* – Chemical, rubber, plastic production; *nmm* – Manufacture of non-metallic mineral products; *nfm* – Manufacture of non-ferrous metals; *ele* – Electronic equipment; *ome* – Other machinery and equipment; *hydro* – Hydro; *wind* – Wind; *oth_ely* – Other electricity; *trd* – Trade; *otp* – Land transport; *wtp* – Water transport; *atp* – Air transport; *ofi* – Financial services; *isr* – Insurance; *obs* – Business services; *osg* – Public administration and defence, Health, Education; *Rest*.

Table A2 Irish households' budget shares

Share	*HH1*	*HH2*	*HH3*	*HH4*	*HH5*	*HH6*	*HH7*	*HH8*	*HH9*	*HH10*
ely	2.5	2.3	2.0	1.9	1.7	1.7	1.5	1.4	1.3	1.1
Rest	36.1	38.9	36.6	33.8	35.1	35.0	33.8	34.0	33.6	39.5
fsh	0.3	0.3	0.4	0.3	0.2	0.3	0.3	0.3	0.2	0.3
coa	0.2	0.3	0.2	0.1	0.1	0.1	0.1	0.0	0.0	0.0
oil	0.0	0.0	0.0	0.0	0.0	0.0	0.0	0.0	0.0	0.0
gas	0.2	0.3	0.2	0.2	0.2	0.2	0.2	0.2	0.2	0.2
omn	0.3	0.3	0.3	0.3	0.3	0.3	0.3	0.3	0.3	0.3
mil	4.0	4.0	3.8	3.1	3.0	2.7	2.5	2.1	1.9	1.6
ofd	13.6	14.6	13.0	11.4	10.8	9.9	8.9	7.5	6.8	5.9
p_c	4.3	3.8	4.5	4.6	4.4	4.5	4.2	3.8	3.9	3.2
crp	4.2	4.0	4.0	4.4	4.1	4.0	4.2	3.9	4.2	3.3
nmm	0.4	0.7	0.3	0.5	0.6	0.4	0.7	0.8	0.7	1.0
nfm	0.0	0.0	0.0	0.0	0.0	0.0	0.0	0.0	0.0	0.0
ele	1.6	1.5	1.3	1.6	1.4	1.5	1.8	1.6	1.4	1.7
ome	1.6	1.3	1.8	1.5	1.7	2.1	1.4	1.4	1.4	1.3
trd	6.4	6.7	6.6	7.9	7.9	8.5	8.7	9.3	9.0	9.0
otp	2.3	1.4	1.7	2.1	2.1	2.1	2.1	2.2	2.4	2.1
wtp	0.2	0.2	0.2	0.1	0.2	0.2	0.1	0.1	0.1	0.2
atp	1.8	2.0	1.8	1.7	1.8	1.8	1.7	1.7	1.7	2.0
ofi	3.8	4.1	3.8	3.5	3.7	3.7	3.5	3.6	3.5	4.1
isr	2.3	2.4	2.5	3.0	3.7	3.7	3.9	4.3	4.7	5.6
obs	8.2	6.4	10.3	12.7	10.0	10.2	12.5	13.2	14.6	10.7
osg	5.9	4.6	4.7	5.5	7.2	7.4	7.8	8.4	8.1	7.2
Total	100	100	100	100	100	100	100	100	100	100

Legend: *fsh* – Fishing; *coa* – Coal; *oil* – Oil; *gas* – Gas; *omn* – Mining; *mil* – Dairy production; *ofd* – Other food; *p_c* – Petroleum, coal production; *crp* – Chemical, rubber, plastic production; *nmm* – Manufacture of non-metallic mineral products; *nfm* – Manufacture of non-ferrous metals; *ele* – Electronic equipment; *ome* – Other machinery and equipment; *ely* – Electricity; *trd* – Trade; *otp* – Land transport; *wtp* – Water transport; *atp* – Air transport; *ofi* – Financial services; *isr* – Insurance; *obs* – Business services; *osg* – Public administration and defence, Health, Education; *Rest*.

Table A3 Closure and closure swaps (tax break scenarios)

Exogenous variables	
pop	Population
ams atm atf ats atd aosec aoreg afcom afsec afreg afall aoall atall	Technical change variables
to tp tm tms tx txs tf tfd tfm tgd tgm tpd tpm toe te tl tll tk	Policy variables
qoe(ENDWNL_COMM,hhlds,REG)	Supply of non-labour endowments
pfactwld	World price of endowments – Numeraire
tradslack endwslack cgdslack profitslack incomeslack psaveslack	Slack variables
au dppriv dpgov dpsave	Distribution parameters
NCTAXB pemp	Carbon tax rate; power of emissions purchases (for emissions trading)
*All other variables endogenous	
Scenario	Swap exogenized var. = endogenized var.
VAT	*del_totaltaxr("IRL") = tp("IRL")*
LABFACT	*del_totaltaxr("IRL") = tl("IRL")*
LABINC	*del_totaltaxr("IRL") = tll("IRL")*
CAPINC	*del_totaltaxr("IRL") = tk("IRL")*

Notes

1 Acknowledgements: I am indebted to Marinos Tsigas and Elisabetta Gotor for sharing with me the code their GTAP variant for multiple households. I am grateful to Alla Golub and Terrie Walmsley for their technical advice. Many thanks also to both Richard Tol, for conceiving and supervising this study, and Denny Ellerman, for his comments.

2 The EU ETS covers conventional electricity generation, mineral oil refinement, production and processing of ferrous metals, mineral industries and pulp and paper industries. In Ireland, the EU ETS sector accounts for about 45 per cent of total CO_2 emissions and 30 per centof total greenhouse gas emissions.

3 'Carbon pricing' is a sufficiently generic term to indicate both carbon taxes and cap-and-trade systems, when the differences between the two need not be considered.

4 Goulder (1995), Bovenberg (1999) and Ballard *et al.* (2005), among others, survey this literature. For a critical perspective, see Fullerton (1999).

5 Early works are those of Pechman (1985) and Poterba (1991). Many more have followed. See Speck (1999) for a then up-to-date literature review; see Fullerton (2009) for a selection of papers.

6 See Decaluwé *et al.* (1999) for a survey of this literature.

7 Thus, only between-group variation is captured, while within-group variation is ignored.

8 The first sub-problem consists in finding general equilibrium prices, household demand being replaced by a single representative agent. The second sub-problem computes partial equilibrium quantities demanded by each of the 15,588 households, given candidate general equilibrium prices. The algorithm finds the equilibrium of the underlying economy if the sequence of general equilibrium prices and partial equilibrium quantities converge to the true equilibrium prices and quantities.

9 FitzGerald and McCoy (1992) had obtained the same result.

10 Weak double dividend means the change in welfare is preferable compared to what is obtained by returning the revenues in a lump-sum fashion.

11 The analysis of first-round effects is based on two assumptions: demand and supply are perfectly inelastic; the tax is fully shifted onto the consumer.

12 See Hertel (1997) and Narayanan and Walmsley (2008) for the GTAP model and database, respectively. More information and resources can be found on the website www.gtap.agecon.purdue.edu/.

13 GTAP users then aggregate regions, sectors and primary factors according to their needs.

14 Multi-tier CES production functions are popular in CGE modelling, as they require only few parameters. They represent separable, constant returns to scale technologies.

15 The Armington elasticities and the respective CES tiers (two) are not shown in this chart and the next one.

16 Table A1, in the Appendix, shows the values used in our application. They vary across sectors (to some extent), not across regions.

17 SplitCom, a GTAP utility program, was used to separate wind and hydro from generic electricity in the GTAP database.

18 GTAP flows are expressed in monetary value ($m). Hence, unit production costs of electricity are needed in order to convert physical data of electricity generation into monetary values. Only then it is possible to split the relevant GTAP flows.

19 It is understood that, in consumption, renewable and conventional electricity are perfect substitutes ($\sigma = \infty$). The modelling of renewable electricity as described is indeed an ad hoc solution: it 'works' empirically, but a treatment more consistent with the theory is desirable.

20 In GTAP notation, EVOA stands for Endowment Value of Output at Agents' prices.

21 Gross domestic savings is given by the sum of households', firms' and government's savings. The GTAP database does not distinguish between these.

22 Making labour supply endogenous (for instance, by linking it to the real wage and the unemployment rate) would be a useful development of the model.
23 In this sense, the model is symmetric. This limitation can be overcome, if needed. It would not require any fundamental change in the model, but only some tedious program coding.
24 This expedient may be useful for future applications as no additional information is needed for the regions whose distributional implications are not of interest and which nonetheless the modeller wishes to include in the model.
25 As the model assumes perfect mobility of labour (and capital) across production sectors, there was no need to split labour further by sector.
26 One recurring problem with survey data is under-reporting of capital income. Thus, the allocation of capital income to the non-resident household, in the way described, may potentially be vitiated by this issue. It is the case, however, that the income of the non-resident household represents 19 per cent of GDP, while the difference between GDP and GNP ('Net factor income from abroad', in national accounts), for the year in question (2004), amounts to 14 per cent of GDP. Therefore, the discrepancy between the income share allocated to the non-resident household and the actual one can only be smaller than 5 percentage points, since GNP also includes incomes received by Irish residents from overseas.
27 The approach was different for the non-resident household. Savings were determined by setting them equal to capital income, and fractions (0.01 per cent) of private and government expenditures were conceded to make the model computationally solvable.
28 For the closure to be valid the number of endogenous variables must be equal to the number of equations and, also, the exogenous variables must be independent (not linked by equations).
29 Table A3, in the Appendix, reports the full closure.
30 This is implemented with 'closure swaps': the share of total tax revenues in GDP is made exogenous and held constant, while the given tax rate is made endogenous.
31 In the GTAP model, government's and households' decisions are not separated and the database does not provide information on household transfers.
32 Technically, we cannot hold the share in question constant, as we do instead in the other scenarios.
33 This makes about 0.9 per cent of all tax revenues.
34 Until the beginning of 2008, Ireland's unemployment rate was below 5 per cent. Then, as a result of the economic crisis, it went up quickly and reached 15per cent, in 2010. It is now (first half of 2013) around 13.5 per cent (source: Eurostat).
35 In fact, in this application, it is the dispersion of GNP, spread across resident households as per equation [1].
36 The percentage change in nominal GDP is the weighted average of these values (however, including that of the non-resident household).
37 The Irish HBS, and household surveys in general, allow depicting consumption patterns in good detail. The indices derived, in Table 8.7, can thus be regarded with justified confidence.
38 In CGE models, price changes are real changes (non-nominal) relative to inflation.

References

Ballard, C.L., J.H. Goddeeris and S.K. Kim (2005), 'Non-Homothetic Preferences and the Non-Environmental Effects of Environmental Taxes', *International Tax and Public Finance*, 12, 115–130.

Beckman, J., T. Hertel and W. Tyner (2011), 'Validating Energy-Oriented CGE Models', *Energy Economics*, 33(5), 799–806.

Bergin, A. and I. Kearney (2007), 'Human Capital Accumulation in an Open Labour Market: Ireland in the 1990s', *Economic Modelling*, 24, 839–858.

Bergin, A., J. FitzGerald and I. Kearney (2004), *The Macro-Economic Effects of Using Fiscal Instruments to Reduce Greenhouse Gas Emissions*, Wexford (Ireland): Environmental Protection Agency.

Bosello, F., L. Campagnolo, F. Eboli, R. Parrado and E. Portale (2011), 'Extending Energy Portfolio with Clean Technologies in the ICES Model', GTAP 2011 Conference paper.

Bourguignon, F. and L. Savard (2008), 'Distributional Effects of Trade Reform: An Integrated Macro-Micro Model Applied to the Philippines', in F. Bourguignon, M. Bussolo and L.A. Pereira da Silva (eds) *The Impact of Macroeconomic Policies on Poverty and Income Distribution – Macro-Micro Evaluation Techniques and Tools*, Washington, DC: World Bank.

Bovenberg, L. (1999), 'Green Tax Reforms and the Double Dividend: an Updated Reader's Guide', *International Tax and Public Finance*, 6, 421–443.

Boyle, G. (2000), *The Competitiveness and Environmental Impact of Energy Taxation on Irish Industry*, Dublin: Irish Business Employers Confederation.

Burniaux, J.M. and T.P. Truong (2002), 'GTAP-E: An Energy-Environmental Version of the GTAP Model', GTAP Technical Paper No. 16.

Callan, T., S. Lyons, S. Scott, R.S.J. Tol and S.F. Verde (2009), 'The Distributional Implications of a Carbon Tax in Ireland', *Energy Policy*, 37(2), 407–412.

CARB (California Air Resources Board) (2010), 'Updated Economic Analysis of California's Climate Change Scoping Plan', Staff Report to the Air Resources Board.

Conefrey, T., J.D. FitzGerald, L. Malaguzzi Valeri and R.S.J. Tol (2008), 'The Impact of a Carbon Tax on Economic Growth and Carbon Dioxide Emissions in Ireland', Working Paper No. 251, Dublin: Economic and Social Research Institute.

Decaluwé, B., J.C. Dumont and L. Savard (1999), 'Measuring Poverty and Inequality in a Computable General Equilibrium Model', Cahier de recherche du CRÉFA, No. 99–20.

FitzGerald, J. and D. McCoy (1992), 'Economic Effects of Carbon Taxes', Policy Research Series, 14, Dublin: Economic and Social Research Institute.

Fullerton, D. (1999), 'The Irrelevance of the Double Dividend', *Proceedings of the National Tax Association, November 1998*, National Tax Association.

Fullerton, D. (ed.) (2009), *Distributional Effects of Environmental and Energy Policy*, Aldershot: Ashgate.

Gotor, E. and M.E. Tsigas (2011), 'The Impact of the EU Sugar Trade Reform on Poor Households in Developing Countries: A General Equilibrium Analysis', *Journal of Policy Modeling*, 33, 568–582.

Goulder, L.H. (1995), 'Environmental Taxation and the "Double Dividend": A Reader's Guide', *International Tax and Public Finance*, 2, 157–183.

Healy, J. (2003), 'Fuel Poverty and Policy in Ireland and the European Union', Studies in Public Policy No. 12, Dublin: The Policy Institute, Trinity College Dublin in association with the Combat Poverty Agency.

Hertel, T.W. (ed.) (1997), *Global Trade Analysis Project: Modeling and Applications*, New York: Cambridge University Press.

Indecon (2002), 'Competitiveness of the Enterprise Sector and the Use of Taxation and Negotiated Agreements for Reducing Greenhouse Gas Emissions in Ireland', Dublin: Forfás.

Jorgenson, D.W., D.T. Slesnick and P.J. Wilcoxen (1992), 'Carbon Taxes and Economic Welfare', *Brookings Papers on Economic Activity: Microeconomics 1992*, 393–431.

Jorgenson, D., R. Goettle, M.S. Ho, D.T. Slesnick and P.J. Wilcoxen (2010), 'The Distributional Impact of Climate Policy', *The B.E. Journal of Economic Analysis & Policy*, 10(2) (Symposium), Article 17.

Leahy, E., S. Lyons, E.L.W. Morgenroth and R.S.J. Tol (2009), 'The Spatial Incidence of a Carbon Tax in Ireland', Working Paper FNU-174, Research Unit Sustainability and Global Change, Hamburg University.

McDougall, R. (2003), 'A New Regional Household Demand System for GTAP', GTAP Technical Paper No. 20.

McDougall, R. and A. Golub (2007), 'GTAP-E: A Revised Energy-Environmental Version of the GTAP Model', GTAP Research Memorandum No. 15.

Narayanan, B.G. and T.L. Walmsley (eds) (2008), 'Global Trade, Assistance, and Production: The GTAP 7 Data Base', Center for Global Trade Analysis, Purdue University.

O'Donoghue, C. (1997), 'Carbon Dioxide, Energy Taxes, and Household Income', Working Paper No. 90, Dublin: Economic and Social Research Institute.

Oladosu, G. and A. Rose (2007), 'Income Distribution Impacts of Climate Change Mitigation Policy in the Susquehanna River Basin Economy', *Energy Economics*, 29(3), 520–544.

Pechman, J. (1985), *Who Paid the Taxes, 1966–85?*, Washington, DC: The Brookings Institution,.

Poterba, J.M. (1991), 'Is the Gasoline Tax Regressive?', NBER Working Papers No. 3578.

Rausch, S., G.E. Metcalf, J.M. Reilly, and S. Paltsev (2010), 'Distributional Implications of Alternative U.S. Greenhouse Gas Control Measures', *The B.E. Journal of Economic Analysis and Policy*, 10(2) (Symposium), Article 1.

Rausch, S., G.E. Metcalf, J.M. Reilly and S. Paltsev (2011a), 'Distributional Impacts of a U.S. Greenhouse Gas Policy: A General Equilibrium Analysis of Carbon Pricing', in G. Metcalf (ed.) *U.S. Energy Tax Policy*, Cambridge: Cambridge University Press.

Rausch, S., G.E. Metcalf and J.M. Reilly (2011b), 'Distributional Impacts of Carbon Pricing: A General Equilibrium Approach with Micro-Data for Households', NBER Working Paper No. 17087.

Rose, A., D. Wei and F. Prager (2012), 'Distributional Impacts of Greenhouse Gas Emissions Trading: Alternative Allocation and Recycling Strategies in California', *Contemporary Economic Policy*, 30(4), 603–617.

Roson, R. (2003), 'Climate Change Policies and Tax Recycling Schemes: Simulations with a Dynamic General Equilibrium Model of the Italian Economy', *Review of Urban & Regional Development Studies*, 15, 26–44.

Rutherford, T.F. and D. Tarr (2008), 'Poverty Effects of Russia's WTO Accession: Modeling "Real" Households with Endogenous Productivity Effects', *Journal of International Economics*, 75, 131–150.

Scott, S. (1992), 'Theoretical Considerations and Estimates of the Effects on Households', in J.D. FitzGerald and D. McCoy (eds), *The Economic Effects of Carbon Taxes*, Policy Research Paper, 14, Dublin: Economic and Social Research Institute.

Scott, S. and J. Eakins (2004), 'Carbon Taxes: Which Households Gain or Lose?', ERTDI Report Series 20, Wexford (Ireland): Environmental Protection Agency.

Scott, S., S. Lyons, C. Keane, D. McCarthy and R.S.J. Tol (2008), 'Fuel Poverty in Ireland: Extent, Affected Groups and Policy Issues', Working Paper No. 262, Dublin: Economic and Social Research Institute.

Speck, S. (1999), 'Energy and Carbon Taxes and Their Distributional Implications'. *Energy Policy*, 27, 659–667.

Van Heerden, J., R. Gerlagh, J. Blignaut, M. Horridge, S. Hess, R. Mabugu and M. Mabugu (2006), 'Searching for Triple Dividends in South Africa: Fighting CO2 Pollution and Poverty While Promoting Growth', *The Energy Journal*, 27, 113–141.

Verde, S.F. and R.S.J. Tol (2009), 'The Distributional Impact of a Carbon Tax in Ireland', *The Economic and Social Review*, 40(3), 317–338.

Wissema, W. (2007), 'Carbon Energy Taxation and Revenue Recycling – An Applied General Equilibrium Analysis for the Irish Economy', PhD thesis, Department of Economics, Trinity College Dublin.

Wissema, W. and R. Dellink (2007), 'Age Analysis of the Impact of a Carbon Energy Tax on the Irish Economy', *Ecological Economics*, 61, 671–683.

Yusuf, A.A. and B. Resosudarmo (2007), 'On the Distributional Effect of Carbon Tax in Developing Countries: The Case of Indonesia', Working Paper in Economics and Development Studies No.200705, Department of Economics, Padjadjaran University.

Part IV

The role of fairness and distributional weights in environmental public goods provision

9 Distributional weights in cost-benefit analysis

Should we forget about them?

Olof Johansson-Stenman

Many argue that it is socially inefficient to use distributional weights in cost-benefit analysis, and that doing so implies large inefficiency losses, when distributional matters can be dealt with through income taxation, instead. Our results question this view, by showing a large range of cases when distributional weights are (second-best) optimal to use. One example is when different provided goods affect tax-revenues equally per dollar spent; utility functions that are separable in the provided goods is sufficient for this. Most results hold for linear and non-linear income taxes and whether they are optimal or not. General policy implications are discussed.

1 Introduction

Cost-benefit analysis (CBA) constitutes a direct link from economic analysis to recommendations for political decisionmakers. Despite this, or perhaps because of this, CBA remains highly controversial. One of the most important reasons is the common practice of focusing solely on efficiency, by simply comparing aggregate maximum willingness to pay (WTP) figures with costs.[1] Indeed, from the political debate, it is clear that distributional matters are often extremely important, especially concerning environmental issues.

However, the current efficiency-only practice is in no way self-evident. Indeed, Alfred Marshall in his inaugural lecture at Cambridge argued that "taking account of the fact that the same sum of money measures a greater pleasure for the poor than for the rich," when computing benefits of various changes is a "task [that] most properly belongs to the economic organ." (Marshall 1885,31). Moreover, distributional concern as reflected by distributional weights were a rather central component of the project appraisal manuals of the seventies, such as Dasgupta, Marglin, and Sen (1972), Little and Mirrlees (1974) and Squire and van der Tak (1975), even though they became gradually less fashionable over time as described by Little and Mirrlees (1991). This is, for example, reflected by the current practice of the World Bank, which in most cases does not use any explicit distributional weights in its CBA.[2] Similarly, recent advanced textbooks in environmental economics, such as Hanley, Shogren, and White (1997) and Freeman (2003), focus very little on distributional concerns, at least within generations.

Despite this, it is still not difficult to find proponents of distributional weighted CBA; see, for example, Dreze and Stern (1987) and Dreze (1998). It is also worth noting that the main financial decisionmaking body in the United Kingdom, H.M. Treasury, has recently, for the first time officially endorsed distributional weights in CBA; the details can be found in their Green Book (H.M. Treasury 2003).

The rationale behind distributional weights are typically based on differences in the social marginal utility of income, that is, the (assumed) fact that one dollar to the poor increases social welfare more than one dollar does to the rich. To illustrate this, consider the frequently used assumptions of a utilitarian social welfare function (SWF) in a society with n individuals, so that $W = U^1 + U^2 + \ldots + U^n$, and that each individual has a utility function characterized by constant relative risk aversion, so that the utility function can be written as $U = y^{1-\sigma}/(1-\sigma)$, where σ is the Arrow-Pratt parameter of relative risk aversion.[3] In social welfare analysis, σ is often seen to reflect social inequality aversion as well; see, for example, Christiansen and Jansen (1978). This implies that the (social) marginal utility of income is given by $U_y = y^{-\sigma}$, and hence, that the monetary benefit for a poor person in the welfare analysis should be given the relative weight of $(y^{rich}/y^{poor})^{\sigma}$ compared to the benefit to the rich. According to Dasgupta (1998), empirical evidence based on choice under uncertainty suggests that σ is around 2 on average, or slightly larger, which is also consistent with questionnaire-experimental evidence by Johansson-Stenman, Carlsson, and Daruvala (2002). Blanchard and Fischer (1989, 44) report that results based on intertemporal choices vary greatly, but are often around or larger than unity. If we assume that $\sigma = 2$, then the benefit to a person who is 100 times richer than another person should be given a weight of only $1/100^2$, that is, 1/10,000, relative to the poor. Obviously, the outcome of the CBA can then be very different with and without weights, for projects that particularly benefit either the rich or the poor.[4]

However, given that equity aspects are intrinsically important, it is still not obvious that one should apply distributional weights in CBA. One may instead, following Harberger (1978), argue that it is more efficient to focus solely on efficiency in CBA and leave distributional considerations to income taxation. A seminal theoretical contribution is due to Hylland and Zeckhauser (1979), authors of "Distributional Objectives Should Affect Taxes But Not Program Choice or Design." They showed that under optimal non-linear taxation and a specific utility formulation (identical for all individuals), which is weakly separable between private and public goods on one hand and leisure on the other, it is indeed optimal to use the basic Samuelson (1954) rule saying that the sum of individual marginal rates of substitution equals the marginal rate of transformation ($MRS = MRT$) between the publicly provided good and a numeraire (such as private income). Hence, given what may seem to be a reasonable preference structure, it is optimal *not* to adjust for distributional concerns (and not for incentive effects either); Christiansen (1981) and Boadway and Keen (1993) have further generalized this result.[5] Moreover, using a utility formulation similar to Hylland and Zeckhauser, Shavell (1981) derived conditions when no distributional concern should be taken in legal rule-making, in a model where people choose their own amount of care to avoid accidents.[6] Another way to express these results is that, for a given degree of inequality, the overall economic pie in terms of social welfare is larger if distributional concerns are dealt with solely through income taxation, compared to a situation where they are also dealt with through public provisions of goods, given the underlying assumptions.

While most of this theoretical literature rarely discusses policy implications outside the specific assumptions made, recently a number of papers and textbooks, including Kaplow and Shavell (1994, 2000), Kaplow (1996, 2004), Frank (2000), Ng (2000a, 2000b), and Frank and Bernanke (2001), have argued more generally against the use of distributional weights in CBA as well as in legal decision-making, based on the premise that such weights make the economic pie smaller. The underlying fundamental theoretical arguments in these contributions can be traced back to the Hylland and Zeckhauser (1979) and Christiansen (1981) papers. A crucial issue, however, is whether we really can say that the economic pie would typically be smaller if we used distributional weights in CBA. As will be shown, we cannot generally do that, and sometimes the pie will even be larger with such weights.

From a policy perspective it is, of course, not sufficient to find clear results under special assumptions, which one typically knows are not strictly fulfilled anyway, but rather aim at gaining information about roughly *how* valid the results are in the real world. For example, if the separability assumptions do not hold, can we then say anything general about distributional concern in CBA? Or, in the example above, can we say, given that we can use income taxation to deal with equity, that the theoretically appropriate weights given to rich and poor people would most likely not differ by more than, say, a factor of 5, unless we make very unreasonable or counterintuitive assumptions?

To analyze distributional concerns in CBA outside the special assumption used by Hylland and Zeckhauser (1979) and followers is the main purpose of this paper. A more specific aim is to investigate whether distributional concerns are warranted in CBA, and if so, to what extent, for the natural benchmark case when different publicly provided goods affect tax revenues, through possible induced labor supply adjustments, equally much per dollar spent on each good. As demonstrated in Section 2, it turns out that distributional weights are warranted then, and that the weights should be inversely related to the social marginal utility of income, implying that they will vary largely with income for empirically realistic values of individual risk aversion. A sufficient condition for this is that utility is separable in the publicly provided goods, instead of in leisure. These results hold for a wide range of tax structures, including poll taxes and linear, piece-wise linear, and nonlinear income taxes, and regardless of whether the taxes are optimal or not.[7] The different separability assumptions are compared in Section 3, and it is argued that there is little substantial basis to argue that one separability structure is more plausible than the other as a general benchmark case. Moreover, it is concluded that using distributional weights is always optimal, irrespective of specific preference structures, unless there are differences in induced tax revenue effects between the goods that work in the direction of off-setting the distributional welfare effects.

In Section 4, we discuss cases that may seem to imply contradictions with earlier theoretical results. First, we analyze strong (additive) separability in the publicly provided goods, which is a case studied by Boadway and Keen (1993). They showed that the condition for when the good should be over-provided relative to the Samuelson rule is independent of the distributional characteristics of the good. Second, we analyze a particular functional form discussed by Kaplow (1996), where both types of weak separability hold *simultaneously*. Since strong separability implies weak separability, it seems that for both of these cases we should simultaneously apply, and not apply, distributional weights, which seems to imply a contradiction. However, as will be shown, this is an illusion since for both of these special cases the marginal WTP for all public goods will vary with income in an identical manner, so that applying weights will make no difference in terms of allocations. Consequently, the allocation would be exactly the same with and without weights in these special cases, implying both that distributional weights are redundant and that they are harmless in terms of efficiency losses. Section 5 summarizes and discusses the results in general within a broader policy context.

2 Choosing between public projects

As the theoretical point of departure, we will use a standard public economics setup in the tradition of Mirrlees (1971), where the government's objective is to maximize a general Bergson-Samuelson SWF:

$$w(U^1, U^2, \ldots, U^n), \qquad [1]$$

subject to a public budget constraint, w is assumed to be increasing and weakly quasi-concave in its arguments, that is, the individual utilities, where U^i is utility for individual i.[8] The government chooses the amount to provide of m different goods (or more generally projects, they need not be pure public goods), such as environmental goods, with different distributional characteristics; some may be preferred mainly by poor people and some by the rich. To simplify presentation, it is assumed that the production technology for these goods is linear, so that the production prices of these goods are fixed. Individuals get utility from private consumption x and leisure l in addition to the publicly provided goods:

$$U^i = u^i (x^i, l^i, G_1, \ldots, G_m). \qquad [2]$$

Individual i's gross income is given by a^iL^i, where a^i is the exogenously given "ability" or productivity, which in equilibrium can be seen as the net wage level, and L^i is the chosen amount of working time to supply. Naturally, the total available amount of time, ω, is limited so that

$$l^i = \omega - L^i. \qquad [3]$$

The individual's consumption is given by the gross income minus the income tax $T(a^iL^i)$, where the tax function T is piece wise continuously differentiable. Thus we have

$$x^i = a^iL^i - T(a^iL^i). \quad [4]$$

At this stage we do not need to specify the tax function T further – it may be optimal or non-optimal, linear, piecewise linear, or non-linear. However, it is essential that the tax can be related only to gross income, and it is assumed to be impossible for the government to directly observe the individual ability or wage level as is standard in the optimal taxation literature. Consequently, we have a second-best problem where the individual choice of working time (and hence leisure) is generally not socially optimal. Substituting [3] and [4] into [2] we get

$$U^i = u^i(a^iL^i - T(a^iL^i), \omega - L^i, G_1, \ldots, G_m), \quad [5]$$

implying the following individual optimum condition with respect to the choice of L:

$$\frac{\partial u^i}{\partial x^i} a^i(1-t^i) = \frac{\partial u^i}{\partial l^i}, \quad [6]$$

where $t^i \equiv \partial T/\partial(a^iL^i)$ is i's marginal tax rate.

The government's objective is to maximize social welfare, that is, eq. [1], subject to an exogenous public budget balance requirement R_0 (which can take any value, including zero), implying the following Lagrangean:

$$w(U^1, \ldots, U^n) + \lambda(\Sigma_i T(a^iL^i) - \Sigma_j p_j G_j - R_0, \quad [7]$$

where p_j is the production price of good j. The social first order optimum condition for the provision of an arbitrary good 1 is then given by

$$\Sigma_i \frac{\partial w}{\partial U^i}\frac{\partial u^i}{\partial G_1} + \lambda\left(\Sigma_i t^i a^i \frac{\partial L^i}{\partial G_1} - p_1\right) = 0, \quad [8]$$

which can be re-written as

$$\Sigma_i \alpha^i MRS^i G_{1x} = \lambda(p_1 - \partial R/\partial G_1), \quad [9]$$

where $\alpha^i = \frac{\partial w}{\partial U^i}\frac{\partial u^i}{\partial x^i}$ is the social marginal utility of income,[9] that is, how much an additional dollar of consumption to individual i contributes to social welfare; $MRS^i_{G_1x} \equiv \frac{\partial u^i}{\partial G_1} / \frac{\partial u^i}{\partial x^i}$ is individual i's marginal rate of substitution between the publicly provided good 1 and x^i (i.e. the marginal willingness to pay for good 1 in terms of x^i); and where we denote $\frac{\partial R}{\partial G_1} = \Sigma_i t^i a^i \frac{\partial L^i}{\partial G_1}$, the induced revenue effect caused by good 1, that is, how much the tax revenues change due to the induced changes in the supplied labor of a marginal increase in the provision of good 1. Combining the first order conditions for goods 1 and 2 then implies

$$\frac{\Sigma_i \alpha^i MRS^i_{G_1x}}{p_1 - \partial R / \partial G_1} = \frac{\Sigma_i \alpha^i MRS^i_{G_2x}}{p_2 - \partial R / \partial G_2} \qquad [10]$$

This result can be compared with the basic first-best Samuelson (1954) rule implying that

$$\frac{\Sigma_i MRS^i_{G_1x}}{p_1} = \frac{\Sigma_i MRS^i_{G_2x}}{p_2} \qquad [11]$$

Thus, we have two deviations from the basic Samuelson rule. The rationale behind the α-factors is straightforward: Since one additional dollar to a poor individual typically implies more social welfare, *ceteris paribus*, than one additional dollar to a rich individual, we need the α-factors as conversion factors, or distributional weights, to correspondingly translate the monetary marginal WTP measures into social welfare units.

The rationale behind the additional term in the denominators is almost as straightforward: Equation [6] implies that each individual (who is working a non-zero amount) on the margin will be indifferent between working one more hour or not. However, the income tax drives a wedge between the private optimum and the social optimum. If individual i works one more hour, the society obtains an additional tax revenue equal to $t^i a^i$, which is of course beneficial for the society as a whole. Hence, the society prefers each individual, on the margin, to work more.[10] Consequently, a marginal increase in the public provision of good 1 implies, for a given tax schedule, that the tax revenues change with $\frac{\partial R}{\partial G_1} = \Sigma_i t^i a^i \frac{\partial L^i}{\partial G_1}$ for the society as a whole, that is, due to the change in all individuals' supplied amount of labor. Again, the utility change of these marginal changes in working hours for each individual is zero, implying that there is no corresponding welfare costs to these tax revenues. Thus, the optimality condition [10] simply implies that the amount of social welfare obtained per unit of dollar-reduction in the social budget should be the same for each good provided. The cost in terms of dollar-reduction in the social budget for good 1, in turn, is equal to $p_1 - \partial R/\partial G_1$ that is, the production cost of good 1 minus the changes in tax revenues that the marginal provision induces.

Although distributional weights do generally seem to play a role in [10], through the α-factors in the nominators, it is not possible to generally say from this equation whether a good preferred by the poor should be over-provided relative to the other good, compared to the basic efficiency rule. The reason is that although the WTPs by the rich are multiplied by smaller a-factors, it is possible that this effect interacts with the tax-revenue effect, which we may alternatively call the efficiency effect, in terms of changes in labor supply. For example, it is possible that the good preferred by the rich induces people to work more on the margin, while the other good has the opposite effect. Whether these effects interact or not depends crucially on people's preference structure, and we will see that different commonly made preference assumptions imply very large differences in policy conclusions regarding the appropriate use of distributional weights.

Let us now consider the natural benchmark case where the tax-revenue effects are the same for per unit of dollars spent on goods 1 and 2, that is,

$$\frac{1}{p_1}\Sigma_i t^i a^i \frac{\partial L^i}{\partial G_1} = \frac{1}{p_2}\Sigma_i t^i a^i \frac{\partial L^i}{\partial G_2} \qquad [12]$$

In this case we have, from substituting [12] into [10], that

$$\frac{\Sigma_i \alpha^i MRS^i_{G_1 x}}{p_1} = \frac{\Sigma_i \alpha^i MRS^i_{G_2 x}}{p_2} \qquad [13]$$

This result implies that for any size of the public budget (optimal or not), and for any taxation system (optimal or not), we should choose the combination of G_1 and G_2 per dollar spent that contributes most to social welfare *ceteris paribus*, since there are no indirect tax-revenue effects through changed labor supply to correct for. In doing so, we need distributional weights, the α-factors, to translate the monetary units of the marginal willingness to pay measures into social welfare units.[11] That is, we need to take the fact into account that a certain WTP of a poor person reflects a higher welfare effect than the same WTP of a rich person.

Separability in publicly provided goods

A sufficient, but not necessary, condition for equal tax-revenue effects is clearly that these effects are zero for both goods, that is, both the left-hand-side and the right-hand-side of equation [12] are equal to zero. A sufficient, but not necessary, condition for this, in turn, is that these effects are zero for each individual, that is, that there are no labor supply effects of the public goods *per se*, so that $\partial L^i/\partial G_1 = \partial L^i/\partial G_2 = 0$, for all individuals. A sufficient, and necessary,[12] condition for this, in turn, is the frequently used structure where utility can be written as weakly separable in the publicly provided goods:

$$U^i = u^i(f(x^i, l^i), G_1, \ldots, G_m). \qquad [14]$$

This formulation implies that the marginal rate of substitution between leisure and private consumption is unaffected by the provision of the publicly provided goods, and the maximization of [14] for the individual simply implies the maximization of the sub-utility function $f(x^i, l^i)$, which is clearly independent of the publicly provided goods. Hence, the (uncompensated) labor supplied is also independent of these goods, so that $\partial L^i/\partial G_j = 0$ for all individuals i and public goods j, which implies that equation [13] holds. Consequently, rather than comparing the aggregate marginal willingness to pay for the public goods, we should compare the *weighted* sums, where the weights are given by the social marginal utility of income. Again, since this holds generally (given the assumed separability), it also holds for optimal non-linear income taxes. Alternatively, we can rewrite [13] to separate out the distributional effects. Using the definition of the expected value of a product, that $E(\alpha MRS) = E(\alpha)E(MRS) + \text{cov}(\alpha, MRS)$, we have that

$$\begin{aligned}&\Sigma_i \alpha^i MRS^i_{G_1x} \\ &= \Sigma_i MRS^i_{G_1x}\left(1+\text{cov}\left(\frac{\alpha}{\bar{\alpha}}, \frac{MRS_{G_1x}}{\overline{MRS_{G_1x}}}\right)\right)\bar{\alpha} \\ &= \Sigma_i MRS^i_{G_1x}(1+\delta_j)\bar{\alpha},\end{aligned} \qquad [15]$$

where an overbar denotes mean value and where

$$\delta_j = \text{cov}\left(\frac{\alpha}{\bar{\alpha}}, \frac{MRS_{G_1x}}{\overline{MRS_{G_1x}}}\right) \qquad [16]$$

is Feldstein's (1972) distributional characteristic of good j. Substituting [15] into [13] we obtain

$$\frac{\Sigma_i MRS^i_{G_1x}}{\Sigma_i MRS^i_{G_2x}} = \frac{p_1}{p_2}\frac{1+\delta_2}{1+\delta_1}. \qquad [17]$$

Hence, the ratio between the sums of the *MRS* should not equal the *MRT* ratio, that is, the production cost ratio, but rather the *MRT* ratio times an expression which compares the distributional characteristics, or the normalized covariances between the marginal willingness to pay for the public goods and the social marginal utility of income. Goods that are relatively more preferred by low-income people should then be over-provided compared to other goods, and vice versa.

It should be noted that although we allow for heterogeneity in preferences, the results hold also when the preferences are identical in the population, as shown in Appendix 1. Hence, the case for distributional weights is not driven by any implicit assumption that poor people have different preferences than the rich.

A transport example

Consider two small[13] and equally costly public projects to be compared: one improv ing the local road infrastructure, and one improving the public transport system. Both projects are assumed to influence tax revenues, through labor supply effects, about equally much. The latter project is preferred primarily by low-income people, since most high-income people will continue not to use public transport irrespective of improvements. Surveys have been undertaken to elicit people's marginal WTPs for small improvements with equal cost in these two areas, and aggregate WTP is found to be 50 percent higher for the improved road infrastructure. As is standard in survey analysis, people's incomes (net of taxes) were asked for, and the WTP income elasticities for these projects, defined as

$$\varepsilon = \frac{\partial MRS_{Gx}}{\partial x}\frac{x}{MRS_{Gx}}, \quad [18]$$

were estimated. The income elasticity was found to equal 1 for the road infrastructure investment, and 0 for the public transport investment. The after-tax income in the economy is assumed to be Gamma-distributed and given by

$$f(x) = xe^{-x}, \quad [19]$$

where $x \geq 0$, implying a Gini-coefficient of about 0.37, which is of the same order of magnitude as for many western European countries. The social welfare function is assumed to be utilitarian, and the representative utility function can be characterized by constant relative risk aversion, implying that

$$\alpha(x) = x^{-\sigma}, \quad [20]$$

where σ is the social inequality aversion, measured as individual relative risk aversion in income. Let us conservatively assume σ to equal 1.

Which project should be preferred? Given constant income elasticities, we can substitute [18–20] into a continuous version of equation [15] and write the distributional characteristic for the publicly provided good as

$$\begin{aligned}\delta &= \frac{\int_0^\infty \alpha\, MRS_{Gx} f(x)dx}{\int_0^\infty MRS_{Gx} f(x)dx \int_0^\infty f(x)dx} - 1 \\ &= \frac{\int_0^\infty x^{1+\varepsilon-\sigma}e^{-x}dx}{\int_0^\infty x^{1+\varepsilon}e^{-x}dx \int_0^\infty x^{1-\sigma}e^{-x}dx} - 1.\end{aligned} \quad [21]$$

Imposing the values for ε and σ into [21] we get that the distributional characteristics are equal to –0.5 for road infrastructure, and 0 for public transport. Imposing these values into [17], where good 1 is the local road improvement, we see that the right-hand-side ratio is equal to 2, which is larger than the aggregate marginal WTP ratio of 1.5. Thus, the road improvement is in this case less socially profitable than the public transport improvement, despite the fact that it would have been more profitable had we only considered efficiency aspects. Expressed alternatively, the size of the pie in terms of social welfare for a given degree of inequality will in this case be larger with distributional weights than without them, even when we have the possibility to use optimal non-linear income taxes to deal with equity.

Separability in leisure

Consider now instead the utility function discussed by Christiansen (1981) and others where utility is separable in leisure as follows

$$U^i = u(f(x^i, G_1, \ldots, G_m), l^i), \qquad [22a]$$

or the slightly more general version discussed by Boadway and Keen (1993):

$$U^i = u^i(f(x^i, G_1, \ldots, G_m), l^i \qquad [22b]$$

Such preferences together with optimal nonlinear income taxes, as thoroughly demonstrated in different ways by the above authors, imply that the basic Samuelson rule for the provision of public goods still holds, that is, it is optimal *not* to use any distributional weights. In order to show that result here, we will adopt a somewhat different strategy than in the previous case.

Consider a combined provision of a good j and its financing, taking possible revenue effects through labor-supply adjustments into account, and denote this combined provision and financing Q_j. That is, a marginal change in Q_j, implying an equally large change in G_j, keeps the public budget unchanged. Without specifying how the goods are financed, we can write the marginal social welfare effect of a marginal change in Q_j as

$$\begin{aligned}\frac{\partial w}{\partial Q_j} &= \Sigma_i \frac{\partial w}{\partial U^i}\left(\frac{\partial u^i}{\partial x^i}\frac{\partial x^i}{\partial Q_j} + \frac{\partial u^i}{\partial l^i}\frac{\partial l^i}{\partial Q_j} + \frac{\partial u^i}{\partial G_j}\right) \\ &= \Sigma_i \alpha^i \left(\frac{\partial x^i}{\partial Q_j} + MRS^i_{lx}\frac{\partial l^i}{\partial Q_j} + MRS^i_{G_j x}\right),\end{aligned} \qquad [23]$$

where MRS^i_{lx} is individual i's marginal value of leisure time in terms of x. At the social optimum, given any particular way to finance the good, this expression must clearly equal zero. An optimal non-linear income tax system implies that any combination of marginal tax parameter changes to raise an additional dollar of revenue is equally good (or bad) in terms of social welfare (by the envelope theorem).[14] Let us now consider a particular way to finance a marginal increase of the good, namely a change in the tax function so that each individual i, through increased income taxes, pays exactly his/her marginal WTP for the good j, so that we have

$$-\frac{\partial x^i}{\partial Q_j} = MRS^i_{G_j x}. \qquad [24]$$

Let us now analyze labor adjustments of this combined provision and financing. Both [22a] and [22b] imply that we can write an inverse function as

$$l^i = \psi(U^i, f^i) = \psi(U^i, f(x^i, G_1, \ldots, G_m)), \tag{25}$$

where ψ; is monotonically increasing in U^i and decreasing in f^i. This formulation implies that any changes in the arguments of f that keep f^i unchanged will imply that l^i, and hence labor, will be unchanged too. Since each individual pays his/her marginal WTP for the increased provision, this means that f^i is unchanged. Consequently, each individual will choose exactly the same amount of leisure (and labor) as before this reform, implying that

$$\frac{\partial l^i}{\partial Q_j} = 0, \tag{26}$$

for all individuals i and financed provisions j. Since the budget is balanced on the margin, this way of financing then also implies that the good will be provided until the sum of the individuals' marginal WTPs for the good equals the per-unit price of it, that is, it implies that the Samuelson rule is applied. In order to see that this provision is socially optimal, substitute [24] and [26] into [23]. This implies that the expression in parentheses in [23] equals zero, and hence that $\frac{\partial w}{\partial Q_i} = 0$, so that the social optimum condition is fulfilled. Thus, we have shown that the basic Samuelson rule, without any distributional concern, is indeed optimal to use in this particular case.

3 Comparing the assumptions and their plausibility

Intuitively, why are the policy conclusions so *very* different for the two commonly used types of separability assumptions discussed? In the case of separability in the publicly provided goods, as in [14], an increase in these goods *per se* does not affect labor choices. Hence, the distributional welfare effects should in this case be taken care of in full, since there are no incentive effects, or "distortionary cost," from the provision of these goods *per se.*

In the case of separability in leisure, as in [22 a and 22b], on the other hand, a *combined* public good and tax increase that is exactly equal to the marginal WTP for all leaves the labor choice unaffected. Thus, a marginal provision increase together with this particular way of financing it have neither any distributional effects nor any efficiency (or tax-revenue) effects on the margin. Intuitively, if we can ignore both induced efficiency effects and distributional effects, then the first best rule can be applied, and hence the efficiency-based Samuelson (1954) rule is optimal. This also means that if one good has large distributional benefits compared to another good, these benefits will always be exactly offset by larger efficiency costs in terms of induced labor supply effects.

Given the large differences in policy conclusions it is of course important to judge which case is more reasonable, and which assumption should be seen as the most natural benchmark case. There is unfortunately little empirical evidence that can be used to compare the realism of these assumptions with each other, and none of the papers cited above refers to any empirical evidence supporting their assumptions. Kaplow (1996, 2004), for example, refers to separability in leisure as part of "standard simplifying assumptions." On the other hand, Starret (1988, 173) argues that "a general project has no obvious net complementarity," supporting separability in the publicly provided goods.

To shed some light on the realism of these assumptions, we will briefly discuss three examples. Consider first a transport-related example that reduces commuting time to work, but has no other effects. It seems reasonable that part of the corresponding time gains may be used to increase working hours, and part to increase leisure. This is consistent with separability in leisure, which gives no prediction regarding sign,[15] but is not consistent with separability in the publicly provided goods, which predicts no change in working hours. However, separability in leisure implies that the value put on the time reduction is independent of the amount of leisure, which seems unreasonable; one would instead believe that the value of time would decrease with the amount of leisure *ceteris paribus.* This prediction is instead consistent with separability in *G.* Hence, in this example, none of the assumptions seems to offer a good approximation of reality.

Next, consider police and defense investments. Presumably, such investments have quite minor effects on the chosen provided amount of labor, which is consistent with both separability assumptions. Separability in leisure also predicts individuals' valuation of an increased public investment to be independent of leisure, which seems reasonably plausible as well.

Finally, consider investments in so-called leisure goods such as theaters, and other cultural or recreational investments that make leisure relatively more attractive. Such investments *per se* tend to increase the chosen amount of leisure, which is consistent with separability in leisure but not with separability in *G.* However, again separability in leisure implies that the monetary value put on increased *G* is independent of the amount of leisure. But in reality one would, of course, expect the value put on an increased provision of a leisure good to increase with the amount of leisure, everything else held constant. Indeed, that is why they are called leisure goods—after all, what is the benefit of increased provision of leisure goods if you have no leisure? Hence, in this example too, none of the assumptions seems to offer a good approximation of reality. Thus, neither of these two frequently made separability assumptions seems to give a representative picture of most public goods, and it appears likely that different assumptions will be more or less suitable for different goods. Which case should serve as the most natural "bench-mark" appears to be an open question.

However, it should again be pointed out that separability in the publicly provided goods is a sufficient, but far from necessary, condition for equal tax-revenue effects between the provided goods. The assumption that two provided goods have equal tax-revenue effects, per dollar spent on them, is therefore much less restrictive than assuming utility functions that are weakly separable in both publicly provided goods.

Moreover, not even equal revenue effects are necessary for the conclusion that taking distributional considerations in the goods provisions is welfare improving. Indeed, recall that [10] implies that distributional adjustments should be made unless the induced efficiency welfare effects, through the tax-revenue effects, off-set the distributional welfare effects. However, it is not even clear that these differences must counteract the distributional welfare effects, even when we do not have equal revenue effects. Indeed, it is easy to think of examples where the distributional welfare effects of using weights are not at all off-set by efficiency-based welfare effects (as is the case given the assumptions used by Christiansen and others) but rather *amplify* the welfare effects by the distributional differences.

Consider a governmental choice between improvements of the local golf course and improvements of the public water-supply system. Naturally, the rich would prefer the golf-course improvement, since they have all invested in private high-quality water supply systems, while the poor would prefer the water-supply improvement, for example, since they cannot afford to play golf anyway. Here we have that the efficiency effects of the project preferred by the rich are expected to be negative, since the golf course improvement makes leisure relatively more attractive.[16] The water supply improvement, on the other hand, can be expected to generate an increased amount of supplied labor due to reduced water-related morbidity. Thus, in this case the good preferred by the poor should clearly be over-provided relative to the other good, compared to the implications of the pure efficiency WTP rule. Moreover, it should also be over-provided relative to [13] or [17], which do include distributional weights, since the induced efficiency effects enhance the distributional welfare effects.

This clearly highlights that the assumptions underlying the conclusion that one should generally focus on efficiency-only, as argued by Kaplow (1996, 2004) and others, are indeed very strong, as noted also by Sandmo (1998) and Slemrod and Yitzhaki (2001), and that they sometimes imply extremely bad approximations of reality. Thus, even though it appears difficult to judge how reasonable, or unreasonable, different preference structures are, it is from a policy perspective sufficient to be able to judge the relative tax-revenue effects. And as long as the good preferred from a distributional point of view is not substantially worse from an efficiency point of view through induced labor supply effects, it is optimal to use distributional weights.

4 Special cases

Additive separability in public goods

Boadway and Keen (1993) derived, using the self-selection approach, a result for the case where the (common for all) utility function is additively, or strongly, separable (and hence also weakly separable) as follows

$$U^i = A(x^i, l^i) + B(G_1, \ldots, G_m). \qquad [27]$$

They showed that, given optimal nonlinear income taxes, a public good should be over-provided relative to the Samuelson rule if $\frac{\partial^2 A}{\partial x \partial l} < 0$, that is, if private consumption and leisure are Edgeworth complements, and vice versa. This condition is clearly independent of the distributional characteristics of the publicly provided goods. Thus, there is no explicit equity consideration here, despite the weakly separable public goods, which seems to contradict the results in [17]. However, as will be shown, this is an illusion. Individual *i*'s marginal WTP for an increase in the provision of good *j* is given by

$$MRS^i_{G_j x} = \frac{\partial B}{\partial G_j} / \frac{\partial A}{\partial x^i}. \qquad [28]$$

Since the utility function is the same for all, we can then use [28] to calculate the corresponding income elasticity in the population as

$$\varepsilon_i = \frac{\partial MRS_{G_j x}}{\partial x} \frac{x}{MRS_{G_j x}} = -x \frac{\partial^2 A}{\partial x^2} / \frac{\partial A}{\partial x}, \qquad [29]$$

which is clearly independent of all publicly provided goods. Hence, the marginal WTP varies with income in exactly the same way for all public goods. Alternatively, we can combine [28] and [15] and write the distributional characteristic of good *j* as[17]

$$\delta j = \frac{\Sigma_i \alpha^i \frac{\partial B}{\partial G_j} / \frac{\partial A}{\partial x^i}}{\Sigma_i \bar{\alpha} \frac{\partial B}{\partial G_j} / \frac{\partial A}{\partial x^i}} - 1 = \frac{\Sigma_i \alpha^i / \frac{\partial A}{\partial x^i}}{\Sigma_i \bar{\alpha} / \frac{\partial A}{\partial x^i}} - 1, \qquad [30]$$

which is clearly independent of all publicly provided goods, implying that the distributional characteristics will be the same for each of these goods, and the right hand side of [17] will then simply be equal to the cost ratio. Thus, given preferences as in [24], comparing two (small) public projects in terms of the cost-benefit ratio will give the same result with and without distributional weights.

Separability in both leisure and publicly provided goods

Consider now the special case discussed by Kaplow (1996) where people's utility functions are given by

$$U^i = f(x^i) + g(G_1, \ldots, G_m) + h(l^i). \qquad [31]$$

This utility function is separable in *both* the publicly provided goods and in leisure. As we have seen, according to the former we should apply distributional weights, but according to the latter we should not, which seems again to indicate a contradiction. However, since [31] is a special case of [27], the same arguments are applicable here. Hence, [17] and the Samuelson rule will hold simultaneously. In Appendix 2, it is shown that a sufficient condition for this result is that utility is *weakly* separable in both leisure and the public goods, simultaneously, so that the utility function can be written as

$$U^i = u(f(x^i, l^i), (G_1, \ldots, G_m) = v(h(x^i, \mathrm{G}_1, \ldots, G_m), l^i). \qquad [32]$$

Consequently, the allocation would be exactly the same with and without weights in these special cases, implying that distributional weights are redundant, but also that they are harmless in terms of efficiency losses.

5 Discussion and conclusions

This chapter has questioned the proposition that distributional weights in CBA typically imply large inefficiency losses, compared to other ways of dealing with equity such as income taxes. Instead it is shown that it is optimal to use such weights in the choice between different publicly provided goods (or projects, more generally), when these goods are expected to affect tax revenues, through changes in labor supply, about equally much per dollar spent on them. For this conclusion, we have not assumed anything further regarding people's preference structures or the characteristics of the implemented tax structure. Still, it has been shown that preferences that are weakly separable in the publicly provided goods are sufficient conditions. Moreover, it has been shown that distributional concerns should be taken unless differences in distributional welfare effects are offset by corresponding differences in tax-revenue effects. This would occur given a set of assumptions used by several authors, but it is demonstrated that these assumptions often constitute very poor approximations of reality.

Of course, if one does not care about equity at all at the social level, then introducing *ad hoc* distributional weights will typically imply large inefficiency losses. Harberger (1978, 1984) provides several examples of the negative consequences of applying distributional weights in cost-benefit analysis. One of the more amusing ones deals with the possibility of sending icecream on camel-back across the desert, from a richer oasis to a poorer one (Har-berger 1978, repeated in Harberger 1984). In an extreme case, when the social inequality-aversion used is large, he asserts (Harberger 1978, S113) that "up to 63/64 of the ice-cream could melt away without causing the project to fail the test." He concludes (Harberger 1984, 458): "Even ways which by the traditional standards would be scandalously inefficient would have to be explored."

However, comparisons with a first-best world is of little help, given that the society cares about equity as reflected by an SWF which is reasonably quasi-concave in income. Decreasing inequality by changes in income taxation will then have large inefficiency losses as well, as pointed out by Dahlby (1998) and Sandmo (1998). To illustrate this, consider again the initial example with a utilitarian SWF, where each individual has an identical utility function characterized by constant relative risk aversion, and where the income of a rich person is 100 times that of a poor. Everything else being equal, a redistribution of one dollar from the rich to the poor through changed income taxes would, in the absence of any inefficiency losses, give the poor individual a utility increase which is 100^{σ} times the utility loss of the rich individual, where σ is again the (constant and common for all) parameter of relative risk aversion. Such redistributions without any efficiency costs are in most cases unrealistic, however. Assume therefore that only the fraction $(1 - \gamma)$ reaches the poor recipient, where γ is the inefficiency loss or the marginal excess burden. Then the social welfare change of the redistribution is positive if (and only if) $(1 - \gamma)100^{\sigma} > 1$. Consequently, this redistribution would be social-welfare improving if the marginal excess burden of this tax change were less than 99 percent for $\sigma = 1$, and 99.99 percent for $\sigma = 2$. Indeed, from a normative perspective one may even argue that these inefficiency losses *should* be large, given what can be considered to be a reasonable SWF—otherwise the re-distributive taxes are simply too low. From a dual formulation of the welfare maximization, where the size of the economy is maximized given a certain inequality level, it follows that these losses are sometimes lower when *only* making tax changes, and sometimes they are lower when *also* taking distributional considerations in CBA.

In this study, as in most other studies, aspects such as simplicity of analysis, administrative costs, and implementation issues are ignored. Presumably, such considerations are often important reasons for not using distributional weights in practice, but sometimes there are also practical arguments in favor of using such weights. The income-tax system works for example very poorly in many developing countries, and equity concerns directed through public projects may then have quite a high distributional accuracy compared to the available alternatives. There are also instances where pure efficiency arguments appear particularly hard to digest. According to the empirical findings of Miller (2000), the WTP-based value of a statistical life is roughly proportional to income. A pure efficiency-based CBA then implies that saving one person with income $10x$ is preferable to saving nine persons with income x (each). In practice, it is hard to imagine that any publicly funded institution uses such priorities and it would be very hard for them to defend them; see for example Usher (2001) and Sunstein (2004).

Finally, the analysis in this paper takes the ethics underlying the (quite flexible) Bergson-Samuelson SWF as a point of departure, and the distributional weights are of course derived conditional on the underlying assumptions. Still, even though many alternative ethical assumptions do exist, it is hard to imagine a consistent and defendable ethical theory that implies *per se* that efficiency-only should guide public policy.[18] Moreover, even though the specific way in which distributional concerns should be made may vary with the alternative ethical assumptions, one can generally not escape the fact that efficiency and distributional concerns must be analyzed simultaneously.

In conclusion, it appears difficult to defend both the proposition that distributional concerns should *always* be used in CBA, and that they should *never* be used. However, the commonly expressed perception that using distributional weights generally imply large efficiency losses appears to be incorrect, or strongly misleading at best.

Acknowledgements

The author is grateful for constructive comments on many different versions of this paper from Fredrik Carlsson, Gilbert van Hagen, Agnar Sandmo, Thomas Sterner, Jason Shogren, Vidar Christiansen, Michael Hanemann, seminar and conference participants at various places, and several anonymous referees. Financial support from the Swedish Agency for Innovation Systems (VINNOVA) is also acknowledged.

Appendix 1

Separability in the publicly provided goods and uniform preferences

When the preferences are identical in the population and separable in the publicly provided goods, they can be written as follows for an individual *i:*

$$U^i = u(f(x^i, l^i), G_1, \ldots, G_m). \quad \text{[A1]}$$

There are many utility functions of this kind that imply different income elasticities for the publicly provided goods, and hence different distributional characteristics. Consider for example the following utility function:

$$U^i = g(G_1(G_2 + x^i l^i)), \quad \text{[A2]}$$

where g is any increasing monotonic transformation (to ensure suitable concavity, etc.). From individual utility maximization with respect to how much to work, we have from eq. [6] that

$$l^i = \frac{x^i}{a^i(1-t^i)}, \quad \text{[A3]}$$

assuming interior solutions. [A3] into [A2] implies

$$U^i = g\left(G_1\left(G_2 + \frac{x^{i^2}}{a^i(1-t^i)}\right)\right). \quad \text{[A4]}$$

The marginal WTP ratio between the publicly provided goods 1 and 2 is then given by

$$\frac{MRS^i_{G_1x}}{MRS^i_{G_2x}} = MRS^i_{G_1G_2} = \frac{1}{G_1}\left(G_2 + \frac{x^{i^2}}{a^i(1-t^i)}\right). \quad \text{[A5]}$$

This is clearly increasing in after-tax income x^i, provided that utility is increasing in after-tax income which is typically assumed. Thus, a richer individual will always value a small increase of G_2, in terms of G_1, higher than a poorer individual will, implying different distributional characteristics. This demonstrates that the case for distributional weights is not driven by any implicit assumption that poor people have different preferences than the rich.

Appendix 2

Weak separability in both leisure and publicly provided goods

A utility function that is weakly separable in both leisure and the publicly provided goods, and which is the same for all, can be written as

$$u(f(x^i, l^i), G_1, \ldots, G_m) = v(h(x^i, \mathrm{G}_1, \ldots, G_m), l^i) \qquad [A7]$$

Using the latter function, the ratio between the marginal WTP for goods 2 and 1 can then be written

$$r = \frac{MRS^i_{G_2x}}{MRS^i_{G_1x}} = MRS^i_{G_2G_1} = \frac{\partial h}{\partial G_2} / \frac{\partial h}{\partial G_1}, \qquad [A8]$$

which is a function of x^i, and $G_1, \ldots, G_m$, and is clearly independent of l^i. But, using the former function, this ratio can also be written

$$r = \frac{\partial u}{\partial G_2} / \frac{\partial u}{\partial G_1}, \qquad [A9]$$

which is a function of $f(x^i, l^i)$ and $G_1, \ldots, G_m$. By combining these implications of [A8] and [A9], we can write

$$r^i = s(x^i, G_1, \ldots, G_m) = t(f(x^i, l^i), G_1, \ldots, G_m). \qquad [A10]$$

Differentiating [A10] with respect to leisure implies that

$$\frac{dr^i}{dl^i} = \frac{\partial s}{\partial l^i} = \frac{\partial t}{\partial f}\frac{\partial f}{\partial l^i}. \qquad [A11]$$

Since s is independent of leisure we have that $\frac{\partial s}{\partial l^i} = 0$, which then clearly implies that

$$\frac{\partial t}{\partial f}\frac{\partial f}{\partial l^i} = 0. \qquad [A12]$$

But since people's marginal utility of leisure is in general non-zero, so that $\frac{\partial f}{\partial l^i} \neq 0$, we must have that

$$\frac{\partial t}{\partial f} = 0. \qquad [A13]$$

Combining [A10] and [A13] implies that r^i is independent of x^i as well. Thus, r^i can be written as a function solely of $G_1, \ldots, G_n$ for all individuals *i*. This means that all individuals, having the same utility function, will have the same *r*. The distributional characteristics are then the same for goods 1 and 2, since

$$\delta_2 = \operatorname{cov}\left(\frac{\alpha}{\bar{\alpha}}, \frac{MRS_{G_2x}}{\overline{MRS_{G_2x}}}\right) = \operatorname{cov}\left(\frac{\alpha}{\bar{\alpha}}, \frac{rMRS_{G_1x}}{\overline{rMRS_{G_1x}}}\right) \qquad \text{[A14]}$$
$$= \operatorname{cov}\left(\frac{\alpha}{\bar{\alpha}}, \frac{MRS_{G_1x}}{\overline{MRS_{G_1x}}}\right) = \delta_1,$$

which should be shown.

Notes

1 See e.g., Bromley (1990, 2004) and Johansson-Stenman (1998) for discussions of other potential problems of deriving policy conclusions based on CBA.

2 On the other hand, since poverty measures are often used to evaluate policy reforms, this can be seen to reflect some kinds of implicit weights.

3 A classical utilitarian framework appears to be the most frequently used in the literature. See Yitzhaki (2003) for an alternative approach, where he derived distributional weights from an SWF which depends directly on inequality indices, such as the Gini coefficient

4 Somewhat similarly, Medin, Nyborg, and Bateman (2001) demonstrate that if one instead of assuming equal marginal utility of income for all (as in conventional unweighted CBA) assumes equal marginal utility of the public good, then the aggregate monetary benefit estimates may change substantially.

5 Hylland and Zeckhauser (1979) showed that a sufficient condition, in addition to optimal non-linear income taxes, for the Samuelson (1954) rule to be applied is that the (identical for all) utility function is separable as follows: $u(f(x + B(x, G)), l)$, where *x* and *G* are private and publicly provided consumption, respectively, *l* is leisure, and *B* is the monetary benefit derived from *G*. Christiansen (1981) showed that it is sufficient that utility can be written as $u\,(f(x, G), l)$. Boadway and Keen (1993), in turn, generalized the result further by showing that it is sufficient that the utility function for any individual *i* may be written $U^i = u^i(f(x^i, G), l^i)$. Hence, it is sufficient that all individuals have an identical sub-utility function *f*; the overall utility function *u* need not be identical for the Samuelson rule to be valid.

6 Sanchirico (2000) is a rare exception in the literature. He analyzed a model of legal rule-making in the tradition of Shavell (1981) and, in that specific setting, made very strong conclusions claiming that it is always optimal to use distributional weights. However, see also the comment by Kaplow and Shavell (2000), who claimed that several conclusions by Sancherico (2000) were unfounded, as well as the rejoinder (in another journal) by Sancherico (2001).

7 Diamond (1975) and Atkinson and Stiglitz (1980, 496–97) have shown that distributional weights should be applied, given this type of separability, in the special case of optimal *linear* income taxation

8 Weak quasi-concavity implies that the government does never prefer that one utility unit would be transferred (hypothetically) from an individual with lower initial utility to an individual with higher initial utility. However, it does not rule out that the government could be indifferent to such a redistribution, as it would be with a utilitarian SWF. Strict quasi-concavity, on the contrary, would rule out utilitarian SWFs.

9 Following the terminology of Diamond and Mirrlees (1971), and hence not the one of Diamond (1975). For a utilitarian SWF we have of course that $\alpha^i = \partial u^i / \partial x^i$,, i.e., the individual marginal utility of income.

10 Note that this conclusion does not depend on whether an increased tax level actually decreases the supplied amount of labor or not, i.e., whether the substitution effect or the income effect dominates. Still, the conclusion depends of course on the (standard) assumptions made. For example, if people also care about relative consumption, i.e., their own consumption relative to those of others, which appears reasonable given existing empirical evidence as well as common-sense reasoning, it is not obvious that it would be socially beneficial if people worked more on the margin; compare with Brekke and Howarth (2002), Johansson-Stenman, Carlsson, and Daruvala (2002), and Alpizar, Carlsson, and Johansson-Stenman (2005).

11 In the case of optimal taxation, our results hold also for a tax reform, by duality, so that it is always optimal to use these distributional weights also if one can change the income tax structure. This is not necessarily true if the initial income tax is not optimal, however.

12 See Goldman and Uzawa (1964).

13 Meaning that the income effect of the good provision is negligible so that the continuous case is a good approximation.

14 Otherwise the first-order optimality conditions would not be fulfilled, and the tax system should be adjusted so that they are fulfilled.

15 Remember that the overall effects of the tax increase and marginal good provision leave the amount of labor unchanged. Since the tax increase on its own can either increase or decrease labor, depending on the relative size of the income and substitution effects, the sign regarding the good provision can also be either positive or negative.

16 Moreover, the efficiency effects are even worse due to the fact that it is the rich persons who work less, since they pay higher taxes per hour.

17 Assuming a utilitarian SWF we get that $\delta = \frac{1}{\bar{\mu} \overline{1/\mu}} - 1$, where μ, is the individual marginal utility of income. Hence, the larger the (after-tax) inequality, the larger the distributional characteristic (in absolute value), reflecting the fact that the public good will then have a more equalizing effect

18 For a critique of ethical justifications of the Hicks-Kaldor compensation criteria, see e.g., Sen (1987).

References

Alpizar, F., F. Carlsson, and O. Johansson–Stenman. 2005. "How Much Do People Care About Absolute versus Relative Income and Consumption?" *Journal of Economic Behavior and Organization* 56 (3): 405–21.

Atkinson, A. B., and J. E. Stiglitz. 1980. *Lectures in Public Economics.* New York: McGraw Hill.

Blanchard, O., and S. Fischer. 1989. *Lectures on Macroeconomics.* Cambridge, Mass.: MIT Press.

Boadway, R., and M. Keen. 1993. "Public Goods, Self-Selection and Optimal Income Taxation." *International Economic Review* 34 (3): 463–78.

Brekke, K.-A., and R. Howarth. 2002. *Status, Growth and the Environment.* Cheltenham, U.K.: Edward Elgar.

Bromley, D. 1990. "The Ideology of Efficiency: Searching for a Theory of Policy Analysis." *Journal of Environmental Economics and Management* 19 (1): 86–107.

——. 2004. "Reconsidering Environmental Policy: Prescriptive Consequentialism and Volitional Pragmatism." *Environmental and Resource Economics* 28 (1): 73–99.

Christiansen, V. 1981. "Evaluation of Public Projects under Optimal Taxation." *Review of Economic Studies* 48 (3): 447–57.

Christiansen, V., and E. Jansen. 1978. "Implicit Social Preferences in the Norwegian System of Indirect Taxation." *Journal of Public Economics* 10 (2): 217–45.

Dahlby, B. 1998. "Progressive Taxation and the Social Marginal Cost of Public Funds." *Journal of Public Economics* 67 (1): 105–22.

Dasgupta, P. 1998. "Population, Consumption and Resources: Ethical Issues." *Ecological Economics* 24 (2–3): 139–52.

Dasgupta, P., S. Marglin, and A. Sen. 1972. *Guidelines for Project Evaluation.* Vienna: United Nations Industrial Development Organization (UNIDO).

Diamond, P. A. 1975. "A Many-Person Ramsey Tax Rule." *Journal of Public Economics* 4 (4): 335–42.

Diamond, P. A., and J. A. Mirrlees. 1971. "Optimal Taxation and Public Production II: Tax Rules." *American Economic Review* 61 (3): 261–78.

Dreze, J. P. 1998. "Distribution Matters in Cost-Benefit Analysis: Comment on K.-A. Brekke." *Journal of Public Economics* 70 (3): 485–88.

Dreze, J. P., and N. Stern. 1987. "The Theory of Cost-Benefit Analysis." In *Handbook of Public Economics* 2, ed. A. J. Auerbach and M. Feldstein, 909–90. Amsterdam: North-Holland.

Feldstein, M. S. 1972. "Distributional Equity and the Optimal Structure of Public Prices." *American Economic Review* 62 (4): 32–36.

Frank, R. H. 2000. "Why Is Cost-Benefit Analysis so Controversial?" *Journal of Legal Studies* 29 (2): 913–30.

Frank, R. H., and B. Bernanke. 2001. *Principles of Economics.* New York: McGraw-Hill.

Freeman, A. M. 2003. *The Measurements of Environmental and Resource Values.* Washington, D.C.: Resources for the Future.

Goldman, S. M., and H. Uzawa. 1964. "A Note on Separability in Demand Analysis." *Econo-metrica* 32 (3): 387–98.

H. M. Treasury. 2003. *The Green Book: Appraisal and Evaluation in Central Government.* London.

Hanley, N., J. Shogren, and B. White. 1997. *Environmental Economics in Theory and Practice.* London: Macmillan.

Harberger, A. C. 1978. "On the Use of Distributional Weights in Social Cost-Benefit Analysis." *Journal of Political Economy* 86 (2): S87–S120.

——. 1984. "Basic Needs Versus Distributional Weights in Social Cost-Benefit Analysis." *Economic Development and Cultural Change* 32 (3): 455–74.

Hylland, A., and R. Zeckhauser. 1979. "Distributional Objectives Should Affect Taxes but Not Program Choice or Design." *Scandinavian Journal of Economics* 81 (2): 264–84.

Johansson-Stenman, O. 1998. "On the Problematic Link between Fundamental Ethics and Economic Policy Recommendations." *Journal of Economic Methodology* 5 (2): 263–97.

Johansson-Stenman, O., F. Carlsson, and D. Dar-uvala. 2002. "Measuring Future Grandparents' Preferences for Equality and Relative Standing." *Economic Journal* 112 (479): 362–83.

Kaplow, L. 1996. "The Optimal Supply of Public Goods and the Distortionary Cost of Taxation." *National Tax Journal* 49 (4): 513–33.

——. 2004. "On the (Ir)Relevance of Distribution and Labor Supply Distortion to Government Policy." *Journal of Economic Perspectives* 18 (4): 159–75.

Kaplow, L, and S. Shavell. 1994. "Why the Legal System Is Less Efficient Than the Income Tax in Redistributing Income." *Journal of Legal Studies* 23 (2): 667–81.

——. 2000. "Should Legal Rules Favor the Poor? Clarifying the Role of Legal Rules and the Income Tax in Redistributing Income." *Journal of Legal Studies* 29 (2): 821–35.
Little, I. M. D., and J. A. Mirrlees. 1974. *Project Appraisal and Planning for Developing Countries.* London: Heinemann.
——. 1991. "Project Appraisal and Planning Twenty Years On." In *Proceedings of the World Bank Annual Conference on Development Economics 1990.* Washington, D.C.: World Bank.
Marshall, A. 1885. *The Present Position of Economics.* London: Macmillan.
Medin, H., K. Nyborg, and I. Bateman. 2001. "The Assumption of Equal Marginal Utility of Income: How Much Does it Matter?" *Ecological Economics* 36 (3): 397–411.
Miller, T. R. 2000. "Variations Between Countries in Values of Statistical Life." *Journal of Transport Economics and Policy* 34 (2): 169–88.
Mirrlees, J. A. 1971. "An Exploration in the Theory of Optimum Income Taxation." *Review of Economic Studies* 38 (2): 175–208.
Ng, Y.-K. 2000a. "The Optimal Size of Public Spending and the Distortionary Cost of Taxation." *National Tax Journal* 53 (2): 253–72.
——. 2000b. *Efficiency, Equality and Public Policy – With a Case for Higher Public Spending.* Basingstoke, U.K.: Macmillan.
Samuelson, P. A. 1954. "The Pure Theory of Public Expenditure." *Review of Economics and Statistics* 36 (4): 387–89.
Sanchirico, C. W. 2000. "Taxes Versus Legal Rules as Instruments for Equity: A More Equitable View." *Journal of Legal Studies* 29 (2): 797–820.
——. 2001. "Deconstructing the New Efficiency Rationale." *Cornell Law Review* 86 (5): 1003–89.
Sandmo, A. 1998. "Redistribution and the Marginal Cost of Public Funds." *Journal of Public Economics* 70 (3): 365–82.
Sen, A. K. 1987. *On Ethics and Economics.* Oxford, U.K.: Blackwell.
Shavell, S. 1981. "A Note on Efficiency vs. Distributional Equity in Legal Rulemaking: Should Distributional Equity Matter Given Optimal Income Taxation?" *American Economic Review (Papers and proceedings)* 71 (2): 414–18.
Slemrod, J., and S. Yitzhaki. 2001. "Integrating Expenditure and Tax Decisions: The Marginal Cost of Funds and the Marginal Benefit of Projects." *National Tax Journal* 54 (2): 189–201.
Squire, L., and H. van der Tak. 1975. *Economic Analysis of Projects.* Baltimore: John Hopkins University Press.
Starret, D. A. 1988. *Foundations of Public Economics.* New York: Cambridge University Press.
Sunstein, C. R. 2004. "Are Poor People Worth Less Than Rich People? Disaggregating the Value of Statistical Lives." Olin working paper no. 207, University of Chicago Law School.
Usher, D. 2001. "Personal Goods, Efficiency and the Law." *European Journal of Political Economy* 17 (4): 673–703.
Yitzhaki, S. 2003. "Cost-Benefit Analysis and Distributional Consequences of Government Projects." *National Tax Journal* 56 (2): 319–25.

10 Fair air

Distributive justice and environmental economics

Olof Johansson-Stenman and James Konow

1 Introduction

A critical issue faced by policymakers across the world is how to distribute the costs and benefits of policies designed to address environmental problems, whether dealing with automobile emissions, water pollution, toxic substances, solid waste or global climate change. Whereas fairness concerns are frequently discussed in many different public policy areas, they appear to occupy a particularly prominent place in environmental issues. In fact, environmental policies, such as green taxes, fuel economy standards and tradable emissions permits, differ dramatically in the distribution of their costs and benefits.

In this paper, we conceive of fairness in rather broad terms as distributive justice, i.e., distributive preferences as distinct from self-interest and other social preferences, such as altruism, reciprocity and honesty. We focus on the contextual factors and the rules, including accountability, efficiency, need and equality, that guide those preferences. Moreover, we note that solutions to real environmental problems are often related to the kind of justice concerns we address here.

Although environmental economics, as well as economics more generally, is largely based on the normative criterion of economic efficiency, it is clear that many people have strong opinions about the perceived fairness of different environmental policies, including policies related to climate change and to the implementation and design of tradable permit systems. These opinions are reflected in the political debate, where fairness arguments are clearly much more prominent than in the environmental economics literature. Thus, although fairness is not a unique concern to environmental issues, it is a prominent theme in real world discussions in this area, even if it has been relatively neglected in the environmental economics literature.

Why, then, do economists not integrate fairness more frequently into their models? There are (at least) three reasons:

1. Such concerns are often seen as highly subjective and amorphous, i.e., they are not (sufficiently) structured to be productively incorporated into such models.

2. They are invoked chiefly in order to benefit the agent employing them, i.e. they are consciously or subconsciously chosen for self-interested reasons.
3. They complicate the models and make the analysis less tractable.

We think there is merit in these arguments but argue that each of these concerns can be satisfactory addressed. First, we certainly do not deny that there are subjective elements in people's fairness perceptions. Nevertheless, even these subjective views obey rules that vary predictably across contexts. Second, it is clear that people often exhibit what we will refer to as a *fairness bias*, that is, they construe fairness in self-interested ways. Stakeholders are frequently focused on the fairness of policies from a biased perspective, and proponents and even opponents of environmental measures often appeal to such arguments, e.g., the latter sometimes claim that gasoline taxes would harm the poor. Thus, even when self-interest insinuates itself into these deliberations, the arguments are often seemingly framed around a shared set of fairness principles (e.g., Lange et al. 2010). Moreover, these views can also be observed empirically under conditions of impartiality and reveal considerable consensus under such conditions. Third, as with all generalizations, it follows that fairness considerations do add a layer of complexity to formal models. But we maintain that the costs of incorporating fairness concerns into the analysis in terms of greater complexity are often outweighed by the benefits, which include improved empirical predictive power, richer descriptive theories, and greater policy relevance. We also believe that environmental economics would have greater influence on the actual environmental policy if fairness considerations were to be taken more seriously.

The reminder of this paper is organized as follows: section 2 discusses different means for measuring fairness concerns with particular attention to the role of fairness biases. Section 3 discusses different fairness rules that people apply and the associated empirical evidence, whereas section 4 discusses further interpretive issues, such as how people handle situations involving tradeoffs between different fairness principles and context dependencies. Section 5 specifically discusses implications for environmental economics, including normative analysis. For example, one position is that fairness principles should inform the overarching goals of environmental policy, if one takes some version of the justice values of real people as relevant to normative foundations (e.g., Konow 2003). Section 6 concludes the paper.

2 Can fairness concerns be measured, and, if so, how?

The fact that fairness judgments require various interpretative decisions introduces the possibility of arriving at very different conclusions. This means that there is rarely unanimity in views of justice, even though impartial judges often exhibit a high degree of consensus. The situation with stakeholders, however, is considerably more difficult, often with polarized views and sometimes even modest levels of consensus a remote ideal. Stakeholders frequently advocate and pursue goals that favor their material interests but that depart from the outcomes preferred, on average, by impartial spectators. We refer to this discrepancy between spectator and stakeholder views as a "fairness bias." This bias can be decomposed into at least two parts.

First, there is a "self-centered bias," which is that part of the discrepancy that is acknowledged by the stakeholder, at least to him-or her-self. For example, a polluter seeking to avoid regulation might recognize its efforts as serving primarily to protect its own profits, even if it does not cite that fact in making its case to regulators. Arguments motivated by this bias might or might not involve fairness, but, if they do, those people advancing them do not actually believe the arguments are legitimate but instead might simply be advancing them to manipulate and exploit the fairness beliefs of others. Second, there is a "self-serving bias," which involves a distortion of the agent's own beliefs about what is fair in the direction of his or her material interests. That is, the self-serving bias is due to self-deception about what is fair. This idea can be found in cognitive dissonance theory (e.g., Festinger 1957), which states that, when people are faced with opposing goals, they can relieve the resulting disutility by altering their beliefs. For example, if the executive leadership of a firm faces a conflict between maximizing profits and bearing their fair share of the costs of reducing emissions, they are likely to underestimate their fair share of abatement costs relative to the view third parties hold.

Babcock and Loewenstein (1997) report the results of a series of studies with their collaborators that investigate self-serving bias in the laboratory and the field. In particular, they find that this bias is significantly correlated with bargaining impasse, that this relationship is causal, and that it affects behavior not only in the laboratory but also has important repercussions in real world bargaining situations with high stakes, e.g., in teacher contract negotiations. In their experimental studies, subjects bargained within a contextually rich framework, a novel departure from the minimalist scenarios of most economics experiments. Research in psychology indicates that such richness feeds self-serving bias: Dunning et al. (1989), for example, find that self-serving evaluations increase with the number of criteria at one's disposal. This suggests that the numerous interpretative decisions inherent to most fairness evaluations facilitate this bias. But the self-serving bias can manifest itself even in relatively sterile contexts. For example, the fairness bias is decomposed in a simple dictator experiment in Konow (2000). Based on actual behavior in economic experiments, around 60% of the overall bias in dictator decisions can be attributed to self-serving bias, whereas about 40% is due to unadulterated self-interest (i.e., the self-centered bias). Such subconscious biases can be expected frequently in environmental contexts, which are often characterized by countless specifics and informational asymmetries. In addition, these same properties can lead to conscious strategic manipulation of fairness concepts. For example, stakeholders, such as polluting firms, frequently possess better information about their costs of complying with environmental objectives than, say, their competitors or government regulators, and one might expect the former to exaggerate these costs and the latter to discount them.

Lange et al. (2010) study fairness bias in international climate policy. They report a survey of almost two hundred individuals actually involved in negotiating climate policy across three continents. Specifically, respondents state their views of the fairness of four rules informed by different interpretations of the fair distribution of obligations to reduce greenhouse gas emissions. They find that individuals in different geographical regions generally favor rules that impose lower costs on their region and higher costs, by implication, on those in other regions, apparently in support of a fairness bias. The data in this study do not allow a decomposition of this bias, but one piece of evidence is suggestive of some role for self-serving bias: the respondents tended to view their own preference of rules as less self-interested than the preferences of others. The latter fact is consistent with a large literature suggesting that most people seem to consider themselves as "better" than the average person in dimensions such as social responsibility. For example, Carlsson and Johansson-Stenman (2009) found that people on average think that others vote more for selfish reasons than they do themselves.

To the extent stakeholders impacted by environmental policy are subject to a self-serving bias, the results from fairness research are not auspicious. In particular, the stakes in real world environmental problems are much higher than in an economics experiment. Yet even in experiments it is quite difficult to dislodge this bias. Babcock and Loewenstein (1997) report various interventions to mediate or purge the self-serving bias among subjects, mostly to little effect. Informing subjects of the bias had no effect, nor did writing an essay arguing the opponent's case, although informing subjects of the bias combined with having them list weaknesses in their own case did significantly reduce the bias. The study of Oberholzer-Gee et al. (1997)suggests that, ultimately, solutions to such conflicts might reside in lessons from procedural justice. They survey a sample of the general Swiss population on their views of the fairness of different procedures for the siting of hazardous waste facilities, viz., waste from nuclear power plants, and also report facts about the actual siting of such a facility. They find strong support for processes that respect impartiality, information, consent and fairness, as well as a greater willingness for people to accept a burden under such conditions.

Given the frequent evidence of fairness biases one may wonder whether fairness perceptions are inherently subjective, and whether it is at all meaningful to talk about objective or impartial measures of fairness? Yet, we argue that it is both meaningful and possible to analyze measures of fairness objectively. We maintain, however, that such attempts should eliminate, or at least minimize, the direct material stakes of the subject whose fairness preferences are measured in order to reduce fairness biases. There are primarily two kinds of broad measures for doing so: (1) survey studies where subjects are asked to state which of different alternatives is the fairest one (e.g. Konow 1996), and (2) experimental studies with real monetary incentives where the subjects act as third party decision-makers who choose allocations for other subjects, implying that their decision will have real effects for the other subjects but not for themselves (e.g. Konow 2000).

3 Fairness rules

Distributive justice, which we use here interchangeably with fairness, concerns moral preferences over the distribution of social and economic benefits and burdens among a group of individuals. As a *moral* preference, it is distinct from self-interest. Viewed as *distributive* preferences, justice also differs from altruism, which in economics typically characterizes an unconditional preference, such as pure altruism or warm glow (see Andreoni 1990). Instead, justice takes a more specific form and might involve some general relationship between preferred outcomes and other factors such as desert, endowments, productivity, need or effort. As behavioral economics has developed over almost three decades, fairness concerns have figured prominently throughout, for example, fairness has frequently been suspected in the results of experimental bargaining games beginning with Güth et al. (1982). But it is only relatively recently that fairness has been analyzed as a possible force in environmental economics, e.g., Brekke and Johansson-Stenman (2008), Lange and Vogt (2003). Numerous experimental and field studies indicate that such preferences have frequent and quantitatively large impacts on economic behavior. Nevertheless, despite certain patterns, including the frequent incidence of equal splits in bargaining experiments, the findings defy explanation according to a single rule or principle. In this paper, we examine four rules that we believe characterize actualized distributive preferences: accountability, efficiency, need and equality.

3.1 The accountability principle

The first rule we discuss is a relative concept of fairness, i.e., it pertains to the allocation of a benefit or burden of a given size among a set of persons. The *accountability principle* states that a person's allocation should be in proportion to the relevant variables he/she controls, but this rule does not hold the person accountable for other differences (Konow 1996). For example, if worker A is twice as productive as worker B, A should earn twice as much as B, if the productivity difference is due to A working more hours or exerting greater effort. But they should earn the same, if the productivity difference is due entirely to factors they do not control, such as innate ability or differing work conditions. Thus, accountability integrates two concepts: proportionality and responsibility.

Justice as proportionality is often referred to as *equity theory* in psychology, sociology and political science. Equity theory states that individuals are motivated to establish or maintain proportionality of agents' inputs (e.g., their contributions to production) to the outputs they receive (e.g., their earnings), although, as usually formulated, equity theory does not restrict the variables that may count as inputs. Empirical studies substantiate the economic importance of proportionality, e.g., Gächter and Riedl (2005), Güth (1994), Selten (1978). Specifically, proportionality emerges as a quite robust finding when impartial preferences are elicited. In Gächter and Riedl (2006), survey participants respond that the fairest division of earnings in a vignette is in proportion to historical performance. In the dictator experiments of Konow (2000), Konow etal. (2009), third parties allocate proportionately to the individual performance of other subjects in a task.

The other part of accountability is responsibility, which is sometimes associated with the concept of just deserts, e.g., Nozick (1974), and is often considered central to normative theories of fair reward, e.g., Bossert and Fleurbaey (1996), Cappelen and Tungodden (2003), Roemer (1998). Alesina and Angeletos (2005), Fong (2001) find that popular support for income redistribution is strongly related the perceived control of recipients over their circumstances. The accountability principle merges proportionality and responsibility: fair outputs are proportional to inputs agents' control. This principle has been corroborated in experiments: in the aforementioned dictator study of Konow (2000), third parties allocate proportionally, when productivity is chosen, but equally, when productivity is due solely to arbitrary differences between subjects. The accountability principle is also related to important work in normative ethics, e.g., Cappelen and Tungodden (2009), which potentially informs policy. In the context of environmental policy, it implies, for example, that those who reduce emissions should benefit proportionately or, conversely, that polluter costs be proportionate to their emissions. Thus, even if the conditions of the Coase Theorem apply and pollution abatement can be as efficiently achieved by assigning property rights to emitters as to the parties affected by the externality, this principle suggests that people are not neutral with respect to the implied distribution of burdens. This is consistent with the survey results in Konow (1996) showing that, even when it is considerably more expensive for the emitter to eliminate the pollution, 84% of 219 respondents find it unfair when the court assigns property rights to the emitter, whereas 80% of 240 respondents find it fair when the court assigns these rights to the affected party.

In terms of burden sharing for global carbon emission reduction, this seems to imply that every person in the world should have an equal initial right to pollute, since it is hard to argue that some individuals have earned the right to pollute more than others. Although such a global distribution of emissions would, of course, imply large inefficiencies, it is, in principle, straightforward to combine it with a market-based instrument that deals with the efficiency aspects. One possibility, for instance, is a global system of tradable permits, where the initial allocation is proportional to the population size in each country. Alternatively, a system with very similar distributional implications is a global tax on emissions, whereby the revenues are distributed back in proportion to population size.[1] Of course, policies that seem ethically appealing (e.g. Kverndokk 1995) are not necessarily politically feasible, and there are also further practical hurdles, such as widespread political corruption in many poor countries, which complicates the picture.

3.2 The efficiency principle

The efficiency principle simply calls for maximizing total surplus. In economics, fairness and efficiency are often considered to be at odds, and much discussion concerns the equity-efficiency trade-off. Tobe sure, the two can conflict, as with a lump sum tax that impacts living standards of low income individuals disproportionately. However, they need not necessarily conflict, for example if pollution permits are allocated so as to favor developing economies as mentioned above. Moreover, survey evidence shows that views of fairness encompass not only equity (i.e., accountability) but also efficiency; indeed, fair allocations reflect trade-offs between competing distributive rules (see Konow 2001). Experimental studies corroborate the trade-off between efficiency and equity; see e.g. Engelmann and Strobel (2004), Fehr et al. (2006), Stahl and Haruvy (2009). In fact, many subjects exhibit a remarkable willingness to sacrifice personal earnings in order to increase the total, e.g., in the dictator games reported in Andreoni and Miller (2002), Charness and Rabin (2002).

The importance of efficiency among distributive preferences is good news for environmental economics, most of which has, to date, stressed efficiency as the normative goal of policy.[2] Indeed, the news only seems to get better, when one considers recent experimental evidence suggesting that surplus maximization also affects the willingness to cooperate. In a voluntary contribution game, Oxoby (2006) allows subjects to constrain the choices of others to more efficient outcomes and finds that, if they can dictate cooperation by others, subjects then voluntarily choose themselves to contribute rather than to free-ride. Nevertheless, collectively, the evidence suggests that efficiency does not exhaust the set of preferences relevant to cooperation. Stahl and Haruvy (2009) argue that the results of their extensive-form games are best reconciled with a behavioral model that incorporates self-interest, efficiency and inequality aversion.

3.3 The need principle

The need principle of distributive justice requires the satisfaction of the basic needs of all individuals. Similar to the efficiency principle, it is an absolute standard, but it pertains to minimum allocations to individuals as opposed to maximization of aggregate allocations. Survey results indicate that people associate fairness with the satisfaction of basic needs, but when needs satisfaction conflicts with accountability or efficiency, there is a trade-off among these goals (e.g., Konow 2001). Some dictator experiments are suggestive of a concern for need. Eckel and Grossman (1996) find that student dictators are less generous toward fellow students than toward the presumably more needy recipients of their donations to the American Red Cross. Crumpler and Grossman (2008) present subjects with a choice of charities, and dictators seem to choose most frequently ones serving those whose basic needs or health is threatened. The results of Konow (2010) provide stronger support for a concern for basic needs: in one treatment, dictators donate to one of two charities that explicitly provide for basic needs and, in other treatments, to fellow students. Transfers in the former significantly exceed those in the latter and are the largest of any laboratory dictator study (the modal gift was the dictator's entire endowment). Moreover, in post-experimental questionnaires, roughly two-thirds of the more generous dictators explain their motivation in terms of a concern for the needs of recipients. Interestingly, many of the more selfish dictators in this study also explain their allocations in terms of need but by appeal to their own needs.

Despite the prominent place given to needs in the early days of economics, e.g., by Malthus (1798) and George (1879), it occupies a considerably less visible position inmost modern economics, excepting, to some degree, in development economics. In particular, most economics experiments and social preference models that have accompanied them do not consider need among the motivations. Perhaps this is related to the fact that most of this research has been conducted in the developed world, where such concerns are not salient in the populations usually studied. Nevertheless, with an estimated 40% of the world's population living on less than $2 per day (World Bank Development Indicators, 2005), need certainly cannot be ignored in an international analysis of justice. In fact, discussions about the fairness of the burden of climate change policy often centers on differences between developed countries and those that have to cope with high rates of poverty. In a survey of agents involved in negotiations over climate change policy, Lange et al. (2010) find strong support for the "ability to pay" rule that favors less developed countries by assigning responsibility for abatement costs based on GDP.

3.4 The equality norm

Probably the most striking stylized fact of experimental studies involving social preferences is the high incidence of equal splits. A frequent, and often the modal, decision is one that creates equal earnings in designs as varied as the dictator game, ultimatum game, and trust game. Most of the major theories of social preferences that have been developed to account for experimental results incorporate equality as an argument, including Bolton and Ockenfels (2000), Charness and Rabin (2002), Fehr and Schmidt (1999), although see also Cox etal. (2007) for one exception. It is usually the case that results of public good experiments are also characterized by equality, but of a different kind, viz., equal contributions. Buckley and Croson (2006), Cherry et al. (2005), for example, conduct linear public good experiments with endowment heterogeneity. To equalize net earnings, those subjects with high endowments should contribute more than those with low endowments. But, instead, there is a pronounced tendency in these studies for subjects to match absolute contributions irrespective of endowments or net earnings. Indeed, such matching of transfers is a stylized fact of many experiments involving cooperation, including Charness et al. (2007), Croson et al. (2005), Fischbacher et al. (2001). These two goals (equalizing earnings vs. equalizing contributions) have very different implications for the distribution of the costs and benefits of environmental policy.

We believe these conflicting goals can be better understood by distinguishing impartial fairness preferences from the potentially biased views of stakeholders. The former are important as guides to normative economics and economic policy and, to the extent they are shared by stakeholders, to descriptive analysis of fairness. The latter are crucial to understanding and predicting behavior in many real world situations in which self-interest is implicated but agents might also have to factor in their distinct fairness preferences from those of spectators. Let us consider and clarify these two perspectives in turn.

Evidence on impartial preferences comes from survey studies of fairness and from experimental studies employing third party decision-makers who choose allocations for other subjects. Based on these, Konow (2003) concludes that equality is not a *principle* of justice, i.e., a general distributive rule endorsed by impartial third parties. The argument is that equality does often emerge for a variety of reasons, but not because of a general, impartial preference for it. One reason for equality is that it is sometimes a *special case* of a general principle that otherwise produces inequality. For example, equality is a special case of accountability, if the contributions individuals control are equal, of efficiency, if equal rewards maximize the total, and of need, if the resources needed to satisfy basic needs are the same across individuals. Often, information about differences that are relevant to general principles is unavailable or unreliable. In such cases, people usually make the *ceteris paribus assumption* about such differences and favor equality by default. A corollary of this last statement is that, when information relevant to other principles becomes available, people will abandon equality in favor of those principles. This is consistent with the survey results on fairness attitudes in Konow (2001) and with the allocation decisions of experimental subjects who reason impartially in Herne and Mård (2006). The ceteris paribus assumption is a plausible explanation for the prominence of equal splits in many economics experiments: in order to focus on a particular question or to avoid inadvertent cues, many of these studies have a very lean design, but then they often lack the contextual elements or means for subjects to apply principles like accountability, efficiency or need. When the information and opportunities exist to act on these principles, subjects typically depart from equality, as seen for the sake of efficiency in Andreoni and Miller (2002), for accountability in Gächter and Riedl (2006), and for need in Konow (2010).

Thus, the evidence casts doubt on equality as a principle of justice, i.e., a general rule endorsed from an impartial or impersonal perspective. Nevertheless, it is clear that equality is frequently employed by stakeholders in personal (as opposed to impartial) relationships, such as with the treatment of co-workers, duties among family members, earnings of counterparts in bargaining experiments, or sharing of a dinner bill among friends. Equality is, therefore, a distributive rule but one of a different kind, which is why we refer to the equality *norm* instead of the equality *principle*. As used here, norm connotes a moral rule distinct to personal relationships, whereas principle denotes a general and impartial rule. A principle might also be valued, of course, in personal relationships, e.g., co-workers might be motivated not only by equality but also by accountability, but a norm is relevant only in personal contexts. This typology is consistent with the results of Konow etal. (2009). Their dictator study involves allocations by third parties, or impartial spectators, as well as by standard dictators, or stakeholders, who vary across treatments in how personal their relationships are to their paired recipients. Spectators allocate strictly according to accountability, whereas stakeholders shift toward equality, and the shift is greater, the more personal their relationship to recipients. These patterns are remarkably robust with respect to a wide range of variables, including nationality (US or Japanese), culture, race, income and gender.

Contributors to a public good are also in a personal relationship: even if they are anonymous, they are matched with other subjects and share earnings in a manner that depends on their individual decisions. Public good experiments often produce marked patterns of equality, but this typically takes the form of a tendency to equalize absolute contributions as in Croson (2007). Cherry et al. (2005) find a similar tendency: high endowment subjects do not contribute proportionately more than low endowment subjects, but the former do contribute significantly more in absolute terms, suggesting that there is an attempt, on average, partially to offset differences in endowments. These results relate easily to debates that occur over the fairness of environmental policies. For instance, negotiations about global warming often revolve around the fairness of rules that require equal contributions, such as the egalitarian rule, versus those that tend to equalize incomes after the costs of abatement, such as the ability to pay rule.

4 Tradeoffs and interpretive issues

The fairness rules described in the previous section are conceptually quite simple, so it seems that applying them should be relatively straightforward. Nevertheless, the frequency and ferocity of debates over fairness make it obvious that their application is anything but straightforward.

A little reflection reveals, however, that, even if there were complete agreement on and clarity about the rules of justice, people would not be able to judge the fairness of allocations without specification of additional variables. What is required is a series of interpretive decisions about contextual factors. First, what is the relative importance of each rule, when the pursuit of one rule conflicts with the satisfaction of another? For instance, how does one balance the efficiency of reducing toxic industrial waste with the potential loss of employment? Indeed, the experimental literature is replete with examples of heterogeneity of types according to their social preferences or their willingness to act on them. Andreoni and Miller (2002), for example, report that about 47% of their dictators are selfish, 30% want equality and 23% prefer efficiency. Studies of cooperation in public good games and other social dilemmas similarly suggest that people fall into different categories, including defectors, conditional cooperators and unconditional cooperators (see Chaudhuri 2009). Agents also differ in their motives, which can include, among others, altruism and warm glow (Andreoni 1990), or reciprocity and conformity (Alpizar et al. 2008).

Even if there is agreement on the first question about how to weigh fairness rules, however, the second set of questions reveals even deeper interpretative issues. Specifically, which people and what variables should be included when evaluating fairness? This question can be contentious, even if one is trying to apply only a single rule. For example, when attempting to determine fair country requirements for the reduction of greenhouse gases according to the accountability principle, should nations with historically higher emissions bear greater costs given that their situation resulted from their choices of inefficient vehicles and dirty technologies, or should their burden be moderated by claims that their higher emissions are partially due to factors outside their control, such as greater travel distances or an outdated infrastructure that is expensive to renovate? As Cappelen et al. (2007) demonstrate in their dictator game study, people sometimes arrive at very different conclusions about what variables are relevant when assigning responsibility. The other question is which people to include when considering the repercussions for fairness of any policies. For example, should one consider the effects of a sulfur dioxide tradeable permits program only on those directly affected, or should one adopt a broader perspective and also consider its effects on their incomes relative to those of others in the region, country or world? With global climate change, the choice seems more obvious, at least for normative matters, that one should include peoples of all countries affected. But then does one also try generally to tackle broader questions of international inequities in income? The evidence on stakeholder behavior suggests people tend to choose a narrower, local view. Ruffle and Sosis (2006), for example, find significant in-group-out-group bias in a field experiment on cooperation among kibbutz members and city dwellers.

Nevertheless, a considerable volume of survey and experimental research suggests that impartial judges often achieve a fairly high of agreement about what is fair, even if stakeholders more frequently disagree (see Konow 2003, for examples, including for the following conclusions). What seems to guide stakeholder views and often create spectator consensus are the particulars provided by the context. First, people typically work with the available information in evaluating the relative importance of fairness rules. Thus, for example, if people in a developed country are presented with the question of how to divide a given salary pool between two workers who have chosen to work different hours, they will apply accountability and favor proportionality, ignoring both efficiency, since the pool is fixed, and need, since the basic needs of workers in developed countries are not typically endangered. Similarly, as previously mentioned, student subjects in dictator experiments are more generous toward charities, responding to the need of their beneficiaries, than toward fellow students, where the equality norm usually applies and requires only equal splits. Second, impartial judges usually exhibit a high degree of agreement about the choice of variables and people relevant to fairness evaluation. Again context provides most direction on and, consequently, answers to these questions. For example, survey respondents view a CEO's high salary as fair, when compared to other similarly paid executives, but as unfair, when compared to the much lower compensation to workers. As this last example illustrates, however, not all information is created equal, and judgments can be sensitive to framing effects. This is useful to know for descriptive analyses of fairness but perhaps troubling for prescriptive work on justice. Nevertheless, even the latter concern seems less serious in light of evidence that spectators can identify morally relevant information and, when they do, arrive at a consensus about fair allocations Konow (2009).

5 Fairness concerns and environmental policy

The studies cited above provide ample support for the claim that people care about fairness. But does this fact have any implication for environmental policy and for how we should systematically analyze environmental problems? We answer these questions in the affirmative for a variety of reasons.

5.1 Cooperation possibilities and fairness concerns

The climate can be seen as a global public good, since we can all benefit from it, but we cannot exclude others from also benefiting. This is, of course, also the core of the problem, since what is rational for a single country in isolation is globally suboptimal. If each country has to pay for its own abatement costs of reducing greenhouse gas emissions, while all countries now and in the future share the benefits, there is clearly room for free-riding, such that each country continues to emit more than what is globally optimal. In order to prevent free-riding, we need agreements on some kind of a cooperative solution, e.g., in terms of coalitions. There is a relatively large theoretical literature on negotiations related to transnational pollution, e.g., Carraro and Siniscalco (1998), Asheim et al. (2006), but almost all of this literature assumes that each negotiating country cares solely about its own material payoff (cf. Barrett 2005). Some of this literature concerns repeated games, i.e., negotiations occur not once, but rather multiple times, and asymmetries between, negotiating parties, i.e., they take account of the fact that some countries are much larger and more powerful than others. Other approaches, so-called differential games, deal both with strategic interaction and dynamic optimization simultaneously. Moreover, parts of the literature allow for collusion, i.e., the possibility that some countries cooperate with one another against other countries.

Carraro and Siniscalco (1993), Barrett (1994) provide the standard approach to studying coalition formation in the climate context. They use a two-period non-cooperative framework in which countries first decide whether or not to join a coalition. Those who join will then behave cooperatively with one another in a second stage. Both the coalition (as an entity) and the remaining countries choose their emission levels non-cooperatively. As shown by Carraro and Siniscalco (1993), Barrett (1994, 1997), the resulting coalition size tends to be rather small.

Lange and Vogt (2003), on the other hand, show that, when countries care not only about their own absolute payoffs but also about fairness, the coalition size tends to be larger, and even the grand coalition (that includes all countries) can be stable. In contrast to Lange and Vogt (2003) who employ a symmetric model, Lange (2006) considers the situation with asymmetries, in which case it is no longer obvious that fairness concerns increase the coalition size.

The above examples show that fairness concerns can, in principle, have significant implications for negotiating parties, providing a rationale for incorporating such concerns into formal environmental economics models. However, the major entities making and attempting to influence environmental policy are often large organizations, such as governments and corporations, rather than the individuals whose decisions often form the basis for the behavioral findings reported previously. That individuals seem to care about fairness does not, of course, imply that the Board of Directors of Exxon and Archer Daniels Midland or the leaders of industrial nations are similarly motivated. Indeed, the fact that decisions about environmental policy are often made by large groups does not seem to bode well for fairness and for international cooperation on the environment, given evidence that groups tend to act in a more selfish way than individuals (e.g., Luhan et al. 2009). Thus, one might expect resistance to environmental initiatives from countries and large corporations. On the other hand, groups, in the end, consist of individuals, who bring their own values into these interactions, as the aforementioned results of Lange et al. (2010) suggest.

Moreover, these organizations are often constrained by the values of others, even if they do not place great value on fairness themselves. Governments (even undemocratic ones) are usually subject, to some degree, to the views and passions of their constituents, and fairness likely plays a significant role in the motives of the latter. Given the negligible instrumental value of voting relative to its cost, Brennan and Hamlin (1998) conclude that an important reason people vote in the first place is for expressive purposes. This claim finds support in field and experimental studies, e.g., see Sobel and Wagner (2004), Tyran (2004), respectively. The putative importance of this expressive motive suggests that voting is a reflection less of a concern for material payoffs than of values, such as fairness. Similarly, corporations must, of course, pay attention to their potential customers, who can engage in boycotts and appeal to state intervention, as evidenced by their public relations campaigns and by adjustments of business practices in response to expressed or expected public reactions.

Thus, although self-interest will certainly influence group behavior, as it does individual behavior, we can also expect fairness to play a role. Moreover, the project of determining the influence of fairness on environmental issues is not aimed at proving that fairness always dominates such issues, but rather at understanding better its distinctive and often significant role, both for descriptive as well as prescriptive analysis.

5.2 Environmental valuation and fairness

In survey-based environmental valuation investigations, such as contingent valuation studies, people are implicitly or explicitly asked to value an environmental improvement, or the avoidance of an environmental damage, in terms of their maximum willingness to pay (or WTP). It is normally assumed that these values reflect their preferences in a manner that corresponds to their individual well-being. There is also evidence, however, from "think-aloud" methodology that the results of environmental valuation studies appear to be influenced by what people believe their fair share of the costs associated with an improvement would be (Schkade and Payne 1994).

Note that this motive is distinct from other non-selfish motives, such as those based on non-paternalistic or paternalistic altruism, cf. McConnell (1997), Johansson-Stenman (2000). Although fairness-based WTP statements might provide the authorities with some valuable information in terms of priorities (see Sect. 5.3 below), it does not make sense to incorporate such responses uncritically into a conventional cost-benefit analysis as if they reflected the respondents' true values in terms of their well-being. There are at least two reasons for prudence in this regard: first, there are questions about the contingent valuation method that have yet to be answered, and, second, there are questions about interpreting preferences (even fairness preferences) as well-being, which we will address in the following sub-section.

On the other hand, these facts do not rule out the usefulness of such studies for purposes of measuring people's preferences over the distributive consequences of solutions to environmental problems, such as to the problem of climate change. For example, Cai et al. (2008) provide a carefully executed web-based contingent valuation study of a hypothetical referendum type that measures willingness to pay for global warming mitigation. They found that people are typically willing to pay more, when the payment vehicle implies that larger cost shares are borne by parties deemed to bear a greater responsibility for mitigation, and when respondents believe that the effects of climate change might be borne disproportionately by the world's poor. These results are, of course, entirely consistent with the *accountability* and *need* principles discussed above. Nevertheless, as useful as stated preference methods may be, it is important to keep in mind that, when it comes to welfare analysis, it is inappropriate to equate people's willingness to pay with individual measures of welfare change.[3]

5.3 The social objective

Let us suppose that people have fairness preferences as outlined above. Does that mean that the social objective function in economic analysis should change accordingly? We argue against the a priori imposition of some social objective, including that of the scientist. Thus, economists should be able to analyze normative problems based on an ethical foundation (e.g. some version of utilitarianism) that the economist does not share. Hence, in our view it makes perfect sense to conclude that based on the ethical assumption A, behavioral assumptions B, and market equilibrium assumption C, that conclusion D follows, even if the economist undertaking the analysis does not share the views underlying the ethical assumption A. Yet, in practice we often have to make some underlying normative assumptions, and we find it different to defend the a priori exclusion of fairness considerations in normative analysis. How incorporating fairness considerations affects the normative analysis depends on at least two broad considerations. Put simply, the one consideration concerns what, exactly, to incorporate, and the other how, exactly, to integrate it. These are addressed in turn below.

Fairness terminology (including the terms justice and equity) is employed with differing levels of specificity, both in theoretical work and in common usage, a fact that has been noted from Aristotle's *Nicomachean Ethics* to modern social science research. That is, at times, it signifies the whole of goodness or virtue, including reciprocity, honesty, charity, etc., whereas, at other times, it represents values that are a proper subset of goodness. Hence, the question "What is fair?" is sometimes the same as the question "What is right?" or "What is good?" In other cases, it signifies something more specific, whereby there is survey evidence that the most specific sense of fairness is equivalent to accountability alone (Konow 2001). We have chosen, in this paper, to define fairness in an intermediate sense as distributive preferences, partly because we believe this represents a close approximation of everyday usage of fairness terminology, which reflects a combination of general and specific meanings. But this implies that evidence on fairness preferences will give disproportionate weight to more specific meanings, like accountability.

To get an intuitive sense of this last claim, consider the following thought experiment. Suppose two workers, A and B, have the same ability, work equally hard, and produce the same amount of output. Which allocation, I or II, below is most *fair*?

I. A earns 100 USD per day, B also earns 100 USD per day
II. A earns 200 USD per day, B earns 150 USD per day

Since both workers have contributed equally to output, allocation I seems fairer, consistent with the accountability principle, which calls for equal allocations in such a case. But consider instead the following question: Which allocation do you think *should* be implemented? Now allocation II seems a more acceptable response. Framed this way, the second question explicitly elicits more general moral preferences, and efficiency, therefore, receives increased weight in the respondent's moral calculus. There is no inconsistency, therefore, in maintaining that I is fairer than II but that II is better than I. In the framework of both welfare economics and consequentialist ethics more generally, goodness can be the overarching goal, even if fairness is an element of goodness. Hence, it does not follow that, if people believe that Policy I is fairer than Policy II, society should prefer Policy I to Policy II.

Thus, any attempt to incorporate moral preferences into a social objective function must first address the question of the level of specificity in those preferences. We advocate a very general approach that incorporates goodness in the broadest terms and believe that the burden of proof, in this matter, must fall on claims for a more narrow definition that excludes some moral preferences. Thus, we choose to treat fairness broadly as distributive justice here, since this encompasses many, if not most, moral preferences in this context. Nevertheless, in the interests of brevity and tractability, we have ignored other important moral preferences, such as reciprocity and honesty, that eventually might be included in a more general analysis.

So, focusing on fairness as distributive justice, should this be incorporated into welfare analysis, and, if so, how? In addressing these questions, we proceed first from the most conservative conclusions implied from the foregoing analysis. The behavioral and survey evidence on fairness strongly suggests that people value it subjectively. That is, put into economic terms, people derive utility (in terms of well-being) from fairness, or equivalently experience disutility from unfairness. If this is the case, fairness has implications for allocations even under standard analysis.

Formally, we may think of a conventional welfaristic social welfare function as follows:

$$W = w(U^1, U^2, ..., U^n), \tag{1}$$

where U^i reflects the utility or well-being of individual i. Assume that each individual's utility depends on his/her own income, x^i, as well as the perceived overall fairness, F^i, so that

$$U^i = u^i(x^i, F^i) \quad \forall i. \tag{2}$$

Let us next assume that i's perceived fairness depends on the distribution of income in the society generally, so that

$$F^i = f^i(\mathbf{x}) \equiv f^i(x^1,...,x^n) \quad \forall i. \tag{3}$$

Note that f^i can reflect issues such as accountability, efficiency and need, and it is, therefore, not at all obvious that it is symmetric with respect to the income levels. For example, i may perceive the allocation to be fairer if individual 2 has twice the income of individual 1 relative to the case in which both have the same income. Substituting (2) and (3) into (1) we obtain

$$W = w\left(u^1(x^1, f^1(\mathbf{x})), u^2(x^2, f^2(\mathbf{x})), ..., u^n(x^n, f^n(x))\right). \tag{4}$$

We can next calculate the corresponding social marginal rate of substitution between an income change for individual i and j, as follows:

$$SMRS^{ij} = \frac{dW / dx^i}{dW / dx^j} = \frac{\partial w / \partial U^i (\partial u^i / \partial x^i + \sum_{k=1}^{n} \partial u^k / \partial F^k \partial f^k / \partial x^i)}{\partial w / \partial U^j (\partial u^j / \partial x^j + \sum_{k=1}^{n} \partial u^k / \partial F^k \partial f^k / \partial x^j)} \quad \forall i, j. \tag{5}$$

Thus, (5) reflects the social welfare increase of giving an additional dollar to individual i, relative to the welfare increase of instead giving the dollar to individual j. Clearly, this ratio depends on several components. First, it depends on the differences in the extent to which incremental utility contributes to social welfare. For example, a frequently made assumption is that w is utilitarian. In that case, $\partial w/\partial U^i = \partial w/\partial U^j$ and (5) reduces to

$$SMRS^{ij} = \frac{\partial u^i / \partial x^i + \sum_{k=1}^{n} \partial u^k / \partial F^k \partial f^k / \partial x^i}{\partial u^j / \partial x^j + \sum_{k=1}^{n} \partial u^k / \partial F^k \partial f^k / \partial x^j} \quad \forall i, j. \tag{6}$$

If w is not utilitarian, it is typically assumed that w is strictly quasi-concave, implying that the same utility increase raises welfare more the lower the initial utility level is. Next, there is a direct effect through the changes in utility levels.

As we have specified the utility function very generally, we can, of course, not say anything in general about comparisons between *i*'s and *j*'s marginal utilities of income, but a commonly made assumption in applied work is that the marginal utility of income is decreasing in the income level.

In addition to these welfare effects, we have the effects through the fairness perceptions. Note that we here have welfare effects for all individuals, since each individual's fairness perception includes the incomes of *i* and *j*. The size of these welfare effects, in turn, depends on the weight the fairness concern carries in each individual's utility function, $\partial u^k/\partial F^k$, as well as on how much each individual *k*'s fairness perception is affected by a small income increase of *i* (or *j*), i.e., on $\partial f^k/\partial x^i$. Thus, even under very modest assumptions acceptable within standard welfare analysis, including utilitarianism, fairness has implications for social welfare.

An alternative approach is to assume that fairness is an intrinsic argument in the social welfare function (SWF), as follows:

$$W = w(U^1, U^2, \ldots, U^n, F). \tag{7}$$

Note that (7) constitutes a *non-welfaristic* social welfare function, following the terminology of Sen (1970, 1979), since it does not solely depend on individual utilities. That is, people might think that the society should value fairness intrinsically. In this case, it can be shown that fairness matters for allocations, even if people individually do not derive utility from fairness. That is, let us here assume that people's utilities (reflecting well-being) are not affected by any fairness concerns, so that we have

$$U^i = u^i(x^i) \quad \forall i, \tag{8}$$

whereas the fairness concerns at the social level can be written as a social fairness function

$$F = f(\mathbf{x}). \tag{9}$$

Substituting (8) and (9) into (7) we obtain

$$W = w\left(u^1(x^1), u^2(x^2), \ldots, u^n(x^n), f(x)\right). \tag{10}$$

The social marginal rate of substitution between an income change for individual *i* and *j* can then be written as:

$$SMRS^{ij} = \frac{\partial w/\partial U^i \partial u^i/\partial x^i + \partial w/\partial F \partial f/\partial x^i}{\partial w/\partial U^j \partial u^j/\partial x^j + \partial w/\partial F \partial f/\partial x^i} \quad \forall i, j. \tag{11}$$

Note that we cannot analyze a utilitarian case here, since utilitarianism is a special case of a welfaristic SWF, and the SWF in (7)is non-welfaristic. Nevertheless, we can still analyze the symmetric case in which each individual's utility carries the same weight in the SWF, similar to the utilitarian case. Then, we have $\partial w/\partial U^i = \partial w/\partial U^j = \partial w/\partial U$, implying that (11) simplifies to

$$SMRS^{ij} = \frac{\partial u^i / \partial x^i + \frac{\partial w / \partial F}{\partial w / \partial U} \partial f / \partial x^i}{\partial u^j / \partial x^j + \frac{\partial w / \partial F}{\partial w / \partial U} \partial f / \partial x^j} \quad \forall i, j. \tag{12}$$

Ignoring the effects through the SWF, welfare effects emerge through the marginal utility of income, as above, and through the social fairness function. The size of the fairness related welfare effect depends on how much fairness is affected by the income change, $\partial f/\partial x^i$, and on the relative weight that is given on the margin to fairness concerns relative to utility concerns in the SWF, i.e., $\frac{\partial w / \partial F}{\partial w / \partial U}$.

We can, of course, also think of the case in which fairness is an argument both of individual utility functions and of the social welfare function. In this case, we can substitute (2), (3) and (9) into (7) and obtain

$$W = w\left(u^1(x^1, f^1(\mathbf{x})), u^2(x^2, f^2(\mathbf{x})), \ldots, u^n(x^n, f^n(\mathbf{x})), f(\mathbf{x})\right). \tag{13}$$

Then, we can write the social marginal rate of substitution between an income change for individual i and j as follows:

$$SMRS^{ij} = \frac{\partial w / \partial U^i (\partial u^i / \partial x^i + \sum_{k=1}^{n} \partial u^k / \partial F^k \partial f^k / \partial x^i) + \partial w / \partial F \partial f / \partial x^i}{\partial w / \partial U^j (\partial u^j / \partial x^j + \sum_{k=1}^{n} \partial u^k / \partial F^k \partial f^k / \partial x^j) + \partial w / \partial F \partial f / \partial x^j} \quad \forall i, j, \tag{14}$$

which, in the symmetric case where $\partial w/\partial U^i = \partial w/\partial U^j = \partial w/\partial U$, can be simplified as

$$SMRS^{ij} = \frac{\partial u^i / \partial x^i + \sum_{k=1}^{n} \partial u^k / \partial F^k \partial f^k / \partial x^i + \frac{\partial w / \partial F}{\partial w / \partial U} \partial f / \partial x^i}{\partial u^j / \partial x^j + \sum_{k=1}^{n} \partial u^k / \partial F^k \partial f^k / \partial x^j + \frac{\partial w / \partial F}{\partial w / \partial U} \partial f / \partial x^j} \quad \forall i, j. \tag{15}$$

Thus, in addition to the welfare effects in (12), we have here also the effects through the individual fairness concerns in each individual's utility function.

Should the government respect people's preferences in these respects? Starting with the effects through people's utility functions, we find it hard to argue that these effects should not count. Indeed, why would utility derived from perceived fairness count less than the same amount derived for any other reason?

The intrinsic fairness effect through the social objective function is perhaps less straightforward. But there are compelling reasons for basing social objective functions on the ethical values that people in the society have. By one view, this is justified as a representation of the moral preferences of an idealized agent. In fact, one can imagine a more radical departure from welfaristic social objective functions that abandons utility as an argument altogether. The social objective function might be written solely as a function of the various functions that, in turn, reflect moral preferences, including, inter alia, accountability, efficiency and need. The arguments of these moral preference functions could be income, as formulated above with the social fairness function, or utility could be reinstated by making the moral preference functions themselves functions of individual utilities.

A related, but mostly separate, discussion has arisen regarding the implications of findings about bounded rationality for social welfare. A growing literature, motivated by behavioral economics insights, points out the hazards of adopting "consumer sovereignty" as a universal guiding rule for welfare analysis. One approach is to assume that what really matters is well-being rather than choice, following, for example, Broome (1999), Ng (1999), O'Donoghue and Rabin (2006), Johansson-Stenman (2008), or, using the terminology of Kahneman et al. (1997), Kahneman and Thaler (2006), to assume that what matters is *experienced* utility rather than *decision* utility.

In conventional welfare analysis, the ultimate goal is often expressed as the maximization of social welfare or well-being, and if we believe that respecting people's preferences, as revealed by their choices, is an effective way of obtaining this goal, then it follows that it would indeed be a good idea for policy makers to respect the principle of consumer sovereignty. This is contingent, however, on the assumption that people do know, and act in accordance with, what is best (in terms of their well-being) for themselves. But suppose, for example, that people have self-control problems, which imply time inconsistency, such that they fail to act in accordance with their own interests. Then the link from consumer sovereignty to welfare maximization does not follow.

As a result, policy measures based on different kinds of paternalism has been proposed. For example, Gruber and Köszegi (2001)argue in favor of cigarette taxation, not in order to internalize *externalities* (which they argue are rather small, anyway), but rather in order to internalize what they denote *internalities*, i.e., in order to help them act consistent with their own ultimate will and interest. Similarly, O'Donoghue and Rabin (2006) argue in favor of "fat taxes," and other "sin taxes." Camerer (2003), Thaler and Sunstein (2008) provide good overviews of such arguments, whereas Sugden (2004), Bernheim and Rangel (2007), Bernheim and Rangel (2009) provide alternative choice-based approaches when people make mistakes.

Concerns for moral preferences and bounded rationality problems sometimes intersect. Bazerman refers to the phenomenon of "bounded ethicality," i.e., the idea that even good people often violate moral norms unawares and as the result of ordinary and predictable psychological processes. For example, Gino and Bazerman (2009) find that people are more likely to accept unethical behavior when allowed to adapt to it more slowly. One can easily imagine serious ramifications of moral preferences under bounded rationality, e.g., if people express political preferences in favor of institutional arrangements that are perceived to be fair but that imply large inefficiency losses, which people systematically tend to underestimate. In fact, there is evidence of this, e.g., Caplan (2002) finds that people, on average, tend to underestimate the benefits from trade and globalization. The question then arises whether the social objective should be based on the values people express or rather on their "informed values."

Thus, considerations of fairness and bounded rationality raise interesting, important and difficult challenges for welfare analysis. Nevertheless, these facts can be seen as a basis for improving and making more relevant this analysis. In the partial equilibrium context of cost-benefit analysis, that is precisely the conclusion at which Bazerman and Greene (2010) arrive, and we believe the same will be found to be true for general equilibrium welfare analysis.

6 Conclusion

This chapter presents empirical evidence that people care about fairness and that it is possible to analyze fairness concerns systematically. Although views of fairness often differ, there is much less heterogeneity regarding impartial fairness concerns, i.e., those expressed by spectators.

We conclude that fairness preferences have important implications for the field of environmental economics through the analysis of (1) individual behavior, (2) the behavior of other decision makers such as policymakers and international negotiators, and also through (3) the overall social objective function. We believe that the benefits in terms of greater empirical predictive power, as well as greater theoretical and policy relevance, of incorporating fairness concerns in the analysis often dominate the associated costs in terms of greater complexity. We also believe that environmental economics would have greater influence on environmental policy if fairness considerations were taken more seriously.

Thus, we think that theoretical and empirical research of fairness in environmental economics is fertile ground for future work. One particularly important and potentially impactful avenue of investigation is empirical analysis of fairness perceptions about alternative policy instruments. Many environmental policy instruments, such as tradable permit systems, can be quite complex and cognitively demanding for laypersons. This contextual complexity, often combined with the previously discussed self-serving biases, present challenges to reaching a consensus on environmental policy that is the result of an informed and thoughtful process. Thus, future work might build on experimental studies, such as those of Frohlich and Oppenheimer (1992), which engage people in discussions aimed at learning and moral reflection and which have sometimes been shown to generate consensus about policies with important distributive consequences.

Acknowledgments

We want to thank Fredrik Carlsson, Magnus Hennlock, Åsa Löfgren, Thomas Sterner and seminar participants at the workshop *Behavioral economics: What can it contribute to environmental and resource economics?* in Bellingham 2009 for very useful comments and discussions. Financial support from Sida to the Environmental Economics Unit at University of Gothenburg is gratefully acknowledged.

Notes

1 Furthermore, one could even argue that poorer countries should have the right to emit more than the richer countries in the future, in order to compensate for their lower emissions in the past.
2 Nevertheless, as discussed further in Sect. 5.3, it is possible that some people value efficiency without considering it to be an element of fairness.
3 At least, this caveat applies, if one means by 'welfare change' changes in actual or expected well-being; if 'welfare change' means something else, that must be specified differently.

References

Alesina A, Angeletos G-M (2005) Fairness and redistribution. *Am Econ Rev* 95(4):960–980

Alpizar F, Carlsson F, Johansson-Stenman O (2008) Anonymity, reciprocity and conformity: evidence from voluntary contributions to a natural park in Costa Rica. *J Public Econ* 92:986–997

Andreoni J (1990) Impure altruism and donations to public goods: a theory of warm-glow giving. *Econ J* 100:464–477

Andreoni J, Miller J (2002) Giving according to GARP: an experimental test of the consistency of preferences for altruism. *Econometrica* 70(2):737–753

Asheim GB, Froyn C, Bretteville HJ, Menz FC (2006) Regional versus global cooperation for climate control. *J Environ Econ Manage* 51:93–109

Babcock L, Loewenstein G (1997) Explaining bargaining impasse: the role of self-serving biases. *J Econ Perspect* 11(1):109–126

Barrett S (1994) Self-enforcing international environmental agreements. *Oxf Econ Pap* 46:878–894

Barrett S (1997) Heterogeneous international environmental agreements. In: Carraro C (ed) *International environmental agreemens: strategic policy issues*. Edward Elgar, Cheltenham, pp 9–25

Barrett S (2005) The theory of international environmental agreements. In: Mäler K-G, Vincent JR (eds) *Handbook of environmental economics, vol. 3*. Elsevier, Amsterdam, p 28

Bazerman M, Greene J (2010) In favor of clear thinking: incorporating moral rules into a wise cost-benefit analysis. *Perspect Psycol Sci* 5(2):209–212

Bernheim D, Rangel A (2007) Toward choice-theoretic foundations for behavioral welfare economics. *Am Econ Rev* 97(2):464–470

Bernheim D, Rangel A (2009) Beyond revealed preference: choice-theoretic foundations for behavioral welfare economics. *QJ Econ* 124(1):51–104

Bolton G, Ockenfels A (2000) A theory of equity, reciprocity, and competition. *Am Econ Rev* 90(1):166–193

Bossert W, Fleurbaey M (1996) Redistribution and compensation. *Soc Choice Welf* 13(3):343–355

Brekke KA, Johansson-Stenman O (2008) The behavioural economics of climate change. *Oxf Rev of Econ Policy* 24(2):280–297

Brennan G, Hamlin A (1998) Expressive voting and electoral equilibrium. *Public Choice* 95(1):149–175

Broome J (1999) *Ethics out of economics*. Cambridge University Press, Cambridge

Buckley E, Croson R (2006) Income and wealth heterogeneity in the voluntary provision of linear public goods. *J Public Econ* 90:935–955

Cai B, Cameron TA, Gerdes GR (2008) Distributional preferences and the incidence of costs and benefits in environmental policy. In: Paper presented at the annual European conference of environmental and resource economics in Gothenburg 2008

Camerer C (2003) *Behavioral game theory: experiments in strategic interaction*. Princeton University Press, Princeton

Caplan B (2002) Systematically biased beliefs about economics: robust evidence of judgmental anomalies from the survey of Americans and economists on the economy. *Econ J* 112:1–26

Cappelen A, Tungodden B (2003) Reward and responsibility: how should we be affected when others change their effort. *Polit Philos Econ* 2(2):191–211

Cappelen AW, Hole AD, Sørensen EO, Tungodden B (2007) The pluralism of fairness ideals: an experimental approach. *Am Econ Rev* 97(3):818–827

Cappelen AW, Tungodden B (2009) Rewarding effort. *Econ Theory* 39(3):425–441

Carlsson F, Johansson-Stenman O (2009) Voting motives, group identity, and social norms. Working paper in Economics no. 366, Department of Economics, University of Gothenburg

Carraro C, Siniscalco D (1993) Strategies for the international protection of the environment. *J Public Econ* 52:309–328

Carraro C, Siniscalco D (1998) International environmental agreements: incentives and political economy. *Eur Econ Rev* 42:561–572

Charness G, Rabin M (2002) Understanding social preferences with simple tests. *QJ Econ* 117(3):817–869

Charness G, Frechette GR, Qin C-Z (2007) Endogenous transfers in the prisoner's dilemma game. *Games Econ Behav* 60(2):287–306

Chaudhuri A (2009) *Experiments in economics*. Routledge, London and New York

Cherry TL, Kroll S, Shogren JF (2005) The impact of endowment heterogeneity and origin on public good contributions: evidence from the lab. *J Econ Behav Organ* 57(3):357–365

Cox JC, Friedman D, Gjerstad S (2007) A tractable model of reciprocity and fairness. *Games Econ Behav* 59:17–45

Croson R, Fatas E, Neugebauer T (2005) Reciprocity, matching and conditional cooperation in two public goods games. *Econ Lett* 87(1):95–101

Croson R (2007) Theories of commitment, altruism and reciprocity: evidence from linear public goods games. *Econ Inq* 45(2):199–216

Crumpler H, Grossman PJ (2008) An experimental test of warm glow giving. *J Public Econ* 92(5–6):1011–1021

Dunning D, Meyerowitz JA, Holzberg AD (1989) Ambiguity and self-evaluation: the role of idiosyncratic trait definitions in self-serving assessments of ability. *J Pers Soc Psychol* 57(6):1082–1090

Eckel CC, Grossman PJ (1996) Altruism in anonymous dictator games. *Games Econ Behav* 16:181–191

Engelmann D, Strobel M (2004) Inequality aversion, efficiency, and maximin preferences in simple distribution experiments. *Am Econ Rev* 94(4):857–869

Fehr E, Schmidt KM (1999) A theory of fairness, competition and cooperation. *QJ Econ* 114(3):817–868

Fehr E, Naef M, Schmidt KM (2006) Inequality aversion, efficiency, and maximin preferences in simple distribution experiments: comment. *Am Econ Rev* 96(5):1912–1917

Festinger L (1957) *A theory of cognitive dissonance*. Stanford University Press, Palo Alto

Fischbacher U, Gachter S, Fehr E (2001) Are people conditionally cooperative? Evidence from a public goods experiment. *Econ Lett* 71(3):397–404

Fong C (2001) Social preferences, self-interest, and the demand for redistribution. *J Public Econ* 82(2):225–246

Frohlich N, Oppenheimer JA (1992) *Choosing justice. An experimental approach to ethical theory*. University of California Press, Berkeley

Gächter S, Riedl A (2005) Moral property rights in bargaining with infeasible claims. Manage Sci 51(2):249–263

Gächter S, Riedl A (2006) Dividing justly in bargaining problems. *Soc Choice Welf* 27:571–594

George, H (1879) *Progress and poverty*. Random House: San Francisco, CA

Gino F, Bazerman M (2009) When misconduct goes unnoticed: the acceptability of gradual erosion in others' unethical behavior. *J Exp Soc Psychol* 45(4):708–719

Gruber J, Köszegi B (2001) Is addiction 'rational'? Theory and evidence. *QJ Econ* 116(4):1261–1303

Güth W (1994) Distributive justice: a behavioral theory and empirical evidence. In: Güth W, Brandstätter H (eds) *Essays on economic psychology*. Springer, Berlin, pp 153–175

Güth W, Schmittberger R, Schwarze B (1982) An experimental analysis of ultimatum bargaining. *J Econ Behav Organ* 3(4):367–388

Herne K, Mård T (2006) *Three versions of impartiality: an experimental investigation*. Department of Political Science: University of Turku, Finland

Johansson-Stenman O (2000) On the value of life in rich and poor countries and distributional weights beyond utilitarianism. *Environ Resour Econ* 17:299–310

Johansson-Stenman O (2008) Mad Cows, terrorism and junk food: should public policy reflect subjective or objective risks? *J Health Econ* 27(2):234–248

Kahneman D, Wakker P, Sarin R (1997) Back to bentham? Explorations of experienced utility. *J Health Econ* 112(2):375–405

Kahneman D, Thaler R (2006) Anomalies: utility maximisation and experienced utility. *J Econ Perspect* 20:221–234

Konow J (1996) A positive theory of economic fairness. *J Econ Behav Organ* 31(1):13–35

Konow J (2000) Fair shares: accountability and cognitive dissonance in allocation decisions. *Am Econ Rev* 90(4):1072–1092

Konow J (2001) Fair and square: the four sides of distributive justice. *J Econ Behav Organ* 46(2):137–164

Konow J (2003) Which is the fairest one of all? A positive analysis of justice theories. *J Econ Lit* 41(4):1186–1237

Konow J (2009) Is fairness in the eye of the beholder? An impartial spectator analysis of justice. *Soc Choice Welfare* 33(1):101–127

Konow J (2010) Mixed feelings: theories of and evidence on giving. *J Public Econ* 94(3–4):279–297

Konow J, Saijo T, Akai K (2009) Morals versus mores: experimental evidence on equity and equality. Manuscript.

Kverndokk S (1995) Tradeable CO_2 emission permits: initial distribution as a justice problem. *Environ Values* 4(2):129–148

Lange A, Vogt C (2003) Cooperation in international environmental negotiations due to a preference for equity. *J Public Econ* 87(9–10):2049–2067

Lange A (2006) The impact of equity-preferences on the stability of international environmental agreements. *Environ Resour Econ* 34:247–267

Lange A, Loschel A, Vogt C, Ziegler A (2010) On the self-serving use of equity in international climate negotiations. *Eur Econ Rev* 54:359–375

Luhan WJ, Kocher M, Sutter M (2009) Group polarization in the team dictator game reconsidered. *Exp Econ* 12(1):26–41

Malthus T (1798) *An essay on the principle of population.* J.M. Dent & Sons, London

McConnell KE (1997) Does altruism undermine existence value. *J Environ Econ Manage* 32:22–37

Ng Y-K (1999) Utility, informed preference, or happiness: following Harsanyi's argument to its logical conclusion. *Soc Choice Welfare* 16:197–216

Nozick R (1974) *Anarchy, state, and Utopia.* Basic Books Inc, New York

O'Donoghue T, Rabin M (2006) Optimal sin taxes. *J Public Econ* 90:1825–1849

Oberholzer-Gee F, Bohnet I, Frey B (1997) Fairness and competence in democratic decisions. *Public Choice* 91(1):89–105

Oxoby R (2006) *Paretian dictators: constraining choice in a voluntary contribution game.* Department of Economics, University of Calgary

Roemer JE (1998) *Equality of opportunity.* Harvard University Press, Cambridge, Mass

Ruffle B, Sosis R (2006) Cooperation and the in-group-out-group bias: a field test on Israeli kibbutz members and city residents. *J Econ Behav Organ* 60(2):147–163

Schkade DA, Payne JW (1994) How people respond to contingent valuation questions: a verbal protocol analysis of willingness to pay for an environmental regulation. *J Environ Econ Manage* 26:88–109

Selten R (1978) The equity principle in economic behavior. In: Gottinger H, Leinfellner W (eds) *Decision theory and social ethics, issues in social choice.* Reifel Publishing, Dordrecht, pp 289–301

Sen AK (1970) *Collective choice and social welfare*, North-Holland, Amsterdam

Sen AK (1979) Personal utilities and public judgements: or what's wrong with welfare economics. *Econ J* 89:537–558

Sobel RS, Wagner GA (2004) Expressive voting and government redistribution: Testing Tullock's Charity of the uncharitable. *Public Choice* 119:143–159

Stahl D, Haruvy E (2009) Testing theories of behavior for extensive-form two-player two-stage games. *Exp Econ* 12(2):242–251

Sugden R (2004) The opportunity criterion: consumer sovereignty without the assumption of coherent preferences. *Am Econ Rev* 94(4):1014–1033

Thaler RH, Sunstein CR (2008) *Nudge: improving decisions about health, wealth, and happiness.* Yale University Press, New Haven

Tyran J-R (2004) Voting when money and morals conflict: an experimental test of expressive voting. *J Public Econ* 88(7):1645–1664

World Bank Development Indicators (2005) http://devdata.worldbank.org/wdi2005/Cover.htm

Index

Bold terms refer to figures, italicized terms refer to tables. Notes are refered to by page number then note number i.e., 10n2 indicates page 10, note 2.

Aaron, H. 58, 69, 72
Abrell, J. 145
accountability 217–218, 221, 223, 226, 227, 231
Africa 40–44, 45
Afroz, R. 79
age 27, 79, 80, 82
aggregated models 132, 137, 138, 147, 150n21
agriculture 38, 40, 44, 45
Ahmed, V. 141
AIDS *see* Almost Ideal Demand System
AIM/CGE model 141
air conditioning 82, 85, 86–90, 96n16
air quality 5–6, 76–98; changes over time 93–94; Conditional Censored Almost Ideal Demand 83–84; data 86–87, 88; household location 92–93, 94; household production function 84–86; literature review 77–82; research results 87–94
Alberini, A. 77
Alesina, A. 218
Allen-Uzawa elasticity of substitution 53, 66, 67, 72
Almost Ideal Demand System (AIDS) 83, 111, 112
altruism 217, 222
Andreoni, James 15, 16, 20, 22, 219, 221, 222
Angeletos, G-M. 218
Anthoff, David 4–5, 34–47
Aristotle 226
arithmetic models 143
Asensio, J. 119
Asheim, G. B. 224
Asia 39, 40–44
Atkinson, A. B. 209n7
averting behavior 77, 78

Babcock, L. 215, 216
Bach, S. 118–119
Bajari, P. 77
Bandyopadhyay, G. 115
Bardazzi, R. 6, 128–156
bargaining games 217
Barrett, S. 224
Bartlett, Bruce 30n3
Basso, L. J. 113
Bateman, I. 209n4
Baumol, W. J. 52
Bayer, P. 77
Bazerman, M. 231, 232
Beckman, J. 141–142
behavioural models 143
Belgium 105, 151n39
benefits: air quality improvements 76; benefit incidence 51–52, 53, 58–61, 68, 70, 72; carbon/energy taxes 120, 159; distribution of 1–2, 3, 4, 70, 131, 213, 220; measures of 57–58
Benkard, L. 77
Bento, A. M. 110, 120
Berger, M. C. 77
Bergin, A. 162–163
Bergmann, A. 80
Bergstrom, T. C. 72–73, 77
Bernanke, B. 193
Bernheim, D. 231
bias, fairness 214–216, 220
biodiversity 40, 78, 81, 82
Blanchard, O. 192
Boadway, R. 192, 194, 200, 203–204, 209n5

Bolton, G. 220
Borcherding, T. E. 72, 73
Bork, C. 119
Bosello, F. 165
Bosquet, B. 139
Bossert, W. 218
bottom-up models 150n21
bounded rationality 130, 231, 232
Bourguignon, F. 159
Bovenberg, A. L. 130
Boyle, G. 163
Braden, J. B. 51
Brännlund, R. 109
Brekke, K. A. 217
Brennan, G. 58, 225
Broberg, T. 81
Broome, J. 231
Buckley, E. 220
Bull, N. 114
Bullard, C. W. III 136
Bureau, B. 120

Cai, B. 8, 226
calibration 140
Callan, T. 119, 163
Camerer, C. 231
Cameron, G. 146
Cameron, T. A. 8
cap-and-trade schemes 161, 162
capital income 172–173, 174, 175, 177, 178, 181, 185n25
Caplan, B. 232
Cappelen, A. 218, 222–223
car ownership 107, 109–110, 111, 112, 119, 120, 122
carbon dioxide (CO_2)emissions 3, 7, 34, 101; carbon/energy taxes 104, 128, 160, 177, 181; fairness 218; G-EMH model 164; GTAP-E model 158; Input-Output matrices 114; Ireland 170–172; *see also* greenhouse gases
carbon/energy taxes 3–4, 128–156; categories of models 106–108, 134–145; country comparisons 103–105; distributional characteristics analysis 121; distributional impact of 101–127, 131–134, 178–181; econometric models 137–140; fairness 218; firms 6–7, 128–156; G-EMH model 164–182; households 6, 101–127; industry sectors 169–170, 171, 172; integrated models 145–147; Ireland 7, 157–188; literature reviews 108–122, 159–163; macroeconomic models 147; market-based instruments 128–129, 130; price and income elasticities 113; welfare 130–131
Carlsson, F. 78, 79, 192, 216
Carraro, C. 224
Carson, R. T. 53, 57, 61, 62, 71
Casler, S. D. 114
CCAID *see* Conditional Censored Almost Ideal Demand
CDE *see* Constant Difference of Elasticities
CES *see* Constant Elasticity of Substitution
CGE models *see* computable general equilibrium models
Champ, P. A. 77
Charness, G. 219, 220
Cherry, T. L. 220, 222
China 79–80, 150n23
Cholesky decomposition procedure 84
Christiansen, V. 192, 193, 200, 203, 209n5
climate change 78, 141; fairness 213, 215–216, 220, 222, 224, 226; income elasticity 4–5, 34–47
Climate Change Levy 104, 145, 151n45
closure 174, 183
coalitions 224
Coase Theorem 218
cognitive dissonance theory 215
COMETR research 150n26
command and control instruments 128–129
Commins, N. 145
COMPASS *see* Comprehensive Model of Policy Assessment
competition 132
competitiveness: carbon pricing 147, 148; firms 131, 133–134, 151n43, 157; industry 102, 132–133; microeconomic models 134; national 103–104, 131, 136, 137, 139, 141, 144, 149n14, 178
complements 53, 69, 71, 204
complexity 214, 232
Comprehensive Model of Policy Assessment (COMPASS) 150n24
computable general equilibrium (CGE) models 112, 115–116, 150n29, 159; closure 174; firms 135, 139, 140–142, 147–148; international literature 160–161; Ireland 7, 157, 163, 180, 181; *see also* GTAP-E model
computation of measures and indices 106, 107, 108, 116–118, 122

Conditional Censored Almost Ideal Demand (CCAID) 83–84
Conefrey, T. 163
constant coefficients hypothesis 137–138
Constant Difference of Elasticities (CDE) 165
Constant Elasticity of Substitution (CES) 164, 165, 182
Consumer Price Index 86
consumer sovereignty 231
consumer surplus 51–52, 57, 58, 61, 72, 110, 119, 120
consumers 52, 54–56, 57–58
consumption 30n5, 30n7, 35; energy 101–102, 106–107, 112, 135, 145, 158; institutional constraints 19–20; public goods 194–195; relative 210n10; returns to scale 20–22; tax on 176, 178, 180, 181; technology constraints 17–18
contingent valuation (CV) 22, 30n4, 30n8, 77; climate change 226; income effects 81–82; income elasticity 78; renewable energy 80
cooperation 219, 222, 224–225
Cornwell, A. 109, 112
cost-benefit analysis (CBA) 1–2, 3, 7, 191–212, 232
costs: distribution of 1–2, 3, 4, 95n1, 131, 213, 220; energy 101, 147; environmental policy instruments 129; household production and demand analysis 83, 85; institutional constraints 15, 19–20; returns to scale 16
country characteristics 27–29, 30
Cox, J. C. 220
Creedy, J. 109, 111, 112
Croson, R. 220, 222
cross-price elasticities 66, 67, 81, 102, 110, 144–145, 151n44
Crumpler, H. 219
CV *see* contingent valuation

Dahlby, B. 205
damage functions 37–38, 44, 45
Dannenberg, A. 139
Daruvala, D. 192
Dasgupta, P. 191, 192
de Mooji, R. 130
Deacon, R. T. 72, 73
Dellink, R. 163
demand: carbon/energy taxes 106, 142; energy 102, 135, 136, 142, 144; fuel/gasoline 113, 119; household production and demand analysis 82–95; income elasticity 5, 52–53, 63, 67, 72, 76, 95n2; Marshallian 55, 65; price elasticity 66, 72, 73
demand system estimation 106, 107, 108–113, 121
demographics 79, 80; carbon/energy taxes 106, 109, 112, 113, 117, 119, 120, 122; energy efficiency demand 81; household production and demand analysis 95; marginal willingness to pay 25, 27
Denmark 114–115, 117
Diamond, P. A. 209n7, 210n9
DICE model 34, 35, 37
Dickie, M. 77
dictator studies 215, 217, 218, 219, 221, 222–223
Diecofis model 144
differential games 224
disaggregated models 132, 134
discount rate 46
distributional characteristics analysis 121
distributional issues 1–2, 3, 4, 5, 51–75; carbon/energy taxes 6, 101–127, 131–134, 147–148, 157–158, 160–163, 178–181; fairness 213–236; G-EMH model 168
distributional weights 7–8, 191–212
distributive justice 213, 216–217, 227; *see also* fairness
Dixit, A. 149n6
double dividend hypothesis 130, 148, 158, 163, 181–182; capital income 177; CGE models 142; literature reviews 159, 160, 161–162; tax reductions 137; weak and strong 149n11, 184n9
Dunning, D. 215
dynamic models 143, 145–146, 150n29, 151n36, 182

E3ME 138–139, 150n25
Eakins, J. 163
Ebert, U. 5, 51–75, 82, 85, 94
Eckel, C. C. 219
Ecological/Environmental Tax Reforms (ETRs) 6, 101–105, 108–109, 112–113, 118–119, 130; econometric models 137, 139; impact on other countries 135
econometric models 134–135, 137–140, 147–148, 150n30
economic development 34–35, 45

economic growth 1, 27; carbon/energy taxes 104–105, 160, 162, 176; climate change 44–45; pollution relationship 13, 14, 16, 29; technology constraints 18
economy-wide models 159–162, 181
education 23, 24, 26, 27, 79, 80, 81
efficiency: carbon/energy taxes 162, 180; distributional weights 191, 192, 201, 203, 205, 206; fairness 213, 218–219, 231
Ekeland, I. 77
Ekins, P. 106, 122, 139
elasticity: benefit incidence 60; carbon/energy taxes 119, 120, 148; Constant Difference of Elasticities 165; expenditure 89; GTAP-E model 142; household production and demand analysis 84; substitution 53, 66–67, 71, 72, 129, 151n35, 164, 165, 182; *see also* income elasticity; price elasticity
electricity 103, 105, 113, 123n4, 161; G-EMH model 165–166; Ireland 171; renewables 158, 176, 184n18
Emissions Trading Scheme (ETS) 144, 145, 157, 184n1
employment 139, 142, 158, 159; carbon/energy taxes 163; Ireland 178, 182; micro-simulation models 144; *see also* labour
energy 78, 80–81, 101, 104; G-EMH model 164–165; IO models 136; micro-simulation models 144; *see also* carbon/energy taxes; electricity
energy efficiency 81
Engelmann, D. 219
Environmental Tax Reforms (ETRs) 115, 122
environmental valuation 225–226
ENV-Linkages Model 141
EPPA model 116
equality norm 220–222, 223
equal-preference model 54, 72
equity 2; carbon/energy taxes 147; climate change 34, 45; distributional weights 192, 205, 206; equity theory 217; trade-off with efficiency 162, 180, 218–219; *see also* fairness
equivalent variation 51–52
Espey, M. 113
ethics 206, 218, 226, 227, 231
ETRs *see* Ecological/Environmental Tax Reforms
ETS *see* Emissions Trading Scheme
EU *see* European Union
Euler's theorem 66
Europe: carbon/energy taxes 103–105, 118, 123n5, 128; climate change 39, 40–44
European Commission 105, 131, 150n26
European Union (EU): carbon/energy taxes 103, 105, 116, 135; climate policy 2; E3ME 138–139; Emissions Trading System 145, 157, 184n1; GINFORS 138
expenditure: carbon/energy taxes 115, 116, 117, 118, 122, 161; demand system estimation 107–108, 110, 111; household production and demand analysis 82, 84, 86–92
experimental studies 215, 216, 217, 218, 219, 220–221
exports 129, 132, 138, 141, 144, 177
externalities 101–102, 105, 129, 136
Ezzedin, R. 146

fairness 2, 8, 213–236; accountability principle 217–218; carbon pricing 129, 147; cooperation 224–225; efficiency principle 218–219; environmental valuation 225–226; equality norm 220–222; interpretive issues 222–223; measurement of 214–216; need principle 219–220; social objective 226–232
Fehr, E. 219, 220
Feldstein, M. S. 198
Finland 103
firms 6–7, 128–156, 158
Fischbacher, U. 220
Fischer, S. 192
Fleurbaey, M. 218
Flores, N. E. 53, 57, 61, 62, 71
Fong, C. 218
forestry 38
fossil fuels 3, 103, 105, 111–112, 129, 136, 157, 164
France 117, 118, 120
Frank, R. H. 193
Freeman, A. M. 51, 52, 77, 191
free-riding 224
Frohlich, N. 232
fuel poverty 163
FUND model 4–5, 34, 35, 36, 37, 38–44, 46

Gächter, S. 217, 221
Galarraga, I. 81

gasoline tax 110–111, 113, 114, 116, 119–120, 123n4
GDP *see* gross domestic product
GEM-E3 model 141
G-EMH model 7, 158, 159, 164–182
gender 79, 80
general equilibrium analysis 3, 4, 7, 118, 123n1, 232; *see also* computable general equilibrium models
general equilibrium theory 140
George, H. 219
Gerdes, G. 8
Gerking, S. 77
Germany 104, 117, 118–119, 138
Ghalwash, T. M. 81
Ghezzi, L. 146–147
GINFORS (Global INterindustry FORecasting System) 138, 139, 150n24
Gini coefficient 106, 107, 117–118, 120, 122, 151n43; distributional weights 199; Ireland 177, 178, 179
Gino, F. 231
Global Trade Analysis Project (GTAP) 7, 140, 141–142, 151n33, 158, 164–165, 172, 174, 181
Goodman, R. P. 72–73
goodness 226, 227
Goodwin, P. 113
Gotor, E. 166
Goulder, L. H. 149n11
Greene, J. 232
greenhouse gases 34, 35, 44, 101; carbon/energy taxes 115, 128, 142, 160; fairness in policy 216, 222, 224; FUND model 38; micro-simulation models 144; *see also* carbon dioxide emissions
gross consumer surplus 51–52, 57, 72
gross domestic product (GDP) 13, 31–32; carbon/energy taxes 132, 133, 161, 176, 179, 181, 182; CGE models 141; DICE model 34; living standards 131; marginal willingness to pay 23–29
Grossman, P. J. 219
Gruber, J. 231
GTAP *see* Global Trade Analysis Project
GTAP-E model 141–142, 151n34, 158, 164, 165, 181
GTAP-MH model 158, 164, 168, 181
Güth, W. 217

Hamlin, A. 225
Hanemann, W. M. 53, 62, 67
Hanley, N. 82, 191
Harberger, A. C. 192, 205
Haruvy, E. 219
Hasselmann, K. 35
health issues: air quality improvements 78–79; climate change 38, 40, 44, 45
Healy, J. 163
heating costs 44, 103–104, 105, 112, 119, 123n4
hedonic approach 77
Herendeen, R. A. 136
HERMES 162, 163
Herne, K. 221
Hertel, T. 141–142
Hicksian measure 52, 53, 57
Hicks-Kaldor compensation criterion 7
high-income countries: climate change 34, 35; institutional constraints 15, 16; marginal willingness to pay 25, 27, 31n11; returns to scale 16, 22; technology constraints 15, 16, 19
Höbky, S. 73, 77, 92
Hoel, M. 35
Hoerner, A. 139
Horowitz, J. K. 35
households: air quality improvements 5–6, 82–95; carbon/energy taxes 3–4, 6, 7, 101–127, 131, 158, 159–162, 164, 166–169, 170–176, 178–180; CGE models 140; integrated models 146, 147; marginal willingness to pay 23, 25, 27; micro-simulation models 142–143; non-resident 169, 182, 185n25, 185n26; production and demand analysis 82–95; total willingness to pay 31n13
Hudson-Jorgenson model 137
Hungary 105
hydro energy 165, 166
Hylland, A. 192, 193, 209n5

imports 137, 138, 177
income 2, 3, 194–195; air quality improvements 76, 78, 79–80, 92, 93; benefit incidence 60–61; carbon/energy taxes 102, 104–107, 110–116, 118–120, 122, 158, 172–180, 181; climate change 36–37; determinants of income effects 81–82; distribution of 51–75; distributional weights 192, 199, 205–206, 207–208; fairness 227, 228–230; G-EMH model 167, 168; lifetime 108, 110, 117–118, 119–120; marginal willingness to pay 22–30; pollution relationship 4, 13, 14, 19, 22; virtual 56, 65

income elasticity 3, 5, 78, 95n2; air quality improvements 76, 96n16; carbon/energy taxes 106, 111, 113; climate change 4–5, 34–47; distributional weights 199; environmental goods 52–53, 56, 61–65, 67, 68–71, 72–73
income taxes: carbon pricing 119, 130, 161, 162, 163, 168; distributional weights 191–193, 195–196, 198, 200, 205, 206, 210n11
Indecon 163
index of air quality (IQA) 87, 88, 89, 93–94
indifference curves 17–21, 63–64, 67
Indonesia 161
inequality 117, 120, 193, 205; distributional weights 199–200; Ireland 178; *see also* Gini coefficient
INFORUM *see* Interindustry Forecasting Project
innovation 130, 149n8
Input-Output (I-O) matrices 106–107, 108, 109, 113, 114–116, 117–118, 121–122, 159; econometric models 138, 139; firms 134–135, 136–137; integrated models 146, 147
institutional constraints 4, 15, 16, 19–20, 22, 27, 29
integrated models 145–147, 148
Interindustry Forecasting Project (INFORUM) 138
IQA *see* index of air quality
Ireland 7, 116, 119, 157–188
Israel, D. 4, 13–33
Italy: air quality improvements 5–6, 76–98; carbon/energy taxes 104–105, 111, 112, 117, 151n39, 160; Diecofis model 144; small firms 151n39

Jacobian matrix 70
Jacobsen, H. K. 117
Jacobsen, J. B. 82
Johansson, O. 113
Johansson, P.-O. 51
Johansson-Stenman, O. 7–8, 78, 79, 191–212, 213–236
John, A. 14, 17
Jones, L. E. 15, 16, 19, 20, 29
Jorgenson, D. W. 159, 160
just deserts 217–218
justice, distributive 213, 216–217, 227; *see also* fairness

Kahneman, D. 231
Kaplow, L. 193, 202, 203, 209n6
Keen, M. 192, 194, 200, 203–204, 209n5
Kerkhof, A. C. 115
Kolstad, C. D. 51
Konow, J. 8, 213–236
Köszegi, B. 231
Kovenock, D. 69
Kristöm, B. 52, 77, 92
Krugman, P. 149n14
Kuznets, S. 30n2
Kwak, S. 80

Labandeira, X. 109, 111, 112, 114, 146
Labeaga, J. M. 109, 114, 146
labour 158, 163, 178; cost of 149n15, 176; econometric models 139; elasticity of demand 137; G-EMH model 7, 169, 172–173, 175, 176; supply 176, 181–182, 184n21, 196–197, 205; *see also* employment
labour income 172–173, 174, 175, 176, 181
land 172–173, 175
Lange, A. 215–216, 217, 220, 224, 225
Latin America 29, 39, 41–44
Leahy, E. 163
Léger, P. T. 79
leisure 160, 163, 192, 194–195, 200–205, 208–209
Leontief, W. 136
LES *see* Linear Expenditure System
Levinson, A. 4, 13–33
LIFT model 150n23
Lin, B. 95n4
Lindahl model 65, 69, 74n6, 74n9
Linear Expenditure System (LES) 111, 112
linear probability models 25–29
Little, I. M. D. 191
living standards 131–132
location 77, 81, 82; air quality improvements 92–93, 94; carbon/energy taxes 113, 115, 122
Loewenstein, G. 215, 216
Lorenz curve 107
low-income countries 1, 13, 14; climate change 5, 34, 35, 220; institutional constraints 16, 19–20; marginal willingness to pay 25, 27, 29; technology constraints 14–15, 16, 17, 19
luxury goods: air quality 76, 89; climate change 5, 35, 37, 45; transport fuels 111

macroeconomic models 134, 135, 137, 139, 140–141, 145–147, 148
Maital, S. 69, 70
Malaysia 79
Mäler, K.-G. 51, 69, 77
Malthus, T. 219
Mansfield, C. 77
Manuelli, R. E. 15, 16, 19, 20, 29
Mård, T. 221
marginal willingness to pay (MWTP) 1, 4, 13–14, 29–30, 55; air quality improvements 82, 90–92; benefit measures 58; distributional weights 194, 195–198, 199, 200–201, 204, 207–208; gross consumer surplus 52, 57; household production and demand analysis 82; income elasticity 5, 53, 56, 61–65, 67, 70–71, 72, 73; institutional constraints 16, 20, 22, 29; returns to scale 16, 21–22, 29; technology constraints 16, 17–19, 29; World Values Survey 22–29, 31–32; *see also* willingness to pay
Marglin, S. 191
market-based instruments 128–129, 130, 147, 149n4, 149n8
markets 51
Marshall, A. 191
Martin, R. 145
Martini, C. 1–9, 76–98, 101–127
maximisation problems 54–55, 106
McConnell, K. E. 225
McGuire, M. 58, 69, 72
median voter theorem 77
medical expenditures 79
Medin, H. 209n4
Menegaki, A. 80
mesoeconomic models 134, 136
Metcalf, G. E. 110, 115, 116–117
micro-simulation models 106, 107, 118–120; firms 134, 135, 142–145, 146–147, 148, 151n38, 159; SWITCH model 163; United Kingdom 151n40
Miller, J. 219, 221, 222
Miller, T. R. 206
Mirrlees, J. A. 191, 194, 210n9
Mozumder, P. 80–81
Mudan model 150n23
Mullahy, J. 79–80
multi-household approach 159, 164, 166, 181
multisectoral models 137, 138–139, 147–148
MWTP *see* marginal willingness to pay

Narita, D. 2
national competitiveness 103–104, 131, 136, 137, 139, 141, 144, 149n14, 178
natural resources 172–173, 175
Neary, J. P. 62
need principle 219–220, 226, 231
neoclassical theory 140
Netherlands 103, 105, 115
neutrality 129, 130, 160, 162
New Zealand 111
Ng, Y-K. 193, 231
Nichele, V. 118
non-behavioural models 143
Noonan, D. S. 80, 92–93, 94
Nordhaus, W. D. 35
Nordic countries 103, 105
Nordström, J. 109
Norway 103–104, 138
Nozick, R. 217–218
Nyborg, K. 209n4

Oates, W. E. 52
Oberholzer-Gee, F. 216
Ockenfels, A. 220
O'Donoghue, C. 141, 163
O'Donoghue, T. 231
OECD ENV-Linkages Model 141
Oladosu, G. 161
Oppenheimer, J. A. 232
ORANI-G 160, 161
Orcutt, G. H. 142, 146
Oum, T. H. 113
Owen, A. L. 30n4
Oxoby, R. 219
ozone 77, 79, 87

PANTA RHEI 138
partial equilibrium analysis 3, 123n1; carbon/energy taxes 106, 108, 118, 159; fairness 232; micro-simulation models 142
Pazienza, M. G. 6, 128–156
Pearce, D. W. 52
Pecchenino, R. 14, 17
personal relationships 221–222
Persson, U. M. 35
pesticides 81
PETRE project 150n26
Pigouvian taxation 129, 130
Poland 105
policy 2, 3, 4, 6, 145–146; air quality 76; carbon pricing 128, 147; command and control instruments 128–129; distributional weights 193, 201;

policy (*cont.*):
  fairness 8, 213, 214, 215–216, 218, 220, 222, 223–232; market-based instruments 128–129, 130, 147, 149n4; micro-simulation models 143; proportionality 218; *see also* carbon/energy taxes; regulation
'polluter pays principle' 128, 129, 132, 147
pollution 4; air conditioning 82; carbon pricing 129; economic growth relationship 1, 13, 14, 16, 29; energy use 101; index of air quality 87; institutional constraints 15, 16, 19–20, 22, 27, 29; proportionality 218; returns to scale 15–16, 20–22, 29; technology constraints 14–15, 16, 17–19, 22, 29; willingness to pay 13–33; World Values Survey 22–29; *see also* air quality; carbon dioxide emissions; greenhouse gases
Porter, M. 130, 149n8
Porter hypothesis 130, 134, 145, 149n8, 149n9
Portugal 105
Poterba, J. 110, 116, 117
poverty 44, 160–161, 220
preferences 4, 52; distributional weights 197, 205; equality norm 220; equal-preference model 54, 72; fairness 8, 213, 216–217, 220–221, 225, 227, 230–231; marginal willingness to pay 13, 29
price elasticity 52–53, 66–68, 72, 73; air quality improvements 88–90; carbon/energy taxes 106, 110, 111, 113, 120, 142; cross-price elasticities 66, 67, 81, 102, 110, 144–145, 151n44; energy products 102, 103
prices: carbon/energy taxes 128, 129, 137, 142, 159; climate change 35; energy 80–81, 101, 102, 106–107, 114, 121, 133, 158; environmental goods 51; market-based instruments 129; virtual 55–56, 62; World Values Survey 23; *see also* willingness to pay
private goods 53, 54, 58, 69, 192
production 101–102, 114
profit maximisation 140
profits 131, 132, 141, 144, 215
progressivity 2, 52, 53, 63, 68, 70, 72; air quality improvements 76; benefit incidence 59–60; carbon/energy taxes 111, 114–115, 117–118, 120, 160–162; costs 95n1
property rights 218
proportionality 217, 218, 223
public goods 51, 52, 58, 65, 72–73, 77, 192; distributional weights 193, 194–200, 201–205; equality norm 220, 221–222; income elasticity 78; separability 207–209
public transport 109–110, 111, 112, 122, 198–199

Quadratic Almost Ideal Demand System (QAIDS) 109, 112

Rabin, M. 219, 220, 231
Rafiqui, A. 114
Rangel, A. 231
Rausch, S. 161–162
regressivity 2, 7–8, 53, 68, 72, 73; air quality improvements 76; benefit incidence 59–60; carbon/energy taxes 106–108, 110, 112, 114–120, 122, 123n5, 157–158, 160, 163, 176, 179–181; costs 95n1
regulation 1, 30n3; costs 129, 132; EU Energy Taxation Directive 105; Porter hypothesis 149n8; *see also* policy
REMI PI model 162
renewable energy 78, 80–81, 104, 158, 176, 184n18
representative household approach 159
reputation 133–134
Resosudarmo, B. 161
responsibility 217–218, 223
returns to scale 4, 15–16, 20–22, 29
revenue: carbon/energy taxes 101–102, 116, 121, 122, 130, 161–162, 176; demand system estimation 108; distributional weights 195–197, 202–203, 205; G-EMH model 168
revenue recycling 6–7, 106, 108, 111, 122–123, 158; CGE models 142, 160, 161; Climate Change Levy 151n45; computation of measures 116–117; econometric models 137–138, 139–140; integrated models 147; Ireland 157, 162–163, 174, 180, 181; micro-simulation models 118–120, 144
Reynolds-Smolensky index 120
Riedl, A. 217, 221
Riera, P. 52, 77, 92
Roberts, K. W. S. 62
Robin, J. 118

Roemer, J. E. 218
Rose, A. 161, 162
Rosen, S. 77
Roson, R. 160
Ruffle, B. 223
rural areas 112, 114, 115, 119, 122, 161
Rutherford, T. F. 162

Sadka, E. 69
SAM *see* Social Accounting Matrix
Samuelson, P. A. 192, 196, 200, 201, 204, 205, 209n5
Sanchirico, C. W. 209n6
Sandmo, A. 203, 205
Santoro, A. 121
Sardinia 1
Savard, L. 159
scenarios: carbon/energy taxes 174–180; econometric models 138; FUND model 38–44
Schelling, Thomas 34, 46
Schelling Conjecture 5, 34, 36, 37, 38, 40, 41, 44–45
Schläpfer, F. 77, 81–82
Schmidt, K. M. 220
Sciclone, N. 146–147
Scott, S. 163
sea-level rise 40
self-centered bias 215
self-interest 214, 217, 219, 220, 225
self-serving bias 215–216, 232
Selten, R. 217
Sen, A. 191, 229
separability 194, 197–198, 200–201, 202, 203–204, 205, 207–209
Shavell, S. 192–193, 209n6
Shipper, L. 113
Shogren, J. 191
Shonkwiler, J. S. 84, 95n4
Siniscalco, D. 224
Sleeman, C. 111
Slemrod, J. 203
Slutsky matrix 70, 71, 85
small firms 151n39, 151n44
Smallwood, D. 95n4
Smith, S. 116
Smith, Z. 111
Snow, A. 65
Sobel, R. S. 225
Social Accounting Matrix (SAM) 140
social marginal rate of substitution 228–230
social marginal utility of income 192, 193, 195, 198
social welfare 2, 119, 193, 195–197, 199–200, 206, 226–232; *see also* welfare
social welfare functions (SWFs) 121, 160, 180; distributional weights 192, 194, 199, 205–206; fairness 229–230; utilitarian 209n8, 210n9, 210n17
Söderqvist, T. 73, 77, 92
Sosis, R. 223
South Africa 160–161
Soviet Union, former (FSU) 39, 40–44
Spain 81, 109, 112, 117, 119, 146, 151n39
spatial micro-simulation 143
Speck, S. 117, 139
Squire, L. 191
Stahl, D. 219
stakeholders 214–215, 216, 220, 223
Starret, D. A. 202
static models 143, 145, 150n29, 151n37
Sterner, T. 35, 117, 118, 119
Sterner Conjecture 5, 35, 37, 38, 40, 41, 44–45
Stiglitz, J. E. 209n7
Stokey, Nancy L. 14, 16, 17, 18, 20, 22, 29
Strobel, M. 219
subjectivity 213, 214, 216
substitution 35, 53, 65–72, 84, 151n35; carbon pricing 129; Constant Elasticity of Substitution 164, 165, 182; energy products 102, 121; marginal willingness to pay 63–64; Slutsky substitution effects 85; social marginal rate of 228–230
Sugden, R. 231
Suits index 106, 107, 117–118
Sunstein, C. R. 231
surveys 216
Sweden 78, 81, 103, 109
SWFs *see* social welfare functions
SWITCH model 119, 163
Switzerland 109–110, 138, 216
Symons, E. 108–109, 117

Tarr, D. 162
tax cuts 130, 137, 161, 174, 176, 177, 178, 181
taxes 3–4, 6, 195; distributional weights 193, 196–197, 206, 210n11; double dividend hypothesis 149n11; fairness 213, 231; Lindahl model 65; tax departures 103; *see also* carbon/energy taxes; income taxes

technology 137, 148; technology constraints 4, 14–15, 16, 17–19, 22, 29
Thaler, R. H. 231
Tiezzi, S. 1–9, 76–98, 111, 115
Tol, R. S. J. 2, 4–5, 34–47, 163
top-down models 150n21
total willingness to pay 31n13, 51–52, 57, 62, 69, 72
tradable permits 135, 145, 213, 218, 223, 232
trade 135, 136–137, 138, 164, 232
transfers 159, 161, 163, 167, 172–176, 178–180, 181
transport: carbon/energy taxes 102, 103, 104–105, 106, 112, 113, 117, 119; distributional weights 198–200; public 109–110, 111, 112, 122, 198–199
Travisi, C. M. 81
triple dividend 160–161
Tsigas, M. E. 166
Tungodden, B. 218
Tyner, W. 141–142
Tyran, J-R. 225

uncertainty 46
unemployment 1, 139, 163, 181–182, 185n33
United Kingdom: carbon/energy taxes 104, 105, 108–109, 111, 116, 117, 138; Climate Change Levy 104, 145, 151n45; distributional weights 192; micro-simulation models 151n40
United States: carbon/energy taxes 115, 116, 120, 160, 161–162; climate change 39, 40–44; LIFT model 150n23
USREP 161
utilitarianism 192, 199, 209n3, 209n8, 210n9, 210n17, 226, 229
utility: CGE models 140; climate change 35; consumers 54–55; distributional weights 192, 194, 200, 202, 203, 204–206, 207, 209n5, 209n8; environmental goods 61, 69–70; fairness 227–231; returns to scale 20; technology constraints 17
Uzawa, H. 66, 67

valuation, environmental 225–226
value added tax (VAT) 109, 163, 180
Van der Linde, C. 149n8
Van der Tak, H. 191
Van Heerden, J. 160–161
VAT *see* value added tax
vehicle ownership 107, 109–110, 111, 112, 119, 120, 122
Vehmas, J. 102, 123
Verde, S. 7, 157–188
Videras, J. 30n4
Vincent, J. R. 77
Vogt, C. 217, 224
voters 72–73, 77, 225

wages 129, 139, 159, 176, 177, 178, 181
Wagner, G. A. 225
Wang, H. 79–80
Wang, Y. 79–80
Warren, R. S. 65
Weisbach, D. A. 105
Weitzman, M. L. 35
Weitzman Conjecture 5
welfare: carbon/energy taxes 3–4, 130–131, 160, 163; distributional weights 203, 205; double dividend hypothesis 158; fairness 226–232; *see also* social welfare
well-being 231
West, G. R. 134
West, S. E. 110, 119
White, B. 191
Wier, M. 114–115, 117
Williams, R. C. III 110
willingness to pay (WTP) 2, 4, 13–33, 51; air quality improvements 5–6, 76–82, 84–86, 90–95; benefit measures 57–58; distributional weights 7–8, 191, 203; fairness 225–226; income elasticity 3, 5; *see also* marginal willingness to pay
wind energy 165, 166
Wissema, W. 163
working hours 194–195, 196
World Bank 79, 191
World Values Survey (WVS) 4, 14, 22–29, 30n4, 31–32
WTP *see* willingness to pay

Yang, Z. 35
Yen, S. 84, 95n4
Yitzhaki, S. 203, 209n3
Yoo, S. 80
Yusuf, A. A. 161

Zeckhauser, R. 192, 193, 209n5
Zhang, Y. 79–80
Zogragfakis, N. 80

For Product Safety Concerns and Information please contact our EU representative GPSR@taylorandfrancis.com Taylor & Francis Verlag GmbH, Kaufingerstraße 24, 80331 München, Germany